FROM
TENEMENTS
TO THE
TAYLOR HOMES

FROM TENEMENTS TO THE TAYLOR HOMES

In Search of an Urban Housing Policy in Twentieth-Century America

Edited by
JOHN F. BAUMAN
ROGER BILES
and
KRISTIN M. SZYLVIAN

The Pennsylvania State University Press
University Park, Pennsylvania

Library of Congress Cataloging-in-Publication Data

From tenements to the Taylor homes : in search of an urban housing policy in
twentieth-century America / edited by John F. Bauman, Roger Biles, and Kristin
M. Szylvian.
    p. cm.
    Includes bibliographical references and index.
    ISBN 0-271-02012-1 (cloth : alk. paper)
    ISBN 0-271-02013-X (pbk. : alk. paper)
    1. Housing policy—United States—History. 2. Urban policy—United
States—History. I. Bauman, John F., 1938– II. Biles, Roger, 1950–
III. Szylvian, Kristin M.
    HD7293.F76 2000
    363.5'0973—dc21   99-055272

It is the policy of The Pennsylvania State University Press to use acid-free paper for
the first printing of all clothbound books. Publications on uncoated stock satisfy the
minimum requirements of American National Standard for Information Sciences—
Permanence of Paper for Printed Library Materials, ANSI Z39.48–1992.

Contents

List of Illustrations   vii

Preface and Acknowledgments   ix

Chronology: American Housing in the Twentieth Century   xi

Introduction: The Eternal War on the Slums   1
    John F. Bauman

Part I: The Roots of Federal Housing Policy

1 From Better Dwellings to Better Neighborhoods: The Rise and Fall of
  the First National Housing Movement   21
    Robert B. Fairbanks

2 The Garden City and Planned Industrial Suburbs: Housing and
  Planning on the Eve of World War I   43
    John S. Garner

3 "No Idea of Doing Anything Wonderful": The Labor-Crisis Origins
  of National Housing Policy and the Reconstruction of the Working-
  Class Community, 1917–1919   60
    Eric J. Karolak

4 Shaping Housing and Enhancing Consumption: Hoover's Interwar
  Housing Policy   81
    Janet Hutchison

5 The Federal Government and Housing During the Great Depression   102
    Gail Radford

6 The Federal Housing Program During World War II   121
    Kristin M. Szylvian

Part II: Federal Housing Policy in Postwar America

7 Public Housing and the Postwar Urban Renaissance, 1949–1973   143
    Roger Biles

8 The Other "Subsidized Housing": Federal Aid to Suburbanization,
  1940s–1960s   163
    Thomas W. Hanchett

9 Why They Built Pruitt-Igoe   180
      Alexander von Hoffman
10 Choosing Segregation: Federal Housing Policy Between *Shelley*
      and *Brown*   206
      Arnold R. Hirsch
11 Planned Destruction: The Interstates and Central City Housing 226
      Raymond A. Mohl
12 Jimmy Carter, Patricia Roberts Harris, and Housing Policy in the
      Age of Limits   246
      John F. Bauman

Epilogue   265
      Roger Biles

Bibliographic Essay   271
List of Contributors   277
Index   281

List of Illustrations

1. Hester Street in New York City   27
2. Inside a Progressive-era tenement   28
3. New York's Forest Hills Gardens   48
4. America's industrial housing estates: Goodyear Heights, Akron,
   Ohio; Eclipse Park, Beloit, Wisconsin   55
5. Eclipse Park Houses   56
6. Houses in New London, Connecticut, and Bath, Maine   68
7. Philadelphia's Carl Mackley Houses   105
8. New York's Harlem River houses   106
9. Brooklyn's Red Hook housing development   113
10. Queensbridge housing development   114
11. Substandard dwelling for defense workers during World War II   123
12. Houses for defense workers, Pico Gardens, Los Angeles   126
13. Avion Village, Grand Prairie, Texas   128
14. Robert Taylor Homes, Chicago   150
15. The Woodlands, Texas   158
16. Levittown, Pennsylvania   167
17. Suburban shopping center   170
18. Pruitt-Igoe housing project in Saint Louis, Missouri   182
19. John J. Cochran Gardens in Saint Louis, Missouri   194
20. Open-air gallery in a Pruitt-Igoe high-rise   196
21. Construction site of W. O. Pruitt Homes, February 1953   198
22. Demolition of Pruitt-Igoe   202
23. Expressway in California   228
24. Chicago's Dan Ryan Expressway   235
25. Patricia Roberts Harris   248

Preface and Acknowledgments

Several years ago, at an informal gathering held after a day of sessions at the biennial meeting of the Society for American City and Regional Planning History in Seattle, this book was born. A number of those assembled at that conference are among the historians who have contributed chapters to this volume that endeavors to fill a perceived void in housing literature. By providing a historical portrait of U.S. housing policy, the authors unveil fresh perspectives on the nation's century-long effort to wrestle with the chronic imperfections in the nation's housing marketplace.

As editors of this book, we wish to acknowledge the dedication and diligence of our contributors, and in particular, their unfailing cooperation, which we believe helped achieve the main purpose of this volume—to provide a readable and comprehensible history of U.S. housing policy. Most important, the contributors' understanding of the social, political, and economic dynamics of housing, their knowledge of the interplay of social and economic forces of race, ethnicity, class, and city building, and their grasp of the impact of government policy in shaping the contours of the housing marketplace make up the form and content of this book.

All historians are forever indebted to numerous people and to institutions, libraries, archives, universities, foundations, and other depositories and funding sources. In the notes, many of the authors have acknowledged such sources and have expressed gratitude for the assistance of librarians, scholars, and others who have critiqued their work and have significantly aided their research. However, the editors wish to recognize a special indebtedness to several people and institutions for helping make this book possible. These include East Carolina University, California University of Pennsylvania, especially the Irene O'Brien Fund, Western Michigan University, Archives II of the National Archives, the photographic archives and the Manuscript Division of the Library of Congress (especially Fred W. Bauman and Michael Flannery of that division), the Southern Regional Education Board, the Dwight D. Eisenhower World Affairs Institute, the Harry S. Truman Library Institute, and the Franklin D. Roosevelt Library.

We are especially indebted to The Pennsylvania State University Press. Peter Potter encouraged this project from the beginning, and his advice and recommendations appreciably contributed to the formation and development of this book. Ann Farkas undertook the burden of copy editing the many chapters. Her prudent queries and wise suggestions for editorial changes served to greatly enhance the quality of the text.

Finally, we wish to thank all the officers and members of the Society for American City and Regional Planning History and the Urban History Association for providing critical forums where new ideas about the evolution and shaping of the urban social, political, economic, and physical landscape are regularly discussed and new understandings and interpretations forged. As noted at the outset, without these forums, this book would not exist.

Chronology
American Housing in the Twentieth Century

1879   New York Housing Act of 1879. The journal *Plumbers and Sanitary Engineers'* contest for the best housing design, which produced the bandbox tenement.

1890   New York Tenement House Act of 1890.

1901   New York Tenement House Act of 1901.

1909   Lawrence Veiller established the National Housing Association founded in New York City.

1917   U.S. Shipping Board, Emergency Fleet Corporation (EFC) created.

1917   U.S. Housing Corporation (USHC) established by the U.S. Department of Labor.

1931   President Hoover's Conference on Home Building and Home Ownership.

1932   Emergency Relief and Construction Act, which created the Reconstruction Finance Corporation (RFC).

1933   Home Owner's Loan Corporation (HOLC) established.
        Federal Deposit Insurance Corporation (FDIC) established.
        National Industrial Recovery Act, which created the Public Works Administration (PWA) Housing Division (HD).

1934   National Housing Act of 1934, created the Federal Housing Administration (FHA).

1935   Works Progress Administration (WPA) created.
        Resettlement Administration (RA) built greenbelt towns such as Greenbelt, Maryland.

1937   RA activities absorbed by the Farm Security Administration (FSA).
         U.S. Housing Act (Wagner-Steagall Act) of 1937, created the United
         States Housing Authority (USHA) and Local Housing Authorities
         (LHAs).

1938   Federal National Mortgage Administration (FNMA, also called Fan-
         nie Mae) created.

1940   Federal Works Agency (FWA) began construction of defense housing
         under the Lanham Act.

1942   National Housing Agency (NHA) absorbed the housing activities of
         the FWA.

1947   Housing and Home Finance Administration (HHFA) absorbed the
         activities of the NHA.

1949   U.S. Housing Act (Taft-Ellender-Wagner [T-E-W] legislation) of
         1949, administered by the HHFA. It established the national housing
         goal of 810,000 units of public housing and "a decent home in a
         decent living environment for every American." It also launched
         urban redevelopment.
         Organizations opposing T-E-W: National Association of Home
         Builders (NAHB), National Association of Real Estate Boards
         (NAREB).
         Organizations favoring T-E-W: National Housing Conference
         (NHC), National Association of Housing and Redevelopment Offi-
         cials (NAHRO).

1954   U.S. Housing Act of 1954, created the Urban Renewal Administra-
         tion (URA).

1961   U.S. Housing Act of 1961, established 221 (d)2 subsidized housing
         and Section 23 Leased Housing Program.

1965   Housing Act of 1965, created U.S Department of Housing and
         Urban Development (HUD).

1968   Housing and Urban Development Act of 1968, created Section 235
         low-income housing subsidy program and Section 236 low-income
         homeownership program. This act also created the Government Na-
         tional Mortgage Administration (GNMA or Ginnie Mae).

1969–71   Adoption of amendments placing a ceiling on rents in conventional public-housing projects introduced by Senator Edwin Brooke of Massachusetts.

1974   Housing Act of 1974, created the Community Development Block Grants (CDBGs) and the Section 8 program allowing low-income families to use certificates to find housing in HUD-approved private rental housing.

Introduction: The Eternal War on the Slums

JOHN F. BAUMAN

"Razing the Slums to Rescue the Residents!" exclaimed a headline in the *New York Times* on Sunday, September 6, 1998. The article focused on the Department of Housing and Urban Development's (HUD's) HOPE VI program to replace massive complexes such as Chicago's notorious cockroach-, crack cocaine–, and heroin-infested Robert Taylor Homes with smaller developments that mixed families of different incomes in privately developed urban communities. The concept of a "mixed" urban community seemed new to HUD in the 1990s. In reality, housing reformers—many discussed in this volume—had been espousing such mixed-housing communities since the turn of the century. Market forces, however, not the vision of community building, have historically driven the construction of such brutal piles whether they are twentieth-century Robert Taylor Homes or nineteenth-century dumbbell tenements. Concentrated poverty and social isolation sealed Robert Taylor's fate. "The Federal Government is helping cities clear slums," announced the *Times*, "but this time they are slums it helped create: public housing projects crippled by flawed policies and mismanagement and overwhelmed by poverty and crime."[1]

All the elements of America's classic housing conundrum appeared in the *Times*'s story. It juxtaposed the vision of a mixed-resident urban community against the eternal reality of troubled poor people for whom decent housing is forever problematic. The story is rooted in the nineteenth century: Whether the housing reformer was Washington, D.C.'s George Sternberg in the nineteenth century or Gotham's Lawrence Veiller in the early twentieth century or, more recently, the Department of Housing and Urban Development, policymakers, as this volume explains, have grappled with the shortcomings of the fiercely competitive and individualistic housing marketplace and have posited a vision of urban community that frequently transcended the harsh economic realities of urban life.

This housing volume explores the history of the United States' efforts to shape a housing policy that, notwithstanding the nation's historical commitment to the sanctity of private property and the goal of homeownership, would overcome the ever-yawning gap between the "modern," "decent" housing enjoyed by the country's upper and middle classes and the increasingly derelict dwellings inhabited by the less advantaged. The book, perforce, focuses on the twentieth century when cities, states, and Washington itself accepted—if slowly at first—the challenge to better house urban America. Each chapter historically investigates this unfolding U.S. housing policy, inquiring into such issues as tenement design, community building, public versus private intervention, policy versus ideology, highways versus housing, housing and race, and housing as part of urban revitalization. All these issues are examined in the framework of a changing urban-industrial economy, the Great Depression, and post–World War II deindustrialization, from the emerging industrial metropolis of 1900 to the sprawling urban-suburban world of slicing freeways, giant malls, and edge cities that marked the eve of the third millennium.

Several themes dominate this housing history: One is the persistence of the so-called Lockean tradition—the fervent, deep-seated national belief in the supremacy of homeownership and the sovereignty and inviolability of the private housing market brought to America and nurtured here in the eighteenth and nineteenth centuries. American housing policymakers, we argue, have succeeded superbly in expanding the opportunities for homeownership while greatly enhancing the quality and amenities of the housing resided in by the nation's sizeable upper- and middle-income families. A second theme concerns the inability of U.S. policy over time to achieve even the semblance of equality in the distribution of good, standard housing to the nation's low-income families. While America has triumphantly produced middle-income housing meeting the highest standards for design and amenities, for abundant space, heating, lighting, plumbing, safety, and neighborhood quality, too many poor and low-income citizens have historically occupied basically substandard, often grossly unfit housing.

A third theme involves the state's role in fostering urban residential decentralization by officially underwriting the rise of suburbia as the locus of the American dream. Indeed, many chapters in this volume deal with the state's role in actively promoting home building in suburbia, by expanding the story to embrace not only the government home-building experiments of World Wars I and II, but also President Herbert Hoover's vigorous support of suburbanization during the 1920s, and the Housing and Home Finance Administration's postwar role in exalting the suburban home. These chapters, therefore, build on the work of the historian Kenneth Jackson whose seminal history of suburbanization, *Crabgrass Frontier* (1985), observed that "suburbanization has been as much a governmental as a natural process."[2] A final theme explores the quest for community, the connection of housing policy with the reconstruction of a harmonious and active urban community.

Another issue explored by many authors in this book concerns the state's role in promoting housing standards. Such standards dictate the crucial housing norms for the number and size of rooms, interior plumbing, lot size and coverage, and amenities. Although the American Public Health Association codified such standards in the early twentieth century, government action by states and cities in the form of housing and planning ordinances, by wartime housing experiments, by Secretary of Commerce Hoover, by New Deal agencies, by the Housing and Home Finance Administration, and by the Department of Housing and Urban Development entrenched these standards as law, as practice, and finally as U.S. housing norms. Although few chapters are expressly concerned with residential architecture, design does appear as an issue, especially in the form of garden-city proposals and the debate over the wisdom of high-rise as opposed to low-rise, garden-type public housing. Housing tenure, that is homeownership versus renting or cooperative ownership of housing, is another issue explored by several contributors.[3]

Overall, the chapters contribute a deeper understanding of the changing contours of American housing policy in the twentieth century. They afford, for example, a fresh perspective on housing reform in the Progressive era by illuminating in particular the shift in the reform focus between 1900 and 1909 from housing as *shelter* to housing as *community building*.

That quest for community has proved elusive. Indeed, the history of U.S. housing and housing policy reveals, deeply rooted in the American experience, tensions that persistently undermine community building. Seeking to explain why Americans in the 1970s lived in cities as if they were "Urban Wildernesses," the historian Sam Bass Warner identified three forces in tension that helped shape the urban American experience: competition (or individualism), community, and innovation. Warner's analysis is equally useful in understanding the history of American housing policy. Blessed with abundant land and absent the ancient class-based traditions of a dying feudalism, seventeenth- and eighteenth-century Americans resisted communal restraints on private landholding and adopted fee-simple land tenure. Americans treated land as a marketplace commodity like food and clothing. However, these entrepreneurial Americans, while embracing the ideas of John Locke and Adam Smith about free competition and the inviolability of private property, favored an American exceptionalism deeply imbued with communalism. America, they argued, was no ordinary place, but a "Citee upon a Hill," a "Holy Experiment," a covenanted community where, theoretically, all—except black slaves—rich and poor, Catholic and Protestant, Christian and Jew—shared the covenant. In fact, seventeenth- and eighteenth-century America still nurtured a primordial sense of community building distinct from housing development. Urban life thrived in the framework of an organic community, where, theoretically at least, solidarity and cooperation prevailed over capitalistic and individualistic tendencies.

By the end of the eighteenth century, virtuous republicans, artisans, journeymen, and apprentices all assaulted the last vestiges of aristocratic privilege, especially the prerogatives of landownership. They proclaimed an American Lockean Commonwealth where all free white male citizens enjoyed an equal right to landed property. In such an egalitarian society, both property rights and personal independence arose from ownership of the product of one's labor. Egalitarianism seemingly militated against community. In housing terms, the vision included a one-and-a-half or two-story clapboard or brick cottage; however, it was neatly arranged among twenty or thirty other cottages surrounding common park land or a town green.[4]

Ennobling the Nineteenth-Century Gothic Cottage

Both images of the unfettered individual and the covenanted community were battered by the rapid economic, technological, and demographic changes that marked the United States' rise to industrial maturity in the nineteenth century. By the 1830s, an increasingly large population of U.S. laborers had glumly traded the vision of the "Citee on a Hill" for the reality of the tenement and the slum. In the preindustrial eighteenth century, wars, epidemics, and widespread indentured servitude, chronic low wages for white common labor, and urban slavery for blacks condemned "the lower sort" to seek shelter in dank, disease-ridden alleys and courts. The American Revolution had ended indentured servitude; the beginning of industrialism, however, produced fortunes for many, while for common labor, now including many hapless apprentices and journeymen, it enlarged the risk of poverty. Work space and living space, formerly joined, now separated, rendering housing conditions for an increasingly large number of workers worse. Lodging and boarding—the dread of nineteenth-century housing reformers—became commonplace. In 1800, a Philadelphia laborer and his family were crammed together with a cordwainer, his wife, and four young children in a typical working-class dwelling: a two-story clapboard domain measuring twelve by eighteen feet.[5]

Early nineteenth-century Americans increasingly glorified the home as a locus of republican virtue whether it was the Jeffersonian row house or the Gothic country cottage publicized by the landscape architect Andrew Jackson Downing. Here children and society could be nurtured to Christian perfection. At the same time, rapid population growth and the rising spirit of entrepreneurship, described by visitors to America from Alexis de Tocqueville to Charles Dickens, eroded the dream of universal homeownership. Artisans faced with the loss of salable skills endured rapidly deteriorating living conditions. Skyrocketing inner-city land values produced densely settled alleys and noisome rear courts. Land values on New York's Manhattan Island rose an estimated 750 percent from 1785 to 1815.[6] The emerging middle class—the proprietors and managers of the new greater scale of production—relocated from the wharf sides of cities such as Philadelphia, New York, Boston, and Baltimore into more spacious and fashionable "uptown" neighborhoods. In the 1840s, capitalist housing production and booming real estate profits more and more governed the shape of the new socially segregated urban residential landscape. Speculative leaseholders, building contractors, and subcontractors might team to erect a block of twenty to thirty spacious, fashionably ornamented three-story townhouses or gothic, Italianate, or Queen Ann piles (with water and sewer services) for middle-class ownership.[7]

This urban-entrepreneurial vigor, observed by foreign visitors, triggered in some a communitarian impulse. Early nineteenth-century New England textile industrialists built several cotton mills at Waltham and along the Merrimack River, at Lowell, replete with community-style housing for their youthful female workforce. At Lowell, the prudent Boston Associates provided a moral community environment for their low-paid young women, safe from the enticements and depravity of the sinful city.[8] In the 1820s, 1830s, and 1840s, deep anxiety about this same industrialism sired a host of utopian, often visionary socialist communities, among them such (Robert) Owen-inspired places as Frederick Rapp's New Harmony (Indiana), John Humphrey Noyes's Oneida (New York), Bronson Alcott's Fruitlands (Massachusetts), and (Charles) Fourier Phalanxes, among them the famed Brook Farm in West Roxbury, Massachusetts and the North American Phalanx at Red Bank, New Jersey.[9] Although relatively few Americans retreated from industrialism to these religious, socialistic experiments in cooperative living, their numbers together with the explosion of millennial Christianity in New England and upstate New York revealed that not everyone welcomed the rampant speculation and business growth of the antebellum period.[10]

Most workers knew little about the "backwoods utopias." Instead, they crowded the narrow alleys and byways left behind by the middle class. In cities such as Philadelphia and New York, a new breed of real estate speculator profited from buying old single homes and subdividing them into tenements. By the 1850s in New York and Philadelphia, tenement houses—defined as residential buildings where three or more families cooked and slept on the premises—had become a commonplace habitation of the working poor. Families crammed every inch of formerly one-family dwellings, including cellars and jerrybuilt courtyard or back alley additions. Moreover, as early as the 1830s in New York's Lower East Side, a new specialized multifamily dwelling unit arose tailored to exploit the crush of new immigration. Flimsily constructed three- and four-story "railroad flats," plagued with internal, windowless, closet-sized sleeping rooms, were jammed onto twenty-five-by-one-hundred-foot lots and housed twelve to twenty-four families. An 1865 report titled "Sanitary Conditions in New York" described 500,000 New Yorkers living in such tenements.[11] Not all cities endured the same congested housing conditions: In 1845, investigators in Boston found less than one-fourth of workers living in tenements. Nevertheless, many cellar dwellings, alley housing, and other unsanitary conditions rendered the housing of the working classes there wretched.[12]

The Birth of Urban Reform

The war against these urban slums began early, in the 1830s, led by both evangelical Christians and "sanitarians," early apostles of the importance of public health. Nineteenth-century philanthropists and social reformers identified slum conditions with slum dwellers and distinguished between the undeserving poor, whose sloth, intemperance, immorality, and other sinful behaviors condemned them by their own action to a wretched existence, and the deserving poor, widows and orphans not responsible for their poverty. Influenced by English social theorists such as Adam Smith, William Cobbett, and Thomas Malthus, Americans generally subscribed to the idea that materially helping undeserving poor people encouraged indolence and improvidence. After 1870, social Darwinists in America, influenced by the English economic philosopher Herbert Spencer, justified the deserving-undeserving distinction by maintaining that it was ordained by the laws of natural selection.[13]

However, these same social reformers railed against the horror of the fetid slums themselves. To the New York philanthropist, Christian evangelical, and leader of the City Temperance Society, Robert Hartley, who in the 1840s distributed religious tracts among the poor people crowding Lower East Side warrens, the utter filth and squalor of slum environments nullified efforts to preach temperance and the merit of hard work. Likewise, New York City health inspectors, believing that "effluvia," the stench produced by offal (animal remains) and other filth, caused disease, blamed the high death rate from the cholera that ravaged the city's poor inhabitants on the "crowded and filthy state in which a great part of our population live."[14] In 1843, Hartley helped found the New York Association for Improving the Condition of the Poor (AICP), which launched the crusade against the slums and the typhoid fever, vice, violence, and intemperance bred there.[15]

Therefore, throughout the nineteenth century, while clinging to a moral definition of poverty, reformers simultaneously wove a theory of environmentalism that traced epidemics, crime, alcoholism, vice, hooliganism, and political revolution to squalid housing. Slums, especially tenements, were the nexus of all civic evil. B. O. Flower, author of *Civilization's Inferno; or, Studies in the Social Cellar* (1893), called them a "moral contagion," a hotbed of physical and moral decay. From the slum crept the "dangerous classes," the "Plug Uglies," "Dead Rabbits," and other gangs that ravaged the city during New York's bloody draft riots of 1862, when Irish immigrant youths, angered at being forced into uniform to battle slavery, murderously rampaged through the city's African American neighborhoods. New York's Children's Aid Society head, Charles Loring Brace, found in the slums the same seeds of destructive social revolution that terrorized Paris during the bloody Commune uprising in the spring of 1871.[16]

By the later nineteenth century, this "social cost" argument—that slums bred crime and disease and that their destruction would reduce the social expense of criminal activity and epidemic disease—was fully formulated, but so too was the "welfare cost approach," which viewed slums in terms of the burden bad housing imposed on the slum dwellers themselves. Less individualistic than the social cost approach, the welfare orientation presumed that bad, unsafe, unsanitary housing constituted a social failure, which by enmeshing its occupants in squalor and ignorance barred them from full participation in the urban community.[17] Ideally, urban authorities should establish standards for good housing and social well-being, below which no citizen or community should fall. Significantly, toward the end of the nineteenth century, the chasm between the quality of middle-class housing and that of working-class housing widened considerably. While wage-laboring families endured shelter devoid of running water and sewer connections and were dependent on noisome water closets and privy vaults, middle-class families in the new streetcar suburbs enjoyed all the modern innovations—paved streets, sidewalks, sewerage, indoor baths, electricity, even telephones.[18]

American government at all levels, however, responded sluggishly to the problem of slum housing because of America's sanctification of private property, as well as its doctrine of laissez-faire. Throughout the nineteenth century, this tradition of "limited government" meant that urban working-class neighborhoods remained without water and other modern sanitary services unless aided by private philanthropy, which strove to ameliorate bad housing conditions, first, as we have seen, by preaching temperance and then by forming model tenement associations, which built housing and tried to keep rents in these dwellings reasonably low by limiting investment dividends. Model tenements, or "Philanthropy at 5 Percent," represented on the whole a vain attempt to induce "enlightened" capitalists to sacrifice high profits on behalf of the "deserving" poor. In fact, the first model tenement, erected in 1854 on New York's Lower East Side by a subsidiary of the AICP, was condemned in 1880 as unfit for human habitation.[19]

In the 1870s and 1880s, model tenements proliferated, together with "friendly visiting," an approach to slum reform pioneered in England in the 1860s by the Octavia Hill Society and brought to the United States by the Philadelphia housing reformer Helen Parrish. Octavia Hill combined the purchase and remodeling of slums into decent housing with the "friendly" instruction of slum dwellers in home economics and moral improvement. (Critics called the visitors "pantry snoopers.") Following the other English example of building model "industrial dwellings," Boston's Robert Treat Paine, Alfred T. White of Brooklyn's Improved Dwellings Company, Elgin R. L. Gould, head of New York's City and Suburban Homes, and Washington, D.C.'s General George Sternberg undertook benevolent, albeit still entrepreneurial, "limited-dividend" housing ventures wherein enlightened investors contented themselves with only modest profits. However, all the late nineteenth- and early twentieth-century model tenement evangelism notwithstanding, "Philanthropy at 5 Percent" made hardly a dent in the housing needs in the industrial city.[20]

Less philanthropic were practical capitalists such as George Pullman, president of the Pullman Palace Car Company, who in 1885 built for his workers the "model" industrial town of Pullman, Illinois. Elsewhere—near Pittsburgh—Apollo Steel's George McMurtry founded Vandergrift, a town that, like Pullman, linked the idea of better housing with improved health, enhanced work habits, and larger profits. Pullman and McMurtry hired prominent architects and landscapers such as George Orth, Frederick Law Olmsted, John Nolen, Charles Elliot, and John C. Olmsted to fully design their towns of solidly constructed brick and clapboard homes with indoor plumbing, sewers, and amenities such as schools, churches, parks, and shopping galleries. Pullman's workers' "utopia" came crashing down in flames amid the violent strike of 1894. Many other industrial towns, often little better than sanitized versions of the notorious coal patches and company towns dotting the industrial landscape of Pennsylvania and West Virginia, failed, like the model tenement, to establish the hoped-for improved standards in U.S. housing. Often jerry built, sharing foul water closets, and without running water, industrial housing like Carnegie Steel's Painters Row and Skunk Hollow, assailed in the *Pittsburgh Survey* (1909), represented the worst of American housing.[21]

The enormity of the housing problem inspired apocalyptic visions. Nineteenth-century utopian novelists such as King Gillette (the razor tycoon) and Edward Bellamy imagined wondrous future cities where workers were communally housed in giant towers or amazing residential complexes, bathed in fresh air, and with shared services such as laundry, child care, and even food preparation. The reformer and New York mayoral candidate Henry George built his vision of a new urban republic around a single tax on the unearned increment in land. Single-taxer George promised to restructure capitalist landholding by confiscating the portion of the profits on urban land attributable to social forces, population growth, and infrastructure building, rather than to individual effort. George's tax would fund an equitable urban community where workers were decently housed.[22] George's vision in *Progress and Poverty* (1879) appealed to social workers such as Frederic C. Howe as well as to wage earners, especially in cities such as Pittsburgh, which enacted George-like reforms. However, neither the "single-tax republic" nor visions of cheap mass transportation making inexpensive worker housing available on the sparsely settled urban periphery gained support sufficient for their realization.[23]

Like Howe and Elgin R. L. Gould, the New York housing philanthropist, Lawrence Veiller, George Ford, and other nineteenth- and early twentieth-century housing reformers regularly visited Europe seeking enlightenment about how to improve working-class dwellings. Housing reformers increasingly beseeched Europeans for guidance on what came to be known as "social politics" as opposed to the entrenched political economy of laissez faire. Indeed, as the historian Daniel T. Rogers observed, Europe provided the model and inspiration for state intervention (often in the form of public ownership of water, gas, and transportation services) to overcome the most serious consequences of unfettered urban industrialization. Together with social insecurity, oppressive factory working conditions, unsewered streets, and unsafe water, execrable working-class housing conditions ranked high among the human degradations that late nineteenth-century European governments in Great Britain, Germany, and Scandinavia sought to redress. A host of American students and other visitors to Europe, among them prominent housing reformers, returned from Europe exhilarated by what they had observed of worker-housing communities, zoning experiments, and city-owned gas plants, waterworks, and transit systems. As many of the chapters in this book explain, American housers in the twentieth century continued to visit Europe and to return enraptured by the Old World's progress in modern housing. European ideas infused the thinking of U.S. housing reformers and especially shaped the garden-city and public housing agendas of the 1920s and 1930s.[24]

Inspired in part by the European example and by the "social cost" argument that slums bred costly crime and disease, American reformers professed that bettering housing involved state and local governments' using their power to protect the public health and safety. Between 1867 and 1901, New York enacted a series of restrictive laws outlawing tenement-building practices deemed dangerous to public well-being. New York's 1868 Tenement House Law required all tenements to have fire escapes; but, as the historian Roy Lubove observed, standards were low—wooden ladders sufficed. Nor did the laws regulate overcrowding. When in 1879 New York at last addressed the issue of extensive tenement lot coverage, a practice that produced narrow railroad flats with dark, airless sleeping quarters, it introduced the atrocious dumbbell tenement design, featuring a narrow central air shaft, which, while supplying tiny interior-room windows, proved more a noxious health hazard than a defense against tuberculosis.[25]

In England, such housing conditions had inspired Parliament to enact workers' housing legislation, and the Lever brothers (soap manufacturers) had built two model worker communities, Port Sunlight and Bourneville, which delighted U.S. housing reformers. American industrialists attempted to follow suit at Pullman, Illinois; Vandergrift, Pennsylvania; Kincaid, Illinois; and Eclipse Park, Wisconsin. Ideally, grateful workers, who would be revitalized by plentiful fresh air, modern sanitation, and other amenities, would reward their philanthropic employers with loyalty, hard work, and high profits. Although, as John Garner observes in this volume, such communities provided an important precedent for turn-of-the-century garden-city planning, they often failed as communities and especially as effective solutions for rehousing the ill-housed working class.[26] It was not until the turn of the century that—armed with statistics, many of which were generated from the emerging science of bacteriology and from knowledge of Europe's housing experience—progressive housing reformers such as Jacob Riis, Lawrence Veiller, Carol Aronovici, John Ford, John Ihlder, and Bleecker Marquette mobilized against slum housing. With their grounding in European housing ideas, they paved the way for the evolution of twentieth-century U.S. housing policy. In New York, the 1894 State Tenement Housing

Commission, chaired by the magazine editor and housing reformer Richard Watson Gilder, assembled statistical data on overcrowding, tenements with private toilets, units with bathrooms, and data linking unsanitary housing to typhoid fever, cholera, and other diseases. For the first time, the ensuing legislation authorized the demolition of structures deemed dangerous to public health. Seven years later, Lawrence Veiller spearheaded passage of New York's first comprehensive housing law that banned the dumbbell tenement, and that, as Robert B. Fairbanks observes in Chapter 1 of this volume, became a national model for restrictive housing legislation. Progressive housers like Veiller marshaled abundant social-cost arguments about slums and crime and about morally and physically stunted children to push for the enactment of strong state housing ordinances. Guided by Jacob Riis, the author of *How the Other Half Lives* (1890), the Settlement House Movement led by Chicago's Jane Addams, and Boston's Robert Woods, reformers also postulated that good, safe, and sanitary housing was central to reconstructed urban neighborhoods where playgrounds, schools, helpful social workers, and clean, spacious, garden-type housing would help mend the tattered social fabric of the urban community and would forge good citizenship.[27]

Twentieth-Century Housing Policy: An Overview of the Chapters

The chapters in this volume explore the history of U.S. housing policy, especially the emergence and evolution of the role of the state in shaping the contours of the middle- and working-class housing marketplace. They chart the rise of government involvement in housing from the Progressive-era penchant for tenement house legislation, through government support for zoning ordinances and boosting homeownership during the 1920s, to the height of federal housing involvement during the Great Depression and the post–World War II era, to the pronounced federal retreat from the low-income housing supply field in the period 1968–2000.

In Chapter 1, Robert B. Fairbanks describes turn-of-the-century, scientific-minded Progressive-era housing reformers such as Lawrence Veiller as focusing their energies single-mindedly on the dwellings of poor people. This obsession produced on the one hand model tenements and on the other enactment of restrictive legislation, namely Veiller's 1901 Tenement House Law that became the model for housing laws everywhere. As Fairbanks also explains, however, many housing reformers, while riveting their attention on wretched tenement buildings, recognized the crucial role slum neighborhoods played in the social adjustment of rural immigrants to urban life. Therefore, by the 1920s, contends Fairbanks, making better dwellings encompassed not only building good homes, but also constructing salubrious, socially edifying communities.

John S. Garner's revisionist essay in Chapter 2 explores housing and planning on the eve of World War I. Garner argues that scholars have overemphasized the importance for American housing and planning history of the English garden city, the vision of the English court stenographer Ebenezer Howard. Garner's essay focuses instead on industrial housing estates, places such as Goodyear Heights, Ohio; Eclipse Park, Wisconsin; and Kincaid, Illinois. These communities, which offered workers attractive, well-designed, affordable domiciles, were conceived entirely by reform-minded capitalists who strove to provide good housing for their employees, while at the same time accomplishing the objective of further regimenting their industrial workforce.

Chapter 3 examines the birth of federal housing and labor policies during World War I. Eric J. Karolak regards World War I as a landmark event in the shaping of U.S. housing policy. The war produced America's first federally built workers' housing, a momentary shift from its hitherto unyielding devotion to laissez faire and the sanctity of the private housing marketplace. Congress and the Wilson administration feared that a wartime shortage of working-class housing was lowering productivity and fueling labor unrest; it believed that well-designed housing communities would both improve worker productivity and strengthen citizenship.

In Chapter 4, Janet Hutchison proposes that during the 1920s the federal government abruptly retreated from its wartime activism in building working-class housing. Nevertheless, although philosophically opposed to direct government intervention in housing supply, Secretary of Commerce and later President Herbert Hoover greatly enlarged the federal government's role in housing, especially, as Hutchison argues, in promoting suburbanization. Hoover substantially backed housing code enforcement and zoning, and through the "Own Your Own Home" campaign and the Better Homes in America movement, he made government a key agent in determining the actual form of the American home and the American neighborhood. Hoover, argues Hutchison, rejected the whole concept of garden communities in vogue in Europe and America in the 1920s and believed that workers shared a common American relationship to the single-family house: that safe behind the facade of a 1920s bungalow, all ethnic, class, and religious differences would fade.

In Chapter 5, Gail Radford carries the housing story into the Great Depression–New Deal era. She explores the origins of New Deal housing policy, especially the efforts of reformers such as Catherine Bauer to fashion a modern, state-directed, affordable housing program, open to all citizens regardless of high or low financial means. What emerged instead, as Radford reveals, was a two-tiered program. One tier, involving home loans, mortgage guarantees, and tax deductibility, aided suburban mobility among middle- and upper-class Americans. The second tier, public housing built to minimum standards and, to the chagrin of Bauer and other housers, limited to low-income families, served poor people. Such restrictions assured that the second tier quickly degenerated from way stations for the victims of the Great Depression into stigmatized poorhouses.

In Chapter 6 on World War II housing policy, Kristin M. Szylvian investigates the significance of the 1940 Lanham housing legislation. Szylvian maintains that this wartime housing legislation offered the final opportunity for New Deal housers to experiment with "modern" communitarian housing ideas. Indeed, the Federal Works Administration head John Carmody regarded wartime housing as a chance to experiment with creative patterns for efficient, affordable postwar housing development, including experimental floor plans, new housing materials, and tenure innovations such as mutual homeownership. Although as Szylvian makes clear, experimental ardor waned by 1942 and was branded "radical" in the 1950s, the experience had importance, ironically, more for postwar suburbanization than for the future of working-class and low-income housing.

During and after World War II, antistatist conservatism—opposed to big government—coexisted warily with pro-urban growth politics, an alliance or partnership of big-city mayors, federal agencies, and downtown business and civic leaders dedicated to enlisting federal dollars in rebuilding cities. Battered by the Great Depression, downtown businesspeople feared that the dual calamity of creeping blight and postwar suburbanization threatened the vital downtown commercial core of retail stores, offices, and apartment towers that made up the heart of the city. Only massive, government-aided redevelopment could stave off disaster. Urban redevelopment, as Roger Biles explains in Chapter 7, seriously affected American low-income housing policy. Biles recounts the dreary saga of public housing and its postwar marriage to city rebuilding. In effect, Biles continues the story of unfulfilled communitarian dreams begun in Chapter 5 by Radford. He sees the vision of pre–World War II housing reformers such as Bauer suffocated by politics, misguided architecture, and, not the least, racism. Postwar urban renewal devastated the modern housing vision. Tethered to urban renewal, starved by an increasingly conservative and tight-fisted Congress, public housing offered a consistently inadequate supply of low-income housing and served a poorer and poorer clientele, those uprooted by urban renewal activity. Vilified as a policy, public housing after 1960 shifted its focus away from the poor and conventional (federally built) housing toward dwellings for older people and toward federally subsidized, privately developed low- to moderate-income units.

Chapters 8 through 11 by Thomas W. Hanchett, Alexander von Hoffman, Arnold R. Hirsch, and Raymond A. Mohl expand and strengthen the critical context for understanding postwar housing policymaking. These chapters explore a number of important factors profoundly affecting postwar housing policy, including suburbanization, high-rise architecture, racism, and interstate highway development. In Chapter 8, Hanchett argues that the federal government never advanced a single, unified housing program for suburbia. Instead, since the 1930s, diverse efforts marked Washington's effort to promote suburban housing, including the Federal Housing Administration (FHA), the Veterans Administration, and other postwar mortgage insurance and tax programs that "revolutionized the scale" of suburban development. Hanchett sees the FHA as favoring the traditional single-family dwelling, but in aiding veterans it also underwrote thousands of garden-type apartments. Many critics hailed suburbia's low-density, reasonably priced homes as the fulfillment of the American dream, but Hanchett also discerns a movement, especially among postwar intellectuals, to oppose racial segregation, advocate "diversity," and decry the "lily white," homogeneous, cookie-cutter suburbs of the postwar era, scathingly depicted in a 1950s folk song as "little boxes all in a row." Social critics such as Charles Abrams, Jane Jacobs, and William H. Whyte stood in the van of this movement, which foreshadowed the fair housing legislation and the FHA's interest in planned unit developments of the 1960s.

In Chapter 9, Alexander von Hoffman treats postwar high-rise public-housing architecture as an urban response to the challenge of suburbia. He traces the roots of Saint Louis's Pruitt-Igoe projects, the epitome of vilified high-rise public housing, to that city's mayor and to urban experts who described the problem of the postwar city as traffic-clogged streets and slums and who blamed the blight on suburban decentralization. Saint Louis first rejected a high-rise future in favor of garden-city ideas. The Gateway City's mayor, however, admired New York City's skyscraper housing. Therefore, argues Von Hoffman, it was the romance of New York, not economics or official contempt for poor people, that swayed Saint Louis toward high-rise public-housing architecture and the debacle of Pruitt-Igoe.

If von Hoffman seemingly exculpates the state, Arnold R. Hirsch in Chapter 10 roundly condemns it. This chapter painstakingly examines Housing and Home Finance Administration policy decisions made between the *Shelley v*

Kraemer Supreme Court decision of 1948, outlawing racially restrictive covenants, and the *Brown v Board of Education* ruling of 1954, abolishing separate but
equal public education. Hirsch, like Hanchett, acknowledges a postwar concern
among intellectuals and some policymakers for racial justice, but unlike Hanchett he emphasizes HHFA's stubborn reluctance to enforce nondiscrimination
in housing. Nor, in the wake of the 1949 and 1954 federal housing and redevelopment acts, did HHFA move to thwart or mitigate the uprooting of black
families from urban renewal areas. Instead, as Hirsch methodically explains,
renewal and public housing actions by state design contributed to entrenching
American apartheid.

The communitarian vision likewise eluded the postwar highway engineer.
Mohl's essay in Chapter 11 emphasizes that the bulldozing of black urban
neighborhoods caused by Interstate Highway building speeded the formation
of new or "second ghettoes." As does Hirsch in his study of HHFA policy,
Mohl finds the process deliberate, not merely the unintended consequence of
an otherwise well-meaning policy. Indeed, Mohl's chapter indicates that Interstate Highway builders invariably sought more than just the creation of better
roadways. In the course of aligning highways, they endeavored to remove
urban blight, but at the cost of ruthlessly destroying both poor white and poor
black communities.

Chapter 12 explores housing policy during the presidency of Jimmy Carter, whose appointment of the first black woman to head HUD, Patricia Roberts Harris, implied a resurgence of federal housing initiatives absent since the
presidency of Lyndon Johnson. In fact, argues John F. Bauman, Harris reinvigo-
rated HUD and with Carter refocused housing policy on cities rather than on
suburbs as had been the case under Richard Nixon and Gerald Ford. Most
significantly, Carter and Harris unfolded a fresh vision of neighborhood revitalization and community rebuilding. Beleaguered by inflation fed by OPEC (Organization of Petroleum Exporting Countries) the Carter administration
targeted scarce federal dollars at the most distressed areas such as New York's
Bronx, Detroit, Newark, New Jersey, and North Philadelphia, areas particularly
affected by deindustrialization, segregation, and social isolation. Ironically,
Carter's urban housing program represented a retreat from U.S. commitment
to increasing the low-income housing supply. Carter's emphasis on business-
government partnerships wedded housing solutions to private, not public, initiatives and to no-strings-attached block-grant monies, part of the "new federalism" for use at the discretion of the states. Rather than producing rehabilitated
neighborhoods as Harris desired, the Carter policies more often produced gentrified urban villages and glitzy downtowns.

Finally, in surveying the history of American housing policy, it is important to reaffirm that the ethos of privatism and the sanctification of homeownership endured and endures as critical influences informing American housing policy and shaping the landscape of the nation's housing. America's vast sprawling post–World War II suburbs proclaim the indelibility of this legacy. However, this entrenched privatism has historically co-existed with an equally enduring concern for community building. Architects of nineteenth-century industrial and philanthropic housing, like progressive reformers, garden-city builders, public housers, and designers of suburbia, all couched their visions of better housing in the language of community building. This communitarian vision in the second half of the twentieth century survived. The dream of revitalized communities scintillated in the rhetoric of the Great Society, in the new town movement of the Kennedy years, and in the neighborhood-rebuilding plans of the Carter administration. Moreover, the epilogue to this book discloses that in the late 1990s, on the eve of the third millennium, new housing policy initiatives such as HOPE VI and the 1998 Housing Act loudly proclaim the goal of rebuilding healthy, diverse urban communities. Alas, that enduring goal aside, questions about housing supply, affordability, and standards of decency remain. How inclusive is the American dream? Reformers still struggle vainly to strike a balance between the deeply embedded ethos of privatism and the broader goal of social justice, the vision of good, safe, and sanitary housing for all.

Notes

1. Pam Belluck, "Razing the Slums to Rescue the Residents," The New York Times, September 6, 1998.

2. Kenneth T. Jackson, Crabgrass Frontier: The Suburbanization of the United States (New York: Oxford University Press, 1985), 11. The process of American suburbanization, as Jackson makes clear, dates from the early nineteenth century, when the affluent began to separate themselves from poor people and sought individually owned, single-family dwellings on spacious lots located on the urban periphery. By the late nineteenth century, a suburban ethos clearly distinguished such suburban from urban settings. See Ann Durkin Keating, Building Chicago: Suburban Development and the Creation of a Divided Metropolis (Columbus: Ohio State University Press, 1988); and Michael H. Ebner, Creating Chicago's North Shore: A Suburban History (Chicago: University of Chicago Press, 1988).

3. For an excellent discussion of housing standards and housing norms, see Earl W. Morris and Mary Winter, Housing, Family, and Society (New York: John Wiley & Sons, 1978).

4. Sam Bass Warner, The Urban Wilderness: A History of the American City (Berkeley and Los Angeles: University of California Press, 1995); Gwendolyn Wright, Building the Dream: A Social History of Housing in America (New York: Pantheon, 1981), xvi, xvii, 26–27.

5. Billy G. Smith, The "Lower Sort": Philadelphia's Laboring People, 1750–1800 (Ithaca: Cornell University Press, 1990), 158–75; and Gary Nash, The Urban Crucible: Social Change, Political Consciousness, and the Origins of the American Revolution (Cambridge, Mass.: Harvard University Press, 1979).

6. Wright, Building the Dream, 26.

7. Stuart M. Blumin, *The Emergence of the Middle Class: Social Experience in the American City, 1760–1900* (Cambridge: Cambridge University Press, 1989), 138–40; Elizabeth Blackmar, *Manhattan for Rent, 1785–1850* (Ithaca: Cornell University Press, 1989), 184–85; Wright, *Building the Dream*, 27.

8. Thomas Dublin, *The Transformation of Work and Community in Lowell, Massachusetts, 1826–1860* (New York: Columbia University Press, 1979).

9. A reaction to the frenetic speculative capitalism of the time. These experiments in primitive communal living often included communal farming and exotic familial arrangements. See Arthur Eugene Bestor, *Backwoods Utopias: The Sectarian and Owenite Phases of Communitarian Socialism in America, 1663–1829* (Philadelphia: University of Pennsylvania Press, 1946).

10. See Mary P. Ryan, *Cradle of the Middle Class: The Family in Oneida County, New York, 1790–1865* (Cambridge: Cambridge University Press, 1981); and Whitney R. Cross, *The Burned-Over District: The Social and Intellectual History of Enthusiastic Religion in Western New York, 1800–1850* (Ithaca: Cornell University Press, 1950).

11. Elizabeth Blackmar, *Manhattan for Rent*, 206–9; Roy Lubove, *The Progressives and the Slums: Tenement House Reform in New York City, 1890–1917* (Pittsburgh: University of Pittsburgh Press, 1962).

12. Blumin, *Emergence of the Middle Class*, 147–48.

13. For a discussion of the distinction between the deserving and undeserving poor, see Gertrude Himmelfarb, *The Idea of Poverty: England in the Industrial Age* (New York: Knopf, 1983), and Michael B. Katz, *Poverty and Policy in American History* (New York: Academic Press, 1983).

14. Lubove, *The Progressives and the Slums*, 4–5.

15. Robert H. Bremner, *From the Depths: The Discovery of Poverty in the United States* (New York: New York University Press, 1956), 35.

16. On B. O. Flower and Charles Loring Brace, see Charles N. Glabb, *The American City: A Documentary History* (Homewood, Ill.: Dorsey Press, 1963), 279, 328–29.

17. Lawrence M. Friedman, *Government and Slum Housing: A Century of Frustration* (Chicago: Rand McNally, 1968), 9–12.

18. Friedman, *Government and Slum Housing*, 4–7; on the gap in housing quality, see Christine M. Rosen, *The Limits of Power: Great Fires and the Process of City Growth in America* (Cambridge: Cambridge University Press, 1986), 12–67.

19. Lubove, *The Progressives and the Slums*, 9.

20. Lubove, *The Progressives and the Slums*; Eugenie Birch and Deborah Gardner, "The Five Percent Solution: A Review of Philanthropic Housing, 1870–1910," *Journal of Urban Housing* 7 (August 1981): 408–38; Bremner, *From the Depths*, 206–8.

21. Stanley Buder, *Pullman: An Experiment in Industrial Order and Community Planning, 1880–1930* (New York: Oxford University Press, 1967); on Vandergrift, see Anne Mosher, "Capital Transformation and the Restructuring of Space" (Ph.D. dissertation, The Pennsylvania State University, University Park, Pa., 1989); Roy Lubove, *Twentieth-Century Pittsburgh: Government, Business, and Environmental Change* (Pittsburgh: University of Pittsburgh Press, 1995), 13–14.

22. John C. Fairfield, *Mysteries of the Great City: The Politics of Urban Design, 1877–1937* (Columbus: Ohio State University Press, 1993); Robert H. Weibe, *The Search for Order, 1877–1920* (New York: Hill and Wang, 1967); idem, *The Distended Society*. On "Urbtopia," see Stanley K. Schultz, *Constructing Urban Culture: American Cities and City Planning, 1800–1920* (Philadelphia: Temple University Press, 1989), 18–32.

23. Fairfield, *Mysteries of the Great City*; Roy Lubove, "Frederic C. Howe and the Quest for Community in America," *The Historian* 39 (February 1977): 270–91.

24. Daniel T. Rodgers, *Atlantic Crossings: Social Politics in the Progressive Era* (Cambridge: Belknap Press of Harvard University Press, 1998).

25. Lubove, *The Progressives and the Slums*, 81–85.

26. Stanley Buder, *Pullman: An Experiment in Industrial Order and Community Planning, 1880–1930* (New York: Oxford University Press, 1967).

27. Allen F. Davis, *Spearheads for Reform: The Social Settlement and the Progressive Movement, 1890–1914* (New York: Oxford University Press, 1967).

PART I

The Roots of Federal Housing Policy

Between 1900 and 1950, the involvement of the federal government in housing significantly increased. At the beginning of the century, housing reformers were divided over the concept of direct federal involvement in the housing market. Two world wars, the Great Depression, and the postwar veterans' housing shortage resulted in a shift of public opinion in favor of federal involvement in housing. By mid-century, there was no longer any question of whether the federal government would intervene in the private housing market; debate focused on which groups of Americans would get housing aid, how much, and in what form. Upper- and middle-income Americans found their ability to secure quality housing greatly enhanced by federal income tax, highway, and other pro-suburban policies. By contrast, Congress proffered increasingly miserly aid to low-income families for whom the goal of homeownership remained plainly unreachable.

During the early decades of the century, social workers, architects, city planning experts, industrialists, and civic leaders studied and visited progressive housing developments in Europe, devoted themselves to the task of exposing the evils of slum housing, and built model housing developments as a means of raising working-class housing standards. Before World War I, most regarded housing as an area of concern primarily to local and state governments, not to the federal government. The World War I housing shortage forced the federal government into the role of housing developer. In 1918, reformers proposed that the U.S. Department of Labor continue the wartime housing work of the U.S. Housing Corporation and the Emergency Fleet Corporation, but the proposal failed.

Under Republican president Herbert Hoover, automobile suburbs flourished (as opposed to the streetcar and railroad suburbs of the late nineteenth century). Hoover, in fact, supported federal aid for the purpose of promoting or protecting homeownership among upper- and middle-income families. Hoover was, however, far more reluctant to become involved in the working-class housing market. The federal government's involvement in housing expanded greatly during the Great Depression. Agencies such as the Federal Housing Administration and the Home Owners Loan Corporation were created by Congress and Franklin D. Roosevelt's administration to help more affluent Americans purchase a home or save their homes from mortgage foreclosure. The passage of the National Industrial Recovery Act in 1933 opened the way for increased federal involvement in the working-class housing market. The Housing Division of the Public Works Administration loaned funds to a handful of limited-dividend housing corporations before directly undertaking the construction of housing for low-income families. The Resettlement Administration (succeeded by the Farm Security Administration in 1937) worked to improve housing standards and the quality of life among rural dwellers.

The low-income public housing program, which targeted low-wage urban workers, was reformulated in 1937 under the U.S. Housing Authority (USHA) to place more initiative in local hands. The USHA faced growing opposition not only from real estate, home-building, and banking interests, but also from residents, particularly homeowners, who did not want public housing projects built in their neighborhoods. An increasingly hostile Congress trimmed USHA's budget, forcing the agency to de-emphasize the construction of facilities designed to foster community life and to allow public housing to function as part of the larger urban fabric.

During World War II, over a dozen agencies were involved in housing before they were consolidated under the National Housing Agency in 1942. Nearly one million units of housing were built for civilian employees of defense contractors, but the majority of these dwelling units were of temporary construction. Efforts were made to capitalize on wartime advances in home design, construction, and finance for the benefit of returning veterans under the Office of the Housing Expediter Wilson Wyatt. None of the prefabricated housing schemes helped the nation quickly resolve its housing shortage. The following chapters illuminate all these issues. They highlight the housing and community-building reforms of Lawrence Veiller and other progressive reformers, Herbert Hoover and the Better Homes movement, and positive federal intervention in housing during the 1930s and 1940s. For many reformers, this intervention was the fulfillment of their visions of the government's bettering living conditions for working-class victims of urban industrialization.

1

From Better Dwellings to Better Neighborhoods

The Rise and Fall of the First National Housing Movement

ROBERT B. FAIRBANKS

The rise of the nation's first housing movement during the Progressive era (1895–1917) proved important but short-lived because of changing definitions of what constituted good housing. The first national housing movement was one of many movements concerned with the immigrant-occupied slum areas of large U.S. cities at the time. It focused on improving the defective dwelling places of poor people, places that reformers feared threatened the physical and moral development of the city's needy, and settings that posed social, political, and health problems to the city as a whole. This response was not the first reaction to the bad housing conditions of urban poor people—health officials in New York, Boston, and Cincinnati had identified bad tenement housing as a problem since the mid-nineteenth century. What distinguished tenement reform in the early twentieth century was the fact that it culminated in the appearance of a national organization, a national conference, and an ongoing dialogue among reformers throughout the nation.

U.S. cities at the turn of the century showed not only the consequences of their rapid growth in the nineteenth century, but the impact of a transportation revolution in which electric streetcars and railroads whisked wealthier residents to the city's fringes and promoted a more segregated land-use pattern than ever before. As increasing numbers left behind the compact walking city of the mid-

nineteenth century, those who could not afford to move stayed near employment opportunities around the central business district, where they were joined
by newcomers who poured into the city. Speculators, lured by the possibilities
of handsome returns on their investment, turned to the possibilities of housing
poor people. Some investors converted abandoned warehouses into residential
use, others divided old single-family houses into multiunit use, while another
group built cheap tenements expressly for poor people. Although these builders
and landlords generally opposed any efforts to regulate their holdings, growing
concerns at the turn of the century about those forced to live in such abodes
seemed to give housing reformers new energy.

Defining the Tenement House Problem

The fact that large numbers of those living in inadequately maintained and
badly constructed urban dwellings were recent European immigrants seemed
particularly threatening at this time. Throughout the Progressive era, reformers
expressed concern about the effects of such places on their occupants and
showed great interest not only in the dwellings themselves but also in what
they perceived as the large, disorganized, and chaotic slum districts.

Settlement-house workers often took the lead in exposing the evils of
slums, or tenement house districts, as contemporaries often called them. Fearful
that such places made it hard for immigrants to adjust to the urban experience
in America, reformers identified an assortment of problems affecting those living there, including horrible congestion, lack of baths, inadequate play space,
and dearth of appropriate social clubs. Although acknowledging that all these
problems were related, turn-of-the-century reformers also believed that each
problem was unique and could therefore be isolated, studied, and responded to.
As a result, the slums or big city tenement districts became, in the words of the
sociologist Ernest Burgess, the "happy hunting ground of movements," not all
of which were equally important.[1] Reformers concerned with slums seemed to
have arranged the various problems hierarchically, and bad housing almost always topped the list of evils.

Indeed, Progressive-era housing reform focused single-mindedly on the
dwelling place of poor people, whether the strategy associated with reform was
that of model tenements, tenement regulation, or tenement management. This
attitude began to change even before the United States entered World War I,
although it did characterize the movement's most significant organization, the
National Housing Association (NHA).

Veiller and Tenement Reform

The Danish immigrant newspaper reporter Jacob Riis, author of *How the Other Half Lives*, was possibly the best-known housing reformer of the Progressive period because of his powerful impressionistic studies of New York City tenement house districts, but it was Lawrence Veiller, organizer of both the Tenement House Committee and the National Housing Association (NHA), who deserves the title "father of modern housing reform."[2] Born in Elizabeth, New Jersey, in 1872 and educated at the City College in New York City, Veiller became particularly interested in housing betterment for poor people after his involvement with the East Side Relief Committee during the depression of 1893. Unlike Riis, who relied on moral suasion to arouse the public and wrote about slum neighborhoods, Veiller reflected the Progressive era's emphasis on specialization and scientific methods and focused almost entirely on the dwelling place so that housing reform would be in reality dwelling improvement.[3]

Riis's writings examined an assortment of slum-related problems in addition to immigrants' housing, but Veiller retained a single-minded emphasis on the dwellings themselves even though he understood that other factors were at work in slum neighborhoods. His efforts in New York City, well documented by the historian Roy Lubove, led to the New York Tenement House Law of 1901. This law was passed after Veiller requested the Charity Organization Society of New York (COS), one of the most influential charity organizations in the nation, to form a permanent tenement house reform body. Although no such group was established, the COS did create the Tenement House Committee as part of its larger organization. That body, established to encourage model tenements, to promote tenement regulation and enforcement, and to encourage tenement renovation and good management practices, provided institutional support for Veiller's reform efforts and operated as a permanent pressure group for housing reform in New York City.[4] It also, in the words of Roy Lubove, "represented a triumph for organization and expertise in housing reform—the maturity of a trend for organization and efficiency which by 1900, had already manifested itself in many areas of American and political life."[5]

Initially Veiller and the Tenement House Committee sought principally to stiffen regulation of New York tenement houses. Legally defined, a tenement was any building in which three or more families lived independently of one another and did their cooking on the premises. Manhattan and the Bronx had about 44,000 tenements, and more than two-thirds of the city's population lived in dwellings that legally qualified as tenements.[6] To Veiller and other reformers, most of the city's tenements suffered from a variety of defects including insufficient light and air, danger from fire, lack of separate water closet and washing facilities, overcrowding, and foul cellars and courts. Built and owned by speculators to house incoming immigrants, the greedy landlords thought only of profit and not of tenants' needs. At the time the commission was founded, the growing number of dumbbell tenements proved particularly disturbing to reformers. Erected on a 25-by-100-foot lot, these five-, six-, and seven-story buildings were developed with fourteen rooms on each floor, which were meant to accommodate four families. Only four rooms on each floor had direct light from the street or small yards—other windows opened on narrow air shafts seldom more than five feet wide. Such buildings allowed for little sunshine and almost no circulation of air and forced tenants to live in a foul-smelling and dark environment. According to Veiller, this setting made "home life almost impossible."[7]

Tenements as a Threat

Indeed, such dwellings, according to reformers, promoted both physical and social pathology. Not only were tuberculosis, diphtheria, and other diseases disproportionately high in tenement house districts, but in the eyes of the reformers, the dwellings also encouraged intemperance, violence, and immorality. This situation was serious in its own right and became particularly problematic in view of the people who lived in tenements—immigrants. It was no accident, therefore, that the modern tenement movement emerged at a time of massive immigration to cities, when many Americans feared that this immigration tide from East and Central Europe threatened the city's future. Tenement reformers seemed influenced by a social theory that embraced race-based cultural determinism and arranged different ethnic and racial groups along hierarchical lines.[8] New immigrants coming into the United States at the turn of the century were generally viewed as inferior to established Anglo-Americans and Western Europeans, and reformers in concert with popular sentiment blamed them disproportionately for the labor unrest, growing crime, and political corruption associated with cities at this time.

Lawrence Veiller may have best captured how fears about these immigrants helped fuel the tenement house movement when he wrote:

> Were this city within a city composed chiefly of native born citizens speaking the same language, activated by a common patriotism, and brought up under the same influences and surroundings, the conse-

quences of this congested population would be serious enough, but where it is in a city composed of people from nations alien to our way of life in nearly every way, ignorant of our language, and brought up under conditions social and political that are entirely foreign to the ones under which they are now living, the results are fraught with the most serious consequences for the community.[9]

E. R. L. Gould, another prominent housing reformer, made the connection between new immigrants and their environment even more clearly when he observed: "Strong-willed, intelligent people may create or modify environment." But "the weak-willed, the careless, and the unreflecting," Gould concluded, "are dominated by environment." He aptly summarized the beliefs of many tenement reformers when he noted that "for all but the exceptionally strong and virile, home environment determines the trend of life."[10] Jacob Riis made a similar observation when he suggested that civilization implied a race in which there were winners and losers. He feared that the new immigrants, "left to their own resources," would become the "victims, not the masters, of their environment." For Riis, the tenement environment was "a bad master."[11] Dr. Charles A. L. Reed, a Cincinnati eugenicist interested in housing reform, may have most succinctly summarized the connection between immigrants and dwellings when he warned that "race culture is most intimately interwoven with general culture." For Reed, the relation between the suffering immigrant and the dwelling was complex. "Is degeneracy the cause of the hovel," he asked, "or is the hovel a cause of degeneracy?" He concluded that "within certain limitations each may be considered as cause and each as effect."[12]

Tenement reformers, then, believed that proper homes were clearly necessary for the Americanization of immigrants, a chief goal of the era. The dwelling shaped the nature of home life, and home life determined the strength of the family that educated the young in matters of health and morality, what those in the nineteenth century called civilization. Defective dwellings would short-circuit the system, result in defective individuals, and retard the Americanization process. This in turn threatened American social and political well-being. Indeed, the commissioner of New York City's Tenement House Department summarized the menace of defective housing when he asserted that "there can be no question that the three great scourges of mankind, disease, poverty, and crime, are in a large measure due to bad housing."[13]

Such a belief led to reformers' single-minded determination to promote better dwellings. Although tenement reformers continued to employ three strategies to remedy the tenement problem—model tenements (as opposed to model communities), enlightened tenement renovation and management as practiced by Octavia Hill, and tenement house regulation—Veiller viewed the last as the best hope and used the COS Tenement House Committee to promote a better tenement house code and a more effective way to enforce it.[14]

Tenement House Regulation in New York City

According to Veiller, what differentiated tenement house laws (and later housing laws) from building codes was their emphasis. Building codes regulated the methods to be employed in the construction of a building—that is, building materials and processes. The tenement code, on the other hand, focused not on the building industry but on living conditions. It governed the environmental conditions in the buildings where many people lived. Tenement house laws, then, concerned themselves "with light and ventilation, plumbing and drainage, intensive use of land, privacy, sewage disposal, egress in case of fire, reasonable fire protection, and to a large extent with maintenance . . . regulating and restricting basement and cellar occupancy, [and] . . . insuring cleanliness and the keeping of buildings in repair, . . . the taking in of lodgers."[15]

Unhappy that the New York Tenement Act of 1895 failed to adequately regulate the city's tenements and had lax enforcement provisions, Veiller, with the help of the COS Tenement House Committee, pushed for new legislation. When early efforts failed, Veiller created a tenement exhibition to prove that workers in New York were "housed worse than any other city in the civilized world." A strong believer in the need to educate the public about the housing problem, Veiller produced an exhibit that used more than one thousand photographs and provided in "accurate, scientific form a number of maps showing the entire tenement city of New York." These maps related the incidence of poverty and disease to the tenement districts. A cardboard model of one tenement house block, which attracted special attention, vividly portrayed the horrors of congestion. The two-week exhibition, held in the old Sherry building on Fifth Avenue, drew more than ten thousand persons and then toured other American cities before being shipped to the Paris Exposition. The exhibition not only educated the public but persuaded New York Governor Theodore Roosevelt to help the cause by creating a state tenement committee.[16]

The commission authored the Tenement Law of 1901, a milestone in the tenement house campaign. It not only outlawed the dumbbell tenement and required private bathroom facilities for each apartment, but it provided stringent fire-protection measures. In addition to setting more demanding standards

1. Hester Street in New York City. Progressive-era reformers feared that the congested living conditions of New York led not only to disease but to intemperance, violence, and immorality.

2. Inside a Progressive-era tenement. Legally defined, a tenement was any building in which three or more families lived independently of one another and did their cooking on the premises. New York City's Tenement Law of 1901 helped start a national movement to improve the living conditions of America's urban poor.

for future tenements, the law required changes in existing tenements, including more windows, better bathroom facilities, fire escapes, lighting for dark halls, and waterproofing of cellar floors. In another important step, the commission established a separate Tenement House Department to enforce its new tenement house law.[17]

Origins of the National Housing Movement

The campaign for the New York tenement law generated much publicity and helped initiate what became a national movement. As had been the case in New York City, Veiller played a critical role in the genesis of the countrywide movement. In 1899, he had tried to promote interest in housing reform by sending a letter to the National Conference of Charities urging it to take up the question of housing at its convention. Veiller justified his request by arguing that "a large part of the present poverty and crime was caused primarily by bad housing."[18] He had also sent a questionnaire about housing conditions to the nation's leading cities, not just to secure information but to make civic leaders think about the problem.[19]

As the chief publicist for better housing, Veiller aided fledgling tenement house movements in other cities by furnishing information on how to address housing evils, particularly ways to formulate and administer regulatory legislation, as well as offering advice about model dwellings.[20] In addition, Veiller along with Robert W. De Forest, president of New York City's Charity Organization Society, edited the two-volume *Tenement House Problem Including the Report of the State Tenement House Commission of 1900*. These volumes assembled the material collected for the Tenement House Commission and more. Along with a lengthy chapter defining the tenement problem and a section on the history of tenement reform in New York City, the book provided chapters dealing with specific tenement-related problems such as fires, back-to-back tenements, sanitation, tuberculosis, and prostitution. Other chapters included statistical studies of New York City's tenement houses as well as entries on housing conditions and tenement laws in American cities and on housing conditions and tenement laws in European cities. The thirty-nine-page chapter on twenty-seven American cities was clearly the most comprehensive study ever done on housing conditions in the United States. This chapter also suggested that even though few cities had experienced the evils of New York City tenements, many had inadequate dwellings for their immigrants and poor people and many had already started addressing these needs through building codes and tenement laws.[21]

Tenement Reform Outside New York City

For instance, Chicago, which had been unsuccessful in its effort to secure a tenement house ordinance in 1874, saw a resurgence of interest in tenement reform around the turn of the century. Although the city had few large-scale tenements like New York's, a desire to prevent the construction of such tenements as well as a concern for the housing conditions of the city's poor people living in smaller tenements explains the housing activity in Chicago. In 1899, social reformers associated with Hull House joined with others to form the

Chicago City Homes Association. The title of their organization suggests they subscribed to Veiller's assertion that bad dwellings destroyed home life. Their first action was to investigate three crowded districts on the West Side, the site of Hull House and the home of large numbers of immigrants. They reported their findings in *Tenement Conditions in Chicago*, published in 1901.

The Chicago investigation approached the housing problem in much the same way that it had been tackled in New York. After acknowledging the dangers stemming from the crowded tenement districts, the report mostly probed the detrimental effects of such dwellings on families and individuals. Tenements were "homeless," the report suggested, and thus created "various forms of social and individual degeneration."[22] After explaining why crowded tenement districts appeared and describing the nature of Chicago's tenements, the document proceeded to report on insufficient housing. Chapters on inside sanitary conditions, defective plumbing and baths, and outside unsanitary conditions took up over 40 percent of the text. The final chapter, "A Review of Remedial Efforts," called for a well-planned building and sanitary code and a single body to regulate tenements. The report also recommended parks and public baths for tenement districts and urged model-housing efforts.[23] As a result of the Chicago Homes Association's investigation and because of its lobbying efforts, Chicago aldermen passed a tenement house ordinance in December 1902.[24]

Even though its tenements differed from those of New York City, Chicago's approach to its housing problem suggests that it shared New York's definition of the housing problem. Thanks to Veiller's efforts to publicize housing problems throughout the nation, many cities embraced New York's approach to the housing problem that focussed on the dwelling.[25] For instance, the well-publicized New York tenement house movement had a direct impact on nearby New Jersey. In 1901, that state passed a new tenement house code that closely followed the one in New York City. Boston, Buffalo, Hartford, Cleveland, and Cincinnati were among the other cities that started or re-energized movements to improve their existing tenements and to prevent future ones like those in New York. Cincinnati's Associated Charities launched a major tenement house campaign in 1901. The group invited Wallace E. Miller, professor of sociology at Southwestern Kansas University, to visit the city and survey the Queen City's tenement conditions. Reformers used Miller's findings both to promote model tenements and to secure a new state tenement house law for Ohio's large cites.[26]

Significantly, the publicity generated by the New York City Tenement House Committee helped promote a growing national awareness not only of tenement houses, but also of the problem of bad housing for the poor. After securing the new tenement house code in 1901, Veiller became increasingly devoted to this emerging national movement.[27] According to Lubove, the COS Tenement House Committee was constantly "swamped with visitors and letters of inquiry."[28] Veiller, the secretary and executive officer of the committee, responded with letters about strategies for attacking housing evils, advised on how to formulate housing legislation, discussed administration of housing laws, and even suggested the best types of model tenements or small housing to develop.[29]

In 1910, to further promote a national housing movement, Veiller wrote *Housing Reform: A Hand-Book for Practical Use in American Cities*. Published by the Russell Sage Foundation, sponsor of the COS, this remarkable book provided step-by-step instructions on how to undertake housing reform. Its first part discussed the housing problem, and later chapters provided guidance on how to organize a housing movement and how to conduct a housing survey, as well as detailed instructions on what proposed housing laws should contain. Along with these specific guidelines, the book offered strategies to secure housing legislation and insight on how to guarantee enforcement of the laws. The book even included sample schedules for housing investigations.[30]

Housing Reform in the Southwest

Housing Reform's influence promoted new awareness of the housing movement throughout the United States, including the sparsely populated Southwest. Starting in November 1911, the *Galveston News* and the *Dallas News* ran a series entitled "The Housing Problems in Texas." Later published as a ninety-three-page pamphlet, the twenty-eight-article tract publicized the intolerable housing conditions in all the state's major cities and defined the housing problem in a fashion paralleling Veiller's definition. Good housing, in the Southwest as in the East, meant better dwellings free of sanitary, structural, and social problems.[31] Although Dallas had no tall tenements like New York City, the *News* pointed out that at least one outsider, the eminent social worker Dr. Charles Stelzle, thought Dallas housing "[v]iler than any he had ever seen in any city in America."[32] Dallas had shotgun houses void of sanitary facilities, adequate privacy, or sunlight and breathing room. Those houses were often built next to one another with no more than three to five feet separating them. Overcrowding it seems was not simply an eastern problem.[33]

The Texas series added a wrinkle to the housing problem not usually discussed in New York City or Boston. Because Dallas had a large transient population, it was hard to secure a permanent worker base to attract more industry. Housing betterment might be a way of overcoming that problem, concluded the *News*. Good housing would "hold them here, [and] cultivate in them a commendable pride of home, [and] develop in them the qualifications of good citizenship and to make them contributors to, as well as sharers in, the general advancement and benefits of society."[34]

The pamphlet ended by discussing how Texas cities could arrest their bad housing and avoid becoming like New York City. It borrowed heavily from (and acknowledged) the guidelines offered by Veiller's *Housing Reform*, including instruction on how to develop a housing body and how to survey and publicize housing needs. The pamphlet also discussed the types of housing laws needed in Texas. Such a series suggests again that the housing movement was indeed national, and similar questions and responses were offered throughout the nation concerning housing.[35]

Creating the National Housing Association

Even more important than his book, Veiller helped establish the National Housing Association (NHA). Shortly after the incorporation of the Russell Sage Foundation in 1907 to organize charity and to professionalize social work, Veiller approached his friend and vice president of the Sage Foundation, Robert W. De Forest, and suggested that Sage help form and finance a national housing association.[36] Two years later, the Sage Foundation agreed to such an offer after Veiller made a formal written proposal. He asked the foundation to provide $10,000 to start the organization and recommended that a thirty-two-member board of directors be selected from around the country to promote a wide interest in housing. The association emerged in 1910 as a result of a meeting held in New York by a number of housing-reform enthusiasts. They selected Robert W. De Forest, head of the COS, as president of the NHA, and John M. Glenn, director of the Russell Sage Foundation, as treasurer. Lawrence Veiller, the driving force behind the association, was named secretary and director.[37]

Reflecting Veiller's belief that the two essential elements undergirding bad housing conditions were neglect and ignorance, the NHA sought to bring home "to each community the importance of right housing conditions and the consequence of bad ones." The first purpose of the association, according to its constitution, was "to improve housing conditions, both urban and suburban, in every practicable way." Toward that end, the NHA would "aid in the enactment and enforcement of laws that [would]: (a) prevent the erection of unfit types of dwellings; (b) encourage the erection of proper ones; (c) secure their proper maintenance and management; (d) bring about a reasonable and practicable improvement of older buildings; (e) secure reasonable, scientific and economic building laws." Note the emphasis here on dwellings. Unlike today, when policymakers see housing as a package of amenities, the first national housing movement accepted Veiller's definition and equated good housing with better dwellings.[38]

Other purposes of the organization included advancing the establishment of housing associations where they did not exist and assisting those already established. The NHA would also "act as a clearing house for such agencies" as well as "promote popular interest in the subject." It would help cities defend their housing laws once enacted and advise cities how to modify such laws "to suit changing conditions and meet new needs as they develop." Reflecting its concern with congestion in the city's tenement house districts, the NHA pledged to study "the causes of drift into the cities, and the methods by which the population ⌊would⌋ be distributed over larger areas." Finally, the new housing organization would help "train and equip workers for various phases of housing reform work."[39]

The NHA's first board of directors included not the proposed thirty-two but thirty-seven members representing nineteen cities from Boston to Los Angeles and Buffalo to New Orleans. Made up of seven women and thirty men, the board included businesspeople, social workers, and professionals. An eleven-member executive committee with participants from Boston, Buffalo, Chicago, New Haven, New York, Philadelphia, and Washington acted as the day-to-day governing body. The NHA also established a number of honorary vice presidents and named prominent reformers like Jane Addams, Jacob Riis, E. R. L. Gould, and Frederick Law Olmsted to these positions. Annual dues were set at five dollars a year with the hope that "the movement may be national, not only in its scope, but in its constituency as well."[40]

The NHA hosted its first conference in New York City in 1911. Held right after the National Conference on Charities and Correction, the meeting drew 137 delegates from sixty-two cities. Participants included representatives from health, building, and fire departments; volunteer citizen groups, chamber of commerce–type groups; real estate professionals; members of building organizations and improvement societies, and those involved in social work.[41] Delegates heard reports from various cites including Detroit, Chicago, Boston, Honolulu, Baltimore, Saint Louis, Atlanta, Cleveland, Youngstown, Columbus, New Bedford (Massachusetts), Philadelphia, Albany, Cincinnati, Nashville, Lawrence (Massachusetts), and Seattle.

At the conference, Veiller delivered a speech entitled "A Program of Housing Reform." Reflecting his scientific approach to housing reform, he argued that such a "program should be . . . broadly comprehensive, at the same time it should be as definite and precise as those very housing laws which we are urging people to enact."[42] Veiller repeated the formula he viewed as critical to a successful better housing movement. He called for the creation of a discrete body to examine the conditions of dwellings and to educate the community about its housing needs. After the community understood the reality of bad housing and its impact on the community's health and social well-being, the movement should then be able to bring about the enactment of legislation to remedy the housing problem. Once that occurred, reformers still had to be committed to seeing the laws enforced. For Veiller, then, housing reform meant securing laws governing dwellings. His formula for success emphasized investigation, education, legislation, and enforcement.[43]

The topics discussed at the first housing conference reflected perfectly the Progressive housing agenda of 1911. They included "The Problems of the Small House"; "Housing Reform through Legislation"; "Privy Vaults"; "City Planning and Housing"; "Alleys, Law Enforcement: The Tenants Responsibility"; "Best Types of Small Houses"; "Garbage and Rubbish"; "Housing Conditions in Small Towns"; and "Sanitary Inspections of Tenements." What all these topics shared was an intense focus on improving individual dwellings. Even Frederick Law Olmsted Jr.'s presentation, "City Planning and Housing," underscored the need to provide more open spaces around tenements to give dwellings better access to light and air.[44]

The National Housing Movement Expands

Although the original movement had been focused on the evils of big-city tenements and promoting legislation to prevent large tenements in smaller cities, the title of the new organization as well as some of the topics at its first meeting reveals—as I have argued—that the original concern with tenements had shifted to housing. Only six or seven cities actually experienced a significant tenement problem. Veiller, in fact, understood that problems in one-and two-family dwellings were more common across the nation and deserved equal attention. If the lack of light or inadequate toilets caused problems in New York City and threatened family stability there, the same could occur in cities with decrepit one- and two-family housing like Columbus, Ohio; Detroit, Michigan; or Buffalo, New York.

Dr. F. E. Fronczak, health commissioner in Buffalo, reported to conferees on a Polish section in his city, which contained mostly small dwellings housing two or three families at most. These tightly packed abodes were overcrowded mainly because many people took in boarders. Detroit endured a different problem with many two-family houses without adequate toilet facilities.[45] It was Columbus, however, that passed a housing code rather than a tenement code to remedy its housing problem. The code covered one- and two-family dwellings as well as larger tenements although its focus remained similar to that associated with regulating the larger tenement houses.[46] Indeed, in his *Model Tenement House Law* published in 1910, Veiller advised reformers that they could apply such a law to model housing simply by replacing the phrase *tenement house* with *dwelling house* in the text.[47] Four years later, Veiller produced a separate volume tackling housing as opposed to tenement house needs and provided a model housing law to boot.[48]

The second NHA conference, held the next year in Philadelphia, was "designed to be as helpful as possible to the medium-sized cities of the country."[49] A variety of papers again emphasized the problems of smaller dwellings and the need to improve them. Several presentations at this conference also discussed garden suburbs and dispersing of poor people to the urban fringes. Presenters argued that such actions would allow more appropriate, less congested dwellings than did inner-city neighborhoods and emphasized the benefits to the dwelling as opposed to the broader neighborhood community.[50]

The NHA, which not only published its proceedings but produced *Housing Betterment*, a quarterly periodical, played a critical role in the nation's growing awareness of its housing problems. Housing reformers around the nation apparently embraced Veiller's definition of bad housing as inadequate dwellings. The second conference drew 231 delegates (including 50 women), 94 more than the number at the first meeting. Besides holding conferences, the NHA published a variety of pamphlets on specific housing issues. Within two years of its founding, it had produced thirteen, a number that increased to forty-one by 1917.[51]

Although the changed emphasis from tenement to housing conditions suggested that the movement had expanded its focus since the turn of the century to include one- and two-family houses, the 1913 NHA conference in Cincinnati reaffirmed that the attention of the nation's housing movement remained on dwellings. John Ihlder, field secretary for the association, made the point when he reminded delegates that "the home furnishes the best method of breaking into the vicious circle of hopelessness that leads to immorality, to disease, to a degrading environment, and again to hopelessness."[52] The Cincinnati model-housing builder Jacob Schmidlapp agreed and concluded: "There is no way in which we can uplift the morals, health, and the social well-being as easily as we can by giving our wage-earners better homes."[53] Although attendance slipped for the third meeting, the field secretary noted that the number of cities involved in the housing movement over the past year had actually increased from seventy-three to ninety-seven.[54]

The housing movement continued to draw more participants even after the United States entered into the war. At the 1917 NHA conference held in Chicago, Lawrence Veiller reported that 473 cities had "manifested a direct interest in the cause of housing reform." One year earlier the number had been 209. The number of housing organizations committed to reform had increased from 135 to 231, according to Veiller. Fifty-seven of those were connected with women's clubs, eighty-nine with Chambers of Commerce, thirty-three with charitable organizations, six with real estate interests; forty-six were separate organizations. Veiller also reported that membership in the NHA had jumped from 521 to 713. Much of this increase, of course, revealed Veiller's strenuous efforts to publicize the nation's housing needs, but it also reflected the national consensus about what constituted the housing problem. Wherever he went, Veiller encouraged a dwelling-based reform movement. In 1917 he wrote over 4,500 letters and visited more than ten cities, from New London, Connecticut, to Detroit, Michigan.[55]

Redefining the Housing Problem

Even as the national movement neared its apogee in 1920, however, it became evident that its close identification with the housing of poor immigrants was being replaced by a different, more comprehensive emphasis that wedded housing and neighborhood. Both were so interrelated, it seems, that one could not be treated without the other. The singular focus on housing as dwelling also gave way to a new emphasis on housing as a dynamic process. At the 1917 conference, George E. Hooker suggested broadening the definition of housing when he observed that "the housing problem isn't, as was supposed a couple of generations ago when it first was attacked, a narrow, small isolated problem, but is a part of that larger idea which has been shaped and labeled within the last two decades as city planning, city building—the community organization problem."[56]

At one level, this was not a revolutionary statement. Since the turn of the century, reformers had understood that a variety of problems in the slum affected the lives of poor people—lack of playgrounds, lack of bathing facilities, inadequate open spaces. However, in some ways the early housing movement, despite understanding the nexus between shelter and community amenities, acted as if the two phenomena could be treated separately. Moreover, reformers appeared to arrange slum needs hierarchically with better dwellings being near if not at the top of the list. By 1915 or 1916, reformers shifted from a preoccupation with dwellings to a definition of housing that emphasized the inextricable connections between dwellings and other neighborhood amenities.[57] After 1915, reformers' solutions to the housing problems started to reflect this new definition of housing. Community development schemes and comprehensive zoning and neighborhood planning now overshadowed model tenements and tenement regulation as the solution to the housing problem.

The Cincinnatian Jacob Schmidlapp's changing involvement in housing reform during the Progressive era helps illustrate this shift to the broader community definition of housing. As we have seen, at the 1913 NHA conference, Schmidlapp espoused the virtues of good housing and indeed built such houses. By 1915, however, he expanded his focus beyond the dwelling and had his Model Homes Company undertake a community development project named Washington Terrace for the city's African Americans. Built for six hundred tenants, his development offered more than safe and sanitary buildings. Employing a "community plan," Washington Terrace included a cooperative store, recreational facilities, an assembly hall for meetings of religious, educational, or community value, and an environment enhanced by architecture and landscape features. Moreover, Schmidlapp created clubs for men and women as a way of fostering community spirit. These clubs also bore the "responsibility of caring for the place and the conduct of its members." This massive reconstruction of the tenants' physical and social world, according to the community's founder, would result in "racial and civic opportunity and a stronger economic position." Freed from the dangers of social disorganization, physical disease, and neighborhood deterioration, tenants could become contributing members of society and could learn the virtues of hard work and participatory democracy.[58] Washington Terrace would improve urban dwellers by arranging urban space to positively influence the social interaction of the group, which in turn would help shape people's attitudes toward citizenship and the city.

The wartime community housing experiments initiated by the U.S. Shipping Board and the U.S. Housing Corporation likewise followed this community model rather than the earlier model tenements or dwellings associated with the distinguished Alfred T. White of Brooklyn or even the earlier efforts of Jacob Schmidlapp. Indeed, the increased coverage given community development projects for war workers in Great Britain by the *Journal of the American*

Institute of Architects in 1917, the establishment of the Committee on Community Planning of the American Institute of Architects in 1919, and developments such as Sunnyside and Radburn in the 1920s pushed the community develop- ment strategy to the forefront of housing reform strategies.[59]

Comprehensive zoning, which sought among other things to create homo- geneous neighborhoods protected from commerce or industry, now engrossed many housing reformers in the same way that tenement regulation had earlier. The New York zoning act passed in 1916, according to David Goldfield and Blaine Brownell, became "the prototype for similar plans in 591 cities through- out the country during the next decade."[60] Writing in 1936, James Ford, the author of *Slums and Housing*, concluded that zoning had "for the first time united two hitherto diverse fields of study and effort, restrictive housing legislation and city planning."[61] It also shifted the focus of better housing advocates from the dwelling to the larger neighborhood setting.

The Decline of the National Housing Association

The decline of the NHA in the 1920s, despite its successes in both publicizing the housing problem and addressing it through the promotion of regulatory legislation, also suggests that its earlier "answers" to the housing problem were no longer as widely shared or as relevant as they once had been. Membership in the organization peaked in 1919 at 1,112 and gradually decreased after that. National meetings of the NHA became more infrequent with only three occur- ring in the twenties. Even those conferences witnessed more discussion of hous- ing problems and solutions that reached beyond the dwelling. For instance, in the NHA's 1923 conference, five papers on zoning and two papers on regional planning were presented. The single-minded focus on the dwelling that had characterized the NHA disappeared, reflecting both the organization's lost vi- tality and the decline of the old definition of bad housing as inadequate dwell- ings.[62]

This shift in emphasis paralleled a contemporary transformation in social theory from race-based to place-based cultural determinism.[63] As we have seen, much of the activism of reformers at the turn of the century stemmed from their fear of the dangers posed by new immigrants to American cities. These people, the theory went, were particularly vulnerable to moral, social, and physical failure, which was best prevented by providing proper home life, something impossible in deteriorating tenements. By 1915, as Zane L. Miller pointed out, there was a shift suggesting that racial, ethnic, and occupational groups "derived their identities from their experience in particular social and physical environments rather than from the genius of their race."[64] Such a social doctrine implied that good dwellings in slum neighborhoods would do little to uplift poor immigrants. Rather, better neighborhoods would provide the social and physical environments necessary for improving poor people. As a result, the broader setting, the neighborhood community, became increasingly important to those who wanted to improve America's ill-housed.[65]

The new shift in housing reform also moved away from the needs of poor people to what constitutes good housing in general. If inappropriate communities threatened poor people in the slums, what about poorly laid-out communities in the suburbs? The process of housing, rather than a simple preoccupation with poor people, became the growing focus of housers after the war, a period that saw a marked decline in the activities of the NHA and the emergence of community builders.[66] Ironically, the few community developments erected in the 1920s were not for poor people but for the middle classes. Indeed, the new emphasis on good housing as a package of neighborhood amenities actually made it more expensive to produce good housing for the poor in the 1920s.

By 1915, then, the focus on the dwelling started to give way to the modern definition of housing, a package of amenities (including the larger neighborhood) that shaped human behavior. No longer would good housing Americanize inferior immigrants as reformers once hoped, but the broader housing context would shape its residents into contributing citizens without necessarily destroying their ethnicity. That commitment altered both the nature and the significance of housing reform in the 1920s and made community development rather than model tenements the focus of those interested in the housing question. When the federal government finally embraced public housing during the Great Depression, it was the community development approach of the 1920s rather than the singular emphasis on the dwelling that most influenced the Public Works Administration's experimental program. At the very time the federal government was initiating public housing, Veiller disbanded the twenty-seven-year-old NHA. On December 31, 1936, the NHA called it quits and turned over its rich files and library to the federal government's Central Housing Committee, a body established by President Franklin Roosevelt to formulate a national housing policy and an organization that embraced the new definition of what constituted good housing, a definition that made community development rather than model tenements the focus of those interested in the housing question.[67]

Notes

1. For more on this approach, see Alan Marcus and Howard P. Segal, *Technology in America: A Brief History* (San Diego: Harcourt Brace Jovanovich, 1989), 139–40. Ernest W. Burgess, ed., *The Urban Community* (Chicago: University of Chicago Press, 1926), preface.

2. Roy Lubove, *The Progressives and the Slums: Tenement House Reform in New York City, 1890–1917* (Pittsburgh: University of Pittsburgh Press, 1962), 118.

3. Ibid., 120.

4. Veiller, "Tenement House Reform in New York City, 1834–1900," in Robert W. De Forest and Lawrence Veiller, eds., *The Tenement House Problem Including the Report of the New York State Tenement House Commission of 1900* (New York: Macmillan, 1903), 1:109.

5. Ibid., 119.

6. Lawrence Veiller, "The Tenement-House Exhibit of 1899," *Charities Review* (March 1900): 20.

7. Ibid., 20–21.

8. For a fascinating look at this social theory, see Henry P. Shapiro, "The Place of Culture and the Problem of Identity," in Alan Batteau, ed., *Appalachia and America: Autonomy and Regional Dependence* (Lexington: University Press of Kentucky, 1983), 131–32.

9. Lawrence Veiller, "The Housing Problem in American Cities," *Annals of the American Academy of Political and Social Science* 26 (1905): 47–48. Philpott pointed out that Chicago tenement reformers also shared race-based assumptions about that city's tenement house residents. Thomas Lee Philpott, *The Slum and the Ghetto: Immigrants, Blacks, and Reformers in Chicago, 1880–1930* (New York: Oxford University Press, 1978), 90–93.

10. E. R. L. Gould, "The Housing Problem in Great Cities," *Quarterly Journal of Economics* 14 (May 1900): 378–89.

11. Jacob Riis, "The Battle with the Slum," *Atlantic Monthly* 83, April 1899, 626.

12. "First Round Table Report," in *Proceedings of the Third National Conference on Housing* [1913] (Cambridge, Mass.: National Housing Association [NHA], 1914), 315.

13. John J. Murphy, "Effects of Bad Housing," in *Proceedings of the Fifth National Conference on Housing* [1915] (New York: NHA, 1916), 82.

14. Octavia Hill bought tenements located in London in the mid-nineteenth century and reno-vated them to rent to poor families. She also provided moral and social guidance to the tenants by visiting them regularly. In 1912, Philadelphia saw the appearance of the Octavia Hill Association, which bought run-down dwellings and repaired them and also offered the "friendly" rent collector to guide and improve the tenants. Lubove, *The Progressives and the Slums*, 105–7; Paul Boyer, *Urban Masses and Moral Order in America, 1820–1920* (Cambridge, Mass.: Harvard University Press, 1978), 14–45.

15. Lawrence Veiller, *A Model Housing Law*, rev. ed. (New York: Russell Sage Foundation, 1920), 12–13.

16. Veiller, "The Tenement-House Exhibit of 1899," 20–21.

17. Lubove, *The Progressives and the Slums*, 134–35.

18. Lawrence Veiller, *Reminiscences* (Columbia Oral History Project), 87.

19. Ibid., 88.

20. Lawrence Veiller, *The National Housing Association: A New Organization to Improve Housing Conditions, Both Urban and Suburban* (New York: NHA, 1910), 5.

21. De Forest and Veiller, eds., *The Tenement House Problem Including the Report of the New York State Tenement House Commission* (New York: Arno Press, 1970 [1903]).

22. Robert Hunter, *Tenement Conditions in Chicago* (New York: Garrett Press, 1970 [1901]), 147, 144.

23. Ibid., 161–78.

24. Edith Abbott, *The Tenements of Chicago* (Chicago: University of Chicago Press, 1936), 59.

25. Robert W. De Forest, "A Brief History of the Housing Movement in America," *Annals of the American Academy of Political and Social Science* 51 (January 1914): 10.

26. Robert B. Fairbanks, *Making Better Citizens: Housing Reform and the Community Development Strategy in Cincinnati, 1890–1960* (Urbana: University of Illinois Press, 1988), 20–22.

27. *The Progressives and the Slums,* 143.

28. Ibid.

29. Veiller, *The National Housing Association,* 5.

30. Lawrence Veiller, *Housing Reform: A Hand-Book for Practical Use in American Cities* (New York: Charities Publication Committee, 1910).

31. *The Housing Problem in Texas: A Study of Physical Conditions Under Which the Other Half Lives* (Galveston-Dallas News, 1911), 89.

32. Ibid.

33. Ibid., 10.

34. Ibid., 36.

35. Ibid., 93.

36. Veiller, *Reminiscences;* David C. Hammack and Stanton Wheeler, *Social Science in the Making: Essays on the Russell Sage Foundation, 1907–1972* (New York: Russell Sage Foundation, 1994), 1–10; Lubove, *The Progressives and the Slums,* 143–44.

37. Veiller, *The National Housing Association,* 5.

38. Ibid.

39. Ibid., 5–6.

40. Ibid., 6–13.

41. "Forward," in *Proceedings of the Second National Conference on Housing* [1912] (Cambridge: NHA, 1913), 3–5.

42. Veiller, "A Program of Housing Reform," paper presented at the National Housing Association Annual Meeting, in *Proceedings of the Academy of Political Science in the City of New York* 2 (1912): 3.

43. Ibid., 4–9.

44. Frederick Law Olmsted, "City Planning and Housing," in *Proceedings of the Academy of Political Science in the City of New York* 2 (1912): 33–34.

45. Discussion, "The Problems of the Small House," in *Proceedings of the Academy of Political Science in the City of New York* 2 (1912): 97–103.

46. Edith Elmer Wood, *Recent Trends in American Housing* (New York: Macmillan, 1931), 11.

47. Lawrence Veiller, *A Model Tenement House Law* (New York: Charities Publication Committee, 1910), 10.

48. Lawrence Veiller, *A Model Housing Law* (New York: Russell Sage Foundation, 1914).

49. "Forward," in *Proceedings of the Second National Conference on Housing* [1912], 4.

50. Andrew Wright Crawford, "Where City Planning and Housing Meet," in *Proceedings of the Second National Conference on Housing* [1912], 129–44; Grosvenor Atterbury, "Garden Cities," in *Proceedings of the Second National Conference on Housing* [1912], 106–13.

51. "Forward," in *Proceedings of the Second National Conference on Housing* [1912], 3–5.

52. John Ihlder, "Housing Progress of the Year," in *Proceedings of the Third National Conference on Housing* [1913] (Cambridge, Mass.: NHA, 1914), 195.

53. "First Round Table Report," comment by Jacob Schmidlapp, in *Proceedings of the Third National Conference on Housing* [1913], 239.

54. Ihlder, "Housing Progress of the Year," in *Proceedings of the Third National Conference on Housing* [1913], 195.

55. Lawrence Veiller, "Housing Progress of the Year," in *Proceedings of the Sixth National Conference on Housing* [1917] (New York: NHA, 1918), 412–15. These numbers were particularly impressive considering that the Sage Foundation had slashed its annual appropriations to the NHA by one-third, from $5,000 to $3,330. Veiller, "Housing Progress for the Year," in *Proceedings of the Fifth National Conference on Housing* [1916] (New York: NHA, 1917), 530.

56. George E. Hooker, "The Problem in the Light of Current Events," in *Proceedings of the Sixth National Conference on Housing* [1917], 302.

57. Fairbanks, *Making Better Citizens*, 35–40.

58. Ibid., 36.

59. Roy Lubove, ed., *The Urban Community: Housing and Planning in the Progressive Era* (Englewood Cliffs, N.J.: Prentice Hall, 1967), 115.

60. David R. Goldfield and Blaine A. Brownell, *Urban America: A History*, 2d ed. (Boston: Houghton Mifflin, 1990), 279.

61. James Ford, *Slums and Housing with Special Reference to New York City: History, Conditions, Policy* (Cambridge, Mass.: Harvard University Press, 1936), 227.

62. Veiller, "Housing Problems in America" [1920], 34; NHA, *Proceedings of the Ninth National Conference on Housing* [1923] (New York: NHA, 1924).

63. Shapiro, "The Place of Culture and the Problem of Identity," 113–24.

64. Zane L. Miller and Bruce Tucker, *Changing Plans for America's Inner Cities: Cincinnati's Over-the-Rhine and Twentieth-Century Urbanism* (Columbus: Ohio State University Press, 1998), 3–10; idem, "The Revolt Against Cultural Determinism and the Meaning of Community Action: A View from Cincinnati," in Jack Salzman, ed., *Prospects: An Annual of American Cultural Studies* 15 (New York: Cambridge University Press, 1990): 415.

65. Clarence Stein's observation in 1930 echoed this theme when he wrote "[the houses'] relation to the community is the thing that really matters." Quoted in Marc A. Weiss, *The Rise of the Community Builders: The American Real Estate Industry and Urban Land Planning* (New York: Columbia University Press, 1987), 2.

66. Weiss, *The Rise of the Community Builders*, 2–78.

67. John M. Glenn, Lilian Brandt, and F. Emerson Andrews, *Russell Sage Foundation, 1907–1946* (New York: Russell Sage Foundation, 1947), 2:649.

2

The Garden City and Planned Industrial Suburbs

Housing and Planning on the Eve of World War I

JOHN S. GARNER

By the second decade of the twentieth century, the garden-city movement had received international attention, and planned housing estates for industrial workers were influencing suburban construction both at home and abroad. The study of housing, together with ideas about town planning, drew on several decades of advances in housing reform, exhibitions at international trade fairs, and landscape design. By the eve of World War I, a number of innovative projects could be seen, studied, and experienced at first hand. Contributing to the garden-city movement in the United States were the international housing congresses, which offered a forum for advocates of housing reform and town planning, and village improvement societies, which concerned themselves with environmental issues.

"Garden suburbs" and "garden villages" were small satellite communities located near larger cities. In many instances, they became attached subdivisions to already existing cities. Their purpose was to house industrial workers in less costly yet more attractive surroundings than traditionally found. Most provided some source of employment in the form of nearby factories. What distinguished them from other small towns and suburbs was their pattern of development and their appearance: All the buildings were new, similar in architectural expression—style and construction—and subordinate to a master plan. The amenities of the countryside were embraced while the drawbacks of the city were excluded.

"New towns," Radburn (1928–29), New Jersey; Norris (1933–34), Tennessee; and Greenbelt (1935–36), Maryland, represented a culmination of the planning principles introduced in the garden-city movement and an advance on the study of vehicular traffic patterns and the use of schools in neighborhood units and spatial organization. Nevertheless, Radburn and the government's Tennessee Valley Administration and greenbelt towns are frequently described as the U.S. response to the British garden city, but are otherwise unprecedented. In fact, they stem from a much older tradition. Their planners, Clarence Stein and Henry Wright, Earle Draper, and Hale Walker, had earlier served an extensive apprenticeship in industrial housing projects.

The Garden-City Myth

In every instance, the term *American garden city* is a misnomer. A more accurate label is *industrial housing estate* or *model company town*, depending on the extent of development. Goodyear Heights (1913) near Akron, Ohio, and Eclipse Park (1915) near Beloit, Wisconsin, sometimes referred to as *garden suburbs*, and Kincaid, Illinois (1914), a company town termed *garden village* (descriptions are provided later), can be included among the better examples of the type, although these are just several among many constructed in the United States during the closing years of the Progressive era.[1]

By World War I, the author of the garden-city movement, Ebenezer Howard (1850–1928), was no longer dismissed as simply another English utopian, but was credited for his environmental approach to development and vindicated for the success of Letchworth, England, the first garden city, founded in 1903. Letchworth employed a number of the social principles of Howard's *Garden Cities of Tomorrow* (1902), but the planning principles set forth in Letchworth, including zoned land uses, contour planning, and large residential blocks with semidetached houses, were not Howard's contribution per se. Rather, Letchworth's planners, Barry Parker and Raymond Unwin, drew on the accumulated knowledge of late nineteenth-century village planning, including their earlier industrial commission for Joseph Rowntree at New Earswick (1901–2), in their eventual layout.[2]

Howard's greater contribution was his vision of urban decentralization through the creation of satellite towns, each self-sufficient and self-contained, girded by a green belt to buffer and nurture them while limiting their populations to a manageable size. That vision was later affirmed by the Barlow Commission and the Reith Report findings during World War II, before Great Britain set about creating the first of its "new towns" in 1946. In the 1960s, France and the United States adopted new-town policies (see Chapter 7) seeking to manage urban sprawl, but at the beginning of the century, Howard was alone in recognizing the need for a national commitment. He did not envision government supervision of town construction and, despite his socialist leanings, held fast to the concept of private subscription.[3]

In operation, garden cities leased land to industrial concerns at attractive rents, land acquired through limited-dividend, joint-stock associations. The principal subscribers were wealthy industrialists and merchants who never intended to make their homes there. The companies that built factories at Letchworth and Welwyn, England, the second garden city, were not required to provide housing, stores, schools, and other public services. These services were commissioned and administered by the town association from revenue raised by the leases, borrowing, and other town-generated sources. In the United States, there was nothing quite comparable. As a result, there continues to be confusion whenever the subject is raised. Co-partnership, the policy behind the garden-city system of land tenure, in which the garden-city association retained title to all property, never caught on in the United States: It smacked of socialism to the U.S. Association of Building and Loan Societies, which considered homeownership to be the arsenal of American democracy. Although similarities in plan can be seen between the English garden cities of Letchworth and Welwyn (1919) and those in the United States, they had nothing in common when it came to land acquisition, housing, tenure, and administration.[4]

International Housing Congresses

Before the garden-city movement received an international following, an earlier international movement had focused primarily on low-cost housing. That movement, initiated in 1889, was the conception of the Frenchman Émile Muller (1823–1889). Numerous housing associations had been founded in the second half of the nineteenth century, but never on an international scale. The International Housing Congresses were held in conjunction with the great trade fairs in Europe and the United States, beginning with the Paris Exposition of 1889. Although the focus was affordable housing, the broader environmental issues of town planning were also discussed.

Muller and his housing initiative deserve greater attention. It should be recalled that, at the turn of the century, American architecture and urban design were influenced more by France than by any other country. Muller was a professor of engineering at the *École Centrale* in Paris between 1864 and 1889, and he also instructed architecture students at the *École Speciale,* a more progressive and technically oriented school than the tradition-bound yet more prestigious *École des Beaux-Arts.* As a young engineer, Muller had designed housing for employees of the Railroad of the East, but in 1852 he received a commission that earned him a reputation as a housing expert and propagandist for labor reform. He designed an industrial housing estate, *une cité ouvriére,* for Dolfus-Meig and Company, a manufacturer of textiles in Mulhouse, France, near the German border. The housing blocks followed the convention of the period in an orthogonal layout with factories to one side and houses to the other. The houses were for the most part semidetached units, and workers' rents could be applied, interest-free, toward purchase. What was important is that the houses were designed for maintaining the integrity and dignity of working-class families; each unit had a door that opened on a small yard and garden that were set back from the street. Services and amenities were planned from the outset; water, gas, and storm drains followed the street layout; and public buildings such as schools, bakeries, savings banks, and baths were also provided.[5]

Early on, Muller distinguished between two types of workers' housing, those constructed in large apartment blocks and those built as smaller, semidetached houses, primarily located outside cities. Of the two, he advocated the semidetached houses, *les petites maisons,* where families lived separately, surveillance of the young was more easily accomplished, disputes among neighbors minimized, and property better maintained. In 1852, Napoleon III had authorized ten million francs for improving workers' housing. The bulk of it went to large apartment complexes in and around Paris, but Muller's project at Mulhouse also received approximately three hundred thousand francs to assist with civic improvements. The issue of whether workers should be housed in large apartment blocks or cottage residences dominated the agendas of housing congresses in the following century and greatly affected the garden-city movement.[6]

In 1867 and again in 1878, Muller succeeded in persuading the French government to mount exhibits of model workers' dwellings at the Paris Expositions, but no medals were awarded. For the Paris Exposition of 1889, however, Muller won full recognition for the entries with gold, silver, and bronze medals awarded. Seven full-size dwellings were constructed on the fair grounds. One of the bronze medals went to the Ludlow Associates of Ludlow, Massachusetts, for their company housing. In addition, a new section of the fair was created under the title "Social Economy." Among Americans attending this section of the fair were E. R. L. Gould, who became president of the City and Suburban Homes Company and a prominent advocate of "investment philanthropy," and Nelson O. Nelson, founder of the model company town of Leclaire, Illinois, who was strongly influenced by the father of French profit sharing, Jean-Edmund Leclaire. Muller's students, Emile Cacheux, Edouard Cheysson, and Jules Challamel, continued his work by organizing the French Society of low-cost housing (Société francaise des habitations à bon marché) in 1890. The society was founded to encourage housing developments and to support the passage of national legislation to facilitate loans for their construction. In particular, it was recommended that tax reductions and exemptions be granted to landlords and investors, that construction loans be advanced by banks, and that mortgage insurance be sought.[7]

Muller's legacy, as carried out by others, was the international review of housing programs, the second at Marséilles in 1892, at Bordeaux in 1895, in Brussels in 1897, and between 1897 and 1907 in cities such as Paris, Düsseldorf, Liége, and London, and in Vienna in 1910. Although World War I cut short plans for a tenth conference, by the 1920s, the international housing movement had initiated so many national organizations that international guidance and support were no longer found to be necessary.[8]

Speaking at the Vienna conference, Robert W. de Forest, who would be named director of the Russell Sage Foundation's Forest Hills Gardens (1911), delivered a paper on municipal housing in the United States. Unlike Europe, America, reported de Forest, eschewed socialist tendencies toward public provision in favor of "[I]ndividual efforts on philanthropic lines." These efforts and more particularly on commercial lines, [are] in large measure solving the problems of American housing." He went on to say that no one in the United States seriously proposed municipal housing as an answer to the housing problem. Nor would he endorse such a proposition, reminding his European audience of 1,400 delegates that "American public opinion as to the proper sphere of governmental action, differs radically from European conditions and European opinion." George B. Ford, who also attended the conference, noted agreement on the desirability of founding garden cities despite disagreement on the issue of co partnership.[9]

Forest Hills Gardens, Long Island, designed by Frederick Law Olmsted Jr. and Grosvenor Atterbury, was very much a philanthropic undertaking, backed by a not-for-profit organization and benefiting from generous open space in the form of a landscaped park in which the housing was arranged. Although intended for working-class families and conceived with the idea of providing

3. New York's Forest Hills Gardens, Long Island, New York, 1909–11, designed by Frederick Law Olmsted Jr. and Grosvenor Atterbury. Forest Hills Gardens was emblematic of the garden city in America (source: *Survey* 25 [November 1910]).

modest homes and townhouses, the financial reality of high land costs and property taxes, and the prospect of renters commuting between home and work, precluded all but a middle-income clientele. Because of its location eight miles from Manhattan, it became a commuter suburb. Forest Hills Gardens identified with the garden-city movement in appearance, landscape design, and architecture, rather than in operation. It was emblematic of the garden city in the United States.

The alternative to philanthropy preoccupied another American participant at the Vienna conference, John Nolen, called the father of American city planning for his part in establishing the American Town Planning Association in 1909. Nolen was one of several early graduates of Harvard University's landscape architecture program under the direction of Charles Eliot and Arthur A. Shurcliff, who had worked with the Olmsted firm and had designed several industrial villages. The early landscape programs at Harvard, the University of California at Berkeley, and the University of Illinois offered classes in civic art as a complement to horticulture, which, together with an occasional civil engineering course, made up the curriculum in town planning. Nolen was an activist who was more at home in the public arena than at the drafting table. A founding member of the [U.S.] National Housing Association and the National Municipal League and an officer of the American Civic Association, he also helped found the American Institute of City Planning (later renamed the American Institute of Planners), patterned on the British Royal Town Planning Institute. Nolen regularly contributed articles in architectural journals about the profession of planning and about his various commissions, including his better-known Neponsit Garden Village (1913) in East Walpole, Massachusetts; Kistler (1915), Pennsylvania; and Kingsport (1916), Tennessee.[10]

Nolen's industrialist clients were eager to avoid the problems associated with company housing and therefore wanted homeownership for their employees. Although the companies hired the architects and constructed the houses, they sought outside financing at terms workers could afford. America's traditional mortgage lenders, banks and insurance companies, rarely lent more than one-half the home's equity to borrowers and then for limited periods of ten years or less. Building and loan associations, which had been in existence in the United States since the 1830s, were tailored to the needs of working families, but were located in cities where membership pools were sufficiently large to supply money for construction. In his paper at the 1910 Housing Congress in Vienna entitled "Organization of Credit for Housing Purposes," Nolen stated:

> In the United States neither the federal government, the states, nor the subordinate political units of the states have so far taken any practical steps toward improving or erecting dwellings. Recently some action has been taken by public authorities toward the investigation of housing conditions. Private capital has been rendered available in some places for improved housing, especially by industrial establishments for their own employees. . . . But the sources of credit available for the erection of inexpensive dwellings [have been limited].[11]

Nolen knew of the nineteenth-century tenement bylaws enforced in Boston, Philadelphia, and New York, and such philanthropic undertakings as Alfred T. White's Improved Dwellings Company, Brooklyn, New York, and the much earlier London projects of the Peabody Provident Trust and Octavia Hill. These were not, however, created by public authority or located outside the largest cities, and rather than providing semidetached and detached housing, they offered apartments in large tenement blocks. Credit for constructing workers' housing went to building and loan associations. Nolen exulted that nearly two thousand building and loan associations, in which 70 percent of the shareholders were working people and which had capital assets of $118 million, offered the means for "showing the elevating relation to citizenship . . . for the encouragement of thrift and home owning." He believed that larger, planned housing estates, benefiting from the backing of large industrial concerns that used creative financing and offered attractive although modest cottage residences, such as those associated with garden suburbs, would enable workers to become homeowners. American housing developments were, above all, capitalist ven-

tures founded by profit-motivated business enterprises rather than by collectiv-
ist associations.[12]

Village Improvement Societies

Nineteenth-century village improvement societies represented the second influence contributing to the garden-city movement. These societies originated
as a regional campaign for beautifying New England's rural villages and bur-
geoned into a national campaign. Village improvement started with the Laurel
Hill Association, Stockbridge, Massachusetts, in 1853. Its founder was Mary
Hopkins, the college-educated daughter of a prominent family, who took it
upon herself to improve the image of Stockbridge by raising money through
private subscription for planting trees along the streets and byways. She next
turned her attention to the village cemetery, transforming a burial ground into
a romantic retreat embowered with flowering shrubs. Landscape improvements
went beyond planting to include road paving, decorative street furniture and
lighting, signage, water supply, and sewerage. Hopkins enlisted in the crusade
the Reverend B. G. Northrup, secretary of the Connecticut Board of Education,
who beginning in 1869 traveled throughout New England encouraging smaller
communities to address environmental issues by forming village improvement
societies. He stressed the importance of women such as Miss Hopkins to their
success: "A society engaging all classes instead of one or two is bound to be
more immediately successful than one that includes one class or 'set.' . . . Most
communities are likely to wait for the impulse of a leader. Many efficient associations have been formed by women, and of nearly all at least a part of the
officers are women. If the executive committee numbers fifteen, I advise that
eight should be women. . . . Women succeed better in getting money and in
securing the cooperation of all classes."[13] Village improvement was not about
the establishment of new communities, but rather the enhancement of existing
ones. Yet its occupation with landscape issues and its popular, domestic appeal,
not to mention its eventual employment of professional landscape architects,
carried over into the design of industrial villages and housing estates. Writing
for *The Nation* in 1874, A. G. Sedgwick acknowledged the similarities between
village improvement and the city parks and suburban movement, noting that
the same enthusiasm exhibited for the creation of parks and suburban improvement in larger cities was visible in rural villages where tree and shrub planting
and the improvement of streets "infus[ed] . . . the inhabitants [with] a pride in
the appearance and reputation of their town." This work, he suggested, would

ultimately overcome the indifference of the "smaller and more disreputable pol-
itician" and "the influx of . . . foreign populations" threatening urban decline.[14]

The 1890s appear to have been the decade of greatest interest in village
improvement as it merged with the new civic art leagues that drew together
women, politicians, and designers. The popularity of this interest continued
until World War I. In 1913, Parris Thaxter Farwell, chairman of the Village
Improvement Committee of the Massachusetts Civic League, published a book
on the history, goals, organization, and management of village improvement
societies. According to Farwell, "a beautiful, healthful, and wholesome environment will go far to solve the most serious problems of society." He further
suggested that employers who made their industrial surroundings attractive to
workers benefited from greater loyalty and satisfaction. Those with a vested
interest in the material well-being of their community, the property owners,
were the benefactors of these societies, although the success of the venture
depended on the participation of all concerned, including the working-class
tenants. Competitions and awards for the better-maintained yards, gardens, and
cottage adornments were some of the inducements used to encourage participation. Albeit paternalistic, this competition contributed to the notion that an
attractive environment was a healthful and prosperous one.[15]

Among the prominent urban professionals calling for village improvement
societies were the civil engineer and renowned crusader for sanitary reform
George E. Waring Jr. and the distinguished landscape architects Frederick Law
Olmsted Jr., Charles Eliot, and Warren Henry Manning (1860–1938). Manning
and Eliot encouraged the members of such village societies to build roads and
bridges and to design new communities without destroying the beauty and
vistas afforded by natural scenery. Addressing the second National Conference
on City Planning in 1910, Manning mentioned that he had participated in "the
improvement of many employees' villages and helped to reduce the cost of
housing in some of these," but that greater opportunity lay in the planning and
construction of new manufacturing villages that, from the outset, provided
houses and services, including water supply and sewerage, together with
schools, parks, and playgrounds. Such improvements could be achieved when
the "capitalist is found who is not afraid to break away from . . . commonplace
methods."[16]

Industrial Housing Estates

Manning found such a capitalist in Franklin A. Seiberling, a self-made business-
man and founder of the Goodyear Tire and Rubber Company. In 1911, he

designed for Seiberling a three-thousand-acre estate, "Stan Hywet," near Akron, Ohio, the city in which Seiberling located his factories. Manning, who like Shurcliff had served an apprenticeship with Frederick Law Olmsted Sr., combined a knowledge of horticulture with landscape design. In 1896, he established an independent firm and rapidly developed a reputation as an environmentalist. He was a founding member of the American Society of Landscape Architects, of which he served as president, a founder of the American City Planning Institute and of the American Civic Association, through which he spoke on village improvement. His early work appeared in Hopedale, Massachusetts, where he designed the housing development Bancroft Park and later a public park bordering the Mill River, for the employees of the Draper Manufacturing Company.[17]

Manning's work with Olmsted had exposed him to resources beyond New England and had given him the opportunity to travel extensively. Seiberling and his wife trusted Manning to create something new, bold, and essentially midwestern. The Stan Hywet estate has recently been restored and is considered one of the United States' finest landscape designs, contributing to the post-Victorian "American style." Aware of Manning's industrial housing developments, Seiberling commissioned him to design housing estates for his employees at Fairlawn Heights and Goodyear Heights in 1912–13. Located on converted farmland, approximately one-quarter mile from the Goodyear factories, Goodyear Heights occupies an irregular sloping terrain that confronted its designer with a challenge: to provide 436 house lots, each with a frontage of fifty feet, paved streets for access, tree-planting for shade, parks, and services, and utilities.[18]

By the onset of the twentieth century, water supply and sewerage, together with electric lighting and telephone service, were requisite to new residential developments in all but the poorest communities, but the capital outlays for these were considerable. Usually, public and private utility companies offered service to existing communities where substantial investment and taxing authority already existed. New developments, with services provided at the outset, created a tremendous burden on developers who had to recoup their investment in the sale of lots that far exceeded the cost of land alone. Home builders could not afford to carry these costs, nor could they borrow the capital to develop large tracts. Howard's garden city was one solution. Letchworth, outside London, was developed by the First Garden City, Ltd., which raised the capital for development through the sale of debentures. Eventually, improvements in the land would entice industry and labor, if one assumed as Howard did that "if you build it, they will come." The problem was that it took more than ten years before the First Garden City, Ltd., provided its stockholders with a dividend. Thomas Adams, first secretary of the Garden City Association, who in later years became a town planner and a tireless promoter of the garden city to American and Canadian audiences, was confronted with the statistical reality of investment and return. The editor of *The American City* in commenting on one of Adams's appeals, "Let Us Have an American Letchworth," pointed out the painful reality of the delay between investment and profit. Adams's project for Temiscaming, Ontario, in 1917, succeeded only because of its single-enterprise backing. Such was the case with Goodyear Heights and other experiments in the United States. The Goodyear Tire and Rubber Company was the sole developer.

Goodyear Heights differed from the garden city not only in conception, but also in plan. There was no civic center, no monumental boulevard leading to village offices, library, and school. House lots and park land took up the site. It remained an industrial housing estate and was subordinate to Akron for employment, entertainment, and government. Another fundamental difference between Goodyear Heights and the English garden city was the type of housing constructed. As a matter of family preference and for purposes of marketing, most of the units were single-family dwellings. Semidetached dwellings, long associated with industrial housing, projected the negative image of company rentals, which Seiberling clearly wished to avoid. Moreover, the houses were designed in a variety of styles to avoid the company housing stereotype.[19]

Through the cost savings of large-scale development, the designers of Goodyear Heights hoped to produce homes affordable to the working class. When finished, the homes cost between $2,000 and $3,000 and were financed through local lenders offering long-term mortgages (up to twenty-seven years) and backed by the Goodyear Tire Company. To discourage speculation, ownership was confined to employees and their families, and mortgage payments were set at local real estate market rates.[20]

Perhaps the finest industrial housing estate constructed before World War I was Eclipse Park near Beloit, Wisconsin, developed by Fairbanks, Morse, and Company, manufacturers of giant stationary engines and other industrial machinery. The founders of the company had built for their workers Fairbanks Village near Saint Johnsbury, Vermont, during the middle decades of the nineteenth century and had long maintained an interest in improved living conditions surrounding their factories. When they relocated their new engine plant to the Midwest, they purchased land near Beloit with the idea of eventually building another model village. For several years, existing housing in Beloit met the company's needs, but with the coming of war in Europe and the demand at home for the company's new line of gasoline-powered engines, additional housing was needed. As was the case in Goodyear Heights, Eclipse Park was set apart from the factories by a belt of undeveloped land, used as a park and athletic field, and lying within a five- to fifteen-minute walk of the new development.[21]

George B. Post and Sons of New York, one of America's more prominent architectural firms, which had designed the Wisconsin state capitol in Madison, was chosen to design Eclipse Park. The landscape architect William Pitkin Jr. assisted Post in developing the fifty-three-acre tract. A contour plan, similar to Goodyear Heights, was imposed on the site to minimize changes in street grade and to create changing vistas along the curving streets. Seventeen blocks were divided into lots varying from 40 to 60 feet in width and between 80 to 110 feet in depth, depending on the type of house purchased. The contour plan was derived from the English garden of the eighteenth century, and by the early nineteenth century, suburban housing schemes near London, Liverpool, and Manchester employed the plan in park-like settings for upper-middle-class families eager to escape the industrial city. Llewellyn Park, Orange, New Jersey, 1853–55, and Riverside, Illinois, southwest of Chicago, 1869, the latter laid out by Frederick Law Olmsted Sr. and Calvert Vaux, were among the first contour plans for residential developments in the United States. Employed in industrial housing in the late nineteenth century, this method of landscape design was well known before being taken up by the garden-city movement. Generous plantings of trees and shrubs, together with meridians of lawn between streets and sidewalks and sidewalks and houses, created attractive neighborhoods for Sunday strolls.[22]

The chief artifacts of these garden suburbs were the houses themselves. At Eclipse Park, George Post and Sons offered a variety of types and styles. The smallest type of unit was a four-room, two-bedroom house featuring Colonial Revival or Craftsman style. Five-, six-, and seven-room houses for larger families in a variety of eclectic styles were also offered. To keep costs as low as possible, construction was frame as opposed to masonry, although exterior wall surfaces were available in stucco. Nevertheless, the attractive assortment of cottages ranging in price from $2,400 to $3,100 (about double the annual salary of the average machinist) was quickly sold, "the demand being extremely great" on the basis of 10 percent down with monthly installments at market rate.[23]

Kincaid, Illinois, differed from Goodyear Heights and Eclipse Park. More than an industrial housing estate, Kincaid was a single-enterprise town. In 1903, Francis S. Peabody, president of the Peabody Coal Company, acquired 40,000 acres of mineral rights in central Illinois for excavating bituminous coal. All too

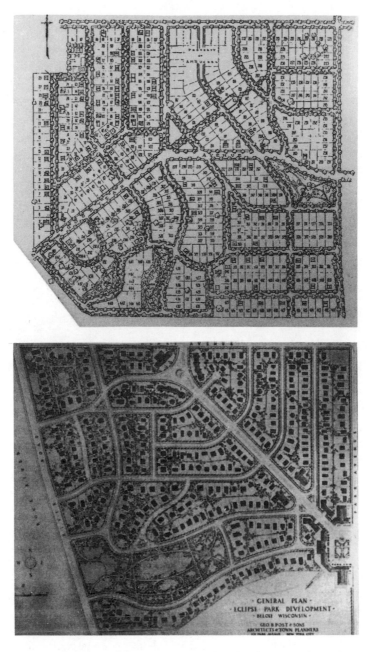

4. America's industrial housing estates. Top, Goodyear Heights, Akron, Ohio, 1912–13, designed by Warren Henry Manning (source: *The American City* 12 [April 1915]). Bottom, Eclipse Park, Beloit, Wisconsin, 1915, designed by George B. Post & Sons of New York. (source: *The Architectural Record* 43 [March 1918]).

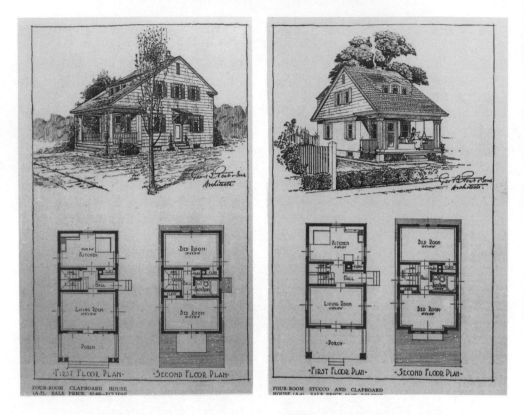

FOUR-ROOM CLAPBOARD HOUSE
(A-7). SALE PRICE. $2,400—ECLIPSE

FOUR-ROOM STUCCO AND CLAPBOARD
HOUSE (A-6) SALE PRICE $2,400—ECLIPSE

5. Eclipse Park in Beloit, Wisconsin, offered residents a variety of types and styles. This is the smallest house, containing four rooms. On the left is the Colonial Revival style; on the right, the Craftsman style. Each house was priced at $2,400 (source: *The Architectural Record* 43 [March, 1918]).

familiar with typical mining towns, Peabody envisioned a model settlement amid several of his mines and in 1912 began acquiring 1,200 acres of surface property six miles northwest of the small town of Taylorville. An electric power plant fed by coal and located in the new settlement was to create "a spotless electric town with every modern utility and convenience," according to the *Taylorville Daily Breeze* of September 29, 1913. Much of the town had been completed by 1914, including a railroad depot, bank, commercial buildings, and school. All the sidewalks and several blocks of the principal street were paved in concrete. Alvord and Burdick, a firm of civil engineers, supervised the site work, but the creative plan was largely the work of Ossian Cole Simonds (1855–1931), the Chicago landscape architect.[24]

Simonds, together with Manning, had helped found the American Civic Association (1897) and the American Society of Landscape Architects (1899). The men may have first met in Chicago in 1893, when Manning supervised the plantings of the World's Columbian Exposition for the Olmsted office. Simonds, like Manning, sought an American expression of landscape design and found it in the broad expansiveness of the midwestern prairies. He eschewed Beaux-Arts formalism for the indigenous and naturalistic style that Frank Lloyd Wright embraced in his plans of residential estates. In 1903, Simonds founded his own firm, designing parks in Pittsburgh, Pennsylvania; Madison, Wisconsin; and Quincy, Springfield, and Lake Forest, Illinois, as well as participating in the extension of Chicago's park system. His work in Lake Forest involved residential layouts, but Kincaid was his only complete town design.[25]

Two site conditions, the Chicago and Illinois Midland Railroad and the south fork of the Sangamon River, influenced Simonds's plan. The twists and turns of the river are reflected in the contoured park and streets located above the flood plain. Main Street was curved to accommodate the city hall, which was set in a hemicycle, and although the principal streets curve, the residential lots are mostly rectangular. The housing was strictly detached single family and consisted of four- and five-room bungalows outfitted with coal-fired furnaces and wired for electricity supplied by the company power plant. In a promotional brochure, architect George W. Maher, who designed the housing and public buildings, made reference to "Garden City Improvements" in justifying the novelty and proven success of such new concepts in town planning and architecture.[26]

The Garden City: Concept and Reality

Those families fortunate enough to purchase a home in Goodyear Heights, Eclipse Park, and Kincaid[27] enjoyed the amenities of attractive surroundings and well-designed houses at affordable prices. Property sales were brisk, suggesting a ready and receptive clientele. The appearance of places like Goodyear Heights, even today, attests to the success of their design. Organized labor did not affect the design of these communities. Plans of each were well under way before strikes threatened the companies behind the developments. Nor did employees have much say in matters of architecture, other than choosing a house type or the number of bedrooms. But they did take pride in their new homes and assumed responsibility for maintaining their neighborhoods as a matter of civic interest.

Thomas Adams and Raymond Unwin, who assisted Howard with his garden city schemes, never tired of promoting the garden-city idea in the United States. Their influence among practitioners, educators, and writers influenced a generation of Americans, beginning with John Nolen, and continuing to Clarence Stein, Henry Wright, Arthur Comey, Henry Churchill, Elbert Peets, Lewis Mumford, Edith Wood, and Tracy Auger, to name a few, who shaped American planning and housing policy in the 1920s and 1930s. It is no wonder that the garden-city image of a suburban development in a park-like setting became so ingrained. When European modernists were dismissing the garden city as quaintly Edwardian, Americans were still carrying the torch. In reality, however, nothing was actually built on the garden-city model in the United States, and this was especially true when it came to housing. Despite sympathy for the Arts and Crafts style of vernacular building forms, the final architectural expression in the United States was derivative of American and not English cottage design.

Development relied on industrial patronage, and property ownership remained in private hands, fiercely independent and guarded by the slogans of building and loan societies. The frame-constructed, detached, single-family house predominated. The earlier Olmsted tradition of landscape design underlay the approach taken by Manning and Simonds in their plans. Most of the places dubbed garden suburbs and garden villages were industrial housing estates—no more, no less.

Notes

1. Neponsit Garden Village (1913) and Indian Hill (1912), Massachusetts; Kistler (1915) and Kohler (1915), Wisconsin; Firestone Park (1916), Ohio; Alcoa (1919), Erwin (1914), and Kingsport (1915), Tennessee; Corey [Fairfield] (1909) and Kaulton (1912), Alabama; Tyrone (1916), New Mexico; and Torrence (1912), California, are additional examples of model housing estates and company towns. A comprehensive survey of similar places can be found in Arthur C. Comey and Max S. Wehrly, "Planned Communities," in *Supplementary Report of the Urbanism Committee*, pt. 1 (Washington, D.C.: Government Printing Office, 1939). See also Joseph L. Arnold, *The New Deal in the Suburbs* (Columbus: Ohio State University Press, 1971), 5–8. A recent study of such communities can be found in Margaret Crawford, *Building the Workingman's Paradise* (New York: Verso, 1995).

2. Ebenezer Howard, *Garden Cities of Tomorrow* (first publ. 1902; London: Faber and Faber, 1945), originally published under the title *To-morrow a Peaceful Path to Real Reform* (1898). For the best overview of the garden-city movement and for a description of New Earswick, see Walter L. Creese, *The Search for Environment* (New Haven: Yale University Press, 1966), 191–202.

3. Creese, *The Search for Environment*, 321; Lloyd Rodwin, *The British New Towns Policy* (Cambridge, Mass.: Harvard University Press, 1956), 21–23; Stanley Buder, *Visionaries and Planners* (New York: Oxford University Press, 1990), 95, 182–83.

4. Mervyn Miller, *Letchworth, the First Garden City* (Chichester, England: Phillimore, 1989), 125–26, 128.

5. *Annuaire de L'École Centrale, 1832–1908* (Paris: Bureaux, 1909), 59–74; Emile Muller, *Habitations ouvrieres et agricoles, cities, bains, et lavoirs* (Paris: Victor Dalmont, 1854), 8–9.

6. Emile Muller and Emile Cacheux, *Les Habitations ouvrieres en tous pays* (Paris: J. DeJey, 1879), 63–64.

7. Jules Challamel, *Les Habitations bon marché* (Paris: F. Pichon, 1895), 17–18; Roy Lubove, *The Progressives and the Slums* (Pittsburgh: University of Pittsburgh Press, 1962), 102, 114.

8. Buder, *Visionaries and Planners*, 147–56; Jonathan Barnett, *The Elusive City* (New York: Harper and Row, 1986), 107–35.

9. Robert W. de Forest, "Municipal Housing in the United States," in *Bureau des Kongresses, Bericht über den* IX. *Internationalen Wohnungskongress* (Vienna: Verlag de Zentralstelle, 1911), 257–58; George B. Ford, "The Ninth International Housing Congress in Vienna," *The American City* 3, August 1910, 81–83.

10. "Garden City Platted by Russell Sage Foundation," *The Survey* 25, November 1910, 309–10; Leland M. Roth, *A Concise History of American Architecture* (New York: Harper and Row), 225–26.

11. Crawford, *Building the Workingman's Paradise*, 152–67.

12. John Nolen, "Organization of Credit for Housing Purposes," in *Bureau des Kongresses, Bericht über den* IX. *Internationalen Wohnungskongress* (Vienna: Verlag de Zentralstelle, 1911), 463–64.

13. Ibid., 468.

14. B. G. Northrop, "The Work of Village Improvement Societies," *The Forum* 19 (March 1895): 104.

15. A. G. Sedgwick, "Village Improvement," *The Nation* 19, September 1874, 149–50.

16. Parris T. Farwell, *Village Improvement* (New York: Sturgis and Walton, 1913), 5.

17. Warren H. Manning, "Villages for the Workingmen and Workingmen's Homes," in *Proceedings of the Second National Conference on City Planning and the Problems of Congestion* (Cambridge, Mass: Harvard University Press, 1910), 103.

18. Blanche Linden-Ward, "Stan Hywet," *Landscape Architect* 77 (July–August 1987): 66–71; *The National Cyclopedia of American Biography* (New York: James T. White, 1947), 201–2; Warren Henry Manning, *The History of Village Improvement in the United States* (reprint from *The Craftsman*, February 1904); John S. Garner, *The Model Company Town* (Amherst: University of Massachusetts Press, 1984), 152–57, 194–96.

19. Warren H. Manning, "A Step Towards Solving the Industrial Housing Problem," *The American City* 12, April 1915, 321–25.

20. "Let Us Have an American Letchworth," *The American City* 15, July 1916, 31–32; Robert Fortier, *Villes industrielles planifiées* (Quebec: Boréal, 1996), 123–25; Perry R. MacNeille, "Ways and Means of Providing Workingmen's Houses," *The American City* 16, May 1917, 508–11.

21. Manning, "A Step Towards Solving the Industrial Housing Problem," 324.

22. Robert H. Morse, *St. Johnsbury, Vt., and Important Industrial Beginnings, 1830, Newcomen Society* (Princeton: Princeton University Press, 1947), 9; Lawrence Veiller, "Industrial Housing Developments in America, pt. 1: Eclipse Park," *Architectural Record* 43, March 1918, 231–56.

23. Albert Fein, *Frederick Law Olmsted and the American Environmental Tradition* (New York: George Braziller, 1972), 32–35.

24. Veiller, "Industrial Housing Developments in America, pt. 1," 234–56; Roth, *A Concise History of American Architecture*, 228–29.

25. "Creating a Model Town," *Geo. W. Maher Quarterly* 1 (April–June 1995): 1–11; "A Big Day in Kincaid. The Bosses Gather for a Check-up on Kincaid," *Taylorville Daily Breeze*, September 29, 1913.

26. Lance M. Neckar, "Developing Landscape Architecture for the Twentieth Century: The Career of Warren H. Manning," *Landscape Journal* 8 (Fall 1989). 88; Mara Gelbloom, "Ossian Simonds: Prairie Spirit in Landscape Gardening," *Prairie School Review* 12 (Winter 1975): 7–8.

27. A. T. Luce, "Kincaid, Illinois—A Model Mining Town," *The American City* 13, July 1915, 10–13; *Kincaid: The Coalectric City* (Kincaid, Ill.: Kincaid Land Association, 1914), n.p. Despite Kincaid's promise, the town did not fare as well as Goodyear Heights and Eclipse Park. Many of the distinctive commercial buildings and the railroad station have been razed. Several mines have closed, and nuclear power has replaced coal as the fuel for producing electricity. Once billed as the "Coalectric City," Kincaid's future has dimmed.

3

"No Idea of Doing Anything Wonderful"

The Labor-Crisis Origins of National Housing Policy and the Reconstruction of the Working-Class Community, 1917–1919

ERIC J. KAROLAK

War is not a process of saving money—it is a test of a nation's imagination in spending it.[1]

World War I marked a watershed in the history of the American state. As part of an unprecedented "total war" effort, the federal government launched the first proactive and coordinated national programs to address the "labor problem" and the "housing problem." Where before there had been only limited efforts to mediate disputes between employers and employees, Washington dramatically expanded its activities to encompass job training, a centralized labor-recruiting plan, separate federal offices concerned with women workers and African American workers, and even a housing program—in short, a wide array of activities aimed to maximize labor productivity and to prevent disputes. Where before there had been only a handful of municipal housing codes and model private developments, Washington embarked on a multimillion-dollar coast-to-coast program of government-funded or government-constructed homes and model "industrial villages" for American workers.[2]

The dramatic departure in housing cannot be fully understood without an appreciation of the circumstances that also gave rise to the first federal labor policy. Congress and President Woodrow Wilson supported the construction of industrial villages, an expanded commuter-transportation infrastructure, and a variety of recreational, educational, and social programs for war workers as a means of coping with the wartime crisis. Scholars of the first national housing programs have slighted the central role played by the war and its attendant labor crisis and have thus afforded themselves only a partial view and limited appreciation of "war emergency housing." Roy Lubove, the first to explore the wartime effort, stressed its significance as a precursor to New Deal housing reforms and as a catalyst in the development of city planning, not as a dramatic departure from previous piecemeal private efforts. Other historians have called the wartime program "an effort to reorganize the proletariat's environment of everyday life in such a way as to render working people more amenable to the goals of capital." However, the housing historian Gail Radford noted that architects and planners designed the war-labor communities much as they had middle-class prewar developments, and she dismissed class analysis as the sole explanatory tool for understanding the wartime departure. Housing profession-als, contended Radford, sought to strengthen the "structure of civil society" and promote "local community life," not to repress workers in the interest of big business.[3]

A heightened appreciation for the complexities of the wartime housing program can be gained through an examination of the contemporary labor cri-sis. The Department of Labor's U.S. Housing Corporation (USHC) and the U.S. Shipping Board's Emergency Fleet Corporation (EFC) were created in 1917 as part of a broad response to the wartime labor crisis. The federal govern-ment built houses partly in an effort to more efficiently channel proletarians into factories and shipyards. However, as this chapter argues, the motives be-hind the war-labor housing experiment were far more complex and were influ-enced by the architects, city planners, and housing reformers who played active roles in wartime housing agencies and seized the opportunity to practice their gospel of community building on a grand scale. Housing became linked to the need to increase labor productivity and to ensure social stability in the volatile wartime atmosphere. As never before, national leaders recognized the impor-tance of working-class home life and also the critical role of the federal govern-ment in improving housing conditions. Yet these new priorities also reinforced the communitarian vision shared by prominent architects, planners, and reform-ers. "There is no such thing as capital and labor," opined one architect promi-nent in the war-labor housing program. Through the model communities he and his colleagues planned and created, they sought to redefine the social iden-tity of U.S. workers and their families and to reconstruct the working class into an idealized image of the American middle class by molding the built environ-ment of the former.[4]

The Dual Emergence of Labor and Housing Policy

Although the "housing problem" had attracted attention before World War I, no consensus had emerged about the state's role in housing reform. By the 1910s, progressives such as the economist Carol Aronovici determined that cities and states had focused unduly on "the pathological aspect of housing," trying to outlaw the tenement rather than to address the fundamental causes of the housing shortage in working-class communities. Prewar working-class home construction remained a private undertaking limited, as John S. Garner in Chapter 2 observes, to company towns and a handful of privately funded model developments employing the garden-city ideal. "Private initiative has failed lamentably," the reformer Edith Elmer Wood concluded. Wood and other housing advocates increasingly called for "constructive legislation" that would offer federal government incentives for greater private investment in working-class housing and more direct government involvement in construction.[5]

The wartime industrial crisis pushed the federal government into the complicated process of working-class community building and changed the terms of the housing debate. Prewar housing reformers supported federal government involvement in housing from concern for the health and moral well-being of working-class families. Architects, city planners, and enlightened builders restructured the debate to emphasize the direct benefits of reducing labor turnover, increasing productivity, and fostering social harmony as primary elements in the brief for federal housing. In short, the demands of the war effort on U.S. industrial capacity dictated a coordinated response to urban congestion, one that would increase productivity and contentment and at the same time improve the morals and health of the laboring classes. Housing became, for a time, clearly an aspect of the "labor problem" and consequently an issue worthy of federal attention.

The economic boom associated with the European war increased demand for labor and contributed to a decline in immigration. The result was a "seller's market" for labor. As workers flocked to new opportunities in congested industrial cities or remote centers of war production, local housing markets quickly became saturated. The housing famine only added to employers' labor woes. Even if war contractors could afford premium wages resulting from the relative scarcity of labor, they might be unable to attract or keep a sufficient labor force because workers could not find adequate housing. Rising housing costs angered and frustrated workers who demanded higher wages.[6]

These developments exerted a pernicious effect on war production. Employers bid against one another for houses as well as for workers. One firm in

Bath, Maine, for example, thought nothing of "hiring occupied houses of work-ers of the Navy, over their heads, evicting the workers of the Navy, and install-ing their own workers." In some shipyards, government investigators estimated, 50 percent of the machinery lay idle "with labor available, because there were no places for the men to sleep."[7]

The housing crisis was in part a result of the scarcity of both capital and building supplies. Tight capital markets, for example, limited the funds local companies could subscribe to a building effort. In late 1917, Bethlehem Steel halted the construction of three thousand houses at its Sparrows Point, Mary-land, mill because of lack of capital. In addition, raw-material priorities regu-lated by the War Industries Board restricted the building of new houses and apartments, as did the general shortage of labor. The Labor Department esti-mated that expenditures for working-class housing had dropped 90 percent from 1916 to 1917. Moreover, local building programs such as those in Bridge-port, Connecticut, and Kenosha, Wisconsin, appeared, for the most part, only in communities where prewar industrial development had already created a housing shortage before the United States entered the war.[8]

Faced with a mounting industrial crisis, Washington moved toward its first housing policy with what Roy Lubove termed "glacial slowness." Congress de-bated the issue of housing in spring 1917, but it delayed appropriations for one year and began construction only months before the Armistice was signed. This twelve-month gestation attested to the magnitude of the departure represented by federally built working-class communities. That it took *only* one year, how-ever, is also testimony to the crisis milieu that attended the birth of the first U.S. national housing policy. Significantly, proponents of federal action relied on a new, production-centered paradigm for understanding the need for work-ing-class housing, rather than on the traditional Progressive emphasis on the relations between housing conditions and health and morals. The war-labor housing program marked a departure, not only in the central place it gave to government in shaping working-class communities, but also in the preeminence it gave to economics *over* social justice in the brief for housing reform.[9]

Washington conceived the war-labor housing program through delibera-tions of the Council of National Defense (CND), a voluntary advisory body formed in 1916 to address U.S. preparedness. Less than one month after the United States declared war, the CND Labor Committee appointed Philip Hiss, a prominent New York City architect, to head its Housing Section. Hiss was joined by Charles H. Whitaker, editor of the *Journal of the American Institute of Architecture*, and John Nolen, the city planner whose expertise included industrial housing. In August, Hiss's group sponsored a conference of leading town planners, architects, and builders. These experts concluded that housing was "the first element in any intelligent plan for speeding up and reducing the cost of industrial production" and maintained that it would be "practically impossible" for the private sector alone to meet war housing needs.

The CND charged the New York construction mogul Otto M. Eidlitz to determine a plan of action. Eidlitz urged the creation of a permanent "executive organization" in government with an initial appropriation of $20 million. In November, Eidlitz met with officials of the Labor Department and U.S. Shipping Board, who concluded that under existing appropriations no agency of the government had the legal ability or sufficient funds to buy, sell, or rent land or housing. In December, Eidlitz drafted a bill to create a central housing organization under the authority of the president. Eidlitz stressed that the housing shortage continued to diminish production, and for the war effort to succeed, "it is imperative that labor be taken care of so as to enable these various localities to hold their men. I am not an alarmist," the builder warned, "but the situation . . . spells disaster under present conditions."[10]

Significantly, nowhere in the government reports and memoranda on the war-labor housing crisis does there appear a case for housing *reform* as a matter of social and economic justice. Indeed, CND officials working on industrial housing eschewed the notion of any broad reform agenda. Hiss explained to a Congressional panel that the wartime industrial crisis rested on "the increasing inefficiency of labor, owing to hard living conditions. We certainly have got to make a man do one and a half or two times as much work as he did before," he stressed, "and to do that we have got to groom him like we do our race horses." Largely rejecting the English example where Parliament used the war to promote the larger cause of working-class housing reform, the final CND report stated bluntly: "Our problem is essentially that of relieving congestion due to war activities and not one directed to the amelioration of general living conditions." Eidlitz stressed that "any Government aid for industrial housing should be considered strictly as a war measure and be rigidly confined to cases where the restriction of output of war materials would otherwise occur." The wartime production crisis, not the general welfare of urban workers and their families, justified the first federal home-building program.[11]

In January 1918, the Senate passed a bill to fund housing construction for shipyard workers under the aegis of the Shipping Board's EFC. Concerned that a fragmented approach would result, Labor Secretary William B. Wilson, with the approval of the president, arranged an interdepartmental meeting at which cabinet secretaries and agency chiefs agreed to "proceed with the object in mind of having the housing problem ultimately administered through the De-

partment of Labor." On March 1, Congress channeled to the EFC appropriations of $50 million for housing construction and $20 million for improving
shipyard transportation logistics. These appropriations were followed in May
and July by acts authorizing the president to address the problem of housing
war workers generally and appropriating a total of $100 million. President Wil-
son delegated control to the Labor Department, which incorporated its Bureau
of Industrial Housing and Transportation as the U.S. Housing Corporation
(USHC) and disbursed the first funds for construction in July.[12]

The EFC and USHC employed different methods to resolve the housing
crisis, but quickly achieved comparable results. Primarily charged with building
ships, the EFC chose to leave house construction in private hands, exercising
strict control by lending federal monies to shipbuilding companies, which then
undertook construction according to federal standards. The Labor Department,
on the other hand, created the USHC specifically to undertake direct construction. However, for both agencies, construction was a last resort, and neither
building program survived a postwar backlash. Still, in less than two years,
between the initial appropriations in spring 1918 and the conclusion of construction late in 1919, the government built more than 16,000 homes at 150
sites from coast to coast, including dozens of completed communities. This
housing sheltered an estimated 95,000 people, half of whom were war workers.
Ironically, most houses were not occupied until after the Armistice. All told,
the USHC and EFC programs in construction, expanded room letting, and
improved transportation logistics helped meet the housing needs of at least
250,000 people. Moreover, because the USHC's Architectural Division, headed
by Eidlitz, oversaw much of the planning and design functions of the EFC as
well, the projects of the two agencies revealed a shared vision of an idealized
working-class community.[13]

What to Build? Family Housing for Contented Worker-Owners

Labor and housing advocates were able to convince Congress and the Wilson
administration to back the creation of the EFC and USHC by emphasizing how
they would help ease the housing crisis. Once the programs were established,
they quickly reached what one war housing official called the "doctor stage,"
when the prescriptions of reformers, town planners, and architects became increasingly influential. As early as October 1917, Hiss suggested involving
prominent architects and reformers in the policymaking process because he
thought "it might be better to have these [individuals] *inside* rather than outside

in our future transactions." Reform-oriented architects and planners recognized the opportunity to break with the past and look beyond the war emergency. The noted town planner and landscape architect Robert Anderson Pope predicted that Washington's actions in 1918 would determine "for better or worse the housing problem in this country for the next ten generations." A federal program, he stressed, would create "at once an entirely unprecedented, unheard of, and in many directions, undesired, high minimum standards [sic] of home and environmental conditions."[14]

Drawing from the cusp of the design and planning fields, housing professionals and social reformers hoped to socially reshape residents by physically reshaping *residences*, to reconstruct the working class by reconstructing working-class communities. Within the limits of wartime exigency, they created communities for workers modeled on prevailing ideals of normative middle-class life. As managers had tried for decades to shape social relations in the workplace, housing officials tried to shape class relations in the homes and neighborhoods of wartime housing projects.[15]

Housing professionals, social reformers, business leaders, and public officials all found common ground in the requirement that working-class housing provide assistance in increasing industrial production. The decision to build primarily permanent housing structures, for example, illustrates this convergence of long-term consequences and short-term concerns. Temporary buildings—shacks or barracks—could hardly provide a middle-class ideal for their residents to model. A Newport News Shipbuilding Company representative stated bluntly, "[W]e do not want the class of mechanics that would live in cantonments." Architects joined with businessmen in favoring permanent construction, arguing that the long-term social consequences of temporary housing could be severe. Market factors reinforced social considerations in favor of permanent construction; Labor Department officials determined that the greater "salvage value" of permanent buildings outweighed the "relatively slight" savings from building decent temporary structures.[16]

A similar admixture of concerns about the short-term impact on productivity and the longer-term social consequences determined the kind of construction undertaken. Although the USHC and the EFC planned a variety of types of structures—row houses, detached and semidetached houses, apartment buildings, and dormitories—in projects that ranged from a few dozen to over two thousand units—detached single-family or two-family houses arranged in planned, self-contained communities distinguished the government's housing program. This configuration would promote homeownership, an outcome war-labor housing officials associated with both increasing productivity and transforming workers' values. Homeownership, they believed, reduced employee absenteeism and labor turnover. Workers with mortgages were more likely to look to the home, rather than the shop floor, union hall, or immigrant aid society, to orient themselves in the world. The housing advocate George Maxwell saw ownership developing "the homing instinct" in workers as strongly "as it is developed in the homing instinct of the pigeon." This conservative influence of homeowning was not lost on businessmen: "Get them [workers] to invest their savings in their homes and own them," stated one industrialist. "Then they won't leave and they won't strike. It ties them down so that they have a stake in our prosperity."[17]

While the strategy of promoting homeownership met both the short- and long-term goals of war housing administrators, it challenged the long-standing consensus among large sections of the industrial working class that homeownership diminished labor's independence. Middle-class reformers and housing professionals in the USHC and EFC preferred homeownership, but "Labor," one federal official acknowledged, "does not entirely concur in this view. The men find some industrial disadvantage in being tied to a house and, consequently, a job." To address this concern, the Labor Department formulated a prearranged buyback program and even considered the "co-partnership" model of selling shares in communities. Faced with reluctance on the part of workers and the need to quickly put families under roof in often-unfinished developments, the USHC opted to lease its properties and to encourage renters to purchase their homes.[18]

As part of the initiative to redefine the working-class community along middle-class lines, government housing was erected in planned suburban communities, often modeled on the garden-city ideal. War-labor housing officials eschewed isolated construction of housing space. Philip Hiss acknowledged that the housing question involved "both the home and the community," and both the EFC and USHC focused on large-scale developments often planned as model communities. Complete communities were built in isolated areas such as the massive Hog Island shipyard facility near Philadelphia or the Sparrows Point shipyards near Baltimore. Both organizations elevated town planning to an exalted position, placing planners rather than engineers or architects at the head of each site's project team. War-labor housing administrators easily assumed the role of community builders because so many had been prominent in the city planning, architectural, and housing reform fields before the war.[19]

Federal housing officials tried to locate communities on the urban periphery, in keeping with the trend in prewar private industrial housing. These suburban communities were planned in contrast to the dirt- and disease-ridden

New London
July 29-1919
B1054 — Looking S.W. along Jefferson Ave from Lincoln Ave.

6. Congress and the Wilson administration created two federal agencies in 1918 to solve the World War I housing crisis. Top, a row of houses in New London, Connecticut, built by the U.S. Housing Corporation (USHC). Bottom, houses in Bath, Maine, built by the USHC.

tenements that concentrated large and often foreign-born populations together in a way that inhibited social and cultural assimilation with middle-class America. A merger of urban and rural, reformers thought, would uplift industrial workers. Strong economic incentives also influenced this push to suburbanize workers. Expensive central-city land values meant that tenements—model or otherwise—were virtually the only cost-effective housing possible. By the 1910s, aided by improvements in commuter transportation, housing experts in Europe and America hailed the promise of cheap, as well as aesthetically pleasing, suburban cottage-communities for workers as a remedy for urban industrial congestion. Such working-class suburbs might offer "an environment more constructive of body and morals," but private entities operating in a market-oriented framework would not build them.[20]

Many war-labor communities incorporated curvilinear streets and landscaping inspired by the garden-city plan and were essentially modeled on the middle-class suburban developments on the cutting edge of prewar town planning. At Union Park Gardens, the EFC development in Wilmington, Delaware, the town planner John Nolen laid out winding streets that followed the natural topography, assuring a pleasant appearance, economy in road-building resources, and a greater degree of traffic control without sacrificing the residential autonomy of the development. Government planners understood that this approach not only added aesthetic value, but also constituted one of the most profitable investments in a housing project when it came to renting or selling the properties.

Federal housing and labor officials believed that working-class access to suburban communities could uplift society's "lower orders" and improve social cohesion. One builder claimed that government support for the garden-city plan demonstrated "an earnest bona fide effort to make conditions better for the poor and for the working-classes" and would "help to relieve the unrest that will certainly follow the War unless the people can see some real, practical effort in their behalf." Federal town planners even went so far as to buy up land adjacent to war-labor communities, as John Nolen did for the EFC's Union Park Gardens, to protect land values by creating buffers against "disreputable shacks and negro hovels" and to prevent the erection of "cheap and unsightly rows of houses or stores."[21]

The community-building process undertaken by the EFC and the USHC resulted in large-scale, centralized construction of worker housing. Frederick Ackerman, apostle of the garden-city movement who became head of the EFC's Design Division, stressed the need to provide for social and community activities. Hiss argued that a centralized war-labor housing administration would enjoy "an unprecedented opportunity, economically and efficiently to plan and carry out consistent community developments with proper health, school, and church facilities." Thus, federal planners dedicated fully 10 percent of the area in war-labor communities to "school, recreational, and community purposes." Among the amenities offered in government housing plans were schools, libraries, churches, and community buildings. In some of its relatively isolated projects, the USHC erected a separate motion-picture theater with "one seat for each family in the community." EFC and USHC planners expected the enhanced standard of living to outweigh the trade-off in cost and number of workers accommodated. As one government engineer put it, "A modern industrial townsite is more than a group of houses; it is a vital, breathing community of homes."[22]

Building and Managing the War-Labor Communities

Housers with the EFC and USHC saw community building as a means to unite a diverse workforce and to further mute class divisions. Lawrence Veiller argued that to ensure efficient and pacific workers committed to their families and communities above all other associations required provision not only for shelter, but for family and community life: "Experience has already shown that the better class of mechanics, who are essential to these industries, will not *stay* even though they may come, unless they can bring their families and have a home life with their wives and children and all the comforts of home life. This is only possible where there are not only houses such as skilled mechanics are accustomed to live in, but also schools, small shops, recreational opportunities, moving pictures, &c."[23]

War-labor communities were designed not only to improve the quality of life, but to promote self-sacrifice and contentment, turning workers away from divisive political or economic associations and toward an idealized image of the American middle class. The architect Electus Litchfield, who designed EFC's Yorkship Village at Camden, New Jersey, reported that his design for the town plan was influenced by two main concerns. The first was "direct and convenient" access to the shipyard. The second was the creation of a town square with a civic building that would, in middle-class fashion, be used by women and children during the day and become a "man's world" in the evening. The USHC attempted to provide "all the necessary facilities for effective self-respecting living and work." At Craddock, Virginia, a relatively isolated community, the USHC justified its temporary recreation hall and movie theater "as a means of solving the labor problem and reducing the turnover." In many war-labor communities, the school doubled as a "day nursery for older children, because mothers as well as fathers were working," proving that, as War Labor Policies Board Chairman Felix Frankfurter put it, "the housing problem—even in its emergency aspects—is a family problem."[24]

In the design and management of its wartime communities, the government sought social harmony. The decisions were made by a design committee made up of a town planner, an engineer, and an architect. The town planner, generally appointed as chairperson, oversaw work on each government project. Such committees made the essential decisions about each project, including number, type, and location of buildings, typically consulting the expertise of committee members' respective professional constituencies in the USHC and EFC as well as the needs and desires of employers in the project area and their workers and families. Federal planners attempted to build what a later generation would call a "stakeholder buy-in." At Quincy, Massachusetts, Labor Department agents "interviewed an appreciable number of the workers as well as their wives" before arriving at a decision it thought "acceptable to the workers in the Fore River plant." Such efforts, however, did not ensure worker satisfaction, and union representatives complained about the Quincy project with little result.[25]

Lawrence Veiller, the head of the USHC Architectural Division, had risen to prominence by drafting the strengthened 1901 New York tenement code. He stood at the forefront of this effort to raise working-class housing standards and authored the model guidelines that ostensibly governed all war-labor housing construction, including those of the EFC. Veiller's minimum standards barred the evils of ordinary working-class housing and permitted architects and planners room enough to impose their notions of the built environments conducive to social assimilation. The standards were fairly detailed, keyed to reducing costs. The USHC adopted one national window standard, accepted by the EFC as well as by the influential War Industries Board, which set production priorities in the war economy. Only a few dozen house types were designed, and only four or five standard types could be used in any one project. Varying modifications and details, either by reversing plans or using different exterior materials and roof styles and the like, assured an aesthetically pleasing appearance and reinforced individualism.[26]

Veiller's standards also reinforced the preference for one- and two-family houses, which accounted for nearly 90 percent of USHC construction. Using the standards as reference, government architects designed homes for workers that mirrored, on a somewhat smaller and simpler scale, the popular styles previously made available only to middle-class home buyers. Floor plans generally imposed the one-room, one-function rule. Before the war, architects designing working-class housing lamented the difficulties they encountered in convincing workers and their families, who desired separate kitchens, dining rooms, and parlors, that "a good living-kitchen would be better and cheaper." In war-labor housing, kitchen and parlor were separate, with two bedrooms above in the four-room model for lower-paid workers.

In the six-room homes for higher-paid workers, architects offered either a large kitchen and parlor or a dining room, kitchenette, and parlor, creating a division between feminine space where food was prepared and family space where it was consumed. Thus, the floor plans suggested a new definition of family roles that paralleled prevailing middle-class notions; husbands provided their labor to the market daily while wives remained at home charged with the social reproduction of labor in child care, meal preparation, clothes washing, and maintenance of the home as a "haven in a heartless world." For government architects and planners, these middle-class qualities were as integral to the design of the war emergency communities as were questions of infrastructure and fixtures. Electus Litchfield, who planned the EFC's landmark project Yorkship Village in Camden, New Jersey, explained that the houses featured permanent materials and the most up-to-date sanitary equipment and were "supplied with electric light, gas ranges, and individual heating plants. Every house," he continued, "has its individual yard, and, so far as possible, back of each group is an open green in which it is planned to plant a few well-placed fruit trees under the shade of which small children can play upon the grass in sight of their mothers working in the kitchen."[27]

EFC and USHC officials worked to promote the virtues of homeownership among all workers, but they focused their efforts on white, skilled workers who were generally provided with five- and six-room, single-family dwellings. Semiskilled or unskilled workers who were presumably less likely to become homeowners after the war were provided with four-room houses of under one thousand square feet. Whereas skilled shipbuilders at Quincy, Massachusetts, moved into homes in a residential area marked by a curvilinear street pattern and located at some distance from the yard, families of the less skilled were confined to smaller homes platted in the traditional grid closer to the work site, and single, unskilled workers lived in dormitories adjacent to the shipyard.[28]

Management of the government's housing projects reflected a desire to shape social relations by reconstructing working-class neighborhoods. The war-labor housing program was supposed to foster community spirit as well as to provide shelter. Thus, the USHC selected project managers and appointed local boards of control to ensure that disputes among worker-residents did not arise or were quickly settled. Rents were collected weekly by women rent collectors who could surreptitiously inspect the home, question tenants, and instruct them to "live properly," as Fred Feld, the rental manager for the EFC's Yorkship Village, put it. Those who failed to meet the standard were subject to "weeding out." Marguerite Walker Jordan, an official at the Altoona, Pennsylvania, project, went so far as to characterize the tenant as "the past under-dog" and the landlord as "the present under-dog." The head of the USHC Homes Registration office reported that "every effort was made to avoid any semblance of paternalism" and noted that participants in local housing advisory committees "were . . . educated to view problems disinterestedly and from the standpoint of the social good." The EFC and the USHC sought to reorient workers away from an individualistic or a class-centered worldview and toward a cross-class, community-centered one. That working-class housing should promote labor efficiency and good citizenship, besides provide shelter, a government housing engineer noted, seemed "above dispute."[29]

Washington also attempted to safeguard and direct the welfare of the war-labor communities. Social workers paid close attention to the conditions of women and children in the government communities, "covering complaints, questions of housekeeping, and the organization of women to handle matters of community interest" as well as encouraging gardening and good health.[30]

By the end of the war, the USHC had added a Commission on Living Conditions, which sought to orchestrate welfare activities not only at government sites but "wherever [bad housing] retarded production." To staff the commission, the Labor Department tapped leading progressive recreation experts, social workers, and corporate welfare work managers, who attempted to coordinate the response of various government offices and private agencies to reports of poor conditions. It aimed at "preventable discontent" and all those community conditions that "render it impossible for the workers to make the maximum contribution of which they are capable." As with housing, welfare measures attracted federal attention when they promised increased output from American workers.[31]

Through the war-labor housing program, the federal government made unprecedented incursions into the private lives of its citizens. It determined the physical context of home life for thousands of workers and their families. USHC and EFC architects established the size of workers' living rooms, influenced the furnishing possibilities of their bedrooms, and defined the outfitting of their kitchens. Through curvilinear streets and nostalgic town squares, they attempted to provide the physical environment necessary for the growth of a sense of community. This work went far beyond the platting of streets and house lots. By determining what kinds of buildings were erected, the government attempted to shape the identities of community members and their institutions. It employed middle-class professionals such as John Nolen, the prominent city planner, who, believing "the problem was a community one as well as a housing one," went so far in his plans as to determine matters such as "the right kind of church for workmen, etc." Washington undertook this departure in its relationship to workers because it developed a new understanding of the place of the home in society.[32]

War-labor housing officials understood the home as a place where labor power was reproduced and thus as a strategically important area for public intervention during the war. Felix Frankfurter, the future Supreme Court jurist who headed the War Labor Policies Board, pointedly linked "conditions inside the plants" to "living conditions outside of plants," both of which intimately affected "the stability and efficiency of the labor force."[33] In its publicity work, the Labor Department cited the reformer Graham Taylor, who linked the war to the defense of the home, and the home to the defense of the nation: "If soldiers and sailors are needed, they must be registered in the home before any government can list them. Mothers and fathers recruit before any sergeant can enlist his man. Camps may mobilize, arm, and train, but the training, equipment, physique, and spirit furnished by the home constitute an army quite as much, if not more than, military discipline, the manual of arms, and 'esprit de corps.' The oath of allegiance to the colors depends for its loyalty upon the standards and the sanctities to which the boy is brought up in the home."[34] The state provided homes for workers, in part, so that working-class families could provide healthy soldiers to the state and contented laborers to industry.

"Bogey Paternalism, Arrant Socialism": The Separation of Labor and Housing Policies in the Postwar Era

With the Armistice in November 1918, the emergency conditions—political and economic—that had spurred the formulation and implementation of the nation's first housing policy began to abate. Almost immediately, Congress ordered construction halted on projects less than 75 percent complete, but under pressure from housing professionals and reform organizations, relented somewhat. In the end, only twenty-seven of the USHC projects were completed as planned. Congress also ordered the government-built houses to be sold at auction. Ultimately, the USHC sold its projects for $27 million, a poor return on the $52 million it had spent. Although worker-tenants were given preference in purchasing, the decision to take the government's model communities to the marketplace disheartened many housing professionals and reformers. They had hoped that the projects would be transferred to worker-tenants on a co-partnership basis in which individuals bought shares in a community, but, in the tumultuous days of 1919 marked by labor unrest and political violence at home and revolutionary activity in Europe, Congress rejected such antimarket initiatives. In 1919, Congress launched an investigation of the USHC, which castigated the agency for lavish design and loose spending by high-minded academics and self-interested housing professionals. The federal housing initiative suffered from a backlash against activist government that followed in the wake of the war. Government construction was halted, the New York architect John Van Pelt opined, by "a general and very laudable tide of public opinion" seeking to reduce taxes and to find "governmental economies." It did not help, he offered, that "the building of houses by the Government smacks not only of the bogey Paternalism, but of arrant Socialism."[35]

The circumstances surrounding the formulation and implementation of the nation's first housing program weakened the position of those who sought continued government involvement in the postwar housing market. The new rationale that had elevated the housing problem in the eyes of policymakers presumed a widespread perception of crisis as a catalyst to action. Even those involved in the war-labor housing program readily acknowledged that the government entered this sphere of working-class life, which had been a wholly private zone before 1917, solely to increase war production and to promote social cohesion. All but gone were arguments based on the health of the poorer classes. Indeed, officials made clear that a lack of housing alone did not warrant the federal construction; communities deserved aid from Washington only to the extent that their housing crisis restricted war output. Otto Eidlitz explained to lawmakers that the purpose of housing legislation "was to secure homes— proper homes—in order to get efficient workers to do this war work. . . . There was no idea of doing anything wonderful; the idea was to make an intelligent development." Not surprisingly, not until faced with the economic crisis of the Great Depression in the 1930s would Washington take dramatic action on the housing problem again.[36]

Federal officials also understood that the war-labor housing program represented an unprecedented departure in the role of the state in the lives of working Americans and an unparalleled opportunity to affect social change. The nation's first housing policy was far more than a plan to better fit proletarian cogs into a capitalist war machine; USHC and EFC architects and town planners endeavored to reconstruct the working class by reconstructing its communities. The USHC and EFC projects were clean slates on which government housing professionals sought to redraw not only the built environment of the working class, but also to redraw the attitudes, values, and beliefs of working people themselves. War housing projects were didactic, consciously intended by their creators to serve as teaching tools. The homes and neighborhoods were models of right living for their residents as well as models of right building for housing and planning professionals. The war emergency offered the opportunity for the substantive reform of working-class housing. "In all the history of the world," wrote one reformer in 1918, "no other nation has ever had such an opportunity to build models of right living conditions."[37]

Conclusion

Housing professionals associated with the war-labor housing program undertook to reshape residents by shaping their residences. Thus, the USHC and the EFC constructed large, suburban garden communities, complete with a range of social institutions from libraries to churches. Government architects designed the houses—the kitchens, bedrooms, and living rooms—of American workers to encourage loyalty, hard work, thrift, and other middle-class values. The war-labor housing projects, Bruce Bustard argued, "followed a distinctly American pattern"; in reality, they followed a distinctly *middle-class* American pattern. Nevertheless, war-labor housing officials measured housing reform through its effect on production.[38]

To a large extent, the war not only changed the rationale for housing reform, but it also made such reform possible. "Due to the present war crisis and the concentration of our working population on war work in certain localities," Eidlitz argued, the government "is given an opportunity for making a constructive demonstration indicating to a slight extent the solution of this great question, and from this experiment it is hoped that some inspiration will be drawn for the final solution of this national problem." The sense of war emergency and of crisis that accompanied the war years influenced many reformers to consider for the first time a direct role in housing reform for the federal government. As one observer reported to the Department of Labor: "War today is an industrial struggle; and all experience, foreign and domestic, shows us that a proper provision for the needs of labor, of which necessary housing is the most important, is essential to its success." War made housing reform possible by providing a production-oriented rationale for uplift; housing professionals and social reformers took the opportunity to attempt to reconstruct the working class by redefining the working-class community in the image of an idealized middle class.[39]

Notes

1. Charles Harris Whitaker, "Foreword," in Frederick L. Ackerman, ed., *What Is a House? Our National Obligation* (Washington, D.C.: Journal of the American Institute of Architects, 1917), 3.

2. On the emergence of the first national labor policy in the United States, see Eric J. Karolak, "'Work or Fight': World War I and the Origins of Federal Labor Policy, 1913–1920" (Ph.D. dissertation, The Ohio State University, 1994); and Bruce I. Bustard, "The Human Factor: Labor Administration and Industrial Manpower Mobilization During the First World War" (Ph.D. dissertation, University of Iowa, 1984). Most treatments of labor and the state during the war focus on dispute-resolution boards. See, for example, Valerie Jean Conner, *The National War Labor Board* (Chapel Hill: University of North Carolina Press, 1983) and Joseph McCartin, *Labor's Great War* (Chapel Hill: University of North Carolina Press, 1997).

3. Roy Lubove, "Homes and 'A Few Well Placed Fruit Trees': An Object Lesson in Federal Housing," *Social Research* 27 (Winter 1960): 469–86; Christian Topalov, "Scientific Urban Planning and the Ordering of Daily Life: The First 'War Housing' Experiment in the United States, 1917–1919," *Journal of Urban History* 17 (November 1990): 14–45; Gail Radford, *Modern Housing for America: Policy Struggles in the New Deal Era* (Chicago: University of Chicago Press, 1996). See also Bruce I. Bustard, "Homes for War Workers: Federal Housing Policy During World War I," *Prologue* 24 (Spring 1992): 33–43, and Kristin M. Szylvian, "Industrial Housing Reform and the Emergency Fleet Corporation," *Journal of Urban History* (July 1999): 647–90. Contemporary views of the war-labor communities are numerous, including John Ihlder, "How the War Came to Chester," *The Survey* 40, June 1, 1918, 243–51; Frederick Law Olmsted, "Lessons from Housing Developments of the United States Housing Corporation," *Monthly Labor Review* 8 (May 1919): 1253–54; Electus D. Litchfield, "Yorkship Village," *North American Review of Reviews* 60 (December 1919): 502–602.

4. Philip Hiss, "Housing as a War Problem," in National Housing Association (NHA), *Housing Problems in America: Proceedings of the Sixth National Conference on Housing* (New York: National Housing Association, 1917), 21.

5. Carol Aronovici, "Housing and the Housing Problem," in *Housing and Town Planning* (Philadelphia: American Academy of Political and Social Science, 1914): 1–2; Edith Elmer Wood, *The Housing of the Unskilled Wage Earner: America's Next Problem* (New York: Macmillan, 1919), 19.

6. Joseph D. Leland, "What the Federal Government Has Done to House the Industrial Army," in NHA, *Housing Problems in America. Proceedings of the Seventh Annual Conference on Housing* (New York: National Housing Association, 1918), 50.

7. Otto Eidlitz to A. Merritt Taylor, June 21, 1918, "Bath, ME" file, Box 32, Entry 10, Records of the U.S. Housing Corporation, National Archives Record Group 3 (hereafter, file/box/entry, USHC); Council of National Defense, *Second Annual Report of the Council of National Defense* (Washington, D.C.: U.S. Government Printing Office, 1918), 84.

8. Grosvenor Atterbury to C. H. Whitaker, September 13, 1917, Box 4, Entries 4 and 5, USHC; Report of the Committee on Housing, October 31, 1917, untitled file, and "Abstract of the Testimony of Mr. Frederick W. Wood," [October 1917], "Committee Reports," Box 3, Entries 2 and 3, USHC; U.S. Department of Labor, Bureau of Industrial Housing and Transportation, *Report of the United States Housing Corporation, December 3, 1918* (Washington, D.C.: U.S. Government Printing Office, 1919), 11; Springfield *Daily Republican*, August 31, 1917.

9. Lubove, "Homes and 'A Few Well Placed Fruit Trees,' " 474, for "glacial slowness."

10. Council of National Defense, *First Annual Report of the Council of National Defense* (Washington, D.C.: U.S. Government Printing Office, 1917), 85; U.S. Department of Labor, Bureau of Industrial

Housing and Transportation, *War Emergency Construction (Housing War Workers): Report of the United States Housing Corporation* (Washington, D.C.: U.S. Government Printing Office, 1920), 1:10; Report of the Housing Section, September 21, 1917, File 118-1D, Entry 8, and Harlean James's untitled memorandum on the August 31 conference, "General Correspondence, 5/3–8/18/1917," Box 4, Entries 4 and 5, USHC; Council of National Defense Committee on Housing to Newton D. Baker, October 30, 1917, October 31, 1917, Box 3, Entries 2 and 3, USHC.

    11. Report of the CND Housing Committee, October 31, 1917, 11, Box 3, Entries 2 and 3, USHC; U.S. Congress, Senate, Committee on Commerce, *United States Shipping Board Emergency Fleet Corporation, Hearings on S.R. 170*, 65th Congress, 2d session, 1918, 1:822.

    12. U.S. Department of Labor, *War Emergency Construction*, 1:12–13; Lubove, "Homes and 'A Few Well Placed Fruit Trees,' " 475; and John Lombardi, *Labor's Voice in the Cabinet: A History of the Department of Labor from Its Origins to 1921* (New York, 1942), 261.

    13. U.S. Department of Labor, *War Emergency Construction*, 1:211–12, 2:385–87; U.S. Shipping Board, Passenger Transportation and Housing Division, Emergency Fleet Corporation, *Housing the Shipbuilders* (Philadelphia: U.S. Government Printing Office, 1920), 1; Miles L. Colean, *Housing for Defense: A Review of the Role of Housing in Relation to America's Defense and a Program for Action* (New York, 1940), 14–26; LeLand, "What the Federal Government Has Done to House the Industrial Army," 69; Topalov, "Scientific Urban Planning and the Ordering of Daily Life," 15, 18.

    14. Harlean James to John Ihlder, October 9, 1917, "Chicago," Entry 1, USHC; Hiss to Gertrude Beeks Easley, October 9, 1917, "Committee on Labor," Entry 2, USHC; R. A. Pope to Eidlitz, December 14, 1917, untitled, Box 3, Entries 2 and 3, USHC; and Ihlder to James, October 3, 1917, "Philadelphia, PA," Box 2, Entry 1, USHC.

    15. On the shop floor parallel, see Daniel Nelson, *Managers and Workers: Origins of the New Factory System in the United States, 1890–1920* (Madison: University of Wisconsin Press, 1975); David Montgomery, *Workers' Control in America: Studies in the History of Work, Technology, and Labor Struggles* (New York: Cambridge University Press, 1979).

    16. F.-J. Gauntlett, Statement, [October 1917], "Committee Reports" File, USHC; W. B. Wilson, Memorandum for Eidlitz, June 13, 1918, File 118-1B, Entry 8, USHC. Temporary housing was built only where rapid postwar depopulation was expected. The USHC emphasized that "shack towns" were "unsightly" and unsanitary, lowered moral standards and property values, and were generally "retarding the development of the community." U.S. Department of Labor, *War Emergency Construction*, 1:17.

    17. J. S. Harlan to Bernard M. Baruch, May 24, 1918, "Recruiting of Labor, Correspondence (April–May 1918)" File, Entry 2, Records of the War Labor Policies Board, National Archives Record Group 1 (hereafter WLPB); G. H. Maxwell to W. B. Wilson, June 8, 1918, File 118-1B, Entry 8, USHC; R. S. Childs, "What Is a House? v," in Charles Harris Whitaker et al., *Housing Problem in War and Peace* (Washington, D.C.: Journal of the American Institute of Architects, 1918), 55.

    18. James to Ihlder, September 21, 1917, "Philadelphia, PA," Box 2, Entry 1, USHC; Hiss to Gompers, January 12, 1918, untitled, Box 4, Entry 5, USHC; Eidlitz to W. B. Wilson, March 20, 1918, File 118-1A, Entry 8, USHC; "Synopsis of the Policy to Be Pursued by the Bureau of Industrial Housing and Transportation, Department of Labor," May 23, 1918, Entry 10, USHC; U.S. Department of Labor, *War Emergency Construction*, 1:44–50, 280.

    19. Hiss to L. A. Coolidge, June 11, 1917, "Housing-General Correspondence, 5/3–8/18/17," Entries 4 and 5, USHC; Mel Scott, *American City Planning Since 1890* (Berkeley and Los Angeles: University of California Press, 1969), 171–72; Topalov, "Scientific Urban Planning and the Ordering of Daily Life," 17–19.

    20. James Ford, *The Housing Problem: A Summary of Conditions and Remedies* (Cambridge, Mass.: Harvard University Press, 1911), 11–14; Margaret Crawford, *Building the Workingman's Paradise: The Design of American Company Towns* (New York: Verso Press, 1996), 101–28.

    21. U.S. Shipping Board, *Housing the Shipbuilders*, 1; W. T. Love to Hiss, October 23, 1917,

"Housing—General Correspondence, August 18," Entries 4 and 5, USHC; Emile G. Perrot, "Union Park Gardens," in *Housing Problems in America: Proceedings of the Seventh Annual Conference on Housing* (New York: National Housing Association, 1918), 101–17, esp. 102 for "negro hovels"; J. H. McFarland to L. K. Sherman, November 13, 1919, and Sherman to McFarland, November 19, 1919, both in untitled, Box 41, Entry 11, USHC.

22. Ackerman, Memorandum on Housing, October 11, 1917, "Special Information," Entries 2 and 3, USHC; Hiss to Gompers, January 12, 1918, untitled, Box 4, Entry 5, USHC; U.S. Department of Labor, *War Emergency Construction*, 1:4, 97–99, 2:46–70; Morris Knowles, *Industrial Housing* (New York: McGraw-Hill, 1920), 17, 73.

23. Veiller to Bell, February 5, 1918, File 89, Entry 56, USHC.

24. Frankfurter to Herbert Swope, October 28, 1918, and draft "Letter to Secretary of Labor," October 25, 1918, both in "Industrial Housing, October 1918," Entry 2, WLPB; Electus D. Litchfield, "Recent Government Housing Developments, Yorkship Village," *Housing Problems in America: Proceedings of the Seventh Annual Conference on Housing*, 85; Frankfurter, Memorandum for Eidlitz, May 25, 1918, "Industrial Housing, May–June 1918," Entry 2, WLPB; Sherman to McFarland, July 10, 1919, untitled, Box 41, Entry 11, USHC.

25. U.S. Department of Labor, *War Emergency Construction*, 1:185–87, 2:497–509; W. B. Wilson to C. U. Mehegan, July 18, 1918; M. T. Joyce to Eidlitz, June 4, 1918, and Joyce to Wilson, June 11, 1918, all in File 118-1B, Chief Clerk's Files, Records of the U.S. Department of Labor, National Archives Record Group 176.

26. U.S. Department of Labor, *War Emergency Construction*, 2:505–9, 1:182–84.

27. U.S. Department of Labor, *War Emergency Construction*, 2:386–87, 398, 506–7; Frank A. Bourne, "The Workingman's Home and Its Architectural Problems," in *Housing and Town Planning* (Philadelphia: American Academy of Political and Social Science, 1914), 51–53; Topalov, "Scientific Urban Planning and the Ordering of Daily Life," 22; and Litchfield, "Recent Government Housing Developments, Yorkship Village," 92.

28. A. C. Blossom to J. D. Leland, September 9, 1918, Box 32, and Minutes of "Conference on Butler, Pa.," "Butler, PA," Entry 10, USHC; H. W. Morton to Eidlitz, February 21, 1918, Bath, ME, blue project folder, File 118/1, Chief Clerk's Files, U.S. Department of Labor; U.S. Department of Labor, *War Emergency Construction*, 1:497–504, 2:323–27.

29. Fred C. Feld, "Some Problems of Management," in *Housing Problems in America: Proceedings of the Seventh Annual Conference on Housing*, 211, 219; "Housing and Community Problems at National Conference of Social Work," *Monthly Labor Review* 9 (July 1919): 241, for "weeding out"; Marguerite Walker Jordan, "What the Tenant Really Wants," in *Housing Problems in America: Proceedings of the Seventh Annual Conference on Housing*, 225, 227; U.S. Department of Labor, *War Emergency Construction*, 1:93, 97; and Knowles, *Industrial Housing*, 293, for "above dispute."

30. Otto Eidlitz to Representative Sherley, October 7, 1918, "Washington, D.C., May 20, 1918," Entry 10, USHC; Mary Conyngton and Leifur Magnusson, "Government Residence Halls, Washington, D.C.," *Monthly Labor Review* 9 (October 1919): 9–15.

31. U.S. Department of Labor, *War Emergency Construction*, 1:387; Lombardi, *Labor's Voice in the Cabinet*, 262; C. P. Howland to W. B. Wilson, September 11, 1918, "Commission on Living Conditions of War Workers, 1918" File, and Frankfurter to W. B. Wilson, September 20, 1918, "Commission on Living Conditions . . . (Members)" File, both in Entry 2, WLPB; U.S. Department of Labor, *Reports of the Department of Labor, 1919* (Washington, D.C.: U.S. Government Printing Office, 1920), 196–98.

32. I. N. Phelps Stokes, Minutes of "Conference on Milton, Pennsylvania," May 15, 1918, File 32, Entry 10, USHC; U.S. Department of Labor, *War Emergency Construction*, 2:505.

33. Frankfurter, Memorandum for the Secretary, September 11, 1918, "Commission on Living Conditions of War Workers, 1918," Entry 2, WLPB.

34. Undated typescript press statement, "A Nation's Homes Its Defense and Hope . . . ," untitled file, Box 462, Entry 105, USHC.

35. Scott, *American City Planning Since 1890*, 172; John Van Pelt, "Government Housing," in *Housing Problems in America: Proceedings of the Seventh Annual Conference on Housing*, 290; Szylvian, "Industrial Housing Reform and the Emergency Fleet Corporation."

36. U.S. Congress, *United States Shipping Board Emergency Fleet Corporation, Hearings on S.R. 170*, 1918, 1:811–12.

37. U.S. Department of Labor, *War Emergency Construction*, 1:44; Bustard, "Homes for War Workers," 38.

38. G. H. Maxwell to W. B. Wilson, June 8, 1918, File 118-1B, Entry 8, USHC.

39. Eidlitz to Stewart, June 19, 1918, "Publicity" File, Entry 10, USHC; Williams, "Government Aid to Housing," 4, 9, 15, in File 5311, Entry 56, USHC. The quotation is on 15.

4

Shaping Housing and Enhancing Consumption
Hoover's Interwar Housing Policy

JANET HUTCHISON

This chapter argues that during the 1920s Hoover's efforts made ownership of a single-family home in a zoned, planned community a primary goal of American housing policy.[1] It introduces four housing organizations—the "Own Your Own Home" campaign, the Better Homes in America Movement, the Architects' Small House Service Bureau, and the Home Modernizing Bureau—that profited from federal endorsement and briefly examines how each marketed the suburban ideal. Tarred by the taint of Depression Hoovervilles, Hoover's housing efforts have been largely overlooked. Even recent scholarship that connects New Deal housing policy to state-sponsored consumerism fails to acknowledge Hoover's groundwork.[2]

After World War I, new federal, local, and voluntary efforts emerged to direct building across the American landscape. Postwar reaction to wartime government construction of industrial housing galvanized antistatist efforts to improve American housing through private channels. Encouraged by the Department of Commerce, under Secretary Herbert Hoover, communities throughout the United States continued to adopt zoning regulations and to standardize building codes. Hoover increased state involvement in promoting material goods and pointed toward a housing policy path in which the state's participation facilitated the flow of real estate capital. This interwar state involvement in housing, along with the recommendation of the single-family residence, responded to the architect Edwin Brown's call to "nationalize the problems of the small home" by aiding in the promotion of Americans as property-owning citizens, furthering the emphasis on the woman as the household technocrat, supporting consumption in the private household, and glorifying a stereotypical American family in a standardized dwelling.[3]

Opposing outright market intervention, Hoover's carefully calculated government policies proselytized Americans about the virtues of suburban homeownership. His encouragement of homeownership and civic participation laid the groundwork for President Franklin Roosevelt's federal housing programs. Hoover eschewed the European-socialist welfare model embraced by more radical American housing reformers. He shifted state involvement away from a prewar laissez-faire stance toward more direct influence.[4]

Drawing on wartime housing programs, government sponsors, manufacturing interests, professional groups, and philanthropic organizations competed against and cooperated with one another to promote single-family detached dwellings. Under Secretary of Commerce Hoover, the federal government endorsed four organizations—the commercial "Own Your Own Home" campaign, the nonprofit Better Homes in America Movement, the professional Architects' Small House Service Bureau, and the commercial Home Modernizing Bureau— that fostered an idealized vision of American home life rooted in the ownership of a suburban residence replete with modern amenities.

By the 1920s, government attention to housing had merged with other interests that encouraged property ownership by depicting the suburban ideal, a single-family dwelling surrounded by a yard, as a secure foundation for American citizenship, an essential consumer arena, and a model for planned, rational living. Hoover's housing efforts marked the federal government's increased interest in determining the actual form of the American residence and the contours of the neighborhood. Although elitist, because only certain Americans could actually purchase or afford such a home, the suburban prototype was couched to appeal to diverse Americans of all classes, furthering an idealized democratic domestic vista.[5]

First established through the Department of Commerce, Hoover's policies drew in part on President Woodrow Wilson's wartime emergency housing programs, the United States Housing Corporation (USHC) and the Emergency Fleet Corporation (EFC). The USHC and the EFC (see Chapter 3) produced housing communities for war workers featuring English-inspired progressive garden-village architecture and landscape design principles with limited dividend and cooperative ownership. Promoters hoped that these developments would establish a precedent for the postwar era,[6] but Hoover's Department of Commerce rejected the alternative economics of limited dividend and cooperative ownership. Concerned that the 1920 census showed a decline in homeownership, Hoover offered a vigorous approach to the housing problem through the application of federal, voluntary, and business cooperative activity. He sought to counter direct government funding, which he believed created a weak, dependent society. In his 1922 bestseller, *American Individualism*, he connected homeownership with independence and initiative, explaining that Americans needed to own homes as part of their national identity. Although Roosevelt's New Deal policies differed from Hoover's New Era decisions about the institutional role that the federal government should take, the 1930s Federal Housing Administration efforts benefited directly from Hoover's vast housing base.[7]

The Suburban Home Ideal

Hoover's housing sponsorship drew on historical currents, from eighteenth-century Jeffersonian agrarianism to the nineteenth-century country house designs articulated by Andrew Jackson Downing, which credited the single-family dwelling with American individualism, Republicanism, and Christian domestic morality. At the end of the nineteenth century, reformers who endorsed these home values condemned urban tenement houses as centers of juvenile vice and disease and denounced middle-class apartment buildings as "human beehives" that fostered sexual immorality, sloth, and divorce. These progressive reformers invested the single-family dwelling with positive moral and physical influences.

Women's work in progressive household reform included the study of spatial needs through municipal housekeeping, consumer surveys, and social work. By the 1920s, earlier activism left a legacy of women's reformist concern with household aesthetics, space, and equipment; the home economics movement advocated active service in the community and educated improvement of the private dwelling. Deliberate government sponsorship that supported women's voluntary reform efforts, architects' professional goals, and business concerns brought the interwar suburban home concerted national attention and support despite the very real challenges offered by other residential prototypes such as apartments and cooperative housing.[8]

The 1920s suburban ideal was a single-family detached dwelling, often a two-story bungalow or a cottage with Colonial Revival elements. A front yard surrounded this building. Visitors gained access via a sidewalk that led onto the portico or porch. On the first floor, a popular suburban house for "modern living" contained a living room and a dining room (occasionally combined) and, to the rear of the house, a small, bright kitchen hailed as the woman's workplace, which might also have an adjacent breakfast nook. New household technology included an electric or gas refrigerator and stove, a telephone, a radio, and a washing machine. Downstairs, the basement, which housed the laundry, frequently had space for relatively new male hobbies such as woodworking. The upstairs had two or three bedrooms and a bath. A proper family limited the number of children, ensured children's privacy, and separated children by gender. Able to own property, the parents maintained a sexual division of labor with a wage-earning father and a housekeeping mother.[9]

Supporting the interwar suburban home ideal offered great potential for business, government, and civic alliances because housing reform had the possibility of resolving a myriad of social and economic tensions. Building single-family dwellings promised to support the construction industry and thus to provide a healthier economic system with more stable jobs, which aided industries and workers. The suburban home ideal promoted emerging professional interest groups such as architects, home economists, and real estate agents. It presented a widespread arena for the consumption of new and more readily available goods and technology from indoor plumbing to gas heating systems and electric conveniences. Finally, encouraging the construction of single-family dwellings with yards incorporated a particular land-use pattern that took advantage of improved public transportation and the automobile, thus expanding residential building beyond earlier boundaries.[10]

During this period, after the passage of the suffrage amendment, an era fraught with debates about women's political activism, focusing on the suburban residence heightened the importance of women's domestic contributions, the home as the woman's proper place, the woman's role as consumer, and voluntary, maternalistic reform efforts to upgrade home environments in the larger community. This era was replete with "dizzying modernisms" from the Charleston to movies, from high school peer culture to automobile backseats, so that concentration on the home reasserted the centrality of the family—emphasizing child rearing, individual psychology, environmental determinism, and good citizenship. Ultimately, in the wake of World War I, this new government involvement that championed the private dwelling for Americans intensified the significance of property as a primary factor for evaluating the citizen's allegiance to the state. The nationalistic vision of Americans invested in home-ownership contained a stable, hard-working citizenry grounded in private property that would defend its own land and democracy from invasion by foreign

influences. These ideas were not new, but they gained increased potency during
the interwar period.[11]

Wartime State Department and Housing Debates

Government attention to housing ills, a concern of late nineteenth-century progressives, had expanded precipitously on American entry into World War I
when industrial mobilization generated critical housing shortages. Congress responded by establishing two new organizations to address housing concerns:
the Emergency Fleet Corporation and the United States Housing Corporation.
These broke with historical precedent by using government financing to construct new developments, introducing state funding into a heretofore private
domain. In 1918, federal involvement in housing increased when the Homes
Registration and Information Division of the USHC adopted the "Own Your
Own Home" campaign, a national real estate marketing program that had operated for a year through local community participation and exhibition of model
houses.[12]

These two state-run housing programs that financed residential development and supported housing campaigns pointed in two directions for the future
of American housing. In one, the government would fund and oversee housing
construction. In the other, the government would entreat builders and real estate agents to construct good shelter. The World War I alternatives marked a
major change in housing policy for the federal government and provided a
touchstone for the 1920s housing programs.

The end of the war led housing critics, congressmen, and real estate agents
to reassess the government's role in housing. Direct government funding drew
widespread opposition from critics who thought that housing should remain a
private enterprise. Many investors feared new state intervention into areas
where financial ventures profited private capital. Some believed that government financing would lead to socialism, a particularly potent fear after the 1917
Bolshevik Revolution. In 1919 after sustained Congressional debate, the federal
government rapidly discontinued funding for residential construction, divested
itself of development at a loss, and terminated its direct supervision of the "Own
Your Own Home" program. Real estate brokers and manufacturers continued
the homeownership campaign through model homes and commercial "educational" displays that frequently featured the endorsement of state officials including Herbert Hoover.[13]

By 1922, the National Association of Real Estate Boards cheered the demise of state-constructed housing. Vocal reformers like Edith Elmer Wood mourned the opportunity for state support. She knew that private philanthropy and business had failed to meet America's shelter needs. Even when successful, earlier limited-dividend corporations, such as the 1911 Cincinnati Model Homes Incorporated, which housed African American residents, had reached very few. In a 1921 draft to Hoover, Wood, writing as the chairperson for the Committee on Housing of the American Association of University Women, called for a "nation-wide program of home building, under government auspices, on a strictly at-cost basis."[14]

Woods was not alone. Demanding "Do Workingmen Deserve Homes?" in *The New Republic*, Bruce Blivens argued: "We must reconcile ourselves to direct aid from the state. If we should do this, we should only be following a well-established European precedent." Facetiously, he acknowledged: "I realize that this sort of state interference in private business goes against a stubborn grain in the American character. We have a feeling that whatever the great god of Business doesn't take on himself ought not be done at all."[15]

At some local levels, continued reform efforts in specific locales did alter taxation and financing during the 1920s. A 1920 New York City property tax exemption sought to make homeownership more accessible. In 1925, Hoover himself had convinced the Chicago philanthropist Julius Rosenwald and the bank president Wilbur Walling to "experiment with alternatives to the usurious second mortgage." Rosenwald and Walling provided a revolving fund for lower-rate, short-term second mortgages, but the fund reached very few. A 1926 New York State Housing Law created a State Housing Board, which regulated conforming corporations that erected multifamily complexes according to board standards, limited rents and dividends, and received tax exemptions. Such financial incentives were only achieved at the federal level on a widespread basis under Roosevelt's New Deal.[16]

Another development option welcomed by many housing reformers came through cooperative housing societies, modeled after German prototypes. The Wisconsin Act of 1919 provided financial incentives for such ventures. The Garden Homes development was built in Milwaukee from 1921 to 1923, but by 1934, the pure cooperative nature of the neighborhood had ended with a gradual shift toward single-family homeownership. The 1926 New York State Housing Law facilitated the establishment of cooperative societies; that year, Brooklyn claimed over twenty-six small cooperative housing organizations. Although cooperative housing never received significant national regard, it continued to present a clear alternative to more traditional American housing.[17]

Private business interests, however, held sway over housing reform alternatives. The debate over the role of government in housing raged throughout the interwar period, but by 1922, the Housing Committee of the National Association of Real Estate Boards could observe with relief: "The danger of municipal or Governmental housing seems to have nearly passed."[18]

Real estate agents who opposed government funding were reassured by the 1921 appointment of Herbert Hoover as head of the Department of Commerce. Widely respected for his business acumen, Hoover embraced voluntary cooperative activity while sanctioning private control of the real estate market and property. According to Hoover, the contemporary crisis in homeownership had potential political ramifications. He worried that insufficient housing would create a class system of tenantry and landlordism that would result in revolution. Amid the postwar economic recession of 1921 Hoover saw construction stimulation as the key to economic recovery.[19]

As head of the Commerce Department, Hoover moved to establish policies that supported his philosophy. The Congressional appropriation for a Division of Building and Housing shifted shelter from a Labor Department issue concerned with stabilizing industrial workers to a Commerce Department challenge where the technocratic application of social-science planning might resolve housing ills. Hoover and his Division Associates James Taylor and John Gries employed scientific management when they tried to standardize the technology, goods, and construction of residences.[20]

Hoover focused on the problems that "cause a blockade on housing." For many Americans, onerous second mortgage rates hampered the path to homeownership. Hoover argued unsuccessfully for state financing to free second mortgage capital. To promote homeownership, Hoover used his dramatic wartime success with "cooperative associationalism" (an approach that linked nonprofits with state interests) as a reference base. He looked to organizational techniques employed in the wartime food conservation campaign where he had enlisted the support of local Chambers of Commerce, magazine editors such as Edward Bok of the *Ladies' Home Journal*, and women's clubs.[21]

The Commerce Department served as a research base: collecting data, organizing conferences, and distributing educational literature. It published pamphlets on city planning and housing, including an "Own Your Own Home" pamphlet, which was then distributed "by the millions." It organized local housing conferences that were attended by representatives from Chambers of Commerce, manufacturers, and building and trade associations. It reviewed zoning legislation; advocated easier access to home-building capital; and oversaw the simplification of municipal building rules, standardization of contractors' specifications, and streamlining of lumber products.[22]

Hoover and his associates attempted to increase homeownership and to improve architectural standards. Hoover later recalled that when he joined the Commerce Department, "thirty percent of our housing was below American ideals of decent family life. The cost of construction was excessive, the designs were wretched, and the sentiment, 'Own Your Own Home,' was losing force."[23]

The Better Homes in America Movement

In 1922, Marie Meloney, the editor of *The Delineator*, a Butterick Company publication with over one million readers, requested Commerce Department sponsorship of her new housing program, the Better Homes in America Movement. Crediting an Ohio "Own Your Own Home" exhibit as her inspiration, she restructured the values of "Own Your Own Home" to fit her own agenda. Unlike the "Own Your Own Home" campaigns that used voluntarism for commercial profit, the Better Homes movement would have women's activities, community service, and home economics education at its core. Meloney envisioned nationwide participation where members of women's clubs, chambers of commerce, churches, and schools would unite to build and decorate a model home in every community. She complained that every American industry had improved working conditions and machinery except one—"the average American home" where "twenty million women toil every day of every year." Meloney borrowed the concept of the demonstration home but reformulated the program as a female-staffed, voluntary forum with a maternalistic reform agenda. Meloney sounded a progressive call: "As is the Home so the Community and the Nation."[24]

Meloney sought government approval for her goals. Urging Commerce Department sanction, Donald Wilhelm, Hoover's publicity agent, advised that Meloney's Better Homes campaign is "exactly the thing needed to shove the whole housing and better homes ideas of the Department over." In this postsuffrage era, Wilhelm recognized the importance of women's interest in housing, the potential political need to cultivate women's allegiances, and the opportunity to enhance the reputation of the new Commerce Department.[25]

Hoover accepted the presidency of the Better Homes in America, which he envisioned as a cooperative solution to American housing ills, rejecting direct government funding of housing and endorsing the single-family residence. Hoover and his Commerce Department advisers regarded the Better Homes movement as a "collateral arm" of the state, moving housing information from the department to the public. By 1925, Hoover reported that under his presidency, Better Homes in America was "practically directed by the Department." The movement served Hoover's larger housing agenda by publicizing the need for better homes, improvement of housing standards, and public participation in reform. However, while the movement did hold annual competitions for the best design of an inexpensive small house, in reality it did little to improve working-class housing.[26]

Sustained by Hoover's support, Meloney obtained the endorsement of twenty-eight state governors and several other national officials including Secretary of Agriculture Henry C. Wallace, Commissioner of Education John James Tigert, and Secretary of Labor James John Davis. She established an advisory council of figureheads from national organizations including the president of the National Federation of Business and Professional Women's Clubs and the president of the United States Chamber of Commerce. The Butterick Publishing Company initially funded the program, and in 1924, Better I lomes gained institutional recognition when the Laura Spelman Rockefeller Memorial Foundation committed one hundred thousand dollars each year for three years. At that time, James Ford, a Harvard University professor of social ethics and former head of the Homes Registration and Information Service of the USHC, became the executive director.[27]

The Better Homes program operated as a nationwide housing competition in which local Better Homes committees reporting to the national headquarters exhibited residences in their communities during a nationally designated Better Homes week. In Washington, a national committee of architects, home economists, and educators reviewed the local reports and photographs and at times visited sites, assessing community participation and ranking aesthetics to select the best American home. Participating governors and organizational representatives selected the women who chaired the demonstration committees. The local committees enlisted schoolchildren, girl scouts, chambers of commerce, and ministers in campaign planning and implementation.

Despite interpretive struggles, the Better Homes program harvested a broad constituency, reaching millions of Americans who toured the homes and read the articles. After only one year, Edwin Brown, president of the Architects' Small House Service Bureau, remarked that the movement had "grown to a surprising extent." Women throughout the country, in communities that included Saint Helena, South Carolina; Atlanta, Georgia; Kohler, Wisconsin; and Santa Barbara, California, organized prize-winning demonstrations. Meloney and Executive Director Ford recorded committee increases from 1922 to 1934, eventually claiming several thousand American committees annually and asserting an international influence in Australia, the Netherlands, and Belgium. Although a major structural reorganization occurred in 1934 when the Better Homes headquarters moved to Purdue University, the movement continued to declare widespread participation, much of it generated by Department of Agriculture professionals. In 1938, over 16,000 committees were reported with over 5,000 houses shown. The program operated until 1942 although it received the strongest national attention under Hoover's tenure at the Commerce Department and during his presidency.[28]

The Architects' Small House Service Bureau

The Better Homes movement relied on female voluntarism as the basis for nationwide housing reform, but it frequently acknowledged professional design authority by recommending the Architects' Small House Service Bureau, an architect-designed mail-order plan service with a central Minneapolis office established in 1920. The Architects' Bureau championed the hiring of professional architects to counter the public's reliance on free plans from lumber dealers and manufacturers, plan books distributed by building companies, and prefabricated housing, such as that sold by Sears Roebuck and Company. The Architects' Bureau provided blueprints and specifications through mail order, recommending the use of a consulting architect to adapt the basic designs to individual clients' needs. The charge for three- to eight-room houses was six dollars per room. Like Better Homes in America, the Architects' Bureau enjoyed the approbation of Hoover who reasoned that use of "expert" designs would eliminate building waste, standardize house plans, and lower construction costs, benefiting the homeowner, the architect, and the building industries.[29]

Like the Better Homes movement, the Architects' Small House Service Bureau marketed its plans through bold advertising. It dispensed information and advice on architecture, design, and construction through a monthly magazine and a nationally syndicated Home Builder's Clinic. Additionally, the national headquarters sold Architects' Bureau plan books. The Bureau launched its publicity campaign with a house underwritten by the *Minneapolis Journal*. A weekly series of articles on land purchase, bank mortgages, and house plans recounted the construction stages for "Mr. and Mrs. John Journal." When completed, the house, a Dutch Colonial Revival dwelling, was opened to the public and sold. Replicas were built throughout Minneapolis and Saint Paul; nationally, the journal house was one of the most popular Bureau plans.[30]

From 1922 to 1942, the Architects' Bureau distributed its plans throughout the United States. Attracted by plan designs in newspapers or magazines, in-

habitants in small towns and metropolitan areas purchased blueprints and specifications. The Depression doused any hopes that the Bureau might achieve
long-term economic stability. Even during its most successful sales period, the
building boom of the 1920s, the Bureau failed to reach a broad housing market.
Economics dictated participation. Most clients desired a minimum of three bedrooms, and many potential customers protested that the construction costs of
these houses were too high. The Bureau sold mainly plans for larger residences;
few plans for less expensive houses were purchased. By the 1930s, a shift away
from owner-built housing and small building ventures toward larger home developments through Federal Housing Authority financing also hampered individual plan sales.[31]

A dense web of connections among government, professional, voluntary,
and manufacturing interests characterized New Era cooperative housing activity. Hoover's sponsorship of the Architects' Small House Service Bureau meant
that the Commerce Department sent requests for house plans to the Bureau as
did the newspapers that publicized the program. Commercial industries and
manufacturers also profited from their affiliation. The Weyerhauser Forest Products Company underwrote the publication of *Your Future Home,* an early Architects' Bureau plan book. The Bureau forwarded public inquiries about paint
colors to Sherwin-Williams, an advertiser in the Bureau's magazine. The Bureau
operated with the support of manufacturing interests, the sponsorship of the
American Institute of Architects, and the endorsement of Hoover's Department
of Commerce. It also benefited from Better Homes in America literature that
recommended Architects' Bureau plans and from local Better Homes committees that constructed demonstration houses from Bureau plans.[32]

The Home Modernizing Bureau

Better Homes in America claimed voluntarism as its base, and Architects' Small
House Service Bureau emphasized professional service; a third organization,
the Home Modernizing Bureau of the National Building Industries, stressed its
commercial goals. In 1928, several prominent members of the building industry,
lumber companies, and building and loan associations organized the Home
Modernizing Bureau. Many participating companies had previous organizational experience through sponsorship of the Architects' Small House Service
Bureau and "Own Your Own Home" campaigns. The Home Modernizing Bureau, which focused on remodeling, served as a natural outgrowth of the older
"Own Your Own Home" programs, which had emphasized new construction.[33]

With the onslaught of the Great Depression, fewer Americans could afford new homes, and the building industries stagnated. A concerned federal government, led by now President Herbert Hoover, believed that a healthy construction industry served as both a base for and an indicator of the U.S. economy. Home renovation offered a way to stimulate building industries and to improve home standards. H. S. Sackett, the secretary and director of the Home Modernizing Bureau, cited a 1926 Hoover housing survey, conducted when the postwar housing construction boom began to decline. Sackett credited the Commerce Department with "the modernization movement," acclaiming Hoover as "the real father" of the program. The 1926 survey unveiled commercial prospects that dovetailed with the saturation of the new house market and the resulting decline of residential construction. According to the survey, three of every five American residences, over twelve million homes, needed modernization. Sackett estimated that a "potential market of $24,000,000,000" existed, because each house would require an average of $2,000. In contrast to the Architects' Small House Service Bureau, which focused exclusively on new houses, the Home Modernizing Bureau proposed to tap the home-renovation market.[34]

The Home Modernizing Bureau opened offices in towns and cities nationwide. Promoters began advertising campaigns through local newspapers from Erie, Pennsylvania, to Long Beach, California. When a house needed renovation, a contractor completed a Bureau form and received sketches of the modernized facade and floor plan at the cost of $2.00 per room. The Bureau hoped to sell new technology and modern living with home metamorphosis.

The house of State Senator Simon E. Lantz of Congerville, Illinois, pictured in the advertising pamphlet, *The Home Modernizer*, epitomized the Bureau goals, by showing the transformation from an 1863 handmade-brick farmhouse that spoke to roadside observers, neighbors, and strangers of tradition and community, to a 1920s suburban residence that was "new according to every modern standard of beauty, comfort, and convenience." The Home Modernizing Bureau used familiar marketing strategies, offering physical sites through demonstration houses and government endorsements for political clout to promote the building industries' products.[35]

Hoover's Housing Legacy

The new government sponsorship of housing organizations—whether professional, voluntary, or commercial—and the corresponding links between those organizations intensified the widespread dissemination of the suburban ideal across the U.S. landscape. Renditions of the single-family residential prototype permeated newspapers, regions, and the American consciousness. Americans cut Architects' Small House Service Bureau plans from such newspapers as the *Harrisburg Telegraph* and wrote to the Bureau for further information. Inhabitants of actual Architects' Small House Service Bureau houses boasted about owning the best colonial house in the neighborhood; local women's club members reported widespread visits to Better Homes sites; the national Better Homes headquarters fielded architectural inquiries; and the Home Modernizing Bureau sold new products. Through extensive publicity campaigns, millions of Americans visited actual sites, listened to radio shorts, and read magazine articles and government publications that promoted the suburban ideal.[36]

Residential construction plummeted during the Depression, and in 1932, Hoover's Conference on Home Building and Home Ownership assessed the state of American housing. Hoover's conference incorporated many of the ideas fostered by the interwar housing programs. The conference proceedings recommended increased homeownership of single-family dwellings, a home mortgage reserve banking system, and a national housing institute.[37]

After 1933, President Franklin Roosevelt's New Deal programs expanded the financial structure of state involvement by providing federally insured funding through private financial institutions. Roosevelt's emphasis on bank and loan corporation financing moved the government-supported programs away from women's domestic reform, evidenced in Better Homes, to a male-centered monetary arena. In 1934, Meloney, who remained committed to Hoover and the Better Homes program, worried: "We can go on with Better Homes . . . or . . . the present administration will do a great deal and reap the harvest." Indeed, the programs from Roosevelt's Federal Housing Administration, created by the National Housing Act of 1934, built on the government-endorsed organizations of the previous decade. Despite new financing systems, the New Deal borrowed from Hoover's housing base by using civic participation to promote homeownership and drawing on Department of Commerce housing expertise to establish new Federal Housing Authority standards.[38]

Established through Title I of the 1934 Housing Act, the Better Housing Program, which provided federally backed bank financing for home modernization, continued the goals of the Home Modernizing Bureau, successfully encouraging local communities to organize modernizing and home-improvement campaigns. Many communities that had actively participated in the Better Homes in America movement quickly moved into the Better Housing Program with promotional banners hung on the streets, women's door-to-door canvassing for the Better Housing campaign, and schoolchildren's poster contests.[39]

Nationwide, the Hoover programs diminished in importance and no longer garnered widespread publicity. The Better Homes Movement continued through voluntarism and Department of Agriculture programs, but neither it nor the Architects' Small House Service Bureau received new presidential recognition. In later years, Hoover claimed the Better Homes program as his most effective housing solution. Of the four interwar housing efforts that he had endorsed, Better Homes in America, with its commitment to voluntary cooperative activity, had enjoyed his closest attention.[40]

The Better Homes program was incorporated into New Deal work. In 1934, C. W. Warburton, director of extension work for the Agriculture Department, suggested that agents coordinate the Civil Works Administration Rural Housing Survey with home-improvement programs during the annual Better Homes week. Individual programs were overshadowed by New Deal initiatives, but public messages about ideal American habitations remained the same. While offering federal mortgage insurance, the Federal Housing Administration (FHA) mandated architectural and construction standards for the single-family home, standards that were first publicized through Better Homes efforts. Indeed, the FHA codified the Better Homes movement's standards and tastes. Like the Better Homes suggestions, FHA designs promoted a Colonial Revival suburban aesthetic as the domestic architecture for Americans.[41]

The consequences for the U.S. landscape were immense. During the building boom of the 1920s, single-family dwellings constituted 60 percent of the family units constructed; during the 1930s, that percentage increased to approximately 90 percent. With the suburban ideal, Americans gained new space, new technology, and new forms of home consumption, but they faced the danger of losing and devaluing much of their visual past and the visual complexity of their culture, replacing these with a landscape that favored a sense of linear progress and greater cultural uniformity. Often, as with Senator Lantz's home, earlier vernacular architecture was rebuilt with "modern" materials. Some who could not afford new home purchases could attempt partial access to the American dream through renovations or product acquisitions. Those who could not, or did not, participate because of class, race, or ethnicity were excluded.[42]

Contemporary critics questioned the efficacy of the ideal, challenging the suburban prototype on the basis of economics, emotional satisfaction, and commercial greed. In their 1919 edition of *American Citizenship*, the progressive historians Charles and Mary Beard cautioned that the reality of American families and residences did not fit the common ideal and commented that the most "commonly pictured average" family with a comfortable wage-earning father, housekeeping mother, and schoolchildren inhabited a home that was often "spoken of as if it were the same thing all over the country and in all sections of the community." In 1922, Sinclair Lewis concluded that Babbitt's house "quite simply, was not a home" for, despite its material goods, it failed to supply contentment. In 1932, the editors of *Fortune* magazine illustrated how the majority of Americans still lacked the "flush plumbing" of Babbitt's "citizenship." Conditions in rural areas were critical. When the Bureau of Foreign and Domestic Commerce completed the 1934 real property inventories of urban housing in sixty-four cities, it found that over 17 percent of urban households had no private indoor water closet, one in four had no bathing facilities, and over one-third cooked with coal or wood stoves.[43]

Despite or perhaps because of the Beards' reminders that "[a]t least a million homes are not that typical American home so fondly pictured by thoughtless orators," the 1920s housing programs sought to standardize American living through the promotion of the single-family residence equipped with modern consumer goods. The housing programs of the interwar era—aided by new technology, advertising techniques, and government—both romanticized and sold the suburban dwelling, marketing property to and attempting to instill desire in Americans of all classes. These civic programs, which advocated self-help and consumer purchasing, failed to address issues of poverty but proffered a suburban home image for all. Writing in *Survey Graphic* in 1936, Stuart Chase depicted Babbitt shouting to Babbitt: "We haven't sufficiently sold the own-a-home idea to the American people" with "old chants" chanting, "old drums . . . beating," and "Uncle Sam . . . asked to sponsor the parade."[44]

Conclusion

This united marketing and acceptance of the single-family detached house form with a surrounding yard dictated widespread land-use patterns, which were furthered by the expansion of the automobile. Around cities and towns, agricultural land was consumed by residential expansion, creating a suburban borderland. In urban and rural areas, new housing standards promoted by government, architects, manufacturers, home economists, and women's clubs intensified land and home consumption. Individual programs faltered—the Better Homes movement lost national visibility when Roosevelt became president, the Architects' Small House Service Bureau failed financially, and both "Own Your Own Home" and the Home Modernizing Bureau lacked widespread commendation from professional and voluntary groups. Nonetheless, together they launched a daunting and impressive campaign that furthered the suburban home ideal.

Long before Levittown, Hoover's weighty encouragement of such organizations as the voluntary Better Homes in America movement, the professional Architects' Small House Service Bureau, and the commercial Home Modernizing Bureau joined business, culture, and state policy, leading to the wider acceptance of the suburban ideal as the American domestic aesthetic. Hoover's application of New Era cooperation to housing issues borrowed from the marketing strategies used during World War I while challenging wartime building programs. Often, the varied housing organizations established a model symbiotic relationship between nonprofit and for-profit activities through the use of civic and state support, which continues to characterize the American social welfare system.

Hoover's widespread endorsement of housing organizations and the suburban ideal increased state entry into private homes and sanctioned consumption. Although the "associative state" was subsumed when New Deal financing replaced nonprofit endeavors as the thrust of government housing policy, Roosevelt nonetheless built on Hoover's popular nonprofit base as a way to enlist support of New Deal projects. The two-tiered housing policy that provided capital but left most U.S. construction in the private sector was selected as the American welfare model over European alternatives. Better Homes failed to offset statist intervention in housing, but contributed to the selection of a largely invisible housing policy for many Americans. Desirable consumer goods in Hoover's Better Homes became tangible household commodities under Roosevelt's New Deal. Historically, Depression Hoovervilles remain in public memory, but the intersections of nonprofit, professional, and commercial organizations upheld by Hoover's housing advocacy defined new state standards for the American home and informed later housing programs.[45]

Notes

1. Edwin Brown, "Report of the Committee on Small Houses (To the Fifty-fourth Annual Convention)," St. Paul: Minnesota Historical Society Architects' Small House Service Bureau (hereafter ASHSB, MHS).

2. Ellis Hawley adopted the term *cooperative associationalism* to depict Hoover's New Era vision of a guiding state overseeing the cooperative activities of business and voluntary groups working together for the public good. See Ellis Hawley, "Herbert Hoover, the Commerce Secretariat, and the Vision of the 'Associative State,'" *Journal of American History* 61 (June 1974): 116–40. For Hoover's commitment to macroeconomic planning in the construction industry, see Fred Bjornstad, "'A Revolution in Ideas and Methods': The Construction Industry and Socio-Economic Planning in the United States, 1915–1933" (Ph.D. dissertation, University of Iowa, 1991).

3. For a longer discussion of these four programs, see Janet Hutchison, "Building for Babbitt: The State and the Suburban Home Ideal," *Journal of Policy History* 9, 2 (1997): 184–210. Portions of this chapter are drawn from this article.

4. See, for example, Ronald C. Tobey's excellent work, *Technology as Freedom: The New Deal and the Electrical Modernization of the American Home* (Berkeley and Los Angeles: University of California Press, 1997).

5. My larger work (*Better Homes in America*, Baltimore: Johns Hopkins University Press, forthcoming) develops the gendered nature of housing reform and consumption through the Better Homes in America campaign, exploring national and local participation.

6. The architects involved included Frederick Law Olmsted Jr., Fred Ackerman, and John Nolen; the communities they built included Yorkship Village in Chester, Pennsylvania. See Michael H. Lang, "The Design of Yorkship Garden Village: Product of the Progressive Planning, Architecture, and Housing Reform Movements," in Mary Corbin Sies and Christopher Silver, eds., *Planning the Twentieth-Century City* (Baltimore: Johns Hopkins University Press, 1996), 120–45.

7. Herbert Hoover, *American Individualism* (New York: Garland, 1922). Joan Hoff Wilson, in *Herbert Hoover, Forgotten Progressive* (Boston: Little, Brown, 1975), clarifies his commitment to civic action. See also William J. Barber, *From New Era to New Deal: Herbert Hoover, the Economists, and American Economic Policy, 1921–1933* (New York: Cambridge University Press, 1985), 191–95.

For a recent discussion of the emergence of the two-tiered housing policy during the interwar period, see Gail Radford, *Modern Housing for America: Struggles in the New Deal Era* (Chicago: University of Chicago Press, 1996). This upper tier, which still often remains invisible to most Americans, contains tax incentives and mortgage financing for particular income levels. Historically, under the Federal Housing Authority, such mortgage financing was disproportionately offered to Americans of European descent. The other tier, "public housing," directed toward low-income citizens, is seen as direct, and negative, "welfare."

For an analysis of the way in which businesses used welfare capitalism to stave off statist action, see Andrea Tone, *The Business of Benevolence: Industrial Paternalism in Progressive America* (Ithaca: Cornell University Press, 1997).

8. There is a wide literature on the history of the American home although much of it fails to address the relation of housing to state policy. For discussions of the single-family detached dwelling as the American dream, see Gwendolyn Wright, *Building the Dream: A Social History of Housing in America* (New York: Pantheon Books, 1981), and idem, *Moralism and the Model Home: Domestic Architecture and Cultural Conflict in Chicago, 1873–1913* (Chicago: University of Chicago Press, 1980); Clifford Edward Clark Jr., *The American Family Home, 1800–1960* (Chapel Hill: University of North Carolina Press, 1986); David P. Handlin, *The American Home: Architecture and Society, 1815–1915* (Boston: Little, Brown, 1979); and Robert Fishman, *Bourgeois Utopias: The Rise and Fall of Suburbia* (New York: Basic Books, 1987).

For analyses of cooperative housekeeping, cooperative options, and apartment living ventures, respectively, see Dolores Hayden, *The Grand Domestic Revolution: A History of Feminist Designs for American Homes, Neighborhoods, and Cities* (Cambridge, Mass.: MIT Press, 1981); Kristin Szylvian Bailey, "The Federal Government and the Cooperative Housing Movement, 1917–1950" (Ph.D. dissertation, Carnegie Mellon University, 1988); and Elizabeth C. Cromley, *Alone Together: A History of New York's Early Apartments* (Ithaca: Cornell University Press, 1990).

9. This description is my synthesis of the houses promoted by the various programs. Other similar descriptions, topology, and an earlier history of the suburban home are found in Alan Gowans, *The Comfortable House: North American Suburban Architecture, 1890–1930* (Cambridge, Mass.: MIT Press, 1986). Gowans uses the term *suburban* to mean "less than fully urban." I would expand the term to include such houses built within the city limits, in developments, and in the countryside. Thus, *suburban* in this context refers to the house form and technological amenities rather than to a political or geographical boundary. See also Sally McMurry, *The Progressive Farmhouse Ideal* (New York: Oxford University Press, 1986).

10. Literature on housing still lacks a clear overview of the history of real estate development over time. The best analysis of real estate development during the interwar period is Marc A. Weiss, *The Rise of the Community Builder: The American Real Estate Industry and Urban Land Planning* (New York: Columbia University Press, 1986).

11. For an analysis of women's responses to suburbanization during this period, see Margaret Marsh, *Suburban Lives* (New Brunswick: Rutgers University Press, 1990). On changing youth culture and concerns, see Paula Fass, *The Beautiful and the Damned: American Youth and the 1920s* (New York: Oxford University Press, 1977).

12. Initially on coming to Washington, the real estate program was temporarily housed in the Department of Labor and was then transferred to the U.S. Housing Corporation (USHC). The USHC oversaw the construction of two government-funded housing developments. Most USHC projects were not completed, and the federal government sold ownership rights after the Armistice. See James Ford, *Report of the U.S. Housing Corporation*, vols. 1 and 2 (Washington, D.C.: U.S. Government Printing Office, 1919).

For a description of the development of one state-financed development, see Richard M. Candee, *Atlantic Heights: A World War I Shipbuilder's Community* (Portsmouth, N.H.: Portsmouth Marine Society, 1985). In 1917, another form of new state involvement occurred with the establishment of federal land banks, which provided farmers with long-term mortgages at low interest rates. Paul Murphy, "Address of Paul C. Murphy, Before the Interstate Realty Convention, Held at Aberdeen and Hoquiam, August 9–11, 1917, Under the Auspices of Grays Harbor Realty Board, Box 482, United States Housing Corporation, National Archives (hereafter referred to as USHC, NA). "Own Your Own Home" originated in 1917 as the "Buy a Home" campaign sponsored by the National Association of Real Estate Boards.

I am grateful to Brian Horrigan, curator at the Minnesota Historical Society, for generously sharing his research on the "Own Your Own Home" movement with me. In particular, my discussion of Murphy and the role of celebrity endorsements uses his analysis of this topic.

13. For example, Senator Albert Fall of New Mexico claimed that these federal developments showed "an insidious concerted effort . . . to socialize this Government of ours, to overturn the entire Government of the United States." Quoted in Kenneth Jackson, *Crabgrass Frontier: The Suburbanization of the United States* (New York: Oxford University Press, 1983), 192. "Own Your Own Home Show Formally Open To-Day," *New York Post*, April 22, 1922, Housing, Clippings, General Accounts, Herbert Hoover Presidential Library, West Branch, Texas (hereafter referred to as HHPL).

14. Edith Elmer Wood, Chairperson, Committee on Housing, American Association of University Women, "An Open Letter to Mr. Hoover," n.d., mentioned in correspondence from Bernard Newman, managing director of the Philadelphia Housing Association, to Wood, October 17, 1921, Housing Association of Delaware Valley, URB3/iii/1478, Box 65, Office Files, 1921–1950, Wood Edith Elmer, 1921–42, Urban Archives, Temple University, Philadelphia, Pa. See also Edith Elmer Wood, *The Housing of the Unskilled Wage Earner: America's Next Problem* (New York: Macmillan, 1919); Charles Harris Whitaker, Frederick Ackerman, Richard S. Childs, and Edith Elmer Wood, *The Housing Problem in War and Peace* (Washington, D.C.: American Institute of Architects, 1918).

15. Bruce Blivens, "Do Workingmen Deserve Homes?" *New Republic*, March 5, 1924, 39–41.

16. *Urban Housing: The Story of the P. W. A. Division, 1933–36*, Bulletin no. 2 (Washington, D.C.: Federal Emergency Administration of Public Works, August 1936), 54–65. Bjornstad, "A Revolution in Ideas and Methods," 306.

17. *Urban Housing*, 57–64.

18. "The Housing Committee of the National Association of Real Estate Board to the Executive Committee at Washington, March 6–8, 1922, by Henry R. Brigham, Chairman," 4, Report of Housing Committee File, Box 35, Idler Papers, NAREB, Roosevelt Presidential Library, Hyde Park, New York (hereafter referred to as RPL).

19. For a thorough examination of Hoover's construction stance, see Bjornstad, "A Revolution in Ideas and Methods."

20. Herbert Hoover, "Good Homes as Investment," *The Delineator* (October 1924): 2. This emphasis on housing as a stable industrial labor force has its antecedents in the nineteenth century. It is no coincidence that government involvement in housing was originally under the purview of the Labor Department. James Taylor and John Gries remained active in government housing policy throughout the interwar period. Herbert Hoover, *The Memoirs of Herbert Hoover* (New York: Macmillan, 1952), 257. Idem, *American Individualism*. For a discussion of Hoover's ideas about social science management and planning, see Barry D. Karl, "Presidential Planning and Social Science Research: Mr. Hoover's Experts," *Perspectives in American History* 3 (1969): 347–409; and Guy Alchon, *The Invisible Hand of Planning: Capitalism, Social Science, and the State in the 1920s* (Princeton: Princeton University Press, 1985).

21. Herbert Hoover to President Harding, February 9, 1922, Commerce Papers, Building and Housing, HHPL. Information on the Food Conservation campaign and women's enlistment can be found in Craig Lloyd, "Aggressive Introvert: Herbert Hoover and Public Relations Management, 1912–1923" (Ph.D. dissertation, University of Iowa, 1970), 48.

22. For articles on standardization, see, for example, "Secretary Hoover's Standardization Plan," *New York City Expert* (April 1922), in General Account Papers, Housing, Clippings, HHPL; and "Government to Squeeze Waste out of Industry: Department of Commerce Plans to Reduce Variety in Practically Every Article of Commerce in Country," *New York American* (July 31, 1922), General Account, Housing, Clippings, HHPL. For his advocacy of a new building code, see "Hoover Presents New Building Code," *The New York Times*, January 22, 1923, General Account, Housing, Clippings, HHPL. Herbert Hoover (unsigned) to Mr. Ernest T. Trigg, President, National Federation of Construction Industries, Commerce Papers, Building and Housing, HHPL. Hoover's stance on the importance of voluntarism remained unchanged. In his memoirs, he asserted that the "free and confident" economy was more successful than the planned economy of Roosevelt's New Deal, citing house numbers constructed per annum as proof. *The Memoirs of Herbert Hoover*, 96. For an excellent discussion of Hoover's optimism about the translation of wartime voluntarism into peacetime efforts, see Robert D. Cuff, "Voluntarism and War Organization During the Great War," *Journal of American History* 64, 1–2 (1977): 358–72.

23. Hoover, *The Memoirs of Herbert Hoover*, 92.

24. Marie Meloney, "Better Homes," *The Delineator* (October 1922): 9. Idem, "Better Homes in America," *The Delineator* (June 1923): 2.

There is a wide literature on the role of maternalist reform in the late nineteenth and early twentieth centuries. Most significant are Theda Skocpol, *Protecting Soldiers and Mothers: The Origins of Social Policy in the United States* (Cambridge, Mass.: Harvard University Press, 1992); Linda Gordan, *Pitied But Not Entitled: Single Mothers and the History of Welfare, 1890–1935* (New York: Free Press, 1994); Seth Koven and Sonya Michel, eds., *Mothers of a New World: Maternalist Politics and the Origins of the Welfare States* (New York: Routledge, 1993); Robin Muncy, *Creating a Female Dominion in American Reform, 1890–1935* (New York: Oxford University Press, 1991); and Molly Ladd-Taylor, *Mother-Work: Women, Child Welfare, and the State, 1890–1930* (Urbana: University of Illinois, 1994).

25. Donald Wilhelm, "Memorandum for the Secretary," June 22, 1922, Commerce Department Bureau of Standards, Commerce Papers, HHPL.

26. "Statement by Secretary Hoover for Christian Science Monitor," March 25, 1925, Building and Housing, Commerce Papers, HHPL. In addition to sponsoring home exhibitions, the national Better Homes office distributed homeownership manuals and zoning primers from the Commerce Department to local committees.

27. Marie Meloney, "Better Homes in America," *The Delineator* (September 1922): 2; Edwin Brown to Mr. Clarence T. Myers, Secretary, Lake Division, A.S.H.S.B., November 26, 1923, ASHSB, MHS; Meloney, "Better Homes in America," *The Delineator* (January 1924): 1; idem, "Better Homes Prizewinners," *The Delineator* (October 1924): 1; idem, "Better Homes in America," *The Delineator* (November 1922): 18.

28. In 1934, for example, Ford claimed over 4,000 participating communities. Annual Reports of the Better Homes Movement, BHA, Hoover Institution of War Revolution and Peace Archives (hereafter refereed to as HIA). Kohler, Wisconsin, showed model Better Homes until 1958, sixteen years after the demise of the national movement. Kohler Company Archives, Kohler, Wisconsin.

29. An overview of the Architects' Small House Service Bureau, including an analysis of cost, is found in Thomas Harvey, "Mail Order Architecture in the Twenties," *Landscape* 25, 3 (1981): 1–9. Lisa Marie Schrenck discusses Bureau marketing, operations, designs, and decline in "The Impact of the Architects' Small House Service Bureau on Early Twentieth-Century Architecture" (Master's thesis, University of Virginia, 1987). Also see Schrenck's introduction in *Your Future Home* (Washington, D.C.: American Institute of Architects, 1992 [reprint of 1922 ed., Saint Paul: Weyerhaeuser Forest Products]). "Report of the Committee on Small Houses," The American Institute of Architects for the Year 1923, American Institute of Architects, Box 1, HIA.

Although the American Institute of Architects endorsed the Architects' Small House Service Bureau, architects in fact contested the efficacy of such a program. Hoover's sponsorship of the Architects' Small House Service Bureau also drew protests. Walter Fawcett, in "Government Endorsements and the Architect," *Architectural Record*, October 1925, 393–94, questioned the ethics of such government endorsements. Hoover refused to revoke his endorsement because the architects were not making excessive profits. John M. Gries to Hoover, October 28, 1925, Building and Housing, Commerce Papers, HHPL.

30. "Economy and Durability Specified for Three Journal Houses," *Minneapolis Journal*, April 15, 1923, 1.

31. For a discussion of Bureau costs, see Harvey, "Mail Order Architecture in the 1920s," 5. Mr. Brogren, "Questionnaire," received January 23, 1924, ASHSB, MHS.

32. Architects' Small House Service Bureau, *Your Future Home* (Saint Paul, Minn.: Weyerhaeuser Forest Products, 1923); other architects criticized this alliance, seeing it as commercializing the Bureau. Robert T. Jones, Technical Director, ASHSB, to Mr. N. M. Collart, Superintendent of Decoration, Sherwin-Williams Company, Cleveland, Ohio, December 21, 1923, ASHSB, MHS; Robert T. Jones, Technical Director, to Mr. N. M. Collart, Superintendent of Decoration, November 19, 1923, ASHSB, MHS. Newspapers often had connections with real estate interests and participated in real estate speculation. Requests for Bureau house plans that cite Better Homes in America as their source are from areas throughout the country including New Jersey, West Virginia, and Texas, ASHSB, MHS. James Ford, "The Plan Service of the Architects' Small House Service Bureau," *American Building Association News*, 5.

33. For example, the Celotex Company and the American Face Brick Association had representatives.

34. H. S. Sackett, Secretary and Director, Home Modernizing Bureau, to George Akerman, Secretary to the President, September 17, 1929, Presidential Subject File—Better Homes Correspondence, HHPL; H. S. Sackett to Santa Maria Construction Company, September 3, 1929, Presidential Subject File—Better Homes Correspondence, Presidential Subject File, HHPL.

35. H. S. Sackett, "What Modernization Means Today," *The Home Modernizer*, 4–7, Better Homes, Presidential Papers, HHPL.

36. John Colville, "Questionnaire," received May 15, 1924, ASHSB, MHS.

37. John M. Gries and James Ford, eds., *Home Ownership, Income, and Types of Dwellings: President's Conference on Home Building and Home Ownership* 18 (Washington, D.C.: President's Conference on Home Building and Home Ownership, 1932).

38. Marie Meloney to Edgar Rickard, March 21, 1933, BHA General, BAEF Collection, HHPL.

39. "Memorandum," March 21, 1934, BHA General, BAEF Collection, HHPL. *Better Housing*, February 14, 1935, 1–3; Leo Henderson, Manager to President Roosevelt, OF 1091, Miscellaneous 1934–36, Box 4, FHA, RPL.

Jackson criticizes the ineffectiveness of Title I citing Albert M. Cole who remarked in 1954 that Title I "is of limited assistance to families of modest income" (*Crabgrass Frontier*, note 49, 364).

40. Hoover, *The Memoirs of Herbert Hoover*, 92.

41. C. W. Warburton, Director of Extension Work, United States Department of Agriculture, March 31, 1934, Special Materials, Box 15, BHA, HIA.

42. Miles L. Colean, *American Housing, Problems and Prospects* (New York: Twentieth Century Fund, 1944), 66. The chart *Estimated Number of Non-Farm Dwelling Units Built Annually by Type of Structure*, FHA, Division of Economics and Statistics, Chart no. 556A (Rev.) March 1, 1939, RPL, shows slightly different percentages. The chart contains a note that no accurate figures exist as to the number of dwelling units built annually in the United States, that estimates are based on census data and on building-permit data reported by the Bureau of Labor Statistics, and that National Bureau of Economic Research Estimates were used for 1920–35. See also *Historical Statistics of the United States: Colonial Times to the Present* (Washington, D.C.: U.S. Department of Commerce, Bureau of the Census, 1970), N 156–69.

43. Charles and Mary Beard, *American Citizenship* (New York: Macmillan, 1919), 25–27; Sinclair Lewis, *Babbitt* (New York: Harcourt Brace Jovanovich, 1922; Signet Classic, 1980), 16; the editors of *Fortune Magazine, Housing America* (New York: Harcourt, Brace, 1932), 1; *Urban Housing* (1936): 6–7.

44. Charles and Mary Beard, *American Citizenship*, 25–27. Stuart Chase, "The Case Against Home Ownership," *Survey Graphic* (May 1938): 263. My thanks to Gail Radford for calling this article to my attention.

45. For a discussion of the transformation of household technology from luxury to commodity, see Tobey, *Technology as Freedom*, 132–56.

5

The Federal Government and Housing During the Great Depression

GAIL RADFORD

"A housing movement based purely on hand-outs from the top down, with all the driving power coming from talk about 'crime and disease,' will never be basically popular in this country, and will necessarily be limited in scope."[1] So warned writer and political activist Catherine Bauer as the United States struggled to shape a permanent federal housing policy during the politically turbulent years of the Great Depression. Just as Bauer predicted, Americans were always lukewarm about programs like public housing, which were aimed specifically at poor people, and in recent years support has cooled practically to the freezing point. Yet, although many people equate federal housing policy primarily or even exclusively with programs like public housing, there is actually a far more important but less visible group of federal programs that deal with housing. These support the commercial market and middle- and upper-class consumers. Like public housing, they, too, originated in the 1930s, but unlike programs for the poor, they have grown steadily more robust since their creation. This chapter, therefore, examines the emergence during the 1930s of a "dual" or "two-tiered" housing policy. At the higher tier, federal dollars buttressed a robust private housing market. When it came to the bottom tier, however, Washington was always penurious. Thus, just as Bauer feared, American public housing came to be regarded as the twentieth-century equivalent of the poorhouse.

At the time this dual pattern was being developed, Bauer worked with an organization called the Labor Housing Conference (LHC) to put forward a very different vision for how the government should deal with the housing issue, a plan often described as "modern housing." As the president of the Pennsylvania Federation of Labor explained to the 1934 annual convention of the American Federation of Labor, the LHC wanted to see public financing of "large-scale planned housing developments on a non-profit basis, designed, constructed, and administered in direct collaboration with bona fide groups of workers and consumers."[2] This program would be the centerpiece of federal efforts, rather than a two-tier approach consisting of building housing for very poor people and reviving the commercial market for everyone else. In contemporary terms, modern housing was a proposal for a "universalistic" policy.

Bauer's 1934 book, *Modern Housing*, became the manifesto of the movement to enroll the government behind this entirely new way of providing American homes. Bauer did not develop the ideas in her book entirely on her own. She explicitly drew on concepts and experiments that were circulating throughout the industrialized world at the time. What differentiated her perspective was the way she connected the two major strands of housing reform, which were usually considered in isolation from each other. In *Modern Housing*, she advocated innovative architectural concepts as well as ideas for decommercializing residential property. As she explicated her approach, she made it clear that modern housing would be built to a standard of majority acceptability. Individual living units would be grouped together similar to garden apartment–type or row house–style construction (today termed "townhouse" or "clustered" developments). This kind of design would cut costs at the same time that it kept land open for nearby parks and playgrounds. More efficient production, made possible by plentiful, low-interest capital as well as by new technologies, would also keep prices down. Neighborhoods would be provided with numerous shared amenities, such as day care for young children and recreational opportunities for older children and adults. Although individual units might be more compact than upscale suburban homes, they could be quite commodious, given the savings possible compared with conventional residential building. Thus the nation could afford to make good housing of a similar character available to everyone, rather than supporting one style for the majority and an inferior and visually stigmatizing alternative for the poor. In addition, this pattern of urban development would encourage a vibrant community life. Bauer illustrated the feasibility of these ideas with an overview of government-supported residential building programs in European countries since the end of the World War I.[3]

Ultimately, the proposal for modern housing failed politically, but its history is nonetheless important. From our perspective of over a half-century later, it is all too easy to assume that the two-tiered pattern of government activity in housing, which emerged by the end of the New Deal, was somehow inevitable. Government policies are not the outcome of natural processes, however. The struggles over housing during the New Deal clearly illustrate how policies result from political choices. From the perspective of the 1930s, the struggle for modern housing is equally significant. Ideas associated with this proposal were taken seriously by architects and urban planners, union activists, and even lawmakers on Capitol Hill. Its design features and emphasis on local community life influenced the first phase of direct federal housing activity in the New Deal under the Public Works Administration (PWA).

The Variety of Early New Deal Housing Programs

The PWA housing program came into existence during the crisis atmosphere that marked the first months of the Roosevelt administration. The National Industrial Recovery Act, which became law in the summer of 1933, established the Public Works Administration (as well as the more controversial National Recovery Administration). The legislation instructed the PWA to engage in "construction, reconstruction, alteration, or repair under public regulation or control of low-cost housing and slum-clearance projects" along with traditional government building projects such as highways and public buildings.[4]

President Franklin Roosevelt named Interior Secretary Harold Ickes to head the new agency. To implement the section of the bill pertaining to the construction of dwellings, Ickes established the Housing Division as a quasi-independent agency in the PWA. The division financed or directly built a total of fifty-eight housing developments around the country, with approximately 25,000 dwelling units, over a period of four years.[5] Much of this housing was very livable. Architect Richard Plunz, writing in the 1970s, noted: "In general, apartment design standards were very high, with sizes, light, and ventilation equal to the best of the 1920s garden apartments."[6] Particularly successful PWA complexes, such as the Carl Mackley Houses in Philadelphia, the Harlem River Houses in New York City, and Lakeview Terrace in Cleveland, have been the subject of numerous positive appraisals over the years by architects, planners, and historians.[7]

7. Philadelphia's Carl Mackley Houses, designed by idealistic trade unionists and architects and built with a loan from the Public Works Administration. The swimming pool was one of many community facilities that distinguished this development. Managed by a labor union rather than a public housing authority, the complex never enforced income ceilings, and the tenant mix included professionals as well as blue-collar workers.

Popular acceptance, not just critical success, greeted the agency's work. Ordinary citizens expressed their approval by moving into the federal developments—even when they might have afforded other accommodations. Senator David Walsh of Massachusetts drew attention to this fact when he complained in 1936 that "the houses which have been constructed [by the PWA] in New York, Cleveland, and Boston and elsewhere are really in competition with private property."[8]

The fact that some moderate-income people not only found PWA housing appealing but were welcomed as residents points to one of the best features of the PWA program in its first years: It was not "means tested." Although using scarce public resources only for the most needy might seem fair and logical, programs limited to only the poorest have debilitating long-range problems.

8. New York's Harlem River Houses, constructed by the Public Works Administration in the 1930s. This development featured an attractive interior park and community services such as a clinic, child care facility, library, and youth recreation programs.

Their narrow constituency makes them more susceptible to budget cuts, and participants are often stigmatized. Only universal programs that do not demean their recipients, such as Social Security, seem able to survive politically in the United States.[9] Initially, PWA housing was open to anyone who cared to apply. This situation ended in 1936 when Congress passed the George-Healey Act, which set income ceilings for the PWA housing projects directly built and owned by the government.[10]

The PWA's direct intervention into the housing field represented only one effort to cope with U.S. housing problems during the early 1930s. As the Roosevelt administration groped for methods of stimulating the economy and responded to demands from various constituencies, it launched a variety of initiatives. Many of these aimed at resuscitating commercial real estate activity, and the most frequently used strategy was to increase the volume of circulating capital in mortgage markets. In good part because of the success of these efforts, the resources and morale of developers and their financial backers began to revive. By mid-decade, these groups were able to respond more energetically and effectively to the threat of publicly aided noncommercial housing than they had at the bottom of the Depression.

The first of these pro-market interventions by the national government predated the New Deal. President Hoover's Federal Home Loan Bank Act of 1932 linked mortgage lenders throughout the country into a federally regulated network with a common credit pool. Although useful to the mortgage industry and still in effect today, this initial federal involvement by itself was insufficient to stop the financial free fall of residential real estate. By 1933, approximately one-half of the twenty billion dollars of national mortgage debt was in default, and foreclosures averaged one thousand per day.[11]

To deal with this crisis, President Roosevelt, soon after taking office, urged creation of the Home Owners Loan Corporation (HOLC) to refinance personal mortgages. In its first year of operation, the HOLC lent more than three billion dollars on over one million mortgages, helping to save 10 percent of all owner-occupied nonfarm residences. Politically, this move was brilliant. Historian Arthur Schlesinger Jr. believes that "probably no single measure consolidated so much middle-class support for the New Deal" as the HOLC.[12]

Although the HOLC moderated the foreclosure crisis, it failed to restore the real estate market to health, much less to reinflate the general economy. Toward the end of 1933, Roosevelt began to cast around for measures by which the government could stimulate home building, believing it to be "the wheel within the wheel to move the whole economic engine." To develop a long-term program, the president appointed a committee that included some of his most prominent advisers, including Harry Hopkins, Henry Wallace, Frances Perkins, Rexford Tugwell, John Fahey, and Averell Harriman. The majority initially favored some kind of large-scale, publicly financed construction program, but Roosevelt's growing unease about budget deficits led him to back a plan involving little direct federal spending. This became the National Housing Act of 1934.[13]

Marriner Eccles, then special assistant to Treasury Secretary Henry Morgenthau Jr. (and later chairman of the Federal Reserve), played a key role in drafting the legislation. As Eccles recounted in his memoirs, he was committed to a program that was "private in character."[14] The act created the Federal Housing Administration (FHA), the most important of several Depression-era federal agencies aimed at pumping life back into the housing market by restructuring its financial underpinnings. The FHA's mortgage insurance program guaranteed financial institutions against default when they adhered to certain guidelines for making home loans. Mortgage lending was thus transformed into a virtually risk-free activity, making more and cheaper capital available for both developers and consumers. Eccles described the mechanism of federal guarantees for commercial loans as a device that "avoided any direct encroachment by the government on the domain of private business, but which used the power of government to establish the conditions under which private initiative could feed itself and multiply its own benefits."[15] That FHA policies succeeded in increasing investor confidence was evident immediately. In 1934, housing starts were up for the first time in eight years. They continued to climb until the war.[16]

Better times emboldened private operators to oppose any role in which government might operate as a competitor (although not those programs that served to support business). Yet, because the PWA was defined from the beginning as a temporary agency, the struggle over how much of the market the government would directly enter was not fought out over the PWA's Housing Division. Instead, the fight occurred over the effort to establish a permanent federal program that would promote the development of a housing sector outside the commercial market.

The Campaign for Directly Aided Housing

In the spring of 1935, Senator Robert Wagner of New York introduced a public housing bill into Congress.[17] The proposed legislation was written by the prominent New York City settlement worker Mary Simkhovitch and her associates in the National Public Housing Conference (NPHC), an organization founded in 1931 to orchestrate the campaign for a federally supported public housing program. Their bill called for terminating the PWA Housing Division and replacing it with a permanent agency in the Department of Interior. Local public authorities would carry out the actual work of building and managing low-rent housing, aided by grants from the national agency. The purposes of the bill were defined in terms of slum clearance, providing housing for the poor, and promoting industrial recovery. In 1935, Wagner was too preoccupied with pushing Social Security and labor relations legislation through Congress to make housing a priority, but he introduced the bill to give his allies in New York reform circles publicity for their program.[18]

Labor Housing Conference leaders eyed the Wagner bill skeptically, believing that it turned over too much initiative to local housing authorities. Furthermore, they objected to the way it placed the program under the authority of Secretary of the Interior Harold Ickes, with whom they found it difficult to work. To influence Wagner, Bauer and her allies drew up what they regarded as a better piece of legislation. Henry Ellenbogen, a sympathetic congressman from Pittsburgh who had been born and educated in Vienna, agreed to work with them and to submit the bill.[19]

The Ellenbogen bill called for establishing a freestanding U.S. Housing Authority to administer the program, rather than putting the new agency inside any cabinet-level department. The authority's funds would come from an initial appropriation, supplemented with revenue from bond sales. The measure gave the national agency more power than Wagner's bill, but at the same time it allowed for more nongovernment participation by providing support to non-profit, limited-dividend, and cooperative building societies.[20] For example, Ellenbogen's bill allowed for grants and loans to not-for-profit bodies on the same terms as fully public ones. Labor Housing Conference leaders believed a variety of mechanisms had to be available so that organized citizens who wanted to create housing for themselves would have a real opportunity to succeed against predictable resistance from locally powerful real estate interests. The LHC took the possibility of hostility from business more seriously than did the National Public Housing Conference, because its hopes of appealing to the broad spectrum of the American population represented a threat to commercial interests not present in the NPHC's emphasis on slum clearance and housing for the very poor.[21]

Impressed by the LHC critique of his original public housing proposal, Wagner invited Bauer and Ellenbogen to help him draft new legislation for the 1936 session of Congress. This relationship continued after his housing bill again failed to pass. In 1937, Wagner introduced a public housing bill for the third time.

The Opposition to Public Housing Legislation

The organizations that mobilized against Wagner's legislation for directly funded, publicly owned housing were the U.S. Chamber of Commerce, the National Association of Real Estate Boards (NAREB), the U.S. Building and Loan League, and the National Retail Lumber Dealers Association.[22] Only the lumber dealers explicitly espoused their own material stake in the battle, stating for the record that they were against a federal residential building program on the grounds that it would use new construction materials such as concrete and steel. Lumber suppliers found such innovation threatening, because wood was the largest single cost item in conventional home construction.[23] Not surprisingly, this type of protest failed to mobilize broad political support.

More politically effective were arguments that coupled private homeownership with the public good. NAREB President Walter Schmidt complained that renting from the government might prove so attractive that "the urge to buy one's own home will be diminished." Harking back to Thomas Jefferson's concerns about the necessity for citizens to own productive farm property so they would be politically independent, Schmidt insisted that "widespread ownership of land . . . is the bulwark of a democratic form of government."[24] Thus, private ownership of homes was connected to themes of freedom and democracy.

Although representatives of real estate groups argued that state-provided shelter amounted to communism or socialism, they never urged the government to withdraw from the housing sector entirely. On the contrary, they welcomed federal interventions such as the FHA and the Federal Home Loan Bank System, which channeled more and cheaper capital into residential real estate. NAREB lobbyist Herbert U. Nelson, who relentlessly opposed publicly subsidized dwellings, insisted that "public credit can be properly used to help sustain homeownership and private enterprise."[25]

In light of what ultimately happened, the alarm sounded by people like Nelson and Schmidt seems disproportionate to the threat that public housing actually posed to their well-being, either ideologically or financially. It should be kept in mind, however, that the issue at this time was not public housing as Americans would later come to know it in the 1960s and 1970s. The threat was the possibility of a broad, "universalistic" program along the lines advocated by the Labor Housing Conference and at times exemplified by the PWA—a program potentially attractive to a sizable segment of the population.

Passage of the Wagner Public Housing Act

Over the vociferous objection of bodies such as the National Association of Real Estate Boards, Wagner's legislation finally passed Congress the third time around and was signed into law by Roosevelt in September 1937 as the United States Housing Act.[26] Although passage of the bill represented a defeat for the business groups that had lobbied against it, the defeat was hardly major because key elements of the proposed legislation had been compromised away. In fact, the political historian James T. Patterson has pinpointed the evisceration of

Wagner's housing bill as the first big victory for the conservative coalition in the Senate.[27]

The legislation created a quasi-autonomous agency called the U.S. Housing Authority (USHA) to administer the program at the national level. While formally under the auspices of the Interior Department, the USHA had its own sources of revenue and was able to function independently. In this respect, the legislation corresponded to what the LHC had suggested in the 1935 Ellenbogen bill. Other LHC ideas fared less well. Congress quickly killed the section on nonprofits and cooperatives. Demonstration projects directed from Washington met the same fate. These changes left all decisions as to where to locate subsidized housing, and even the decision as to whether to build at all, entirely with local government bodies. Such exclusive emphasis on local initiative was unfortunate, because at the local level most politically powerful groups reacted to the idea of public housing with, in the words of one commentator, "the same enthusiasm as they might have greeted the introduction of bubonic plague." Other changes included amendments that kept construction costs minimal, specifically excluded all but the lowest income groups, and mandated elimination of slum property in a quantity equal to new dwelling units constructed.[28]

This last provision of the 1937 Wagner-Steagall Bill, the so-called equivalent elimination clause, formally linked public housing to slum clearance. This proviso meant that private developers would not face significant competition for land on the desirable suburban fringes of American cities. At the same time, commercial landlords would be protected from publicly supported increases in the supply of available apartment units (which might force down rent levels at the bottom end of the market). Focusing on slum clearance also meant that the increased land costs required to purchase already-developed property would consume more of the limited resources allocated to public housing.

Of all the alterations made to Wagner's proposed housing bill, the cost limitation amendment added by Senator Harry Byrd of Virginia was probably most devastating to the hope that government building programs might eventually develop a widely appealing new residential architecture—one of the most radical possibilities of Bauer's modern housing concept. Senator Byrd, perturbed by what he regarded as the excessive costs and threatening "socialistic" implications of the Resettlement Administration's cooperative farms, was determined to hold federally subsidized housing to minimal expenditures. The Resettlement Administration, headed by President Roosevelt's brain truster Rexford Tugwell, sought to build cooperative farm communities for "stranded" agricultural and industrial workers. Byrd's efforts resulted in spending caps far below what the bill's backers envisioned: The absolute limit per unit was $5,000.[29]

A comparison with the money spent by the Housing Division gives a sense of the constraints imposed on the new program. Under the PWA, the *average* price per dwelling unit was $4,975, almost exactly the absolute upper limit allowed under the permanent legislation (and possible only in the largest cities with the highest land and labor costs). The PWA expenditures, moreover, included the South as well as cities with under a half-million in population, locations where costs were considerably lower.[30] Thus, it becomes clear that the permanent legislation mandated a markedly diminished physical standard for what Americans would come to know as "public housing," compared with the work of the PWA.

Proponents of public housing were distressed, but supported the final version as the best they were likely to get. As it turned out, some later regretted their decision. Charles Abrams, a subsidized housing advocate who had initially been positive about the Wagner Act, wrote in the 1960s that "in retrospect, I believe that the compromises that were made in the 1937 debate on the public housing measure lastingly impaired it and will ultimately contribute to its demise."[31]

The Two Tiers of U.S. Housing Policy

The passage of the 1937 United States Housing Act was a major setback for the hopes of those who advocated a modern housing policy direction, and choices about how to implement the legislation further dimmed the prospects for an expansive, popular program. The Byrd Amendment mandated austerity, but the United States Housing Authority (USHA) was even more parsimonious than required. Nathan Straus, Roosevelt's choice to head the newly formed authority, initiated this administrative approach.

Straus was part of the public-spirited family that owned Macy's department stores. A New Deal supporter, Straus had a long-standing interest in housing reform. He had sponsored a limited-dividend project in the Bronx called Hillside Houses in the first phase of the PWA housing program and had served on the board of the New York City Housing Authority. Sincerely devoted to the cause of public housing, Straus hoped that by keeping costs to a minimum he could garner political support and at the same time produce the greatest amount of shelter. In the authority's 1939 annual report, he wrote proudly that "despite the doubts of many who felt that these statutory limitations [on expenditures] would seriously retard the rehousing drive, the average room and unit dwelling-facilities costs under the U.S.H.A. program are well below the statutory maxima *and are constantly being driven even further downward.*"[32] Overall, the new agency spent an average of 30 percent below PWA levels on its construction in the period before World War II.[33]

The cuts had a severe impact. Red Hook and Queensbridge, the first two complexes built in New York City under the new legislation, cost approximately one-half as much per room as the two projects built in the city by the PWA.[34] Lewis Mumford, writing in the *New Yorker*, complained that both developments were "unnecessarily barrackslike and monotonous." He found Red Hook, with its "Leningrad formalism," particularly inhumane.[35] The authority carried out its self-proclaimed "policy of eliminating all nonessentials" in a variety of ways.[36] Doors were left off closets, kitchens were not separated from living areas, and interior partitions were cheap and flimsy. At Red Hook, there were no elevator stops at the second, fourth, and sixth floors of buildings.[37]

The USHA's constrained approach to building, which began under Straus's

9. Brooklyn's Red Hook housing development, one of the first complexes built in the public housing program established by the 1937 Housing Act. Cost-cutting under the permanent program markedly diminished the attractiveness and convenience of public housing, as compared with PWA developments.

10. Queensbridge housing development. Lewis Mumford complained that both Queensbridge and Red Hook were "unnecessarily barrackslike and monotonous."

administration, ultimately proved politically disastrous. Its miserly practices meant that it produced precisely what one architect supporter of the Labor Housing Conference had hoped to avoid: construction the public would identify as "those buildings which the government built to house poor people."[38] Those who hated public housing remained hostile, while the minimal buildings produced by the USHA attracted no new allies and discouraged many old ones.[39]

Notably, at the same time the USHA was delegitimating the idea of a noncommercial housing sector, the Federal Housing Administration was successfully restructuring the private real estate market so that it could serve a larger proportion of the population. The FHA, by promising to insure mortgages for homes in stable neighborhoods that passed its guidelines, made it easier and cheaper for speculative builders to secure working capital from private financial institutions. With more money available, developers ran bigger and more cost-efficient operations. Meanwhile, consumers found it easier and cheaper to borrow, thanks to the new format for mortgages instituted by FHA regulations and the fact that the government insured their loans. Residential property became a safer investment for all concerned, because developers had to comply with FHA planning specifications to get approval for government mortgage insurance.[40]

The FHA's accomplishments were impressive. In the early years of the twentieth century, social workers had put forward minimum standards for urban dwellings, calling for such things as adequate ventilation, running water, and a flush toilet for each dwelling unit. Such amenities had seemed impossible at a mass level even in the prosperous 1920s. After World War II, the most modest of the FHA-insured tracts supplied shelter that met or exceeded these standards, at prices that the majority of Americans could afford.[41]

Yet even as we acknowledge the achievements of the Federal Housing Administration, we should note the ways it not only failed to achieve the possibilities envisioned by advocates of modern housing, but actively worked against them. For example, FHA policies encouraged low-density building at the periphery of cities, making Americans increasingly reliant on the automobile. In addition, as historian Kenneth Jackson demonstrated (see also Chapter 10, this volume), the agency "exhorted segregation and enshrined it as public policy." Until 1950, the FHA itself engaged in racially discriminatory practices with regard to insuring loans, and afterward it continued to work with private builders who refused to sell homes to African Americans. Thus, even affluent black families had trouble escaping decaying inner cities.[42] Meanwhile, whites sorted themselves out by income level in the new subdivisions where houses sold for roughly the same price. Finally, federal housing programs on behalf of the market did a much better job of producing environments for individual families than for neighborhood life, thus reinforcing existing trends toward privatism in the United States. Few speculative builders could afford to supply their housing tracts with generous playground and park spaces, let alone institute social programs like day care, clinics, or supervised recreation.

Conclusion

At the depth of the Depression in the early 1930s, the near-collapse of the real estate market, combined with a liberal upsurge, opened up a small political space for people committed to a new kind of American housing. Those influenced by the innovative ideas and values that were then circulating internationally with regard to housing found limited but real opportunities for experimentation in the temporary housing program of the Public Works Administration. Labor Housing Conference supporters hoped that this period would see the birth of a significant noncommercial housing sector in the United States, in the same way that so-called social housing had taken root in European countries after World War I.[43]

As things worked out, advocates of modern housing were not able to have any major part of their plan institutionalized in long-term policies. How can we explain this? One obvious answer is that the plan failed because Americans would never embrace alternatives to the ideal of single-family homeownership. This explanation does not seem justified by evidence, however. Rank-and-file trade unionists responded enthusiastically when Bauer traveled around the country presenting the program of the Labor Housing Conference to union gatherings. Also, interviews with individuals who lived in PWA complexes indicate a high level of satisfaction, particularly about their quality of life in the years that social programs were available.[44] It seems clear then that even with minimum publicity there was a real, if small, audience for new ideas about housing design and noncommercial ownership forms. Unfortunately, most Americans never heard about alternative possibilities, much less saw attractive, well-functioning examples of noncommercial neighborhoods. Thus, it seems probable that there was a sizable minority who would have chosen a more community-oriented residential option, at least during some part of their life cycle.

In trying to understand why public policy took the direction it did, what we *do* know is that modern housing activists had far less political influence with

Congress than did real estate investors. Facing the small, fragmented, and poorly funded coalition in favor of federal support for nonmarket, community-oriented alternatives were real estate business groups throughout the country, one of the strongest political forces in American political life. Although temporarily stunned at the outset of the decade, real estate developers and financial institutions linked to the property market were on the upswing by the mid-1930s, thanks in good part to public aid.

In most European countries, where movements supporting noncommercial housing met with greater success, groups with a financial interest in residential real estate had far less political influence than in the United States. In Vienna, for example, the municipal government erected enough shelter to rehouse 10 percent of the population during the 1920s. Export-oriented big industrialists positively welcomed the Social Democrats' housing programs, caring little about how they disadvantaged the private rental sector. In England, which also instituted a large-scale program of noncommercial housing, property capital was politically weak as well. The social and economic isolation of landlords gave them no voice in the policies of the Liberal and Conservative Parties before World War I, nor any input into the Labor Party afterward. Not surprisingly, therefore, the crisis of the early twentieth-century English housing market was resolved at the expense of private landlords through unfavorable taxation policies, rent control, and ultimately the displacement of a large part of the private rental sector by council (or public) housing.[45]

In the United States, with its long tradition of land speculation as a central economic activity, the configuration of political forces was very different. Here, property investors possessed much greater political power than did those in European nations, especially at the local level where more political decisions were made. With regard to housing decisions made in Washington, D.C., real estate entrepreneurs, economically bulwarked by Depression-era reforms, exerted enormous power in every Congressional district in the country and pursued their interests in Washington through well-funded lobbying organizations. Furthermore, property interests were less isolated from other sectors of capital than in most European contexts. While leading industrialists did not join in fighting the Wagner Act, neither did they, as was the case in England or Vienna, actively support large-scale public ownership of residential real estate.

By the end of the 1930s, a long-term pattern for federal housing policy had emerged. It consisted of two tiers. The top one, largely implementing the proposals that business groups had been making since the end of World War I, consisted of mortgage insurance and other institutional arrangements organized and subsidized by the federal government. These allowed financial markets to provide low-cost capital to producers and consumers of market-supplied housing. The core programs of the top policy tier were managed mainly by the FHA (but were supplemented by other agencies, such as the Home Loan Bank Board, the temporary Home Owners Loan Corporation, and the Federal National Mortgage Association, better known as Fannie Mae). The Wagner Act (1937), which established public housing as we know it today, defined the lower tier. Wagner's housing legislation, as it ultimately emerged from Congress, created a form of directly assisted housing that was stingy, physically alienating, and means tested. The final program did not support cooperatives or other private organizations interested in developing noncommercial alternatives, nor did it provide possibilities for residents to participate in administering publicly owned housing. These two tiers, created by the housing legislation of the thirties, established the framework for the development of the U.S. housing system for the next several decades.

The modern housing vision of a unified federal program characterized by compact neighborhoods, community facilities, and noncommercial ownership failed to leave its mark on the final New Deal legislative outcome for housing. Nevertheless, many concepts associated with the modern housing proposal continued to inspire design professionals and urban reformers in the years that followed.

Notes

1. Quoted in Mary Susan Cole, "Catherine Bauer and the Public Housing Movement, 1926–1937," (Ph.D. dissertation, George Washington University, 1974), 673.

2. Resolution by John A. Phillips, president of the Pennsylvania Federation of Labor, in *Report of the Proceedings of the Fifty-Fourth Annual Convention of The American Federation of Labor* (Washington, D.C.: Judd and Detweiler, 1934), 580.

3. Catherine Bauer, *Modern Housing* (Boston: Houghton Mifflin, 1934).

4. Timothy L. McDonnell, *The Wagner Housing Act: A Case Study of the Legislative Process* (Chicago: Loyola University Press, 1957), 54–55, 29. Citations from *The National Industrial Recovery Act*, 48 Stat. 195.

5. Different authors calculate the total number of projects in different ways. Statistics given here conform to the data published in Ickes's 1937 Congressional testimony. Harold L. Ickes, "Activities of Housing Division of the Federal Emergency Administration of Public Works," Report Submitted to Senate Committee on Education and Labor, 75th Congress, 1st Session (1937), *Hearings on S. 1685* (Washington, D.C.: Government Printing Office, 1937), 20.

6. Richard Plunz, "Institutionalization of Housing Form in New York City, 1920–1950," in Richard Plunz, ed., *Housing Form and Public Policy in the United States* (New York: Praeger, 1980), 178.

7. See, for example, the influential article by Richard Pommer, "The Architecture of Urban Housing in the United States During the Early 1930s," *Journal of the Society of Architectural Historians* 37 (December 1978): 263. For an overview of PWA housing efforts, see Gail Radford, *Modern Housing for America: Policy Struggles in the New Deal Era* (Chicago: University of Chicago Press, 1996).

8. Cited in McDonnell, *The Wagner Housing Act*, 166.

9. R. Allen Hays, *The Federal Government and Urban Housing: Ideology and Change in Public Policy* (Albany: State University of New York Press, 1985), 92–93.

10. 49 Stat. 2025.

11. Gertrude S. Fish, "Housing Policy During the Great Depression," in Gertrude Sipperly Fish, ed., *The Story of Housing* (New York: Macmillan, 1979), 185–86.

12. Kenneth T. Jackson, "Race, Ethnicity, and Real Estate Appraisal: The Home Owners Loan Corporation and the Federal Housing Administration," *Journal of Urban History* 6 (August 1980): 421; Arthur M. Schlesinger Jr., *The Coming of the New Deal* (Boston: Houghton Mifflin, 1958), 298.

13. 48 Stat. 1246.

14. Marriner S. Eccles, *Beckoning Frontiers* (New York: Alfred A. Knopf, 1951), 144–52, quotation from 144.

15. Eccles, *Beckoning Frontiers*, 149, 151.

16. U.S. Housing and Home Finance Agency, *Tenth Annual Report, 1956* (Washington D.C.: Government Printing Office, 1957), Table A-1, 266.

17. S. 2392, 74th Congress, 1st Session, 1935.

18. McDonnell, *The Wagner Housing Act*, 88–92. Wagner's 1935 bill, S. 2392, 74th Congress, 1st Session (1935), reprinted in McDonnell, *The Wagner Housing Act*, 405–25. J. Joseph Huthmacher, *Senator Robert F. Wagner and the Rise of Urban Liberalism* (New York: Atheneum, 1968), 207.

19. McDonnell, *The Wagner Housing Act*, 97–99. John W. Edelman, *Labor Lobbyist: The Autobiography of John W. Edelman* (Indianapolis: Bobbs-Merrill, 1974), 109.

20. Ellenbogen's bill, H.R. 7399, 74th Congress, 1st Session (1935), reprinted in McDonnell, *The Wagner Housing Act*, 404–24

21. Differences in outlook between the two groups are described in Eugenie Ladner Birch, "Edith Elmer Wood and the Genesis of Liberal Housing Thought, 1910–1942" (Ph.D. dissertation, Columbia University, 1976), 195.

22. Nathaniel S. Keith, *Politics and the Housing Crisis Since 1930* (New York: Universe Books, 1973), 29–30; McDonnell, *The Wagner Housing Act*, 60–62.

23. Michael J. Doucet and John C. Weaver, "Material Culture and the North American House: The Era of the Common Man, 1870–1920," *Journal of American History* 72 (December 1985): 570.

24. Quoted in McDonnell, *The Wagner Housing Act*, 138–39.

25. Quoted in John H. Mollenkopf, *The Contested City*, (Princeton: Princeton University Press, 1983), 70.

26. 50 Stat. 888.

27. James T. Patterson, *Congressional Conservatism and the New Deal: The Growth of the Conservative Coalition in Congress, 1933–1939* (Lexington: University of Kentucky Press, 1967), 155.

28. McDonnell, *The Wagner Housing Act*, 301–2, 323–59, and 389–402; Lawrence M. Friedman, *Government and Slum Housing: A Century of Frustration* (Chicago: Rand McNally, 1968), 111–12; Hays, *The Federal Government and Urban Housing*, 90–91, quotation from 90; Bruce Headey, *Housing Policy in the Developed Economy: The United Kingdom, Sweden, and the United States* (New York: St. Martin's Press, 1978), 204–5.

29. McDonnell, *The Wagner Housing Act*, 326–32, 394–95; Friedman, *Government and Slum Housing*, 112–13.

30. Miles L. Colean, *American Housing: Problems and Prospects* (New York: Twentieth Century Fund, 1944), 277. Herman B. Byer and Clarence A. Trump, "Labor and Unit Costs in PWA Low-Rent Housing," *Monthly Labor Review* 49 (September 1939): 579

31. Charles Abrams, "Housing Policy—1937 to 1967," in Bernard J. Frieden and William W. Nash Jr., eds., *Shaping an Urban Future: Essays in Memory of Catherine Bauer Wurster* (Cambridge, Mass.: MIT Press, 1969), quotation from 35–36.

32. United States Housing Authority, *Annual Report for Fiscal Year 1939* (Washington D.C.: U.S. Government Printing Office, 1940), 5, emphasis added.

33. Computed from Colean, *American Housing*, Table 60, 439.

34. Pommer, "The Architecture of Urban Housing in the United States During the Early 1930s," 256.

35. Mumford, "Versailles for the Millions," *The New Yorker* 16, February 17, 1940, 44, 42.

36. "26 Million To Be Saved in Development Costs," *Public Housing Weekly News*, June 25, 1940, 4.

37. Described in Plunz, "Institutionalization of Housing Form in New York City, 1920–1950," 180–81. See also idem, "A Lesson in Cost Reduction," *Architectural Forum*, November 1938, 405–8.

38. Draft of a letter by Oskar Stonorov to the PWA housing Division, March 25, 1935, Box 2, Stonorov File, Records of the Executive Secretary of the Labor Housing Conference, State Historical Society of Wisconsin.

39. Mark I. Gelfand, *A Nation of Cities* (New York: Oxford University Press, 1975), 64.

40. Marc A. Weiss, *The Rise of the Community Builders: The American Real Estate Industry and Urban Land Planning* (New York: Columbia University Press, 1987), chapter 6.

41. Minimum requirements for a good dwelling formulated by the National Conference of Charities and Correction, as cited in Edith Elmer Wood, *Recent Trends in American Housing* (New York: Macmillan, 1931), 39–40.

42. Kenneth T. Jackson, *Crabgrass Frontier: The Suburbanization of the United States* (New York: Oxford University Press, 1985), chapter 11, quotation from 213. Arnold R. Hirsch, "With or Without Jim Crow: Black Residential Segregation in the United States," in Arnold R. Hirsch and Raymond A. Mohl, eds., *Urban Policy in Twentieth-Century America* (New Brunswick: Rutgers University Press, 1993), 84–94.

43. For the influence of the European social-democratic housing movement on American urban reformers, see Radford, *Modern Housing for America*, chapter 3; and Daniel T. Rodgers, *Atlantic Crossings: Social Politics in a Progressive Age* (Cambridge, Mass.: Harvard University Press, 1998), 381–401.

44. Radford, *Modern Housing for America*, chapters 5 and 6.

45. These interpretations are based on work by Peter Marcuse and M. J. Daunton. See Marcuse, "A Useful Installment of Socialist Work: Housing in Red Vienna in the 1920s," in Rachel G. Bratt, Chester W. Hartman, and Ann Meyerson, eds., *Critical Perspectives on Housing* (Philadelphia: Temple University Press, 1986), esp. 581–83; idem, "The Housing Policy of Social Democracy: Determinants and Consequences," in Anson Rabinbach, ed., *The Austrian Socialist Experiment: Social Democracy and Austromarxism, 1918–1934* (Boulder, Colo.: Westview Press, 1985), 201–21; Daunton, "Introduction," in Daunton, ed., *Councillors and Tenants: Local Authority Housing in English Cities, 1919–1939* (Leicester, England: Leicester University Press, 1984), 1–33; and idem, *House and Home in the Victorian City: Working Class Housing, 1850–1914* (London: E. Arnold, 1983).

6

The Federal Housing Program During World War II

As the United States mobilized for war in 1940, workers migrated from rural to urban areas in search of employment in defense industries. Within a year, the population of certain cities and towns on the East, West, and Gulf Coasts and in the upper Midwest doubled or in some cases tripled. Holly Ridge, North Carolina, for example, had a population of twenty-six before the 1941 construction of Camp Davis, a U.S. Army antiaircraft-training facility capable of housing twenty thousand troops.[1]

Whether or not this migration represented the "greatest voluntary migration of free men and women in history," there is no question that the shortage of housing in centers of defense activity was a critical economic and social problem.[2] By late 1940, many workers who found employment at defense plants and military bases discovered their housing options were limited to moving in with another family or occupying an apartment in a converted attic, basement, or garage. Trailers, railroad cars, automobiles, and even grain bins were enlisted to provide shelter for housing-hungry defense workers.[3]

Elmer Honeycutt, a machine tool operator who migrated to San Diego in early 1941 for a job at the Consolidated Aircraft Company, was typical of thousands of defense workers nationwide. Honeycutt's employment nearly ended a short time after it began because the only dwelling he could find for his wife and children was a condemned two-room tourist cabin where sanitary facilities were shared among fifty persons.[4]

What made Honeycutt atypical or unusual among the defense workers who found it nearly impossible to locate decent, affordable rental housing was that he was presented with the option of leaving the overburdened private housing market for the public housing market. The Honeycutts were among an estimated forty-four thousand defense workers and their families nationwide who were residing in public housing by October 1941. They were also among the first three thousand families who, in 1941, moved to Linda Vista, the nation's largest defense public housing development.[5]

This chapter will examine the goals that guided the formulation and administration of the federal housing program created during World War II. It argues that housing policy goals changed over the course of the war. Three distinct phases emerged during the wartime housing program, each with its own unique set of policy goals. When the Defense Phase began in mid-1940, the federal government reestablished itself as a force in local and regional planning and development in a manner reminiscent of the early days of the New Deal.

The War Phase commenced in February 1942 with the reorganization of the federal housing bureaucracy under the National Housing Agency (NHA). During the War Phase, the home-building, real estate, and banking interests regained much of their pre-Depression ability to oppose direct federal involvement in local and regional planning and development, especially for purposes of economic and social reform.

The third phase of the wartime housing program, the Disposition Phase, began shortly after the war ended in 1945 and extended for over a decade. During this time, conservative interests pressured the NHA and its successor agency, the Housing and Home Finance Agency, to liquidate the homes and communities constructed under New Deal, defense, and war housing programs and to distance the public housing program from its previous association with economic and social reform. This chapter focuses mainly on the Defense Phase because of its broader implications for postwar housing policy.

The Defense Phase

The goals of the Defense Phase of the wartime housing program can best be understood when examined in the larger context of how Congress and the administration of President Franklin D. Roosevelt approached the wartime housing shortage. Determined to avoid a change in the nation's housing status

11. America needed defense workers during World War II, but a shortage of housing forced many workers and their families to live in substandard dwellings such as the one shown here in Pennsylvania.

quo, they supported the use of federal power to ensure the economic survival of the commercial housing market and to reinforce the importance of home-ownership.[6]

The Defense Phase began in June 1940 when Congress authorized the U.S. Housing Authority (USHA) to build twenty public housing developments for civilian employees of the armed forces and defense contractors, with funds originally appropriated for low-income public housing. One month later, President Roosevelt appointed the former Atlanta realtor Charles F. Palmer to the post of Defense Housing Coordinator. Palmer's job was to determine where the shortage of housing threatened defense production and to estimate the quantity of private and public housing necessary to ease the crisis.

With the support of President Roosevelt, Palmer concentrated his efforts on helping the private home-building industry respond to the need for housing in centers of defense activity. He worked closely with officials from the Defense Homes Corporation (DHC), created in 1941 to provide financial aid to private contractors who built homes for defense workers. The Defense Housing Coordinator was also closely linked to the Federal Housing Administration (FHA) and supported the agency's efforts to encourage defense workers to become homeowners by reducing or eliminating down payments and increasing opportunities to obtain mortgage insurance.

Working in collaboration with Palmer's Division of Defense Housing Coordination, the DHC and the FHA helped ease the housing shortage among defense workers who wished to purchase homes. These agencies were not, however, effective in expanding the supply of housing for families who could not afford to purchase a home. Convinced that the private home-building industry was unable to provide an adequate supply of rental housing, representatives from organized labor and housing and social welfare organizations supported a bill introduced by Representative Fritz G. Lanham (Democrat, Texas) in September 1940, calling for the construction of public housing for defense workers.[7]

Lanham not only received the backing of liberals who favored the expansion of the public housing program for defense workers, but also of home-building, real estate, and banking interests who opposed public housing legislation. He secured conservative support by taking steps to ensure that defense housing would not compete with private-sector efforts. The bill stipulated that defense housing could be built only in those cities and towns inadequately served by the private home-building industry.

Lanham's known hostility toward the low-income public housing program created by the 1937 Wagner-Steagall Act further solidified the support of home-building and allied interests. Determined that low-income public housing would not benefit as a result of his bill, he refused to place the USHA in charge of the defense housing program despite the fact that the agency presided over a nationwide network of local public housing authorities. He later erased any ambiguity about the postwar fate of the housing constructed under his bill by securing an amendment prohibiting the conversion of defense public housing into low-income public housing without specific Congressional authorization.[8]

In October 1940, Lanham's bill was signed into law by President Roosevelt. The National Defense Housing Act, also known as the Lanham Act, authorized the Federal Works Agency (FWA) to construct housing for "persons engaged in national defense activities and their families," including noncommissioned officers and civilian employees of defense contractors.[9]

The Lanham Act's conservative agenda notwithstanding, FWA Administrator John M. Carmody, who had previously served as administrator of the Rural Electrification Administration, regarded the Lanham Act as an opportunity for federal housing officials to reestablish themselves as a force in local and regional planning and development on a level that was equal to or exceeded the New Deal. Lanham Act funds also gave Carmody a chance to revive the program of experimentation in low-cost housing architecture and design, construction techniques and building materials, and finance that had begun when "modern housing" was introduced to the United States by the Public Works Administration.[10]

Looking ahead to postwar housing needs, Carmody foresaw an expanded role for public housing if large-scale public works projects were necessary to ease unemployment while the economy converted back to peacetime production. As a result, he regarded the defense housing program as an opportunity to design and build communities that would "set a pattern for the future development of housing in America."[11]

To develop prototypes for postwar housing, Carmody created research and pilot projects in architecture and design, construction, and home finance. Several FWA constituent agencies developed and implemented experimental housing programs, including the USHA, which had administered the federal low-income public housing program since 1937, and two FWA administrative subagencies, the FWA's Defense Housing Division (DHD) and the Mutual Ownership Defense Housing Division (MODHD).

Under the leadership of the embattled administrator Nathan Straus, the USHA made a twofold contribution to defense housing innovation. First, the agency hired leading International Style architects who were sympathetic to modern housing goals. Eliel and Eero Saarinen, the Finnish father and son architectural team, worked in collaboration with J. Robert F. Swanson on the USHA's 276-unit Krammer homes in Center Line, Michigan; George Howe and Louis I. Kahn designed the 450-dwelling unit Pine Ford Acres in Middletown, Pennsylvania. Presented as showcases for postwar urban housing, both developments featured comprehensive site planning and facilities designed to promote community interaction.[12]

Second, the USHA advanced housing research and experimentation by selecting certain defense housing developments for the establishment of "small laboratories," where architects functioned as the "chief scientists."[13] The USHA authorized the architect Antonin Raymond and his associate Edwin Schruers to use a small percentage of the dwelling units at the 168-unit Parkridge Homes in Bethlehem, Pennsylvania, to test new designs, construction techniques, and

12. The National Defense Housing Act, also known as the Lanham Act, authorized the construction of houses for defense workers. The result was houses such as these built by the National Housing Agency at Pico Gardens in Los Angeles.

building products. The experimental dwelling units at Parkridge Homes offered an open floor plan, large windows, and sliding glass doors, features that proved to be widely popular with postwar homeowners.

The DHD, founded in April 1941, shared the USHA's innovative approach to defense housing. Defense Housing Division Director Clark Foreman, who had previously served as an adviser on racial policy to the Works Progress Administration (WPA), was directed to find ways to integrate prefabrication into the defense housing program. Foreman's job was made more complicated by the disappointing results of the Public Buildings Administration's earlier prefabricated defense housing demonstration project at Indian Head, Maryland.[14]

Foreman convinced Walter Gropius and Frank Lloyd Wright, two of the world's foremost architects, to accept the challenge of designing low-cost prefabricated housing for defense workers. Gropius, Wright, and other renowned architects accepted Foreman's offer to design prefabricated defense housing for patriotic and, in some cases, economic reasons, and also because they were intrigued with the prospect of developing a prefabricated housing system that might ultimately revolutionize the entire field of housing.[15]

The MODHD pushed the limits of housing experimentation even further than the USHA and the DHD. Under the direction of Lawrence Westbrook, an engineer and attorney who had previously served with the Federal Emergency Relief Administration and the WPA, the MODHD built eight defense housing developments in New Jersey, Pennsylvania, Ohio, Indiana, and Texas. Ranging in size from 250 to 1,000 units, each MODHD development featured prefabricated homes designed by leading modern architects such as the Austrian Richard J. Neutra, who had established an architectural practice in Los Angeles in the 1920s. Site plans were based on Neutra's Park Living Plan, which was similar to the Superblock concept used at Radburn, New Jersey. At MODHD developments such as South Bend's 250-unit Walnut Grove, pedestrians could reach the community center, a cooperative grocery store, and a nursery school by traveling through an interior park.[16]

The eight developments built by the MODHD were noteworthy not only for their architecture and design, but also because they were slated for sale to the residents on a cooperative or mutual basis. Conceived during the Great Depression when homeownership was an economic liability for many workers, the Mutual Home Ownership Plan was developed by Westbrook in consultation with John Green, the president of the Industrial Union of Marine and Shipbuilding Workers of America, a member union of the Congress of Industrial Organizations (CIO). Labor and prominent liberal reformers regarded the Mutual Home Ownership Plan as a viable economic and social alternative to traditional homeownership. Dorothy Rosenman of the National Committee on the Housing Emergency regarded it as the best means of ensuring that defense housing would provide "attractive, valuable neighborhoods long after the war is over."[17]

Through research and pilot projects undertaken by the USHA, the DHD, and the MODHD, Carmody sought to regain the ground that federal housing agencies lost in local and regional planning and development when the public housing program became the subject of political attack in 1938–39. By contrast, Defense Housing Coordinator Palmer sought to limit federal government involvement in housing and planning and to return to the pre-Roosevelt housing status quo, when the private home-building, real estate, and banking interests had little competition for influence in federal housing policy formation.[18]

The differences between those who favored and those who opposed

13. Each dwelling unit at Avion Village was photographed before the 216-unit defense public housing project was sold to the residents on a mutual basis in 1948. Designed by architects Roscoe P. DeWitt, Richard J. Neutra, and David R. Williams, the Grand Prairie, Texas development was one of eight pilot projects built by the Federal Works Agency's Mutual Ownership Defense Housing Division in 1941. Seven of the eight original pilot projects, including Avion Village, are still owned by the residents on a cooperative basis today.

greater federal activism in housing and urban planning can perhaps best be seen in the case of Willow Run, Michigan. The shortage of housing for workers employed at the famous Ford Motor Company's B-24 Bomber factory created a national scandal that, by 1942, had attracted the attention of U.S. Senator Harry S. Truman and his defense investigatory committee. Carmody supported the 1941 plan proposed by United Automobile, Aircraft, and Agricultural Implements Workers of America (UAW) official Walter Reuther, calling for the FWA to use Lanham Act funds to construct an entire "Defense City" for twenty thousand bomber workers. Determined to establish Detroit as the starting place for the economic and social revitalization of urban America, Reuther urged that Defense City be designed by leading International Style architects and sold to its residents on a mutual or cooperative basis.[19]

Palmer joined the industrialist Henry Ford and other politically conservative interests in opposing Reuther's Defense City plan. Reuther's proposed "laboratory for post-war housing and life" filled conservatives such as Palmer and Ford with alarm because of the potential that twenty thousand UAW-CIO workers and their families offered for altering the existing balance of economic, political, and social power. Palmer helped to defeat the Defense City plan by delaying action on it and supporting the construction of several smaller, scattered developments. The fact that temporary housing units and dormitories made up the bulk of the housing provided for Willow Run bomber workers was an indication that a fundamental shift in wartime housing policy would soon emerge.[20]

During the Defense Phase, Carmody and other leading defense housing officials challenged architectural and design conventions and introduced or improved new building materials and construction techniques. They also helped boost the growth of the noncommercial housing sector when they offered workers access to cooperative homeownership. Carmody and his supporters did not, however, attempt to alter the racial status quo in public housing or to use the wartime housing crisis as an opportunity to desegregate public housing. Despite the fact that "local custom" and "prevailing racial patterns" were used to determine the racial composition of defense housing, the construction of housing for African American defense workers still triggered protests in Detroit and other cities and even contributed to racial violence.[21]

Two hundred and seven defense housing projects had been completed and occupied nationwide by January 1942. An additional 171 defense housing projects had been authorized for construction. Despite these accomplishments, the defense housing program had largely failed to provide housing when and where it was needed. Housing analysts and organized labor warned that the efficiency of the defense housing program had to be markedly improved if bottlenecks in war-related industrial production were to be avoided. In February 1942, President Roosevelt approved a reorganization plan proposed by his adviser Samuel I. Rosenman. Roosevelt's Executive Order 9070 transferred the housing activities of sixteen federal housing agencies to the newly created National Housing Agency (NHA).[22]

The creation of the NHA resulted in the consolidation of all defense housing activities under the NHA's subagency, the Federal Public Housing Authority (FPHA). It also led to a major personnel shake-up among war housing officials. Foreman, Westbrook, and other liberal defense housing officials who had not departed in October 1941, when for health reasons Carmody resigned as FWA administrator, were replaced by a new breed of housing officials led by NHA Administrator John B. Blandford Jr. Blandford rejected Carmody's New Deal view of housing as a tool of economic and social reform and adopted a more businesslike approach to housing.[23]

The War Phase

In 1942, the FPHA completed work on two defense housing developments that closely resembled those built by its predecessor agency, the FWA, as models for postwar living. The George Washington Carver Court in Coatesville, Pennsylvania, offered African American war workers an opportunity to live in a development that featured comprehensive site planning and International Style architecture. Richard J. Neutra, who had collaborated on an MODHD project with Westbrook one year earlier, designed Channel Heights, an FPHA-constructed development for San Pedro, California, shipyard workers. The development not only offered residents homes with a Pacific Ocean view, but also the benefit of living in a comprehensively planned community with a day care center, a supermarket, and a gardening education center.[24]

Carver Court and Channel Heights gained the FPHA architectural acclaim. Overall, however, modern housing was the exception, not the rule, for the agency. The FPHA adopted a series of policies that, according to Herbert Emmerich, who served as the agency's commissioner from 1942 to 1944, helped to transform the war housing program into one of "streamlined production and enlightened business management."[25]

NHA Administrator Blandford changed the focus of the war housing program from the construction of permanent housing developments (that might serve as starting points for postwar urban revitalization) toward the provision of minimalist temporary housing that would be torn down when the war ended. Blandford directed the FPHA to build temporary housing unless a demonstrated and ongoing need for permanent housing existed in a particular community. Blandford's decision to favor the construction of temporary housing over permanent housing was supported by home-building, real estate, and banking interests and their allies in Congress, who were convinced that building permanent housing would depress real estate values.[26]

Although they had supported the 1942 reorganization of the federal housing bureaucracy, organized labor and housing reform organizations opposed this new emphasis of the war housing program. They feared that trailers and other forms of temporary housing were potential postwar slums that would discredit all public housing. They further maintained that temporary and other types of stopgap housing did not adequately meet workers' shelter needs. Such claims were supported by studies of the University of Michigan sociologists Lowell J. Carr and James E. Sterner, who went undercover, took production-line jobs at the Ford Motor Company's B-24 Liberator Bomber plant in Willow Run, Michigan, and resided in Willow Lodge, a dormitory constructed by the FPHA.[27]

During the War Phase, the quality of the housing provided for war workers under the Lanham Act declined. Temporary dwellings built according to standardized plans, often with so-called victory building materials as a substitute for scarce, top-quality building materials, predominated. Still, however, two accomplishments emerged from the War Phase. First, FPHA officials strengthened their relationship with state and local governmental bodies that had been pushed aside during the Defense Phase when the FWA and other federal agencies built defense housing without regard for local planning initiatives, building codes, and zoning regulations.

Second, the War Phase saw increased attention to the housing needs of African American workers. As the percentage of African Americans employed in war industries rose, so too did the percentage of war housing reserved for black occupancy. In 1941, for example, only 4,050 units of defense housing were reserved for African American occupancy. Within a year, that figure rose dramatically to 31,357. By 1944, 11.2 percent of all public housing built for war workers was reserved for black occupancy. Still, Blandford and other federal housing officials refused to desegregate public housing.[28]

Looking back on his years as FPHA commissioner, Herbert Emmerich identified 1942 as a turning point in federal housing policy. During that year, "tempting Utopian schemes of only postwar significance" were "reluctantly rejected." In reality, however, Emmerich's boss, NHA Administrator Blandford, acted with little reluctance in restoring greater local and regional control over planning and development and replacing the social and economic reform focus of the Defense Phase with an emphasis on low-cost temporary housing. According to Emmerich, once the "[i]deological hatchets" were buried and the New Deal–inspired experimentation and innovation came to an end, "remarkable cooperation between private and public initiative" was created.[29]

Convinced that under the FPHA, the war housing program would not benefit the low-income public housing program, Congress lessened its hostility. Still, it favored housing agencies that encouraged war workers to become homeowners such as the Federal Housing Administration (FHA). By the close of 1945, the FHA had insured mortgages and made other financial commitments for private-sector defense housing totaling $1.6 billion.[30] Thus, the War Phase reinforced the two-tier system of federal housing aid described by Gail Radford in Chapter 5.

The Disposition Phase

In May 1948, the Columbia River flooded, destroying Oregon's second largest city, Vanport City. Consisting entirely of temporary structures, Vanport City had been built by the FPHA six years earlier. It housed 44,000 Kaiser Shipyard workers and their families. The disaster left homeless approximately 18,000 veterans and their families who resided in the homes once occupied by defense workers. Ironically, the flood ended the bitter political debate over the postwar fate of Vanport City. In other cities and towns across the nation where defense housing was located, the process of selling or tearing down wartime housing, known by federal housing officials as "disposition," was a far more complicated and time-consuming task.[31]

From the outset of the defense housing program in 1940, concern arose over the postwar fate of the over 700,000 units of Lanham Act housing built for the men and women who labored on the U.S. industrial home front. Although by 1945 over 546,112 family dwellings, 94,206 dormitory rooms, and 74,079 trailers and other types of stopgap defense housing had been built at the cost of more than $2 billion, no plan existed for its ultimate disposition.[32]

In its original form, the Lanham Act contained a vague provision indicating that defense housing was to be disposed of at the end of the war in the public interest. As noted earlier, the Lanham Act was amended in 1941 to require Congressional action to convert defense housing into low-income public housing. Washington expected that after the war temporary housing would be torn down and permanent housing sold to residents or private investors; no net increase in the number of housing units in the public domain was anticipated.

Between 1947 and 1955, FPHA officials and their successors in the Public Housing Administration developed a series of policies and procedures for defense and war housing disposition. FPHA applied the same guidelines to over five thousand units of housing in communities developed under the New Deal such as the Greenbelt Towns and the Subsistence Homesteads.

The development and implementation of disposition policy for the New Deal and wartime public housing became a complicated, time-consuming, and expensive process for several reasons. The severity of the postwar housing shortage made it impossible for federal housing officials to evict war workers and returning veterans and their families who moved into vacant war housing apartments. The Korean War prompted President Harry S. Truman to temporarily halt the disposition process in 1950. Finally, various disputes among the federal housing agencies, local governments, veterans' organizations, tenant groups, organized labor, and home-building and real estate interests also delayed the disposition process.

Despite the numerous delays, by March 1955, nearly a decade after the war ended, 87 percent of all defense and war housing had been liquidated. Approximately 270,000 temporary units were moved to college campuses and other sites and rented to veterans and their families. The remaining temporary units were torn down or sold to private investors who converted them into permanent homes and commercial buildings.[33]

The disposition of the permanent housing presented far more complex problems than did temporary dwellings. Congress allowed a small number of the permanent, family-type defense housing developments, about 1.9 percent of the total, to be conveyed to local public housing authorities for the use of low-income families. Most of these developments, such as the 140-unit Blair Heights in Clairton, Pennsylvania, had originally been built for occupancy by African American workers. By 1955, approximately 182,000 units of permanent, family-style units had been sold to residents, veterans, and private investors.[34]

The most significant and long-lasting accomplishment of the Disposition Phase was the sale of an undetermined number of defense housing developments of permanent construction, perhaps as many as fifty nationwide, to the residents under a modified version of Westbrook's Mutual Home Ownership Plan. Despite the opposition of real estate and business interests, thirteen defense housing developments in the Pittsburgh area alone, including Aluminum City Terrace, the defense housing development designed by Walter Gropius and Marcel Breuer, have been mutually owned by their residents for over fifty years.[35]

Conclusion

For nearly half a century, most historians and urban policy analysts have either overlooked the wartime housing program or have criticized it for its lack of administrative efficiency. In his classic 1956 study of the role of American industry in World War II, Francis Walton argued that "the housing tragedy of

World War II was not to be confused with, or compared to the New Deal rallying cry of a 'nation one-third ill housed.' It was scandal piled on earlier neglect."[36]

During the 1970s, the historian Philip J. Funigiello concluded that the "need for good inexpensive housing—which might have served hundreds of thousands of families from the slums, as well as returning veterans—went largely unfilled."[37] In 1985, the policy analyst J. Paul Mitchell wrote what might be considered the war housing program's epitaph: "War housing added nothing to, indeed subtracted from, the design of and implementation of a coherent national housing policy."[38] Only recently have scholars found that the wartime housing program had both positive and negative affects on housing and urban planning in postwar California.[39]

Most assessments of the war housing have failed to take into consideration that the goals of wartime housing changed over time. During the Defense Phase, housing visionaries such as Carmody prepared for an ambitious postwar public works and housing program by hiring leading architects to design model housing for the postwar years. The model housing developments built by the FWA and its constituent agencies never served as models for postwar housing, in part because no large-scale public works and federal housing program was created to aid in the reconversion process. In addition, the Truman administration responded to the postwar housing shortage by authorizing Veterans' Emergency Housing Expediter Wilson Wyatt to work primarily with private-sector prefabricated housing manufacturers in solving the problem. Bills calling for the resumption of public housing construction failed to secure passage until 1949.[40]

Another reason that the defense housing developments designed by Gropius and other prominent modern architects never served as models for postwar housing was that the Servicemen's Readjustment Act (widely known as the G.I. bill), FHA mortgage insurance, and other direct and indirect housing subsidies made it possible for workers to purchase a home in a suburban or recently developed urban neighborhood. The ranch homes and Cape Cod–style dwellings built in the two decades following the end of the war emphasized individualism, not the collective action that was a part of the modern housing vision. Furthermore, there was no need for wage earners to consider mutual homeownership when they could obtain the American dream of traditional homeownership.

In contrast to the lack of interest in wartime experimentation in low-cost housing architecture and finance, the building products and construction techniques developed or improved as a result of defense housing research received considerable attention during the postwar period. Plywood, plastic, Plexiglas, fiberglass, and other building materials that were first used or perfected in defense and war housing became common in postwar housing. In addition, the mass-production building techniques employed in famous postwar suburban developments such as Levittown were perfected in the defense housing laboratory.[41]

The use of federal power during World War II to preserve the commercial nature of housing and to reinforce the economic and social importance of homeownership stood in marked contrast to the approach employed in Europe—most notably England. Throughout much of Europe, World War II reinforced the post–World War I trend toward noncommercial and public housing.

Despite the conservatism of the U.S. war housing program, new directions in housing were proposed, and models of communities that set new standards in low-cost housing architecture, site planning, building materials, construction techniques, and financing were established. Architecture and design in particular were enlisted to help foster the growth of a sense of community among highly mobile war workers. What if defense housing developments such as Aluminum City Terrace had actually served as a model for postwar housing? It is impossible to say whether such a model might have altered the direction of postwar housing from its commercial, architecturally stale, and highly individualistic path toward a policy that emphasized a "people-centered" pattern of urban revitalization. As current policymakers seek solutions to the chronic U.S. shortage of low-cost housing, perhaps they will find that the defense and war housing program deserves a reconsideration.

Notes

1. "Holly Ridge Awaits Coming of Huge Anti-Aircraft Training Camp," December 10, 1940, Camp Davis Scrapbook, New Hanover County Library, North Carolina Collection, Wilmington, N.C. On the defense housing shortage and federal housing policy during World War II, see Philip J. Funigiello, *The Challenge of Urban Liberalism: Federal-City Relations During World War II* (Knoxville: University of Tennessee Press, 1978), 80–119; Greg Hise, *Magnetic Los Angeles: Planning the Twentieth Century Metropolis* (Baltimore and London: Johns Hopkins University Press, 1997); Gwendolyn Wright, *Building the Dream: A Social History of Housing in America* (New York: Pantheon Books, 1981), 242; Kenneth T. Jackson, *Crabgrass Frontier: The Suburbanization of the United States* (New York and Oxford: Oxford University Press, 1985), 240–41; John F. Bauman, *Public Housing, Race, and Renewal: Urban Planning in Philadelphia, 1920–1974* (Philadelphia: Temple University Press, 1987), 1–75; Lawrence M. Friedman, *Government and Slum Housing: A Century of Frustration* (Chicago: Rand McNally, 1968), 116; Francis E. Merrill, *Social Problems on the Homefront: A Study of Wartime Influences* (New York: Harper, 1948), 235; Richard Boyden, "'Where Outsized Paychecks Grow on Trees': War Workers in San Francisco Shipyards," *Prologue* 23 (1991): 253–59; James B. Allen, "Crisis on the Homefront: The Federal Government and Utah's Defense Housing in World War II," *Pacific Historical Review* 38 (1969): 407–28; and Lorraine McConaghy, "Wartime Boomtown, Kirkland, Washington, a Small Town During World

War II," *Pacific Northwest Quarterly* 80 (April 1989): 43, 45. For a fictional account of life in a defense housing development, see Harriet Arnow, *The Dollmaker* (New York: Macmillan, 1954).

2. National Housing Agency, *War Housing in the United States* (Washington, D.C.: National Housing Agency, 1945). See also "1940–1945: The Story of World War II Housing from Construction to Disposition," *Journal of Housing* 7 (May 1955): 152.

3. Merrill, *Social Problems on the Homefront*, 235; "Workers Urge Defense Housing for 5 Cities," *Public Housing* 2, no. 3 (July 16, 1940): 4; "Housing Hampers the Defense Job," *The New York Times*, March 30, 1941, p. 10E; U.S. Federal Works Agency, *Second Annual Report* (Washington, D.C.: U.S. Government Printing Office, 1942), 25; and "New Homes for Old," *CIO News*, July 15, 1940, 7.

4. U.S. Federal Works Agency, *Defense Housing, 1941* (U.S. Government Printing Office, 1942), n.p. On San Diego's wartime housing shortage, see Christine Killory, "Temporary Suburbs: The Lost Opportunity of San Diego's National Defense Housing Projects," *Journal of San Diego History* 39, no. 2 (1994): 33–49.

5. U.S. Federal Works Agency, *Second Annual Report* (Washington, D.C.: U.S. Government Printing Office, 1942), 54.

6. Twentieth Century Fund, Housing Committee, *Housing for Defense: A Review of the Role of Housing in Relation to America's Defense and a Program for Action*, Factual Findings by Miles L. Colean; the Program by the Housing Committee (New York: Twentieth Century Fund, 1940).

7. Cecil Owen, "New Homes for Old: Housing and Defense," *CIO News*, July 15, 1940, 7.

8. P.L. 409, 77th Congress, 1st Session. On Lanham's motives, see U.S. Congress, House of Representatives, Representative Lanham speaking for the Amendment of the Lanham Act, House Res. 6128, 77th Congress, 1st Session, December 1, 1941, *Congressional Record* 87 (1941): 9278. See also Charles Abrams, "Housing the War Workers," *New Republic* 105, 1941, 886–88.

9. P.L. 849, 76th Congress, 3d Session.

10. Catherine Bauer, *Modern Housing* (Boston and New York: Houghton Mifflin, 1934), xvi; and Catherine Bauer Wurster, "The Social Front of Modern Architecture in the 1930s," *Journal of the Society of Architectural Historians* 24 (1965): 48–52. See also Gail Radford, *Modern Housing For America: Policy Struggles in the New Deal Era* (Chicago: University of Chicago Press, 1997), 99–104.

11. U.S. Federal Works Agency, Press Release No. S-9, October 12, 1941, National Archives and Records Administration (hereafter NARA), Records of the Federal Works Agency, RG 162, Series 8, Box 5. Wartime housing experimentation was also undertaken by the Navy, which investigated the use of steel to frame housing and by the Tennessee Valley Authority, which refined designs for demountable dwellings that could be assembled, transported, and reassembled with minimum waste and cost. The Farm Security Administration tested the practicality of rammed earth as a durable building material. A prefabricated house built of composite material that included cotton was placed in the courtyard of the Department of Agriculture's Washington, D.C., office complex, where it attracted thousands of visitors. Numerous other examples abound.

12. "War Housing," *Architectural Forum*, May 1942, 281–84, 307–8. See also Peter S. Reed, "Enlisting Modernism," in Donald Albrecht, ed., *World War II and the American Dream: How Wartime Building Changed a Nation* (Cambridge and London: MIT Press, 1995), 2–41. On Straus, see Roger Biles, "Nathan Straus and the Failure of U.S. Public Housing, 1937–1942," *The Historian* 53 (Autumn 1990): 33–46.

13. O. Klime Fulmer, quoted in Antonin Raymond, "Working with [the] USHA Under the Lanham Act," *Pencil Points* 22 (November 1941): 693. See also "Install Novel Features," *The New York Times*, September 7, 1941, p. xi, 2.

14. Frederick Gutheim, "Indian Head Experiment in Prefabrication," *Pencil Points* 22 (1941): 724.

15. Walter Gropius and Martin Wagner, "How to Bring Forth an Ideal Solution of the Defense Housing Problem?" in Walter Gropius Papers, Houghton Library, Harvard University. The western Massachusetts defense housing development designed by Wright was never built as a result of political controversy. See Talbot Wegg, "FLW Versus the USA," *Journal of the American Institute of Architects* 53

(February 1970): 48–52. On Aluminum City Terrace, see Kristin M. Szylvian, "Bauhaus on Trial: Aluminum City Terrace and Federal Defense Housing Policy," *Planning Perspectives* 9 (1994): 229–54.

16. Kristin Szylvian Bailey, "The Federal Government and the Cooperative Housing Movement, 1917–1950," (Ph.D. dissertation, Carnegie Mellon University, 1988), and idem, "Our Mutual Friend: A Progressive Housing Legacy in the 1940s," *Cite: The Architectural and Design Review of Houston* 33 (1995): 17–19, 43. On Walnut Grove, see Richard A. Meussel, "Appraisal for Walnut Grove Mutual Housing Project," mimeograph copy, September 7, 1946, Walnut Grove Mutual Housing, Inc., South Bend, Indiana.

17. Dorothy Rosenman, "Housing to Speed Production," *Architectural Record* 91, 1942, 45; "FDR Approves Defense Housing Start; Camden Project Gets Underway," *Shipyard Worker* 5, no. 22, November 29, 1940, 1; and National Public Housing Conference, "Program for National Public Housing Conference," mimeograph copy, 5, NARA, Records of the Housing and Home Finance Agency, RG 207, Series 22, Box 2.

18. Funigiello, *The Challenge to Urban Liberalism*, 84. See also "Stop Public Housing!" *National Real Estate Journal* 45 (March 1944): 11; "Nation's Home Builders Lash Out Against Public Housing in Fiery Session," *National Real Estate Journal* 44 (December 1943): 16–18; and "Dallas Builds a New City Within a City," *Dallas Magazine*, March 1941, 11, 23.

19. John M. Carmody, [handwritten note on] Oscar Stonorov to John M. Carmody, Philadelphia, Pa., October 1, 1941, Papers of John M. Carmody, Franklin D. Roosevelt Library, Hyde Park, N.Y., Box 103. See also Alan Mather, "Backhousing for Bomber Plants," *Pencil Points* 23 (December 1942): 69–74.

20. Walter Reuther, International Executive Committee Board Member, United Automobile Workers Union, "Memorandum on Defense City in the Detroit Area," 12, Washington, D.C., September 26, 1941, Papers of John M. Carmody, Franklin D. Roosevelt Library, Box 103.

21. Margaret Crawford, "Daily Life on the Homefront: Women, Blacks, and the Struggle for Public Housing," in Donald Albrecht, ed., *World War II and the American Dream: How Wartime Building Changed a Nation* (Cambridge and London: MIT Press for the National Building Museum, 1994), 106–17.

22. U.S. Federal Works Agency, *Third Annual Report* (Washington, D.C.: U.S. Government Printing Office, 1942), 99.

23. Despite leaving the FWA for health reasons, Carmody was soon an appointed commissioner of the U.S. Maritime Commission. On Blandford's honeymoon relationship with Congress, see "War Housing & Vice Versa," *Architectural Forum* 76, July 1942, 33.

24. Lisa Ann Greenhouse, "Oskar Stonorov: Building Community on Shifting Ground," (Master's thesis, George Washington University, 1997); Richard Sheppard, "U.S. Wartime Housing," *Architectural Review* 96 (1944): 45, 49–50; "Channel Heights Housing Project," *Architectural Forum* 80, March 1944, 65–74.

25. Herbert Emmerich, "World War II Housing," *Journal of Housing* 7 (July 1955): 233. See also Gordon Walter, "Cities While You Wait in Washington and Oregon," *Pencil Points* 24 (April 1943): 48–55; and Ruth G. Weintraub and Rosalind Tough, "Federal Housing and World War II," *Journal of Land & Public Utility Economics* (May 1942): 159.

26. "Nation's Home Builders Lash Out Against Public Housing in Fiery Session," 16–18.

27. Lowell J. Carr and James E. Sterner, *Willow Run: A Study of Industrialization and Cultural Inadequacy* (New York: Harper, 1952), 133–73. See also Herman H. Field, "The Lesson of Willow Run," *Task: A Magazine for Architects and Planners* 4 (1943): 10.

28. U.S. National Housing Agency, *Third Annual Report* (Washington, D.C.: U.S. Government Printing Office, 1945), 32.

29. Emmerich, "World War II Housing," 233.

30. On Palmer, see Charles F. Palmer, "Defense Housing Program as Seen by the Government," *Pencil Points* 22 (February 1941): 130. See also "Congress in Defense Housing Snarl," *Business Week,*

September 14, 1940, 20. On federal aid to private home builders, see U.S. National Housing Agency, *Third Annual Report* (Washington, D.C.: U.S. Government Printing Office, 1944), 4.

31. "1940–1955," 154.

32. U.S. National Housing Agency, *Fourth Annual Report* (Washington, D.C.: U.S. Government Printing Office, 1945), 196.

33. U.S. Housing and Home Finance Agency, *Fourth Annual Report* (Washington, D.C.: U.S. Government Printing Office, 1950), 395–97.

34. "1940–1955," 154; and "U.S. to Sell 11 Projects Here," January 27, 1953, clipping file, Electric Heights Mutual Housing Association, Turtle Creek, Pa.

35. "1940–1955," 158.

36. Francis Walton, *The Miracle of World War II: How American Industry Made Victory Possible* (New York: Macmillan, 1956), 65.

37. Funigiello, *The Challenge to Urban Liberalism*, 83.

38. J. Paul Mitchell, "Historical Overview of Direct Housing Programs," in J. Paul Mitchell, ed., *Federal Housing Policy and Programs: Past and Present* (New Brunswick: Rutgers University Center for Urban Policy Research, 1985), 194.

39. For example, see Hise, *Magnetic Los Angeles*, 165–67; and Roger Lotchin, "World War II and Urban California: City Planning and the Transformation Hypothesis," *Pacific Historical Review* 62, no. 2 (1993): 143–71.

40. Richard O. Davies, *Housing Reform During the Truman Administration* (Columbia: University of Missouri Press, 1966).

41. Greg Hise recently examined the influence of the Farm Security Administration on postwar housing and of planning initiatives on the Kaiser Community Homes initiative. See Hise, *Magnetic Los Angeles*, 151–61. Henry Kaiser benefited from the research and pilot programs undertaken by the FWA as well. He even met with Lawrence Westbrook of the Mutual Ownership Defense Housing Division to discuss the possibility of building housing under a version of the Mutual Home Ownership Plan.

PART II

Federal Housing Policy in Postwar America

The wartime struggle that pitted New Deal housers and architects bent on harnessing wartime Lanham Act housing to their vision of a modernist, progressive housing future against a resurgent real estate industry that was determined to block further government encroachment on private housing markets fizzled amid the prosperity of the 1950s. Privatism triumphed, all but dooming a communitarian future based on cooperative or mutual housing. Indeed, as the next six chapters show, the second half of the twentieth century revealed the full consequences of the flawed "two-tiered" housing policy enacted with the Housing Act of 1937. Middle-class homeownership programs such as those administered by the Federal Housing Administration, and for World War II heroes by the Veterans Administration, buttressed by a generous federal mortgage-interest-tax deduction, unleashed sprawling postwar suburbanization. In U.S. cities, racism, urban renewal, public housing policy, and deindustrialization spawned alienating, hypersegregated black slums.

Policymakers hammered out the U.S. postwar housing program amid a cold war psychology inimical to New Deal experimentalism. It took a severe housing shortage following the war, and the tireless crusading of Catherine Bauer Wurster and organizations such as the National Association of Housing Officials and labor groups, to produce the Taft-Ellender-Wagner (T-E-W) Law of 1949. First introduced as the Wagner-Ellenbogen bill in 1945, the original legislation was defeated by Republicans who enjoyed the support of southern and other conservative Democrats. Portions of Wagner's 1945 bill appeared in various guises until 1949 when the most important postwar piece of housing legislation was passed. Title II of the 1949 housing law established a national housing goal of a "decent home in a decent environment for every American" and set a six-year target of 810,000 units of public housing, 135,000 per year. Ominously, Title I of the 1949 law appropriated $1.5 billion to enable local authorities to clear and redevelop city slums. This sum, however, paled before the $13 billion in federal mortgage guarantees, which the Housing and Home Finance Administration, the successor agency to the wartime National Housing Agency, poured into the mushrooming suburbs.

Moreover, in 1954, a reluctant Congress appropriated monies not for 135,000, but for barely 20,000 units of public housing, a tribute to the successful assault on the program undertaken by foes such as the National Association of Real Estate Boards, which branded the policy a "communist plot" and the "road to serfdom."

Public housing survived by wedding itself to urban renewal. Betrothed in 1949, the Housing Act of 1954 consummated the marriage. The 1954 law made public housing a refuge for central-city families uprooted when their aging housing was demolished to accommodate expanding universities, hospitals, convention centers, or downtown malls. Other postwar laws had a similar impact. The 1956 Highway Act accelerated the development of the Interstate Highway system, unveiled in 1944. The new freeways and expressways also boosted the attractiveness of suburbia while—often by design—displacing thousands of inner-city, disproportionately African American, families.

The unloved handmaiden of urban renewal, public housing, frequently tower design, degenerated into a warehousing strategy for very poor people and an increasingly African American urban population. Once its champion, now a critic, Catherine Bauer Wurster in 1957 assailed public housing as a "Dreary Deadlock." Jane Jacobs agreed, vilifying the policy in her 1961 classic, *Death and Life of American Cities*.

In 1961, President John F. Kennedy, politically astute, shifted federal housing policy away from benighted, government-built public housing toward subsidized privately built low-income units. Moreover, his housing administrator, Marie McGuire, also switched emphasis from families in need to elderly people. In 1961, the Housing and Home Finance Agency introduced Section 23 "leased housing" and Section 221 (d) (3), which offered below-market interest rates to developers who built dwelling units for low- and moderate-income families. After considerable pressure from the black community who had backed him in the 1960 election, Kennedy issued Executive Order 11063, finally outlawing segregation in all federally built and subsidized housing.

Epitomizing the activist president, Lyndon Baines Johnson in 1965 created the Department of Housing and Urban Development (HUD), the first cabinet-level urban agency, and to head it tapped Robert Weaver, an African American long involved in government housing. HUD launched a bevy of urban programs and aggressively pursued the privatization of public housing begun under Kennedy. The 1968 Housing Act established an ambitious new housing goal of twenty-six million new housing units, six million for low- and moderate-income families. To meet the latter goal, HUD established Sections 235 and 236, subsidized interest rate programs, which by 1971 were deeply enmeshed in scandal.

In 1973, these scandals helped convince President Richard Nixon to declare a moratorium on all federally subsidized housing programs. Nixon ordered a reassessment of HUD's low-rent housing programs, which produced in 1974 Section 8, a program that allowed low-income families to seek on their own HUD-approved housing that they rented for one-third of their income. Washington's subsidy amounted to the difference between what tenants could afford and the market rent for the unit.

No Presidential administration since 1974, including the Carter administration, examined in Chapter 12, diverged from this rigid course of privatization. Not until the late 1990s did Washington address the crisis long plaguing the nation's low-income housing policy: Neither rental income from low-income families nor the government's annual contribution to local housing authorities (meant to ensure low rents) adequately met the maintenance and administrative costs of the housing projects. In fact, in 1969, the Massachusetts congressman Edwin Brook amended the 1937 housing law to prevent local housing authorities from raising tenant rents to cover rising maintenance costs. By the late 1970s, many distressed big city housing authorities, awash in maintenance problems, faced or had declared bankruptcy. With federal approval, cities summoned the wrecking balls. Significantly, many of these cities such as Baltimore, Philadelphia, Chicago, and Saint Louis maintained long waiting lists of people seeking shelter in public housing. The next six chapters of this book help illuminate this paradox and other housing issues, among them enduring privatism, entrenched racism, highway building, suburbanization, and deindustrialization, which undermined the nation's housing goals and stifled efforts to make community building or neighborhood reconstruction part of the nation's urban housing policy.

7

Public Housing and the Postwar Urban Renaissance, 1949–1973

ROGER BILES

This chapter considers how the housing reformers' dream of community building faded in the years between the passage of the Taft-Ellender-Wagner Housing Act of 1949 and President Richard M. Nixon's announcement of a moratorium on all housing involving federal subsidies. In the 1930s and 1940s, Lewis Mumford, Clarence Stein, Henry Wright, Catherine Bauer, and other reformers envisioned a government housing program that would provide modern dwellings as well as ready access to recreation centers, child care facilities, playgrounds, schools, health care clinics, and other amenities that would foster a sense of community among middle-class and low-income residents. After World War II, these so-called housers resumed their crusade but clashed with entrenched economic interests opposed to government's presence in the private housing market and with conservative politicians dedicated to a tightfisted fiscal conservatism. Policymakers in Washington opted for slum clearance with the passage of major housing bills in 1949 (urban redevelopment) and 1954 (urban renewal), while the provision of low-income housing assumed secondary importance.

At the same time, public housing projects became the repositories for society's unfortunates; by the early 1950s, monstrous high-rise edifices isolated low-income occupants by race and social class and obviated any notion of community. Beset by criticisms from conservative banking and building interests, public housing received a modest but steady stream of Congressional appropriations in the 1950s and 1960s, which allowed for continued construction at a languid rate. Moreover, as suburbanization and deindustrialization proceeded apace, urban renaissance schemes focused on downtown revitalization and upscale housing while failing to provide an adequate stock of low-income dwellings for displaced former-residents. Massive slum clearance and towering public housing projects no longer seemed the best solutions for the shortages of low-income housing; continuing to reject the reformist vision of large-scale subsidization of public housing communities, policymakers began experimenting with new kinds of low-income housing, rent supplements, and decentralization schemes. The reformers' hopeful endorsement of high-rise construction and urban renewal paid few dividends; by the end of the 1960s, the goal of creating community rarely figured in policy discussions about low-income housing.[1]

Post–World War II Initiatives

For four years after the conclusion of World War II, Senator Robert F. Wagner and his Congressional allies introduced a series of measures to revive the public housing initiatives left dormant during the conflict. The public housing provisions of the 1949 housing law provoked the most opposition in Congress, avoiding deletion in the House of Representatives by only five votes. The Taft-Ellender-Wagner Housing Act of 1949, the only major piece of President Harry S. Truman's Fair Deal legislative program passed by Congress, identified as its goal the provision of "a decent home and a suitable living environment" for every American family, yet public housing survived in this law only as an adjunct to slum clearance and downtown revitalization. Planners, big city mayors, bankers, and builders all supported the bill, causing Catherine Bauer, the influential author of *Modern Housing*, to observe wryly: "Seldom has such a variegated crew of would-be angels tried to sit on the same pin at the same time." The law's Title III provided for the construction of 810,000 units of public housing in the next six years, a whopping rate of 135,000 units per year, which dwarfed the earlier appropriations of the 1930s and 1940s. At the same time, however, Title I authorized huge subsidies for urban redevelopment whereby slum clearance would elevate depressed property values, boost property tax revenues, and encourage private investment in beleaguered central business districts. The law mandated that the redevelopment be "predominantly residential," in that at least 50 percent of either the buildings cleared or the new construction had to be residential—a requirement that proved elastic in future years. Seduced by the prospect of a low-income housing bonanza, reformers supported what ultimately turned out to be largely a vehicle for constructing office buildings, parking garages, swank apartment complexes, and shopping centers.[2]

A postwar preoccupation with slum clearance and downtown development, a highly successful campaign by the real estate lobby to block the selection of local slum sites for project construction, and President Truman's executive order to conserve building materials during U.S. intervention in Korea severely limited the amount of public housing completed. By December 1951, more than two years after the passage of the Taft-Ellender-Wagner Act, construction had commenced on just 84,600 public housing units (a far cry from the 135,000 units per year allocated in 1949). By the time Truman left the White House in 1953, local housing authorities had started or completed a paltry total of 156,000 units and contracted for just 53,000 more.[3]

Reformers suffered another setback in 1950 when they attempted to secure legislation for cooperative housing. Intended for the "forgotten third" of Americans whose moderate earnings fell short of the amount needed to purchase a home but exceeded the eligibility standard for public housing, cooperatives appealed to organized labor, women's groups, and such veterans' organizations as the American Legion and the Veterans of Foreign Wars. Title III of the Housing Act of 1950 created the National Mortgage Corporation for Housing Cooperatives, an independent agency empowered to grant fifty-year low-interest loans to cooperatives. President Truman supported the bill, but the powerful real estate, home-building, and banking lobbies conducted an aggressive campaign in opposition. Spokespersons for such organizations as the National Association of Real Estate Boards, National Association of Home Builders, and United States Savings and Loan League variously assailed cooperatives as communistic, socialistic, and insidiously un-American. Senator John Bricker (Republican, Ohio) successfully introduced an amendment that eliminated Title III, and the Housing Act of 1950 became law without any mention of federal aid to cooperatives.[4]

Urban renaissance, not unmet housing needs, drew Congress's attention. On January 25, 1954, President Dwight D. Eisenhower sent to Congress a special message on housing that underscored his preference for slum clearance and downtown revitalization. The Republican administration's housing proposal, which the president promptly submitted in the form of omnibus legislation, added to the redevelopment program of 1949 new urban renewal opportunities based on Federal Housing Administration (FHA) financing for housing rehabilitation in blighted areas as well as for slum clearance. The new law allowed local housing authorities to spend up to 10 percent of federal grants on projects not situated in predominantly residential areas. (Amendments to the Housing Act of 1961 later raised the amount of funds allocated for nonresidential uses to 30 percent.) The Housing Act of 1954 called for the construction of 35,000 public housing units during the next fiscal year and mandated that new construction be limited to communities with existing slum clearance and urban renewal projects. The president argued for the additional low-income housing units as a necessary concomitant to urban renewal, yet promised that "the continuation of this program will be reviewed before the end of the four-year period."[5]

The Housing Act of 1954, which the Republican administration lauded as the most significant piece of housing legislation ever enacted, coupled urban renewal with urban redevelopment programs to launch a massive assault on slums and blight in American cities during the 1950s and 1960s. Such groups as the American Institute of Planners and the U.S. Conference of Mayors endorsed the law believing that the cause of public housing would benefit accordingly, but subsequent developments showed that slum clearance did not necessarily result in the construction of more low-income dwellings. Ira Robbins, president of the National Housing Conference, noted that the eradication of blight inherently did nothing to increase the supply of low-income housing and inevitably created the problem of relocating uprooted slum dwellers. Worse, the amount of public housing planned in 1949 had still not been completed, and, even as the shortage of affordable dwellings increased each year, the government authorized the construction of fewer and fewer low-income units. Wary liberals noted that, although President Eisenhower had no history of opposition to public housing, he failed to object when the Congressional leadership of his party cut appropriations; only the actions of liberal Democrats in the Senate preserved the modest number of low-income units provided in the 1954 legislation.[6]

According to the historian Stephen Ambrose, Eisenhower intended to replace government involvement in public housing with a package of long-term loans to private homeowners. The World War II hero had come to the presidency with very little specific knowledge about low-income housing but a predisposition against it—a predisposition based on a conservative's suspicion of costly social programs and aversion to centralized government. Hamstrung at first by what he called a "skimpy majority" of Republicans in Congress, Eisenhower initially adopted a cautious approach and attempted no straightforward challenges to the existing program. In part, the president's acquiescence to the construction of at least some public housing stemmed from his recognition of the need to relocate families displaced by urban renewal. By the time of his

1956 reelection, however, Eisenhower's latent misgivings gave way to a more active opposition to public housing. Having requested 35,000 new units in each piece of legislation he submitted from 1953 to 1956, Eisenhower requested no additional units thereafter. The lame-duck president spoke of the need to block the nation's "deadly drift" toward socialism and sought what Albert Cole, the chief administrator of the Housing and Home Finance Agency (HHFA), called a "fair and feasible way to terminate the program." Because of Democratic gains in Congress, however, public housing construction continued at a substantially reduced rate through the 1950s, averaging a meager 26,750 units annually from 1957 to 1960.[7]

The Dreary Deadlock

In her landmark article "The Dreary Deadlock of Public Housing," Catherine Bauer assayed the status of public housing in 1957 and sadly concluded that "after more than two decades, [it] still drags along in a kind of limbo, continuously controversial, not dead but never more than half alive." To Bauer and other disillusioned reformers, the problem was not just that government had declined to construct the amount of low-income housing outlined in the Taft-Ellender-Wagner Act but that the projects built by local housing authorities were subject to criticism on so many levels. The design of the high-rise projects—which Bauer acidly called "watered-down modernism"—contrasted sharply with the splendid units completed in the 1930s under the auspices of the Public Works Administration (PWA). "Life in the usual public housing project is just not the way most American families want to live," Bauer observed, lamenting the decision of big city housing authorities to meet rising costs by building high-density, skyscraper apartment buildings bereft of innovative or attractive design rather than single-family homes. Mammoth high-rise projects occupying superblocks, many of which had been built to accommodate urban renewal, existed in stark isolation from surrounding neighborhoods. Segregated and readily identified as charity cases, warehoused by society in gray fortresses that loomed menacingly over the cityscape, public housing residents had vacated crumbling tenements only to be placed in sterile silos. This was not what Bauer and other housers intended in the 1930s.[8]

Echoing the complaints of frustrated reformers, public housing tenants detailed the many shortcomings of the projects built in the post–World War II era. Operating under restricted budgets, architects built spartan accommodations that had small rooms, cement floors, closets without doors, and many fewer trees than the sumptuously landscaped projects completed under the PWA's imprimatur. Residents bristled at the intrusiveness of public housing's management. Local housing authorities dictated policies on pets, visitors, and the amount and arrangement of furniture; project managers even chose the color of paint to be applied in apartments and established schedules for use of laundry facilities. With fewer dollars allocated for security, projects became less safe, and courtyards degenerated into empty wastelands. In its role as landlord, the government treated public housing tenants in a manner that smacked of paternalism. Not surprisingly, complained the residents, such an arrangement hardly allowed for the creation of cohesive residential communities.[9]

In the 1950s and 1960s, much of the negative publicity aimed at public housing centered on the new high-rise projects that appeared in the nation's metropolises. Impressed by the tower-in-the-park design propounded by the Swiss architect Le Corbusier, housing reformers and architects in the United States enthusiastically endorsed the high-rise project as an innovative solution to the dearth of open space, the prohibitive cost of land, and the rapid rise of urban construction costs after World War II. (Construction costs doubled within fourteen months during 1946–47, for example.) By building vertically rather than horizontally, municipal officials purportedly could spend tax dollars more efficiently, shelter more people in less space, accommodate the growing number of families uprooted by the new urban renewal initiative, and still provide project residents with large courtyards and other open spaces for recreation.

Enthusiasm for the bold experiment in low-income housing eventually dissipated along with the chronic mechanical breakdowns, high incidence of vandalism, and rising vacancy rates that increasingly plagued the projects. Studies also revealed that, because of the inflated value of inner-city real estate, the expense of complex construction, and the recurring maintenance charges, the high-rises cost more than low-rise projects. In perhaps the most devastating critique of high-rise public housing, Oscar Newman claimed that apartment towers invariably created unsafe environments. In his highly influential *Defensible Space*, he called for the greater opportunity for surveillance and more accessible space for public interaction afforded by low-rise buildings. In the postwar years, however, planners and policymakers ignored such jeremiads and eagerly built a vast number of high-rise projects in America's largest cities.[10]

The high-rise projects first appeared in New York City where Robert Moses reigned as chairman of the Mayor's Committee on Slum Clearance for fourteen years beginning in 1948. A devotee of the tower-in-the-park idea and the most powerful bureaucrat in the city, Moses used slum clearance on a massive scale to complete his ambitious design of expressways, parks, bridges, and other public works in and around New York City. Ruthlessly evicting slum dwellers and vanquishing opposition to his proposals, he set an example of how cities could make use of Title I redevelopment funds, which other communities promptly followed. In 1956, at the height of the public housing building boom in New York City, all seventeen projects proposed by the Mayor's Committee on Slum Clearance involved high-rise construction. During the Moses era, the city erected public housing towers in East Harlem, the South Bronx, and central Brooklyn, as well as mile after mile of high-rise projects in the Lower East Side of Manhattan, an agglomeration of drab, hulking towers that contained 148,000 apartments and over one-half-million tenants.[11]

Although the news media widely reported the existence of serious problems by the late 1950s, the federal government continued to underwrite the construction of massive high-rise projects. From 1957 through 1968, the Chicago Housing Authority (CHA) built 15,591 units of family housing, 14,895 units of which were in high-rise buildings. In 1960, the CHA authorized construction of Robert Taylor Homes on a ninety-five-acre site one-quarter mile wide and two miles long. The largest public housing project in the world at the time of its completion in 1962, it consisted of 4,415 units in twenty-eight identical sixteen-story buildings. Adjacent to Stateway Gardens, an austere high-rise project completed in 1958, which contained 1,684 units in two seventeen-story buildings, the Taylor Homes originally housed twenty-seven thousand people (of whom approximately twenty thousand were children, all were poor, and almost all were black). Dissatisfaction surfaced almost immediately. The architecture critic W. Joseph Black called the completed Taylor Homes "one of the worst tragedies that architects have created, and surely among the world's ugliest buildings." The newspaperman M. W. Newman called it a "seventy-million-dollar ghetto."[12] In a seven-part Chicago *Daily News* series, one demoralized resident of what came to be called the "Congo Hilton" complained: "We live stacked on top of one another with no elbow room. Danger is all around. There's little privacy or peace and no quiet. And the world looks on all of us as project rats, living on a reservation like untouchables."[13]

The Robert Taylor Homes-Stateway Garden complex formed a monument to social engineering in America's Second City, a clear example of how public housing could be used to bolster existing patterns of racial segregation. Separating the projects from white neighborhoods just a few blocks to the west was the Dan Ryan Expressway, a fourteen-lane demarcation between the white and black South Sides completed by Mayor Richard J. Daley in 1967. For the many motorists daily traversing the "world's busiest expressway," the overwhelmingly white crowds attending Chicago White Sox baseball games at Comiskey Park

14. Robert Taylor Homes, Chicago.

on the west banks of the Dan Ryan, and the thousands of white homeowners in nearby neighborhoods, the towering projects just across the Dan Ryan Expressway were hallmarks of segregation. Between 1955 and 1966, Chicago's city council approved fifty-one public housing sites, forty-nine of which were situated in the ghetto areas of the South, West, and Near North Sides. In the fifty-four family housing projects operated by the CHA in 1968, 91 percent of the units lay, by the city's own account, "in areas which are or soon will be substantially all Negro." For Daley and other big city mayors concerned with the political fallout from rising black populations and white flight to the suburbs, public housing provided a means of preserving racial ghettos and—as the historian Arnold Hirsch has shown for Chicago—fashioning "second ghettos."[14]

The confinement of public housing to existing black residential enclaves conformed to a custom established by the PWA of not altering the racial composition of neighborhoods where projects were built. Problems arose when local officials hinted at the construction of public housing units on vacant land in white neighborhoods rather than in the more congested ghettos. In Chicago, where CHA Executive Secretary Elizabeth Wood sought the integration of public housing in white neighborhoods, violence flared at a number of sites.

Although no large-scale outbreaks involving massive destruction of property or significant loss of life resulted, the decade following the end of World War II saw a continuation of territorial clashes in what Hirsch called "chronic urban guerrilla warfare." Precisely the same pattern unfolded in Philadelphia where Mayor Richard Dilworth articulated a policy of desegregation. Just during the first six months of 1955, according to John F. Bauman, 213 racial incidents erupted, and Mayor Dilworth's hortatory rhetoric notwithstanding, the boundaries of the North Philadelphia ghetto remained firm. In Detroit, the issue of race and public housing crested in the 1949 mayoral election when Albert Cobo, with the endorsement of white homeowners' associations, bested the liberal city councilman George Edwards, who advocated the location of public housing in outlying sites. The new mayor immediately replaced liberal members of the Detroit Housing Commission with businessmen who supported his campaign pledge to limit public housing to inner-city black neighborhoods. In fact, as Thomas J. Sugrue has shown, Cobo effectively terminated the construction of any public housing in the Motor City.[15]

The bitter struggles over the federal government's involvement in race and housing policy became an issue in the 1960 presidential campaign, and John F. Kennedy boldly promised to champion a federal law banning racial segregation in housing. Shortly before the election, Kennedy pledged that all federally financed housing would be "desegregated by the stroke of a presidential pen." On November 10, 1962, he signed Executive Order 11063, mandating the prevention of discrimination in housing provided wholly or partially with federal assistance. Kennedy's order applied only to new public housing, however, and exempted all low-cost units built or planned before November 20, 1962. Throughout the rest of the decade, the HHFA—and its successor, the Department of Housing and Urban Development (HUD)—monitored the impact of Executive Order 11063 and found compliance erratic. Local housing authorities continued to perpetuate racial segregation through their site-selection procedures.[16]

Many whites who resisted the location of low-cost units in their neighborhoods insisted on a policy of consigning public housing to racial ghettos because of what they perceived as a negative change over the years in the projects' clientele. Public housing projects had been racially segregated since the 1930s, but increasingly whites fled the projects and blacks—and in some large cities, Hispanics—made up the vast majority of residents. In the early days, working-class families with at least one employed member (usually the male head of household) predominated; by the 1960s, fatherless families, frequently collecting some form of public assistance, became the norm.

The 1969 Brooke Amendment limited the rent that local housing authorities could charge to 25 percent of a public housing tenant's net income. This new policy penalized employed tenants and paved the way for an increase in the percentage of tenant population receiving unemployment benefits and other forms of government assistance. Once scrupulously careful about admitting tenants, local housing authorities became less discriminating and relaxed screening procedures. Families less frequently used public housing as a springboard, because upward social mobility became less common among the new breed of residents. Instead, families remained indefinitely, children spent all their formative years in the projects, and intergenerational public housing families became commonplace. To many Americans, residents and onlookers alike, public housing had metamorphosed into a dumping ground for society's unfortunates and an absolute last resort for anyone who could not possibly do better elsewhere.[17]

Journalists and social critics commented at length on public housing's disastrous descent from way station to welfare center. In a landmark series of articles for the *New York Times* on post–World War II American culture, Harrison Salisbury called the tenants of New York City's Fort Green Homes "a living catastrophe . . . [generating] social ills and requiring endless outside assistance." Based on his study of a Puerto Rican family that floated in and out of New York City's public housing, the anthropologist Oscar Lewis coined the term *culture of poverty* to describe the antisocial behavior he observed there. Assistant Secretary of Labor Daniel Patrick Moynihan's controversial study of black poverty and the sociologist Gerald D. Suttles's investigation of life in Chicago's Jane Addams homes similarly ascribed many of the ills of a developing urban underclass to the culture of poverty incubated in the hellish public housing projects.[18]

Disillusionment with Urban Renewal

The corrosive effect of public housing on deteriorating inner-city neighborhoods frequently dovetailed with the upheavals engendered by urban renewal. In the program's early years, slum clearance regularly led to the construction of a substantial amount of moderately priced housing. By the late 1950s and early 1960s, however, local planners increasingly invested in flashier ventures that promised greater financial rewards often at the cost of affordable housing— especially after the Housing Acts of 1959 and 1961 provided cities with greater freedom to spend urban renewal dollars on commercial enterprises. The list of dazzling urban renewal creations included Lincoln Center for the Performing

Arts in New York City, Charles Center in Baltimore, and Gateway Center in Minneapolis, to name just a few; and such institutions of higher education as Fordham University in New York City and Saint Louis University used urban renewal largess to expand their campuses.[19]

The remarkable transformations of decaying downtowns into glittering showplaces notwithstanding, a growing legion of dissenters questioned the relative costs and benefits of urban renewal for the cities. Between 1949 and 1968, the program razed 425,000 units of housing but constructed only 125,000 units nationwide (the majority of which were luxury apartments). By the 1960s, both conservatives and liberals assailed the program as a costly failure that spent exorbitant amounts of money while exacting an especially terrible toll on the city's lower classes. Right-wing critics opposed to the extensive involvement of the federal government in local affairs decried the fact that over eight hundred communities had participated in urban renewal activities by 1964. In the polemical *The Federal Bulldozer*, the conservative Martin Anderson aimed a comprehensive critique at the federal program and argued strenuously for its cancellation. He charged that the federal government's intrusive presence in the cities disrupted the private housing market, wasted millions of taxpayers' dollars, and undermined hundreds of small businesses in neighborhoods designated for redevelopment. Moreover, he contended, urban renewal projects devoted only 62 percent of new construction dollars to housing, and over 90 percent of the replacement housing charged rents that proved unaffordable to former area residents.[20]

Members of the liberal intelligentsia grew equally displeased with urban renewal; their most trenchant criticisms were summarized in Jane Jacobs's romantic *The Death and Life of Great American Cities*. Outraged by the New York City renewal agency's designs on her own Greenwich Village neighborhood, Jacobs composed a passionate defense of the well-worn portions of cities erroneously termed slums by ravenous developers. She called for dense populations, the preservation of old buildings, and mixed economic functions—in short, the retention of the heterogeneity and diversity that made metropolises vibrant and exciting places in which to live.[21] The toll of urban renewal on the urban housing stock she calculated as follows: "Low-income projects that become worse centers of delinquency, vandalism, and general social hopelessness than the slums they were supposed to replace. Middle-income housing projects which are truly marvels of dullness and regimentation, sealed against any buoyancy or vitality of city life. Luxury housing projects that mitigate their inanity, or try to, with vapid vulgarity. . . . This is not the rebuilding of cities. This is the sacking of cities."[22]

The published attacks on urban renewal by Anderson, Jacobs, and others resonated with much of the public because of the program's disappointing outcomes in city after city. In many instances, charged activists, the federal bulldozers destroyed vital communities and thereby exacerbated housing shortages. Massive public housing projects proved no substitute for cohesive neighborhoods. In the celebrated case of Boston's West End, approximately 7,500 residents of a primarily Italian neighborhood singled out for removal vehemently objected and mounted a protracted grassroots protest. The demonstrators lost their highly publicized battle with city hall, then helplessly stood by as wrecking balls pulverized their homes and developers erected luxury apartment buildings. In subsequent years, the sociologist Herbert Gans's *The Urban Villagers* chronicled the Italian Americans' emotional attachment to their doomed neighborhood, and the clinical psychologist Marc Fried wrote extensively about the grief experienced by the uprooted West Enders. The housing expert Chester Hartman contended that nearly one-half of these "slum dwellers" lived in perfectly good housing and reported that the median monthly rents for the 73 percent of dislodged people for whom the city found new housing rose from $41 to $71.[23]

Similarly, the residents of Chicago's Near West Side mobilized to protect their homes and communities as the city sought to exercise its right of eminent domain to build a branch campus of the University of Illinois. Sympathetically portrayed in the press as embattled Davids gamely fighting against the Goliath of Mayor Richard J. Daley's powerful Democratic machine, the predominantly Italian, Greek, and Mexican residents of "the Valley" repeatedly marched on city hall while seeking restraining orders in state and federal courts. Prolonged litigation delayed the start of construction for more than one year, but a 1963 U.S. Supreme Court decision finally upheld the city's right to seize the land.

The plucky neighborhood protesters scored numerous public relations victories in the media and made their plight a local cause célèbre, but they lacked the political power necessary to thwart a powerful mayor who was solidly backed by the city's business leadership. The campus dislodged an estimated 8,000 people and 630 business establishments, while several thousand other residents left along with families and friends or departed out of fear of displacement. "All that housing they were going to put up for us?" asked Florence Scala, the leader of the resistance movement. "I think they put up forty-four units in one place and about fifty units in another. And most of it was too high-priced for the people who lived there." For Daley and growth-oriented businesspeople concerned with the revitalization of the downtown, the campus became an island of higher land values nearby, which slowed the entry of black and Latin populations into the area.[24]

The incidents in Boston and Chicago clearly illustrated the powerlessness of citizens unfortunate enough to reside in areas designated for renewal and also underscored how ethnic and racial minorities, who often possessed negligible political clout in city halls, could be especially vulnerable. Because blacks inhabited so many of the slums selected for clearance, they repeatedly found their domiciles singled out for condemnation and redevelopment. Urban renewal authorities usually invested little time and money on the relocation of uprooted slum dwellers—only one-half of 1 percent of total federal expenditures between 1949 and 1964, according to one study—so that poor blacks were frequently left to fend for themselves in a racially segregated housing market that charged prohibitively high rents. As a consequence, blacks shifted from one ghetto to another—often ending up in public housing—with the net effect being a worsening of crowded conditions. Angry civil rights leaders and their white liberal allies sardonically referred to urban renewal as "negro renewal" and "negro removal."[25]

New Varieties of Reform

By the late 1950s and early 1960s, with the proponents of the communitarian ideal lamenting the shortcomings of the federal government's public housing program, policymakers in Washington, D.C., began to embrace very different varieties of housing reform. Beginning in the Eisenhower administration, the federal government devoted less attention to the troublesome problem of family housing and more resources to shelter for older people. From 1956, when the elderly first became eligible for low-income housing, until 1960, they constituted approximately 10 to 12 percent of total admissions. The real breakthrough came with the Housing Act of 1961, which allocated fully one-half of new public housing units to older people. Catering to the potential political power of the growing number of old people in the U.S. electorate and sensitive to the attacks on family public housing, members of Congress also thought that older tenants would cause fewer problems than did low-income families. As the legal historian Lawrence Friedman concluded, the 1961 law successfully identified "the only remaining reservoir of poor people who are also white, orderly, and middle-class in behavior. Neighborhoods which will not tolerate a ten-story tower packed with Negro mothers on AFDC might tolerate a tower of sweet but impoverished old folks." The federal government devoted steadily increasing proportions of its low-income housing to the elderly, so much so that in later years it became the centerpiece of public housing.[26]

For the low-income families that had traditionally served as the federal government's clientele, Congress provided alternatives to the formula of federally underwritten projects built and operated by local housing authorities. The Housing and Urban Development Act of 1965 initiated the program of rent supplements whereby the FHA insured mortgages for nonprofit enterprises, limited-dividend corporations, or building cooperatives to provide housing for low-income families. The law also empowered HUD to provide rent supplements to bridge the gap between market rents and the amount families could afford to pay (defined as one-fourth of their income). Section 23 authorized persons of low income to lease existing units from private landlords with government subsidies provided by local housing authorities. The bill also provided for "turnkey" housing, which was originally proposed by Joseph Burstein, former general counsel of the Public Housing Administration, and first implemented at Claridge Towers in Washington, D.C. Under this program, a developer acquired land and contracted with the local housing authority to construct public housing according to its specifications. Only after completion of the project did the developer "turn the key" over to the city agency.[27]

The Housing and Urban Development Act of 1968 added other programs that sought to privatize low-income housing. Section 235 of the law, which provided federal subsidies for home purchases, and Section 236, which was designed for rental housing, employed FHA and Federal National Mortgage Administration (Fannie Mae) instruments such as the Below Market Interest Rate and accelerated depreciation to induce builders to supply decent housing for low- and moderate-income families. Unfortunately, fiscal shortcomings and scandals tarnished the record of the new assisted housing programs. HUD relaxed inspection requirements for Section 235 housing, a fatal error when local housing authorities failed to educate prospective homeowners about the importance of maintenance. HUD's laxity proved disastrous in cities like Detroit and Philadelphia where corrupt real estate agents lured home buyers into shabbily constructed or poorly renovated housing. Having invested as little as $200 in the Section 235 housing, low-income buyers simply slammed the door and walked away when problems arose. Meanwhile, Section 236's accelerated depreciation allowance seemed more a boon to wealthy tax dodgers than to the less affluent renters for whom the program was intended. The rental program saddled tenants whose annual incomes totaled only $6,000 with the repayment of loans designed for residents making $10,000 a year. Beset in the mid-1970s by negative publicity and saddled with rising subsidization costs, housing officials terminated Section 235 and kept 236 alive with an infusion of funds from other HUD coffers.[28]

In its most innovative attempt to address the inadequacy of affordable housing, Lyndon Johnson's administration advanced the idea of expanding the housing stock by constructing new towns financed by the federal government and patterned after Ebenezer Howard's garden-cities model. Instead of haphazard development with no attention to the environment, each new town would be part of a comprehensive regional plan encompassing transportation, public utilities, leisure facilities, and housing for approximately 20,000 people from varied social and economic strata. Not bedroom communities or satellite cities entirely dependent on the central city, the new towns would enjoy a solid economic foundation based on the existence of industrial and commercial as well as residential zones.[29]

During the life of the program, the federal government provided loan guarantees and direct grants for thirteen new towns and grant assistance for three others. On September 30, 1983, after fifteen years and the expenditure of $590 million in unrecoverable loan guarantees and grants, HUD officially terminated the new towns effort. With the lone exception of The Woodlands, Texas, all the new towns went into receivership and fell into the hands of private developers. Like many other Great Society programs that foundered in the less congenial environment of the Nixon era, the new towns suffered when the Republican White House suffocated the program in bureaucracy and refused to provide the financial support authorized by Congress—a precarious situation exacerbated by a stagnating national economy in the early 1970s, which undermined the real estate market and made such large-scale speculative building ventures hazardous. Simply put, the new towns perished in floods of red tape and red ink. The demise of the new towns effort constituted another setback for the housing reformers who sought to create healthy communities along with sound dwellings for all families.[30]

The Housing and Urban Development Act of 1968 prohibited the construction of high-rise public housing projects for families with children, tacit recognition that the grand experiment of the previous generation had failed. The following year, the National Commission on Urban Problems, an investigatory group appointed by President Johnson and chaired by former U.S. Senator Paul Douglas, published a report that dealt at length with the shortage of suitable low-income housing. Extremely critical of the high-rise projects and urban renewal ventures completed in the nation's large cities in the previous

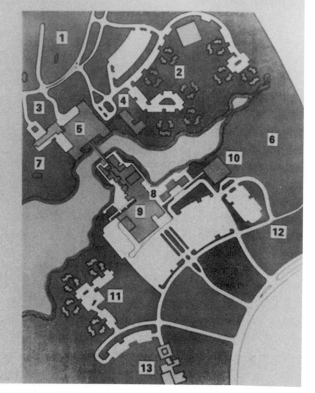

Legend:

1. Golf Course 18 Hole
2. Guest Condominiums
3. Country Club
4. Hotel Guest Rooms
5. Conference Center
6. Village Park
7. Practice Green
8. Offices
9. Village Square
10. Information Center
11. Apartments
12. Automobile Service Center
13. Community Center
   & Aquatics Center

15. The Woodlands, Texas, the most successful of the so-called new towns built by the federal government as part of Johnson's Great Society. Unlike other new towns, The Woodlands survived the Nixon years.

twenty years, the commission members called for the annual construction of an unprecedented 500,000 units of low-income housing on scattered sites. Recommending a full-blown commitment to public housing, Douglas and his cohorts urged that, if state and local agencies failed to show satisfactory progress in meeting the goal, the federal government should become the builder of last resort—in effect, a return to the practice of the 1930s in which the PWA directly built dwellings.[31]

Spurning the ambitious recommendations of the Douglas Commission, the federal government soon moved in new directions under Republican leadership. At a time that President Nixon recounted the virtues of fiscal restraint and proposed a new federalism in which state and local governments were being induced to supplant Washington in social welfare provision, any call for increased spending sounded a discordant note in the White House. As his principal housing program, George Romney, Nixon's choice as Secretary of HUD, championed the ill-fated Operation Breakthrough, a technique for the assembly-line mass production of single housing units, which gave short shrift to public housing of any stripe. To be sure, HUD continued to build considerable amounts of public housing but mostly for older people and increasingly under the auspices of the new subsidy programs. In January 1973, saying that "this high-cost no-result boondoggling by the Federal Government must end" and touting rent subsidies as the best means of disassociating government from the construction and operation of housing, President Nixon declared a moratorium on all housing activities involving federal subsidies.[32]

In 1972, the federal government made available for occupancy the last of the 810,000 public housing units authorized by the Taft-Ellender-Wagner Act twenty-three years before. By that time, even reformers acknowledged that the slow and uneven pace of construction since 1949 may have been fortuitous. Urban renaissance plans had failed to reverse metropolitan decentralization and all too often replaced dilapidated structures with housing that merely proffered a different kind of slum. Drab, institutional high rises became reservations for society's misfits, new problems rather than solutions. A developing consensus for privatization and attention to the needs of the elderly followed a repudiation of the approaches taken in the postwar generation. High-rise public housing and urban renewal had become examples to many Americans of fatally flawed public policy that had done little to rescue the nation's crumbling inner cities. Developments of the 1950s and 1960s left unrealized the communitarian vision of an earlier generation of housers, whose voices became fainter in the postwar years. Sadly, the task of housing the low-income residents of the nation's metropolises seemed no closer to completion.[33]

Notes

1. Catherine Bauer, "The Dreary Deadlock of Public Housing," *Architectural Forum*, May 1957, 140–42, 219–21.

2. *United States Statutes at Large*, 81st Congress, 1st Session, 1949, 63, part 1, 413 (first quotation); Catherine Bauer, "Redevelopment: A Misfit in the Fifties," in Coleman Woodbury, ed., *The Future of Cities and Urban Redevelopment* (Chicago: University of Chicago Press, 1953), 9 (second quotation). On the passage of the 1949 Housing Act, see Richard O. Davies, *Housing Reform During the Truman Administration* (Columbia: University of Missouri Press, 1966). Also see the extensive discussion of urban redevelopment in Mark I. Gelfand, *A Nation of Cities: The Federal Government and Urban America, 1933–1965* (New York: Oxford University Press, 1975).

3. Nathaniel S. Keith, *Politics and the Housing Crisis Since 1930* (New York: Universe Books, 1973), 101–9. On the real estate interests' campaign against public housing, see "'Grass-roots' Opposition to Public Housing Has 'Canned' Flavor," *Journal of Housing* 7 (May 1950): 158–60; and Catherine Bauer, "Three-Way War in Housing: Lenders v. Builders v. Reformers," *The Reporter* 10 (June 22, 1954): 19.

4. Kristin Szylvian, "Cooperative Home Ownership and the Housing Act of 1950" (Paper presented at the annual meeting of the Social Science History Association, October 10, 1996); Richard O. Davies, *Housing Reform During the Truman Administration*, 118–20.

5. Congressional Quarterly Service, *Housing a Nation* (Washington, D.C.: Congressional Quarterly Service, 1966), 32–33; "Message to the Congress on Housing," January 25, 1954, Dwight D. Eisenhower Papers as President, Box 6, Folder "Message to Congress on Housing, January 25, 1954," Dwight D. Eisenhower Library, Abilene, Kansas (quotation); *Public Papers of the Presidents of the United States: Dwight D. Eisenhower, 1954* (Washington, D.C.: Government Printing Office, 1960), 197. Also see Richard M. Flanagan, "The Housing Act of 1954: The Sea Change in National Urban Policy," *Urban Affairs Review* 33 (November 1997): 265–86.

6. U.S. Senate Committee on Banking and Currency, *Hearings Before the Committee on Banking and Currency*, 83d Congress, 2d Session, 1954, part 1, 836; John Sparkman, "Demand Exceeds Supply," *New Republic* 132, January 17, 1955, 13. For a discussion of the very different reasons that reformers and building interests supported urban redevelopment, see Catherine Bauer, "Redevelopment," 7–25.

7. Stephen E. Ambrose, *Eisenhower: The President* (New York: Simon and Schuster, 1984), 158; Roger Biles, "Public Housing Policy in the Eisenhower Administration" (Paper delivered at the annual meeting of the Social Science History Association, October 10, 1996) Gilbert Y. Steiner, *The State of Welfare* (Washington, D.C.: The Brookings Institution, 1971), 142 (quotation); "Requests and Authorization of Additional Units of Low-Rent Public Housing," White House Central Files, Official File 120, Box 616, Folder "1959-2," Eisenhower Library.

8. Bauer, "The Dreary Deadlock of Public Housing," 140–41, 221.

9. Gwendolyn Wright, *Building the Dream: A Social History of Housing in America* (New York: Pantheon, 1981), 233–39.

10. Roy Strickland, "Public Housing," in Kenneth T. Jackson, ed., *The Encyclopedia of New York City* (New Haven: Yale University Press, 1995), 955; Oscar Newman, *Defensible Space: Crime Prevention Through Urban Design* (New York: Macmillan, 1973).

11. Richard Plunz, *A History of Housing in New York City* (New York: Columbia University Press, 1990), 270–74; Joel Schwartz, *The New York Approach: Robert Moses, Urban Liberals, and Redevelopment of the Inner City* (Columbus: Ohio State University Press, 1993), 290–96; Robert A. Caro, *The Power Broker: Robert Moses and the Fall of New York* (New York: Vintage Books, 1974), 7–8; Strickland, "Public Housing," 955. For a defense of Moses's record, see his *Public Works: A Dangerous Trade* (New York: McGraw-Hill, 1970).

12. Roger Biles, *Richard J. Daley: Politics, Race, and the Governing of Chicago* (DeKalb: Northern Illinois University Press, 1995), 89. The best account of the project's history appears in Devereux

Bowly Jr., *The Poorhouse: Subsidized Housing in Chicago, 1895–1976* (Carbondale: Southern Illinois University Press, 1978).

13. Chicago *Daily News*, April 10, 1965.

14. Biles, *Richard J. Daley*, 89–90. See Arnold R. Hirsch, *Making the Second Ghetto: Race and Housing in Chicago, 1940–1960* (Cambridge: Cambridge University Press, 1983); and Raymond Mohl, "The Second Ghetto and the 'Infiltration Theory' in Urban Real Estate, 1940–1960," in June Manning Thomas and Marsha Ritzdorf, eds., *Urban Planning and the African American Community* (Thousand Oaks, Calif.: Sage Publications, 1996), 58–74. For a contrasting view of race and slum clearance, see Robert B. Fairbanks, *Making Better Citizens: Housing Reform and the Community Development Strategy in Cincinnati, 1890–1960* (Urbana: University of Illinois Press, 1988).

15. Elizabeth Wood, *The Beautiful Beginnings, The Failure to Learn: Fifty Years of Public Housing in America* (Washington, D.C.: National Center for Housing Management, 1982), 62; John F. Bauman, *Public Housing, Race, and Renewal: Urban Planning in Philadelphia, 1920–1974* (Philadelphia: Temple University Press, 1987), 160–61; Thomas J. Sugrue, *The Origins of the Urban Crisis: Race and Inequality in Postwar Detroit* (Princeton: Princeton University Press, 1996), 81–88; June Manning Thomas, *Redevelopment and Race: Planning a Finer City in Postwar Detroit* (Baltimore: Johns Hopkins University Press, 1997), 58–60. The best case study of how race influenced site selection is found in Martin Meyerson and Edward C. Banfield, *Politics, Planning, and the Public Interest* (New York: Free Press, 1955).

16. Carl M. Brauer, *John F. Kennedy and the Second Reconstruction* (New York: Columbia University Press, 1977), 43 (quotation), 205–10; John F. Bauman, *Public Housing, Race, and Renewal*, 171–74.

17. Jon C. Teaford, *The Twentieth-Century American City: Problem, Promise, and Reality* (Baltimore: Johns Hopkins University Press, 1986), 124; John F. Bauman, Norman P. Hummon, and Edward K. Muller, "Public Housing, Isolation, and the Urban Underclass: Philadelphia's Richard Allen Homes, 1941–1965," *Journal of Urban History* 17 (May 1991): 273–86; Eugene J. Meehan, *The Quality of Federal Policymaking: Programmed Failure in Public Housing* (Columbia: University of Missouri Press, 1979), 103. On the press presenting a distorted image of public housing, see A. Scott Henderson, "'Tarred with the Exceptional Image': Public Housing and Popular Discourse, 1950–1990," *American Studies* 36 (Spring 1995): 31–52.

18. *The New York Times*, March 26, 1958; Oscar Lewis, *La Vida: A Puerto Rican Family in the Culture of Poverty* (New York: Random House, 1966); Daniel Patrick Moynihan, *The Negro Family: A Case For National Action* (Washington, D.C.: U.S. Department of Labor, 1965); Gerald D. Suttles, *The Social Order of the Slum: Ethnicity and Territory in the Inner City* (Chicago: University of Chicago Press, 1968).

19. Jon C. Teaford, *The Rough Road to Renaissance: Urban Revitalization in America, 1940–1985* (Baltimore: Johns Hopkins University Press, 1990), 145–47; Congressional Quarterly Service, *Housing a Nation*, 40–42. Also see Marc A. Weiss, "The Origins and Legacy of Urban Renewal," in J. Paul Mitchell, ed., *Federal Housing Policy and Programs, Past and Present* (New Brunswick, N.J.: Center for Urban Policy Research, 1985), 253–76.

20. Wright, *Building the Dream*, 234; Martin Anderson, *The Federal Bulldozer: A Critical Analysis of Urban Renewal, 1949–1962* (Cambridge, Mass.: MIT Press, 1964); Keith, *Politics and the Housing Crisis Since 1930*, 153.

21. Jane Jacobs, *The Death and Life of Great American Cities* (New York: Vintage Books, 1961).

22. Ibid., 4.

23. Herbert J. Gans, *The Urban Villagers* (New York: Free Press of Glencoe, 1962); Marc Fried, "Grieving for a Lost Home: Psychological Costs of Relocation," in Leonard J. Duhl, ed., *The Environment of the Metropolis* (New York: Basic Books, 1963); Chester Hartman, "The Housing of Relocated Families," in James Q. Wilson, ed., *Urban Renewal: The Record and the Controversy* (Cambridge: MIT Press, 1966), 293–335. Also see Thomas H. O'Connor, *Building a New Boston: Politics and Urban Renewal, 1950–1970* (Boston: Northeastern University Press, 1993).

24. Biles, *Richard J. Daley*, 77 (quotation). The most complete recounting of the episode is George Rosen, *Decision-Making Chicago Style: The Genesis of a University of Illinois Campus* (Urbana: University of Illinois Press, 1980).

25. Herbert J. Gans, "The Failure of Urban Renewal," *Commentary* 39, April 1965, 30–35; Keith, *Politics and the Housing Crisis Since 1930*, 154. Also see Ronald H. Bayor, "Urban Renewal, Public Housing, and the Racial Shaping of Atlanta," *Journal of Policy History* 1, no. 4 (1989): 419–39; and idem, *Race and the Shaping of Twentieth-Century Atlanta* (Chapel Hill: University of North Carolina Press, 1996).

26. "Housing Act of 1961 Background Papers," Housing and Home Finance Agency Papers, Microfilm Roll 5, John F. Kennedy Library, Boston, Massachusetts; Housing and Home Finance Agency, *Fifteenth Annual Report, Housing and Home Finance Agency* (1961), National Archives II, College Park, Md.; Morton J. Schussheim, *Toward a New Housing Policy: The Legacy of the Sixties* (New York: Committee for Economic Development, 1969), 11; Lawrence Friedman, "Public Housing and the Poor," in Jon Pynoos, Robert Schafer, and Chester W. Hartman, eds., *Housing Urban America* (Chicago: Aldine, 1973), 454 (quotation).

27. "Rent Supplement Program," James Gaither Office Files, White House Central File, Aides Files, Box 13, Folder "Rent Supplement Program," Lyndon B. Johnson Library, Austin, Texas; U.S. Department of Housing and Urban Development, *Department of Housing and Urban Development, Second Annual Report* (1966), National Archives II; Elizabeth Brenner Drew, "The Long Trial of Public Housing," *The Reporter* 32 (June 17, 1965): 17–18.

28. R. Allen Hays, *The Federal Government and Urban Housing: Ideology and Change in Public Policy* (Albany: State University of New York Press, 1985), 87; Bowly, *The Poorhouse*, 156; Schussheim, *Toward a New Housing Policy*, 22, 55; Willem van Vliet, ed., *The Encyclopedia of Housing* (Thousand Oaks, Calif.: Sage Publications, 1998), 514–16.

29. Roger Biles, "New Towns for the Great Society: A Case Study in Politics and Planning," *Planning Perspectives* 13 (April 1998): 113–32.

30. Cedar-Riverside Project Area Committee, "Position on Solution to the New Community Development Crisis," January 9, 1976, General Records of the Department of Housing and Urban Development, New Community Development Corporation, Record Group 207, Box 11 (Briefing Books), Folder "December 10, 1976-1," National Archives II; "New Towns in Metropolitan Development," Background Paper no. 5 (1965), Joseph Califano Papers, Box 93, Folder Model Cities Legislative Background, Part One, Lyndon B. Johnson Library; Mary-Margaret Wantuck, "Those New Towns, Fifteen Years Later," *Nation's Business* 71 (October 1983): 43; *Washington Post*, January 14, 1975.

31. Paul H. Douglas et al., *Building the American City: Report of the National Commission on Urban Problems* (New York: Praeger, 1969), 192 (quotation); Paul H. Douglas, *In the Fullness of Time* (New York: Harcourt Brace Jovanovich, 1971), 405. The National Advisory Commission on Civil Disorders recommended the construction of six million units of public housing over the next five years. The National Advisory Commission on Civil Disorders, *Report of the National Advisory Commission on Civil Disorders* (New York: New York Times, 1968), 475.

32. Anthony Downs, "The Success and Failure of Federal Housing Policy," *The Public Interest* 34 (Winter 1974): 135–36; J. Paul Mitchell, "Historical Overview of Direct Federal Housing Assistance" in Mitchell, ed., *Federal Housing Policy and Programs*, 195; Anthony Jackson, *A Place Called Home: A History of Low-Cost Housing in Manhattan* (Cambridge, Mass.: MIT Press, 1976), 284 (quotation). For a summary of the Nixon position on public housing, see Draft of Task Force Report by E. C. Banfield, January 4, 1969, White House Central Files, Subject Files, Box 2, Folder "[EX] FG 221-1 Urban Affairs, 1969–70," Richard M. Nixon Presidential Materials Staff at National Archives II. On Operation Breakthrough, see the copious materials in the White House Central Files, Subject Files, HS 2, Box 5, Nixon Presidential Materials Staff.

33. Most public housing existed in small- and medium-sized cities, about 25 percent of such units in communities with populations in excess of 500,000. Henry J. Aaron, *Shelter and Subsidies: Who Benefits From Federal Housing Policies?* (Washington, D.C.: The Brookings Institution, 1972), 120–21.

8

The Other "Subsidized Housing"
Federal Aid To Suburbanization, 1940s–1960s

THOMAS W. HANCHETT

How should government help Americans achieve better housing? That question emerged as an important one in the decades around 1900 as people poured into cities to work in the new factories and offices generated by the Industrial Revolution. Initially, there was no government involvement except for rudimentary local building codes. Americans depended purely on the private market to provide housing, which produced packed tenements threatening public health. Therefore, housing reformers began pushing government to get involved. Better local laws, such as New York City's 1901 Tenement House Law requiring indoor plumbing in each apartment, made some headway, yet slums still existed.[1] Activists began campaigning for federal dollars to demolish bad housing and to erect decent, affordable multifamily dwellings for America's lower-income workers. That vision began to be realized in the 1930s and 1940s. Under the New Deal of the 1930s, Washington started providing dollars to build public housing projects, and in 1949 amid great publicity it launched slum clearance.

These efforts on behalf of poor people, however, turned out to be only a tiny portion of the new government assistance to housing. In the decades following World War II, suburbanization, not slum clearance and low-income apartments, emerged as the twentieth century's most sweeping change in the

American metropolis. Beginning in the 1930s and blossoming after World War II, Washington launched major programs that aided middle- and upper-income citizens, particularly in the suburbs.[2] It can be said with considerable truth that the vast landscape of suburban ranch houses and apartment complexes that sprawled outward from every U.S. city during the late 1940s, 1950s, and beyond was—no less than the grimmest public housing project—"federally subsidized housing."

Three types of federal actions shaped the new suburban environment. All affected the number of buildings that got built and had considerable impact on the kinds of communities that took shape. First, Washington offered direct financial incentives targeted explicitly toward suburbia, particularly Federal Housing Administration (FHA) and Veterans Administration (VA) mortgage aid. A second type of subsidy came in the form of financial initiatives that indirectly made building in the suburbs easier, ranging from expressway construction to tax breaks for homeowners and real estate developers. Third were Washington actions that affected the character and composition of suburbia, such as Supreme Court decisions on deed restrictions and civil rights. Never has there been a single unified federal housing policy for suburbia. Instead, diverse Washington efforts have interacted often unexpectedly to push suburban development in ways that changed considerably over the decades.

Direct Dollars for Suburban Housing

Federal mortgage assistance, introduced during the New Deal of the 1930s and expanded in the mid-1940s, emerged as a powerful factor in metropolitan development after World War II.[3] The practice was conceived as a way to shore up America's tottering banking industry during the Great Depression. The newly chartered FHA used federal dollars to insure mortgage loans, promising to repay the bank should the home buyer default. This meant that home loans suddenly became a very safe and desirable business for America's bankers. In 1944, Congress created a second similar program as part of the G.I. Bill aimed at rewarding America's war-weary military forces. The VA mortgage program offered such generous insurance that banks not only made more loans but also slashed the cash down payment a home-buying veteran was required to provide.

Both agencies explicitly favored loans to new construction in the suburbs, routinely refusing to underwrite mortgages in existing built-up districts.[4] "Interior locations" in the metropolis "have a tendency to exhibit a gradual decline in quality," warned the FHA's *Underwriting Manual*.[5] The historian Kenneth Jackson's examination of internal agency records showed that in Saint Louis, for instance, five times as much FHA mortgage aid went into the suburbs as into the city itself—despite the fact that more single-family homes were constructed inside the city than outside. In Washington, D.C., the ratio was seven to one. Older industrial centers particularly bore the brunt. "As late as 1966, for example," wrote Jackson, "FHA did not have a mortgage on a single home in Camden or Paterson, New Jersey, both declining industrial cities."[6]

The FHA and VA programs dramatically changed down payment and payback requirements, a revolution that extended to the finance industry in general. Previously, home loans had been short-term affairs available primarily to the relatively well-to-do. The buyer typically had to have enough cash to pay 50 percent of the home's purchase price as a down payment and then had to pay off the balance in five years. Now, thanks to FHA-VA guarantees, banks were willing to accept much lower down payments and much longer loans. The consumer needed just 10 percent down payment for an FHA loan (0 percent for some VA loans!) and for either a VA or FHA loan could take up to thirty years to repay. Those terms quickly became the standard for conventional mortgages as well. Suddenly millions more Americans could afford a home of their own. Before FHA-VA, barely 45 percent of U.S. housing units were owner-occupied. Once the federal subsidies took hold, that number advanced to close to 65 percent, where it remains today.[7]

The FHA-VA programs also revolutionized the scale at which suburban developers worked. Home loans became so desirable that lenders now actively sought projects to bankroll, the bigger the better. As soon as FHA approved a development for mortgage insurance, lenders eagerly advanced cash to the developer to get the dwellings built. Savvy developers found themselves commanding virtually unlimited capital—very little of which they actually had to supply themselves—which enabled construction on a scale virtually unknown in U.S. history. Where the typical builder of the 1920s had only one or two homes under construction at a given moment, post–World War II firms commonly erected hundreds at a clip. FHA-VA officials, thinking that mass production promoted efficiency, actively funneled federal loans away from small craft builders and instead explicitly favored gigantic "operative builders" who "assume responsibility for the product from the plotting and development of the land to the disposal of completed dwelling units."[8]

The most famous builder to use FHA-VA financing in the postwar era was William Levitt, who created three sprawling communities under the name Levittown. Levitt had begun developing mass building techniques during World

War II when he won a government contract to erect 2,350 units of defense housing at the Norfolk, Virginia, naval base. Once the war was over he purchased 4,000 acres of potato farms on Long Island just beyond the edge of New York City. Next he got FHA-VA commitments to guarantee mortgages for an initial 4,000 houses.[9] Paper in hand, he found lenders eager to supply capital. Levitt hired teams of workers to pour concrete slabs (omitting basements saved money), hammer together framing, and finish out look-alike cottages a street at a time. Sales began in 1947 amid heavy publicity, and by 1951 Levittown held over 17,000 houses, with similar projects in the works in Pennsylvania and New Jersey. "NO CASH DOWN for Veterans, $65 monthly buys your home!" trumpeted Levitt's newspaper ads. With an FHA mortgage, "civilians need only $790 down, $68 monthly!"[10] *Life* magazine reported that it was cheaper to move out to Levittown and buy a new house than to keep renting an existing apartment in the city, an astonishing testimonial to the power of the federal mortgage subsidy.[11]

The FHA-VA did much to dictate what sorts of communities the fast-spreading suburbs of the postwar era would be. Drawing on America's wealthy and exclusive neighborhoods as models, Washington's vision of the ideal society emphasized privacy and homogeneity rather than diversity.[12] Both agencies strongly favored single-family dwellings, with none of the small-scale rental housing traditionally intermingled in U.S. neighborhoods. Pamphlets counseled developers not to arrange streets in an old-fashioned grid of blocks. Instead, they recommended curving avenues and cul-de-sacs to promote "privacy of the residential area."[13] There would be no corner groceries; if there were any stores at all, they would be grouped into a single shopping center. The FHA *Underwriting Manual* emphasized that suburbs must be arranged to promote strict separation of land uses.

Most important—and quite surprising to us today—the FHA-VA ideal of homogenenous communities included blatant discrimination on the basis of gender, race, and class. For many years, FHA did not approve mortgages for female-headed households.[14] The *Underwriting Manual* required developers to guard against "invasion" by lower-income residents or minorities. Builders were explicitly advised to write restrictive covenants into all deeds, legally blocking purchase by specific groups. "If a neighborhood is to retain stability," the manual stated emphatically, "it is necessary that properties shall continue to be occupied by the same social and racial classes."[15] Between 1945 and 1959, less than 2 percent of all federally insured home loans went to African Americans.

By the start of the 1970s, eleven million Americans had purchased dwellings thanks to FHA-VA financing. Almost one-fourth of new houses in the

16. Levittown, Pennsylvania, one of three such sprawling suburban communities, all named Levittown, built by William Levitt with the help of favorable financing terms in the postwar era. The other two Levittowns are in New Jersey and on Long Island.

United States during the 1940s–1960s received FHA-VA subsidy, with the high point at 40.7 percent in 1955. The impact of the agencies' policies extended far beyond that impressive figure. A developer might sell just a few houses in a subdivision through the FHA-VA, but only if the whole subdivision met federal standards. As a result, FHA-VA ideas quickly became the accepted wisdom among American developers and ordinary home buyers as well and as such remained in force long after federal policy officially changed. Levittown, Long Island, had not a single African American among its 82,000 residents as late as 1960, more than a decade after the Supreme Court declared racially exclusive deed restrictions legally unenforceable.

Although the FHA favored mostly single-family dwellings, one high-impact program brought a new kind of rental housing to suburbia in the late 1940s: the garden-apartment complex. The idea of creating large apartment projects with abundant green space had been kicking around for a half-century, inspired by such visionaries as Ebenezer Howard and Le Corbusier.[16] The public housing projects of the 1930s incorporated this thinking, and a handful of private developers played with it in scattered cities, but the land costs involved and the sheer newness of the notion made it a rarity in most of the United States. Then in 1946, to ease tight housing as veterans returned from overseas, the FHA announced its "608" program: For builders of garden apartments, the federal government would insure mortgage loans for virtually 100 percent of estimated construction cost.[17] Developers could borrow all the cash needed to construct an apartment complex, then set rents to cover expenses and repay the loan *and* pay themselves a profit on their "investment." Lax FHA officials allowed many to do even better. Numerous builders succeeded in getting loans—at low 4 percent interest—for substantially more than the project cost and pocketed the surplus. Outraged, Congress terminated the giveaway in 1950, but not before seven thousand projects had received FHA 608 subsidies. Garden apartments for middle- and upper-income tenants now existed in the suburbs of nearly every American city.

Indirect Financial Incentives

Along with the direct actions of the FHA and VA, many other programs of the federal government had indirect impacts in suburbia. The urban renewal slum clearance programs that demolished great swaths of inner-city housing in 1949–72 (discussed in Chapter 7) pushed those residents to find new accommodations, with repercussions often echoing into the suburbs. Policies about public housing had similar ripple effects, especially starting in the 1970s as Washington began to require "scatter site" housing, no longer clustering low-income residents in the center city. Here it is appropriate to explore three other federal initiatives that worked to make suburban development more economically attractive from the mid-1940s onward. Aggressive highway and sewer construction, tax breaks for homeowners, and creation of tax shelters for commercial developers all at first blush seemed to have little to do with suburbia. Yet each had the effect of reinforcing Americans' rush to the city's rim.

When first proposed, construction of big new expressways into U.S. cities seemed a sure ticket to downtown vitality, not suburban sprawl. For the first half-century of automobile travel, cities were hell. Between towns ran handsome federal highways aided by Washington beginning in 1916, but once a traveler hit town there was only the tedious stop-and-go of choked city streets laid out in horse-and-buggy days. Planners urged that sweeping limited-access expressways be sliced through, taking interstate travelers off city streets and making it easier for everyone to get downtown to offices and shopping. During the 1930s, a few isolated urban examples of the new kind of highway appeared: New York's Henry Hudson Parkway, Chicago's Lake Shore Drive, Los Angeles's Arroyo Seco Freeway.[18] The immense costs of assembling and clearing land made further such projects seem unlikely.

Congress's long-standing emphasis on rural highway funding started to shift in 1944. Proclaiming a "new departure in federal highway legislation," that year's Federal Aid Highway Act for the first time allowed Washington dollars to be used for roadway construction inside city boundaries.[19] In separate legislation, Congress announced it would help pay for highway land-acquisition costs, a burden that states and cities had previously shouldered alone—often the largest single component in an urban project. Municipalities across the United States rushed to prepare plans for broad boulevards and expressways, and the bulldozers began biting into inner-city neighborhoods. By 1949, federal highway officials reported 25 percent of their budget going to construction in metropolitan areas, including Atlanta's six-lane North-South Expressway, Charlotte's Independence Boulevard, Dallas's Central Expressway, Houston's Gulf Freeway, Pittsburgh's Penn-Lincoln Parkway, the Eastshore Freeway in Oakland, California, and the Edsel Ford and John C. Lodge Expressways taking Detroit commuters to northern suburbs.

The rumble of machinery rose to a roar with passage of the Interstate Highway Act of 1956.[20] President Dwight Eisenhower, the popular general who had led the United States to victory in World War II, convened a committee in 1954 to study the nation's highway needs. The panel recommended construction of a massive network of National Defense Highways, multilane and limited access so that convoys of military vehicles might move quickly to meet any Cold War attack. Such a system would also be a boon to travelers and businesspeople. The vision became law in 1956, earmarking over $27 billion for 42,500 miles of expressways by the end of the 1960s, the most expensive public works project in the history of the world. Half of that amount went to the fifty-five hundred miles of freeways that cut through urban areas.

Ironically, leaders in America's cities wholeheartedly embraced expressway construction. Washington put up 50 percent of the money for each mile of highway under the 1944 Act, a figure that increased to 90 percent under the Interstate program. Building a freeway meant thousands of jobs for local laborers and construction firms at virtually no cost to the local government. Just as important, businesspeople imagined that the new roads would help funnel suburban shoppers downtown. Instead, the projects had the opposite effect. Expressways opened up cheap land beyond the urban rim for new development, allowing shoppers to stream outward, and beltways around cities facilitated suburb-to-suburb commuting. Soon shopping malls and office parks at suburban expressway exits were stealing the traditional functions of America's downtowns, and the demolition required to bulldoze highways through the urban heart disrupted neighborhoods and created ugly scars that further weakened cities' health.

Highway funding set the model for a second type of growth subsidy, federal aid to sewer construction. Much less glamorous and much less visible than the majestic sweep of the Interstate expressways, the humble underground sewer pipe nevertheless facilitated suburbanization. In 1956, Congress signed legislation offering U.S. government grants to communities for up to 55 percent of construction costs for sewerage treatment facilities This aid helped cities

17. Suburban shopping centers flourished in the postwar years thanks to cheap land outside cities and easy commuting via expressways. Northgate Shopping Center, built five miles from downtown Seattle in 1950, was the nation's first to feature a central pedestrian walkway or "mall."

improve existing systems, of course, but it also meant that suburban municipalities could more easily extend lines out into the periphery. Developers who had previously bumped up against the limits of private septic systems now could hook onto the public sewer line and happily convert more cornfields to housing tracts. The subsidy hit its zenith in the 1970s. The Water Pollution Control Act of 1972 increased federal aid to 75 percent with annual appropriations of up to $6 billion per year.[21]

Like highway and sewer construction, Washington's tax breaks for homeowners also had the indirect effect of supporting suburban expansion after World War II. Federal income tax rules have always given property owners special write-offs. The amount paid for mortgage interest and local property taxes does not count as income; thus the income tax is lower for homeowners than for renters. Until World War II, this rule had little effect on most Americans, because the federal government remained small and only the wealthiest people had to pay any income tax at all. The huge military build-up to fight the war, and later the continued expenditures for the Cold War against Communism lasting through the 1950s, '60s, and '70s, however, meant that virtually all citizens owed the Internal Revenue Service taxes each April 15th. In this situation, the deductions for owning a home began to be alluring to the majority of Americans.

By the mid-1960s, the homeownership deductions were costing the U.S. Treasury $7 billion per year—Washington's "largest and most significant aid to housing," in the words of the economist Henry J. Aaron.[22] By 1984, the subsidy totaled $53 billion annually, nearly five times greater than all direct federal expenditures for housing.[23] Poor Americans reaped no benefit from these homeownership subsidies. Middle-income taxpayers saw small individual gains. The deductions were largest for the nation's wealthiest citizens, who had the greatest income to shelter. For people in both moderate and upper tax brackets, the law offered yet another reason to quit renting in the city and instead to buy one of the new houses springing up in suburbia.

Another quirk in the tax code helped ensure that suburban homeowners would never give up their houses, even when children were grown and a small center-city apartment might seem attractive. Under a 1951 federal tax law, a person who sold his or her residence was required to pay capital gains tax on the profit—unless the money was used to buy another house of equal or greater value. Not only did this regulation push people to continue owning homes longer than they might otherwise, but it also bolstered the market for ever-more-expensive dwellings, according to careful studies by Thomas Bier.[24] Because new houses in the suburbs tended to be larger and more costly than "used" structures in the city, the law had the effect of making suburbia yet more financially alluring. Like the deductions for ownership, the capital gains policy applied to dwellings inside the city but was felt most strongly in suburbia.

In addition to promoting suburban homeownership, U.S. tax policy also subsidized new commercial construction beginning in the 1950s. The mechanism was an arcane bit of Internal Revenue Service law called "accelerated depreciation."[25] Since the income tax was instituted in 1913, businesspeople had been allowed a deduction for wear and tear on their buildings, typically one-fortieth of the building's cost each year for forty years. In theory, this deduction provided cash to replace or update the structure—but in reality a businessperson could use the tax-free dollars for any purpose. In 1954, intending to spur industrialists to update factories, Congress changed the law and enabled businesses to take most of the depreciation deduction in the first years of the structure's life. If the "loss" from depreciation exceeded the profit on the building, the owner could apply it against any other income he or she might have. Building construction, in other words, became a lucrative tax shelter.

As investors discovered the twist, money began pouring into real estate development. Though intended to spur factory modernization, the law's language referred simply to "income-producing" buildings, which included stores, offices, and rental housing, as well as industrial structures. "Profits in Losses: Real Estate Investors Turn Depreciation Tax Write-Offs into Gains" headlined an enthusiastic 1961 front-page story in *The Wall Street Journal*.[26] By the mid-1960s, the tax break was costing the U.S. Treasury more than $700 million per year. By comparison, Washington had spent virtually that same amount over *ten* years of the Urban Renewal Program aimed at revitalizing America's central cities.[27]

Accelerated depreciation rules inadvertently favored suburbia. The write-off was greater for new construction than for renovation, and new construction was usually easiest on the open lands of the urban periphery. Also, the law forbade write-offs for depreciation of land, so that developers often shied away from urban projects with high land costs. Any income-producing project could reap the tax shelter: shopping centers, motels, offices, apartments. Indeed, all such projects increased sharply beginning in the late 1950s, contributing to the trend toward self-sufficient suburbs independent of downtown.[28]

Accelerated depreciation's impact was perhaps most dramatic in housing. Since 1945, single-family homes had accounted for nearly all the nation's housing starts, with multifamily homes running just 5 to 8 percent of the total. In 1957, multifamily homes suddenly broke into double digits and hit 42 percent by the late 1960s, the highest figure since record keeping began in 1900.[29] The shift was nowhere more remarkable than in Los Angeles, America's suburban metropolis, where apartment building permits began to outnumber those for single-family construction shortly before 1960.[30] "The key to the profit in apartments is accelerated depreciation," builders' magazines advised.[31] The "upturn owes more," stated *Architectural Forum*, to the "Internal Revenue Law than to the market itself."[32] By the end of the 1960s, sprawling apartment complexes were an omnipresent feature of America's suburban landscape.

The rise of shopping and office employment at the urban rim, the proliferation of rental as well as single-family homes, and the growing possibility of suburb-to-suburb commuting along federally financed beltways together changed the very meaning of suburbia. America's suburbanization had begun in the early nineteenth century when it became possible to commute by railroad or streetcar between downtown and the new residential communities at the city's edge.[33] Suburbs were literally, as the word suggests, "sub-urbs": less than cities. They were envisioned as secluded family retreats, predominantly residential, and inhabitants expected to travel downtown daily to office jobs and major shopping. During the 1950s and 1960s, however, that traditional commuting pattern dropped substantially in importance in most American cities. Suburbia was becoming increasingly self-sufficient—no longer "sub" at all, as Robert Fishman pointed out, but instead a new kind of community. Dependent on the automobile, with land uses carefully separated into homogeneous pods, and lacking any central coming-together place where citizens of all backgrounds mingle and interact, this new "metropolitan region" or "galactic metropolis" was unlike any urban society in the previous history of the human race.[34]

Indirect Federal Actions and the Changing "Suburban Ideal"

As suburbia became predominant in American life during the postwar decades, attitudes toward it underwent considerable changes. Initially, suburban development seemed a holy grail that would heal all the nation's metropolitan ills. By the 1970s, however, many assumptions underlying this vision of community were being questioned, particularly the belief that land uses should be homogeneous, with each racial and income group set off by itself. Historians today are just beginning to probe how and why attitudes changed. They are finding that, just as Washington had played many roles in creating the suburbs, U.S. government actions had much to do with reevaluating suburbanization.

The landscape of America's postwar suburbs reflected a widely shared philosophy that valued newness and order. Since the nineteenth century, reformers had blamed the old densely jumbled city for contributing to social chaos. Architects and planners including Clarence Stein, Frank Lloyd Wright, and Le Corbusier had sketched schemes for new low-density, decentralized environments where land uses would be sorted out into orderly zones.[35] In the postwar era, those dreams could become reality on a gigantic scale. The United States emerged from World War II untouched by battle, possessing the richest economy on the face of the earth. It seemed only right that the government should channel some of that wealth into programs that would realize the brave new world. When the FHA frankly subsidized suburbs over center cities or required deed restrictions to screen out "incompatible" groups, when Interstate Highways bulldozed old low-income neighborhoods or tax policies made shopping-center construction an investor bonanza, Washington was merely acting on assumptions that were widely held in U.S. society. To a large extent, suburbia as it developed by the 1960s looked just like what Americans had dreamed two decades before.[36]

Suburbia, however, turned out to be no ideal world. In the mid-1950s, a handful of intellectuals began questioning the suburban ideal. Was the carefully ordered world creating bland and mindlessly regimented citizens? So argued works with titles like *The Organization Man*, *The Crack in the Picture Window*, and "Homogenized Children of New Suburbia."[37] A more fundamental critique came from African Americans. The racial exclusion so overt in the FHA and deeply embedded throughout the rest of the United States government became the focus of concerted activism during the 1940s. In World War II, the nation had mobilized its forces against Germany's Adolf Hitler and his ugly vision of an Aryan super-race. How could Americans countenance giving unequal opportunity to their own citizens on the basis of skin color? In 1948, the National Association for the Advancement of Colored People succeeded in convincing the U.S. Supreme Court to declare racial deed restrictions unconstitutional. This victory set the stage for the famed *Brown v Board of Education* decision of 1954.[38] The Supreme Court's ruling in that case explicitly outlawed segregation of black and white children in schools, but the Justices' statement rang much deeper: "Separate," they declared, was "inherently unequal."

This bold statement may perhaps be seen as the turning point in a much wider moral reevaluation in the United States. For generations, the nation's most thoughtful and compassionate planners and policymakers—liberals and conservatives alike—had urged Americans to achieve better cities by sorting themselves out, by becoming more "separate." But now, as citizens thought through the implications raised by Brown and the Civil Rights movement, segregation of all kinds began to seem less desirable. It seems more than a coincidence that "diversity" now began to replace "homogeneity" as the watchword of planners and others concerned with creating better urban environments. Planning writers led by Jane Jacobs and William H. Whyte now celebrated urban density and the joys of diverse land use.[39] Americans by no means abandoned all their tendencies to set groups apart in the metropolis—indeed the Court's school desegregation decisions triggered measurable white flight from areas having multiracial schools—but urban activists no longer talked about homogeneity as a supreme goal. This philosophical shift deserves more study by historians.

Four federal initiatives in the 1960s and 1970s stand as symbols of the fresh thinking. In the early 1960s, the FHA wrote new regulations that permitted mortgage insurance for "planned unit developments." Instead of building identical housing units, planned-unit developers could mix lot sizes, single- and multifamily uses, and other land uses.[40] In 1968, Congress passed the Fair Housing Act, making it unlawful to refuse to sell or rent a dwelling on the basis of race, religion, or national origin. The Justice Department filed some two hundred cases enforcing the act during its first six years, making a small step toward dismantling the barriers the federal government had helped erect beginning in the 1930s.[41] In 1976, Congress approved an income tax break to reward the historic preservation of older structures. Business buildings—stores, offices, apartments—listed in the National Register of Historic places now qualified for the same type of tax treatment that new suburban structures had enjoyed since 1954. The result was a wave of inner-city reinvestment. Retail centers blossomed in once-decaying buildings, such as the Strand Historic District in Galveston, Texas, and Brightleaf Square in Durham, North Carolina. Residential projects ranged from historic hotels rehabbed as elderly apartments (Bangor House in Bangor, Maine) to the upgrading of low-income housing (the Victorian District in Savannah, Georgia). A fourth important law came in 1977. The Community Reinvestment Act (CRA) required banks and other lenders to actively invest in all neighborhoods, not just suburban areas.[42] In places such as Pittsburgh's Northside Manchester neighborhood, community activists used CRA dollars to spark noticeable revitalization.

The momentum of suburbanization is hard to stop, however. In the 1980s and 1990s, the two most popular trends in urban development were "neotraditional neighborhoods" and "edge cities." Neotraditional (also known as "New Urban") architects and planners scorned post–World War II suburbia. They celebrated mixed land use and old-fashioned density and walkability, both in existing metropolises and in new developments such as the much-publicized model communities of Seaside and Celebration in Florida.[43] In stark contrast to this cozy pedestrian-friendly picture stood the much more numerous "suburban downtowns," which sprang up by the late 1980s outside nearly every American city. In places such as Tyson's Corner south of Washington, D.C., or the Galleria area north of Dallas, sprawling shopping centers, office buildings, and parking lots created a concrete landscape dominated by the automobile. In these edge cities, the ideals of America's post–World War II suburban developers seemed very much alive and undimmed.[44]

As America passed the year 2000 milestone, citizens continued to wrestle with the issues raised during the nation's rapid post–World War II suburbanization. Amid the ongoing debate over the proper shape of the metropolis, it is important to recognize the extent to which the landscape has been molded by Washington's actions. Federal policy can also be a powerful tool to reshape that world, if people so choose.

Notes

1. Richard Plunz, *A History of Housing in New York City: Dwelling Type and Social Change in the American Metropolis* (New York: Columbia University Press, 1990), 45–49.

2. Some useful works on suburbanization and the history of federal policy since World War II include Kenneth Jackson, *Crabgrass Frontier: The Suburbanization of the United States* (New York: Oxford University Press, 1985); Gwendolyn Wright, *Building the Dream: A Social History of Housing in America* (Cambridge, Mass.: MIT Press, 1981); Matthew Edel, Elliott Sclar, and Daniel Luria, *Shaky Palaces: Homeownership and Social Mobility in Boston's Suburbanization* (New York: Columbia University Press, 1984); J. Paul Mitchell, *Federal Housing Policy and Programs, Past and Present* (New Brunswick: Rutgers University Press, 1985); Mark Gelfand, *A Nation of Cities: The Federal Government and Urban America, 1933–1965* (New York: Oxford University Press, 1975); R. Allen Hays, *The Federal Government and Urban Housing: Ideology and Change in Public Policy*, 2d ed. (Albany: State University of New York Press, 1995); Irving Welfield, *Where We Live: A Social History of American Housing* (New York: Simon and Schuster, 1988); Peter O. Muller, "Everyday Life in Suburbia: A Review of Changing Social and Economic Forces That Shape Daily Rhythms Within the Outer City," *American Quarterly* 34 (1982): 262–77; Barry Checkoway, "Large Builders, Federal Housing Programs, and Postwar Suburbanization," in Rachel G. Bratt, Chester Hartman, and Ann Myerson, eds., *Critical Perspectives on Housing* (Philadelphia: Temple University Press, 1986), 119–36; Mason C. Doan, *American Housing Production 1880–2000: A Concise History* (Lanham, Md.: University Press of America, 1997).

3. Washington insured 90 percent of the mortgage for a house costing up to $9,000. Jackson, *Crabgrass Frontier*, 132–22, 196–97, 204; Harvey Green, *The Uncertainty of Everyday Life, 1915–1945* (New York: HarperCollins, 1992), 92–95.

4. Gelfand, *A Nation of Cities*, 123, 217–19. Michael N. Danielson, *The Politics of Exclusion* (New York: Columbia University Press, 1976), 202–4.

5. Federal Housing Administration, *Underwriting Manual: Underwriting and Valuation Procedure Under Title II of the National Housing Act* (Washington, D.C.: Federal Housing Administration, 1938), section 909.

6. Jackson, *Crabgrass Frontier*, 210, 213.

7. David Berson and Eileen Neeley, "Homeownership in the United States: Where We've Been, Where We're Going," *Business Economics* 32 (July 1997): 7–11.

8. Federal Housing Administration, *Circular 4: Operative Builders* (Washington, D.C.: U.S. Government Printing Office, 1937), 1. An informative memoir by one of the West Coast's largest opera-

tive builders is Ned Eichler, *The Merchant Builders* (Cambridge, Mass.: MIT Press, 1982), especially 38–61.

9. Checkoway, "Large Builders, Federal Housing Programs, and Postwar Suburbanization," 126.

10. *New York Daily News*, Saturday, May 9, 1953, reproduced in Alexander O. Boulton, "The Buy of the Century," *American Heritage*, July–August 1993, 62–69. On the subsequent history of Levittown, see Barbara Kelly, *Expanding the American Dream: Building and Rebuilding Levittown* (Albany: State University of New York Press, 1993)

11. Cited in Delores Hayden, *Redesigning the American Dream: The Future of Housing, Work, and Family Life* (New York: Norton, 1984), 6.

12. Jackson, *Crabgrass Frontier*, 206. Checkoway, "Large Builders, Federal Housing Programs, and Postwar Suburbanization," 127.

13. Federal Housing Administration, *Planning Neighborhoods for Small Houses*, Technical Bulletin no. 5 (Washington, D.C.: U.S. Government Printing Office, 1936); Federal Housing Administration, *Circular No. 5: Subdivision Standards for the Insurance of Mortgages on Properties Located in Undeveloped Subdivisions*, FHA Form 2059 (Washington, D.C.: U.S. Government Printing Office, 1938). On other types of FHA requirements, see, for instance, Ronald Tobey, *Technology as Freedom: The New Deal and the Electrical Modernization of the American Home* (Berkeley and Los Angeles: University of California Press, 1996).

14. Hayden, *Redesigning the American Dream*, 7.

15. Quoted in Jackson, *Crabgrass Frontier*, 208. In 1950, the FHA officially backed away from requirements for restrictive covenants, because of the Supreme Court's 1948 *Shelley v Kraemer* ruling, but FHA underwriters continued to encourage exclusion through unwritten "gentlemen's agreements." Richard O. Davies, *Housing Reform During the Truman Administration* (Columbia: University of Missouri Press, 1966), 124–25; Gelfand, *A Nation of Cities*, 220–21; Tobey, *Technology as Freedom*, 196–201; Danielson, *The Politics of Exclusion*.

16. Carl F. Horowitz, *The New Garden Apartment: Current Market Realities of an American Housing Form* (New Brunswick: Center for Urban Policy Research, Rutgers University, 1983).

17. Not all FHA 608 loans went to suburban projects, but that was where the program's largest impact registered. "FHA Impact on the Financing and Design of Apartments," *Architectural Forum*, January 1950, 97–108; Irving Welfeld, *HUD Scandals: Howling Headlines and Silent Fiascoes* (New Brunswick, N.J.: Transaction Press, 1992), 5–17; Mitchell, *Federal Housing Policy and Programs, Past and Present*, 87–88, 95; Louis Winnick, *Rental Housing: Opportunities for Private Investment* (New York: McGraw-Hill, 1958), 16–17, 156–57, 166; Gail Sansbury, "Calculating Cost and Value: The 1954 Investigation of the Federal Housing Administration" (unpublished paper for the UCLA Department of Urban Planning, September 1995); "FHA's Five-Year-Old Scandal," *House and Home* 5, May 14, 1954, special section; Joseph B. Mason, *History of Housing in the U.S., 1930–1980* (Houston: Gulf Publishing, 1982), 68.

18. Christopher Tunnard and Boris Pushkarev, *Man-Made America: Chaos or Control?* (New Haven: Yale University Press, 1963), 159–70.

19. Thomas W. Hanchett, "Roots of the 'Renaissance': Federal Incentives to Urban Planning, 1941 to 1948," in Mary Corbin Sies and Christopher Silver, eds., *Planning the Twentieth Century American City* (Baltimore: Johns Hopkins University Press, 1996), 289–91; Federal Works Agency, *Sixth Annual Report, 1945* (Washington, D.C.: Federal Works Agency, 1945), 2; idem, *Tenth Annual Report, 1949* (Washington, D.C.: Federal Works Agency, 1949), 42–69. The new policy on land acquisition became law in 1943. Henry J. Kaltenbach, "The Federal Highway Program and Its Significance to Real Estate," *Appraisal Journal* 24 (July 1956): 377–84.

20. Mark Rose, *Interstate: Express Highway Politics, 1939–1989*, rev. ed. (Knoxville: University of Tennessee Press, 1990), Tom Lewis, *Divided Highways: Building the Interstate Highways, Transforming American Life* (New York: Viking Penguin, 1997); Jackson, *Crabgrass Frontier*, 248–50.

21. A. Myrick Freeman III, "Water Pollution Policy," in Paul Portney, ed., *Public Policies for Environmental Protection* (Washington, D.C.: Resources for the Future, 1990), 97–149, especially 98–101, 134–40. Thanks to Rolf Pendall for this citation.

22. Henry J. Aaron, *Shelter and Subsidies: Who Benefits from Federal Housing Policies?* (Washington, D.C.: The Brookings Institution, 1979), 53–66; Cushing Dolbeare, "How the Income Tax System Subsidizes Housing for the Affluent," in Rachel G. Bratt, Chester Hartman, and Ann Myerson, eds., *Critical Perspectives on Housing* (Philadelphia: Temple University Press, 1986), 264–71; Christopher Howard, *The Hidden Welfare State: Tax Expenditures and Social Policy in the United States* (Princeton: Princeton University Press, 1997). For an argument that effects of the write-off were small, see Welfeld, *Where We Live*, 58–59.

23. Jackson, *Crabgrass Frontier*, 294–95.

24. Before 1951, a seller had to pay capital gains tax for any sale, which tended to encourage people to stay in their existing neighborhoods. The real estate industry proposed the 1951 revision, arguing it would promote mobility. Thomas Bier and Ivan Maric, "IRS Homeseller Provision and Urban Decline," *Journal of Urban Affairs* 16:2 (1994): 141–54. Thanks to Bier's work, Congress finally changed the law in 1997, abolishing the tax for any sale up to $250,000. Neal R. Pierce, "New Tax Law's Sleeper: Boon for Cities," *Nation's Cities Weekly* 20, August 18, 1997, 4.

25. Thomas W. Hanchett, "U.S. Tax Policy and the Shopping Center Boom of the 1950s and 1960s," *American Historical Review* 101:4 (1996): 1082–110.

26. *The Wall Street Journal*, July 17, 1961.

27. Hanchett, "U.S. Tax Policy and the Shopping Center Boom of the 1950s and 1960s," 1107.

28. John Jakle, Keith Sculle, and Jefferson Rogers, *The Motel in America* (Baltimore: Johns Hopkins University Press, 1996), 45–47, 54–56; Hanchett, "U.S. Tax Policy and the Shopping Center Boom of the 1950s and 1960s."

29. Robert Schafer, *The Suburbanization of Multi-Family Housing* (Lexington, Mass.: Lexington Books, 1974), 1, 126–27.

30. Charles E. Silberman and Todd May, "The Coming Changes in Housing," *Fortune* 60, August 1959, 89–93, 194–96; Victor Gruen, *The Heart of Our Cities: The Urban Crisis—Diagnosis and Cure* (New York: Simon and Schuster, 1964), 267.

31. "There Are Big Profits in Small Apartments and Duplexes," *House and Home* 20, July 1961, 166–67.

32. Richard A. Miller, "The Rise in Apartments," *Architectural Forum*, September 1958, 105–10; Max Neutze, *The Suburban Apartment Boom: Case Study of a Land-Use Problem* (Washington, D.C.: Resources for the Future/Johns Hopkins University Press, 1968), 31–34, 91–93, 157–63; Wallace F. Smith, *The Low-Rise Speculative Apartment* (Berkeley and Los Angeles: University of California Center for Real Estate and Urban Economics, 1964).

33. Henry Binford, *The First Suburbs: Residential Communities on Boston's Periphery, 1815–1860* (Chicago: University of Chicago Press, 1985); Robert Fishman, *Bourgeois Utopias: The Rise and Fall of Suburbia* (New York: Basic Books, 1987).

34. Fishman, *Bourgeois Utopias*; Peter O. Muller, *Contemporary Suburban America* (Englewood Cliffs, N.J.: Prentice Hall, 1981); Peirce F. Lewis, "The Galactic Metropolis," in Rutherford Platt and George Macinko, eds., *Beyond the Urban Fringe* (Minneapolis: University of Minnesota Press, 1983), 23–49.

35. Clarence Stein, *Toward New Towns for America* (Cambridge, Mass.: MIT Press, 1957). Robert Fishman, *Urban Utopias in the Twentieth Century: Ebenezer Howard, Frank Lloyd Wright, and Le Corbusier* (Cambridge, Mass.: MIT Press, 1982). Fishman, *Bourgeois Utopias*.

36. Greg Hise, *Magnetic Los Angeles: Planning the Twentieth Century Metropolis* (Baltimore: Johns Hopkins University Press, 1997).

37. William Whyte, *The Organization Man* (New York: Simon and Schuster, 1956); John Keats, *The Crack in the Picture Window* (Boston: Houghton Mifflin, 1956); Sidonie Gruenburg, "Homogenized Children of New Suburbia," *The New York Times Magazine*, September 19, 1954, 14.

38. Richard Kluger, *Simple Justice: The History of Brown v Board of Education and Black America's Struggle for Equality* (New York: Vintage Books, 1975).

39. Jane Jacobs, *The Death and Life of Great American Cities* (New York: Vintage Books, 1961); William Whyte, *City: Rediscovering the Center* (New York: Anchor/Doubleday, 1988).

40. Robert Burchell, *Planned Unit Development: New Communities American Style* (New Brunswick: Center for Urban Policy Research, Rutgers University, 1972); Federal Housing Administration, *Planned Unit Development with a Homes Association* (Washington, D.C.: U.S. Government Printing Office, 1963).

41. Kluger, *Simple Justice*, 760–61.

42. Gregory D. Squires, ed., *From Redlining to Reinvestment: Community Responses to Urban Disinvestment* (Philadelphia: Temple University Press, 1992).

43. Philip Langdon, *A Better Place to Live: Reshaping the American Suburb* (Amherst: University of Massachusetts Press, 1994); Peter Katz, *The New Urbanism: Toward an Architecture of Community* (New York: McGraw-Hill, 1994); James Howard Kunstler, *Home from Nowhere: Remaking Our Everyday World for the Twenty-first Century* (New York: Simon and Schuster, 1996); Richard Moe and Carter Wilkie, *Changing Places: Rebuilding Community in the Age of Sprawl* (New York: Henry Holt, 1997).

44. Joel Garreau, *Edge City: Life on the New Frontier* (New York: Doubleday, 1991); William Sharpe and Leonard Wallock, "Bold New City or Built-Up 'Burb? Redefining Contemporary Suburbia," *American Quarterly* 46 (1994): 1–30.

9

Why They Built Pruitt-Igoe

ALEXANDER VON HOFFMAN

The Pruitt-Igoe housing project in Saint Louis, Missouri, is arguably the most infamous public housing project ever to have been built in the United States. Its progression from architectural monument to crime-ridden slum to demolition foreshadowed the fate of the high-rise public housing projects that are currently being destroyed by housing authorities across the nation.

This mammoth development—actually two adjacent housing projects consisting of thirty-three eleven-story modernist-style slabs—was developed under the federal public housing program of the post–World War II era. Only a few years after it was completed in 1956, disrepair, vandalism, and crime plagued Pruitt-Igoe. The project's recreational galleries and skip-stop elevators, once heralded as architectural innovations, had become nuisances and danger zones. Large numbers of vacancies indicated that even poor people preferred to live in the slums rather than at Pruitt-Igoe.

In 1972, after spending over five million dollars in vain to cure the problems at Pruitt-Igoe, the Saint Louis Housing Authority demolished three of the high-rise buildings. The demolition was highly unusual both as an experiment in exploding large apartment buildings with dynamite and as an exercise in the destruction, as opposed to the creation, of public housing. Moreover, it was visually dramatic. Newspapers, national magazines, and television news broadcasts reproduced pictures of the demolition, treating it as a great event. As the images of destruction of modern high-rise buildings saturated the mass media, the Saint Louis Housing Authority and the U.S. Department of Housing and Urban Development added an exclamation point in 1973 by declaring Pruitt-Igoe unsalvageable and razing the remaining buildings.[1]

So great was the fiasco that after its destruction Pruitt-Igoe lived on as an icon of failure. Most observers agreed that the story of the housing project seemed to symbolize a crisis in the nation's public housing program. Liberals declared that Pruitt-Igoe exemplified the government's appalling treatment of poor people. Many architectural critics condemned Pruitt-Igoe for its use of high-rise apartment buildings for family residences. Oscar Newman blamed the design of Pruitt-Igoe for allowing crime to flourish and the federal government for allowing criminals to move in. Christopher Jencks claimed that the destruction of Pruitt-Igoe demonstrated the fallacies and demise of the modernist style of architecture.[2]

Yet for all the discussion of Pruitt-Igoe and the many ways it failed, little is known about why the Saint Louis Housing Authority decided to build the project as a massive complex of high-rise apartment buildings. One popular theory blames the Swiss architect Le Corbusier and his influential conception of a modernist city of high-rises. Another points to racist policies aimed at confining African American residential areas to the inner city. By restricting the location of public housing to high-cost inner-city land, the theory goes, the Saint Louis Housing Authority was forced to build tall elevator-buildings to accommodate the need for low-income housing. Perhaps the most widely accepted theory holds the federal government to account. The Public Housing Administration (PHA) in Washington, according to this reasoning, laid down restrictive cost guidelines for public housing that required the construction of a megalithic high-rise project.[3]

These theories, however, have not been specifically connected to the case of Saint Louis and Pruitt-Igoe. Le Corbusier's influence, white racist attitudes, and federal guidelines were more or less general across the United States. Yet among large U.S. cities, only New York, Chicago, Saint Louis, and Philadelphia built high-rise public housing to any significant degree before the 1960s, and only one city, Saint Louis, built the behemoth Pruitt-Igoe.[4]

This chapter reveals that a particular convergence of circumstances led to the decision to build the mammoth public housing scheme in Saint Louis. As in other cities that were losing their middle-class population to the suburbs, the civic leaders of Saint Louis desperately grasped at urban redevelopment as a way to save their city. The city elected a new mayor, Joseph M. Darst, a bricks-

18. Pruitt-Igoe housing project in Saint Louis, Missouri, designed by the architect Minoru Yamasaki. City leaders believed that such modernist projects would solve the social problems of the poor, but Pruitt-Igoe, containing 2,870 units in 33 high-rise buildings, was plagued by crime, vandalism, and disrepair within only a few years of completion in 1956. (Photo courtesy of Missouri Historical Society, Saint Louis)

and-mortar type of municipal official, who was enamored of the skyscrapers of Manhattan. Saint Louis began to rebuild its inner core, and the public housing authority hired Minoru Yamasaki, an ambitious young architect who specialized in tall modernist buildings. Redevelopment in Saint Louis took the form of a grandiose high-rise building program for public housing projects, such as Pruitt-Igoe, as well as commercial residential developments. The city leaders believed that building such shiny monumental structures would reverse suburban migration and solve the social problems of the poor. The fundamental scheme for Pruitt-Igoe reflected these unrealistic assumptions. During the development of the housing project, spiraling costs created more difficulties by forcing Yamasaki to accept higher population densities and fewer basic amenities than those in his original plan.

A Program to Save the Cities

During the middle decades of the twentieth century, observers of the urban scene became increasingly apprehensive. Since 1920, population growth in most of the nation's great cities had slowed from the previous century's breathtaking pace to a crawl, and in a few cities the population had even declined. Yet suburban towns continued to attract people. Even more disturbing, affluent urban dwellers were defecting in increasing numbers to the suburbs, and the downtown commercial districts and the posh residential areas that depended on them began to decline. Big city newspaper publishers, department-store owners, members of the chambers of commerce, and government officials became alarmed that the loss of tax revenues threatened the economic survival of America's cities.

Urban experts and leaders believed the problems of the city were essentially physical in nature. They associated "decentralization"—the movement of people and businesses from the city to the suburbs—with the spread of slums and blight from the inner-city industrial areas to the residential neighborhoods. To retain middle- and upper-class residents and to reverse the spread of blight, the defenders of the city wanted to upgrade the aging building stock, rebuild inadequate street plans, and promote new downtown development.[5]

The promoters of urban redevelopment encountered two difficulties. First, slum landowners were often reluctant to sell their properties, and second, slum lands cost more in their present profitable state than after they were redeveloped. To solve these problems, the National Association of Real Estate Boards in 1941 proposed setting up metropolitan redevelopment commissions, which would acquire blighted areas through the power of eminent domain and, using subsidies known as write-downs, sell them to private developers at below-market prices. The idea caught on, and between 1941 and 1948, legislatures in twenty-five states, including Missouri, passed urban redevelopment acts. Yet because all but two of the states refused to provide subsidies, big city mayors were forced to turn to the federal government for financial aid for redevelopment.[6] A conflict between two major lobbying groups, however, stymied the efforts to pass an urban redevelopment bill in the Congress between 1943 and 1948. On one side, a liberal coalition—including the Truman administration and social welfare, housing, and mayors' organizations—insisted that public housing was essential to a successful urban revival program. Cities needed public housing, their leaders argued, to redevelop the slums and alleviate the postwar housing shortage. On the other side, the conservative real estate and banking industry adamantly opposed the funds for public housing as a "socialistic" intrusion in the private market. Finally, Harry Truman's come-from-behind victory in the 1948 presidential election provided the liberal forces with the political momentum to pass the Housing Act of 1949.[7]

The Housing Act of 1949 finally gave big-city officials the money to carry out their long-deferred dreams of urban redevelopment. Title I authorized one billion dollars in loans to help cities acquire slums and blighted land for public or private redevelopment. It also allotted one hundred million dollars for write-down grants to cover two-thirds of the difference between the cost of slum land and its re-use value. The act stated that local governments had to pay the remaining one-third, but lightened the burden by allowing them to do so either in cash or in kind by building needed public facilities. The act's other major provision, Title III, authorized $1.5 billion to finance the construction of 810,000 units of public housing and another $308 million to help pay the difference between the cost of the projects and the rents of the low-income tenants.[8]

The Housing Act of 1949 inaugurated a wave of building projects that reshaped urban politics and planning across the United States. Although the actual appropriations for public housing fell short of the goals set forth in the law, the act made public housing an important part of the urban redevelopment program. The provisions for subsidizing slum clearance and rebuilding were even more popular with city officials who used them to replace slums with both public and private housing, stadiums, and even parking lots. In the 1960s, both public housing and urban renewal (as redevelopment later became known) were engulfed in controversy, but in the years following its passage, the Housing Act of 1949 inspired a sense of optimism about the possibilities of reviving the American city.

Saint Louis: Progress or Decay?

During the postwar era, no city in the United States was more ripe for redevelopment than Saint Louis. The town's business and political leaders felt anxious about the fate of the Gateway City. Its population had declined by six thousand people in the decade from 1930 to 1940, making it one of the four cities in the United States to have lost population.[9] The city's proportion of total metropolitan population had plummeted from 79 percent in 1900 to 51 percent in 1950. Writing for the City Plan Commission in 1947, the nationally known planner Harland Bartholomew grimly observed, "We cannot have a city without people."[10]

The obvious deterioration of the city's neighborhoods gave a more visible form to the city's economic and population decline. Bartholomew calculated that slums and blighted districts—as measured by substandard dwellings and outdoor privies—occupied 35 percent of Saint Louis. He warned that "this cancerous growth may engulf the entire city if steps are not taken to prevent it."[11] A Saint Louis department-store executive predicted that if the entire city turned into a slum, the downtown would not survive, an eventuality that would have dire implications for the city as a whole.[12]

In 1950 the Saint Louis *Post-Dispatch* ran a thirteen-week series of articles about Saint Louis's problems, which attracted national attention and stirred up local leaders. The title of the series posed stark alternatives for the city: "Progress or Decay?" The city was either going to take positive steps to save itself, or it would disappear. Following the thinking of the City Plan Commission, the *Post-Dispatch* preached that most of Saint Louis's difficulties, including the problems of unskilled and poor blacks, would be solved by destroying the slums and creating environments that would attract people of all backgrounds and wealth to the city. It was a message in which Saint Louis's leaders—including businessmen such as Augustus Busch of the Anheuser-Busch Company—believed.[13]

In its plan of 1947, the City Plan Commission laid out a strategy to revive and bring people back to Saint Louis. This strategy ignored the issue of race, the increasing numbers of low-income black residents in Saint Louis, or for that matter any social issue. Instead, reflecting the approach to planning that prevailed in the 1940s, the City Plan endorsed physical improvements such as neighborhood redevelopment, better traffic routes, more parks, and separation of land uses. The city had improved its civic center over the years and now with the federal government planned to convert a large section of the downtown riverfront into the Jefferson National Expansion Memorial park, complete

with an impressive monument. It remained for the City Plan to lay out a strategy for making the other elements of the city function effectively.

For the neighborhoods of Saint Louis, the plan envisioned a progression of
residential areas from the inner city, where population density would be highest, to the more sparsely settled outskirts. The inner-city neighborhoods would
be cleared of slums and rebuilt at the same or higher densities. To meet its ends,
the commission strongly supported legislation for clearance, redevelopment,
and public housing.

The plan designated two Saint Louis neighborhoods as "extremely obso-
lete" in the city and provided detailed site plans for their reconstruction. The
first district was DeSoto-Carr, an area of approximately 180 acres, which was
considered by many to be the worst neighborhood in the city and would eventually become the site of the Pruitt-Igoe housing projects. (The other neighborhood was Soulard.)

A Garden-City Plan for Saint Louis

At the time the Saint Louis City Plan Commission produced its report, communitarian traditions of planning and design exerted a strong influence on American city planning. The garden-city movement, begun in England at the turn of
the century, fostered the notion that designers could plan towns that combined
the culture and economic opportunity of the city with the natural landscape
and healthy life of the country. In England, the movement spawned planned
towns such as Letchworth and suburbs such as Hampstead Garden Suburb
whose designs emphasized an abundance of greenery and cozy homes with
shared open spaces.

In the United States, the garden-city movement inspired a variety of innovations. In New York City during the 1920s, reform-minded architects invented
the garden apartment building, a four- to six-story-high apartment block with
landscaped interior courts, to replace the crowded tenement buildings. About
the same time, a group of designers and intellectuals organized the Regional
Planning Association of America (RPAA), to convince Americans to develop
planned communities and to protect green spaces from sprawl and blight. Two
RPAA architects, Clarence Stein and Henry Wright, designed the Sunnyside
section of Queens, New York City, and the planned town of Radburn, New
Jersey, with "superblocks," large residential areas with interior garden spaces, to
remove unwanted automobile through traffic from the vicinity of people's
homes. Clarence Perry, a social worker, contributed the concept of the neigh-

borhood unit, centered on communal facilities such as an elementary school, shops, and a central meeting place, to community planning.[14]

At the same time, modernist styles of architecture also gained a foothold in the United States. Catherine Bauer, an RPAA member and leader of the movement to establish a public housing program in the United States during the 1930s, championed the experiments of European designers in her influential book *Modern Housing* (1934). Bauer and an increasing number of American architects admired the modernist streamlined, rectilinear apartment buildings with flat roofs and plain window frames. Bauer described site organizations for the modernist garden apartments as well, especially the *Zeilenbau* arrangement developed by Walter Gropius and his followers in Germany. The *Zeilenbau* organization consisted of parallel rows of two- to four-story apartment buildings aligned along an east-west orientation and situated in superblocks.[15]

The communitarian town planning and modernist architecture styles made their mark on the administration of Franklin D. Roosevelt. Designers incorporated community facilities, superblocks, landscaped thoroughfares, residential cul-de-sacs, and sleek flat-roofed apartment buildings into the public housing projects and planned "Greenbelt" towns built under the auspices of the New Deal. Roosevelt's Federal Housing Administration also encouraged developers to use superblocks, tree-lined streets, and residential cul-de-sacs in suburban subdivisions.

Harland Bartholomew's proposals for redeveloping Saint Louis's neighborhoods reflected his strong belief in community planning. The plan for the De-Soto neighborhood proposed the virtual clearing of the site and the creation of a large public park, DeSoto Park, that included such community facilities as an athletic field, swimming pool, community center, and two new schools. Drawing on the work of Stein and Wright at Radburn, the residences were arranged on large superblocks to discourage through traffic; commercial areas were grouped into shopping centers; and there was landscaping throughout.

The plan for DeSoto-Carr specifically called for "two- or three-story row-type apartment buildings generally except for a few multistory apartment buildings."[16] As the plan and a Hugh Ferris drawing of 1950 show, Bartholomew and the commission envisioned arrangements of garden apartment buildings with verdant pedestrian courts. The redeveloped areas would adapt the work of Wright and Stein and the *Zeilenbau* model to produce residential complexes similar to the better-designed public housing projects of the 1930s such as Carl Mackley Houses in Philadelphia and Techwood Homes in Atlanta.

Thus, in the early postwar years, support for urban redevelopment ran strong in Saint Louis, but the Bartholomew plan for the inner-city neighborhood of DeSoto-Carr called for modern low-rise garden-city communities, not the monolithic high-rise slabs of Pruitt-Igoe. The election of a new mayor in 1949 provided the catalyst that transformed the redevelopment plans for De-Soto-Carr.

The Mayor Who Would Rebuild Saint Louis

Joseph M. Darst, Saint Louis's new chief officer, typified the new breed of big city mayors who came to power in the postwar period. These mayors distanced themselves from the old-style political bosses and looked for support from downtown interests. They campaigned for the revival of their aging cities and promoted large-scale physical building programs that included highways, airports, and especially downtown and neighborhood redevelopment.[17]

Darst believed it was imperative to rebuild Saint Louis and make it once again a vital and growing urban center. In his 1949 campaign for mayor, he placed the solution of the housing crisis, particularly "the great need of rental housing for the lower-income groups," as the first item on his fifteen-point campaign platform.[18] In his inaugural address, Darst again stressed the housing issue and explained the importance of slum clearance and redevelopment. "If we can clear away the slums and blighted areas of this city, and replace them with modern, cheerful living accommodations, people will stop moving out of the city into the [suburban] county, and many will start moving back." If this were done, Darst argued, property values and real estate assessments would rise, and the increasing property tax revenues would solve the city's pressing financial problems.[19]

Darst's passion for redevelopment may have had something to do with the experience he brought to the mayor's office. With family roots in Saint Louis extending back to the 1830s, Darst ran the family real estate business (two large Saint Louis subdivisions bore the family name). During the New Deal years, Darst had served under the Democratic mayor Bernard Dickmann as the city's director of public welfare where he played the role of builder, overseeing the construction of five hospitals, the city sanitarium, and three community centers. In 1947, he was appointed director of the Federal Housing Administration for eastern Missouri, but resigned the following year to protest the failure of the Republican Congress to pass the Taft-Ellender-Wagner housing bill.[20]

Darst's principal achievements of his single term in office—heart disease forced him to retire from politics and killed him in 1953 at the age of sixty-four—were in the field of housing and redevelopment. Aided by the recent

passage of the Missouri Urban Redevelopment Corporation Act (which authorized redevelopment corporations to receive tax relief) and the Housing Act of
1949, Darst pushed for several major slum clearance projects. He lobbied the
federal PHA to allocate to Saint Louis 12,000 public housing dwelling units, of
which 5,800 were authorized. As a result of Darst's efforts, four large high-rise
public housing projects—among them Pruitt-Igoe—containing 5,466 apartments were built between 1949 and 1961. Darst initiated the $18 million Plaza
Square project, which redeveloped a flophouse district near the downtown into
high-rise apartment buildings with 1,090 units of housing for middle-income
families. He initiated the enormous Mill Creek industrial valley redevelopment,
which, when completed during the 1960s, rebuilt an entire one-hundred-block
area, and also encouraged other housing developments financed by private capital.

Public housing, Darst believed, was a key part of the strategy to revitalize
Saint Louis. The city had completed its only two projects, one for whites and
one for blacks, each with just under 650 dwelling units in low-rise buildings, in
1942, by which time the war had shut down any further development. Within
weeks of assuming office in April 1949, Darst took steps to revive plans for a
public housing project intended for white occupancy, which had lain dormant
during the war. Two days after the passage of the Housing Act of 1949, Darst
demonstrated his close contacts with the Truman administration—he was a personal friend of the president—and unveiled plans for the proposed housing
project that the housing authority planners called Missouri 1-3 (or M-3) and
after construction named John J. Cochran Gardens. The new plans for M-3
doubled the original size of the project; less than two weeks later, federal housing officials granted preliminary approval.[21]

Darst thought it was essential that the M-3 project present a fresh and
appealing image that differed from that of Saint Louis's earlier public housing
projects, both of which were composed of simple brick two- and three-story
buildings typical of many smaller public housing projects built in the late 1930s
and early 1940s. The mayor recalled that he had been director of public welfare
when Clinton-Peabody Terrace, the white-occupancy project, was built, and
that it had been "a horrible disappointment" to him.

Darst did not like these plain low-rise buildings, but instead greatly admired the public housing projects that the New York mayor William O'Dwyer
had shown him on a recent visit to New York. In showing his Saint Louis guest
around, the New York mayor no doubt pointed out the new elevator-building
projects built in Manhattan: East River Houses, a 1941 East Harlem project of
six-, ten- and eleven-story buildings that set the precedent for the many high-

rise public housing projects to come in Harlem, and Jacob Riis Houses, six-, thirteen-, and fourteen-story buildings, just completed on the Lower East Side in 1949. Surely O'Dwyer did not miss the opportunity to show off Robert Moses's pioneering urban renewal development, Stuyvesant Town, a massive but elegant enclave of thirteen-story buildings, also newly built and located near Jacob Riis Houses in the old gasworks district.[22]

Of course, New York City had more than just housing with which to impress the mayor of Saint Louis. Although New York suffered from some of the same ills as other U.S. cities, it still retained an aura of urban excitement and dynamic growth. It was still the great American metropolis with its famous landmarks, Times Square, Broadway, and the dramatic skyline of skyscraper office buildings. Even during the Depression, imposing new monuments, the Empire State Building and Rockefeller Center, had arisen in midtown Manhattan. In the postwar period the metropolis could claim to be the capital of the world. The United Nations had chosen to locate in New York, and the sleek modernist-style design of the organization's headquarters was creating a sensation.

Ironically, New York's tall buildings originally inspired high-rise modernism. In the 1920s, the Swiss-born designer Le Corbusier combined the anti-congestion rhetoric of the housing reform movement with dramatic renderings of futuristic-looking skyscrapers to create what became known as tower-in-the-park planning. His "contemporary city" consisted of monumental structures, high-speed automobile highways, and lush park lands below. He placed the inhabitants in honeycomb-like complexes, which lacked the neighborhood scale and facilities that characterized communitarian planning. In the 1930s, German architects, including Walter Gropius and Marcel Breuer, further interpreted Le Corbusier's tower-in-the-park with designs of stark high-rise slab blocks set in green open spaces.[23]

In New York City, the shift from garden-city communities to towers-in-the-park came early. After years of debate over the most economical building type for public housing, the city's public housing authority abandoned low-rise garden apartment buildings in favor of elevator buildings in the early 1940s. In 1949, *Architectural Forum* acclaimed the slab-block style designs of four public housing projects under development by the New York housing authority as a "major revolution in the housing field." In most other American cities, the effort to recreate the image of Le Corbusier's airy visions did not begin in earnest until the 1950s.[24]

Returning to Saint Louis with visions of New York skyscrapers dancing in his head, Darst immediately rebuffed the original architect for the M-3 project, who had produced plans along the "rowhouse type design of Clinton-Peabody Terrace." Instead, the Saint Louis mayor pushed the housing authority to hire a new firm, that of George F. Hellmuth. Arthur Blumeyer, chairman of the Saint Louis Housing Authority, directed Hellmuth to give special attention to the appearance of the new projects because the city's earlier public housing had been criticized as "ugly and barren."[25]

The architect whose firms would design a generation of high-rise buildings for the Saint Louis Housing Authority was well situated to obtain the position. His father was a prominent Saint Louis architect, and Hellmuth had served as architect for the city's Division of Bridges and Buildings in the 1930s at the same time that Darst had been director of public welfare. During the 1940s, he had worked for a large Detroit architecture-engineering firm on large-scale projects. Apparently assured of housing authority commissions, Hellmuth returned to Saint Louis to take over his father's firm with two colleagues from the Detroit firm, Joseph W. Leinweber and the man who designed Cochran Gardens and Pruitt-Igoe, Minoru Yamasaki.[26]

Yamasaki's professional background held him in good stead with the mayor who was committed to redeveloping Saint Louis in the image of Manhattan. An ambitious—even driven—young architect, Yamasaki had spent ten years in New York and risen through the ranks of large firms such as Shreve, Lamb, and Harmon, the architects of the Empire State Building, and Harrison and Abramovitz, Nelson Rockefeller's house architects and the designers of Rockefeller Center. (Many years later, Yamasaki would crown his career by designing the mammoth World Trade Center Towers in Manhattan.) While working in Detroit, Yamasaki met the designer Eero Saarinen—whose giant Gateway Arch design for the Saint Louis riverfront won the 1948 competition—when their two firms collaborated on the General Motors Technical Center.

In the throes of an intense infatuation with Manhattan and its modernist monuments—an infatuation that would bring high-rise buildings, including the Pruitt-Igoe public housing project, to Saint Louis—Mayor Darst and other Saint Louisans invited a group of movers and shakers connected to Nelson Rockefeller to help rebuild their city. In 1949, the high-flying New York real estate developer William Zeckendorf, head of the Webb and Knapp Company, and a Saint Louis insurance executive, Sidney Salomon, had invested in a shopping center in the Saint Louis neighborhood of Hampton Village, which they hoped to develop. Salomon then enticed Zeckendorf in his capacity as representative of Nelson Rockefeller's International Basic Economy Corporation (or IBEC) to consider Saint Louis as a site for housing development for African Americans.[27]

Declaring "If there is one thing I ought to know how to do, it is to sell real estate," Mayor Darst threw himself into the effort to persuade Zeckendorf and Rockefeller to develop the industrial Mill Creek basin east of downtown Saint Louis. The sales pitch succeeded, and in March 1950 Darst hosted a delegation from New York including Zeckendorf, George A. Dudley, the president of the IBEC Housing Corporation, and Wallace K. Harrison, principal of Harrison and Abramovitz, architects of the imposing United Nations complex in Manhattan. (Zeckendorf and Rockefeller had maneuvered the United Nations to accept the Manhattan site.) Soon, Rockefeller and IBEC pledged from six to fifteen million dollars for a 1,000- to 2,500-unit African American development in the Mill Creek area and a middle-income housing project at Hampton Village.[28]

Although eventually the redevelopment project would not fall to Zeckendorf, for a time the possibilities of the New York–Saint Louis connections seemed limitless. In late March, Hellmuth's firm, now designated as the local consultants to IBEC, scheduled a trip to confer with Harrison and Abramovitz about the Saint Louis development. As the "key man in the work" of low-income housing and a former member of the Harrison and Abramovitz firm, Yamasaki went east. In the meantime, Darst, who had visited Zeckendorf in New York, also invited the developer to build one of his current enthusiasms, a spiral-shaped (helix) apartment building designed by I. M. Pei.[29]

Saint Louis's midcentury craze for Manhattan Moderne, however, was by no means restricted to the mayor. In April 1950, a Saint Louis real estate developer boasted that his proposed $3.9 million twelve-story apartment house would be "a modern architectural type" of building that included bands of windows resembling those in "the United Nations building in New York." Later that year, a syndicate headed by the president of the Saint Louis Fire Door Company announced the construction of a fourteen-story apartment building "of modernistic contemporary design" adjacent to downtown in a neighborhood of run-down mansions, which the mayor hoped would be redeveloped into an area of high-rise buildings to house white-collar office workers.[30]

The Saint Louis *Post-Dispatch* applauded the efforts to create a New York cityscape in the heartland city. It reprinted an article by a New York investment banker urging cities to build high-rise apartment buildings ("Cities Must Grow UP, Declares New York Investor") and breathlessly reported all the activities concerning Zeckendorf and the IBEC development. The newspaper even sent a reporter to New York to interview Nelson Rockefeller about his plans for the Mill Creek development.[31]

Feelings of provincial inferiority may have helped engender this fascination with the New York style of building. Prominent businessmen supported the slum clearance and housing schemes because they would revive the downtown and make Saint Louis a first-class city. When an alderman changed the zoning to prevent Zeckendorf's development at Hampton Village, Darst charged that the amendment "makes it look like we're just a hick town trying to embarrass the people who are trying to develop our city."[32]

A Monumental Design for Public Housing in DeSoto-Carr

The impact of the mayor's enthusiasm for New York–style housing projects became clear as the new architectural firm began developing plans. On June 30, 1949, the very day that he was hired, George Hellmuth presented a scheme for the M-3 project that foreshadowed the massive uniformity of Pruitt-Igoe. Hellmuth proposed replacing the prewar plan of two- and three-story buildings with twelve thirteen-story buildings containing 1,000 dwelling units. After citizens' groups complained that the plan created too high a population density, the Saint Louis Housing Authority and the architects scaled back the project slightly to 704 units distributed among six six-story, two seven-story, and four twelve-story buildings. They justified the substitution of elevator buildings for low-rises as a way to alleviate the postwar housing shortage and to preserve open space on the site.[33]

The buildings were divided into two blocks with a recessed elevator and stairwell tower in the center. Each floor had a central corridor with apartments on each side, and each apartment had its own separate balcony—which the architects, revealing a weakness for optimistic metaphors, described as an elevated "front porch." When it was completed in 1953, John J. Cochran Gardens, as M-3 was named, won a Gold Medal from the Saint Louis Chapter of the American Institute of Architects and an Honorable Mention at the annual exhibition of the Architectural League of New York.[34]

In December 1949, the city began to shape its plans for DeSoto-Carr, the neighborhood long scheduled for redevelopment and the future location of Pruitt-Igoe. From the beginning, the Saint Louis Housing Authority intended to demolish all but a few structures on the large site and to replace all the homes of the 3,200 families (or 11,200 people) with new residences.

Initially city officials hoped to construct two-thirds of the new housing as middle-income units (developed privately) and one-third as public low-rent dwellings, a plan they said responded to the preference of the federal PHA for a mixed and therefore stable neighborhood. This scheme for transforming the

19. John J. Cochran Gardens, Saint Louis's first high-rise housing project and a forerunner of Pruitt-Igoe. Mayor Joseph Darst scuttled earlier plans for modern low-rise garden-city communities in favor of New York–style "tower-in-the-park" housing projects. (Photo courtesy of the Frances Loeb Library, Graduate School of Design, Harvard University)

social character of DeSoto-Carr, however, was soon scrapped. Although some whites lived in the northeastern section of DeSoto-Carr, the planners now slated all the new housing for the city's African American residents, who lived in the worst housing conditions.[35]

Under pressure from Darst to move the plan along, in January 1950 the Saint Louis Housing Authority revised the earlier redevelopment scheme of the City Plan Commission and proposed carving the DeSoto-Carr neighborhood into four black housing districts, two schools, and a large park in the center of the neighborhood. Three of the housing districts would hold huge public housing projects: M-4 (later Pruitt) on the west consisting of 1,000 low-rent dwellings, M-5 (later Igoe), immediately to the north, containing 680 low-rent dwellings, and M-6 (later George L. Vaughn Apartments), on the other side of the park in the southeastern section of the site, another 810 low-rent dwellings. In the northeast corner of the site, where whites were living, the planners proposed that an urban redevelopment corporation build 750 middle-income dwellings.[36]

As to the height of the housing projects, the preliminary plans called for six-story buildings at M-4 (Pruitt) and two- and three-story row houses at M-5 (Igoe) and M-6 (Vaughn). Nonetheless, architects Hellmuth and Yamasaki stated that although the largest units of three to five bedrooms would probably be built in the two-story row houses, they were considering "a new type of apartment dwelling in which the floors are served by elevators in units of three," a reference to what would become known as the skip-stop elevator building.[37]

Sure enough, by May 1950 the housing authority added an unspecified number of elevator buildings to the large-family row houses in its plan for De-Soto-Carr. Yamasaki's creative scheme called for eight-story buildings using a straight line or slab design instead of the cross-shaped layout used in recent tall public housing buildings in New York and Chicago. To obtain the slab form, Yamasaki employed the skip-stop arrangement—every third floor had an elevator stop and was connected by stairs to the floors above and below.[38]

Before Pruitt-Igoe, only a few skip-stop elevator buildings had actually been built, but modernist architects such as Oscar Neimeyer and Le Corbusier had been toying with this form since the 1930s, and the idea had begun to catch on in the late 1940s. The advantages of the scheme were that it was economical—fewer elevators and door openings and a simpler structure than the cross- or H-shaped plans—and that the slim-looking slab form conformed to the modernist aesthetic.[39]

In his plans for the M-4 and M-5 projects, Yamasaki designed window-lined corridors eleven feet deep by eighty-five feet long for the floors with elevator stops. The use of deep corridors, or galleries as they were called, was another innovation that architects had begun to use to give residents of tall buildings convenient access to elevators. Yamasaki presented the galleries as an answer to the frequent criticism that high-rises were not conducive to normal family life, especially to supervision of small children. The row of windows in the gallery would create light, open-air hallways; the gallery would function as an accessible playground for small children without recourse to the elevator; and laundry and storage rooms off the gallery would be convenient to the household apartments. "Mother can be doing laundry within sight and hearing of child playing in sun," a writer for *Architectural Forum* described the cheerful scenario of life in the new projects. "And all this is not too far away from whatever may be cooking on the apartment stove." Imagining that the design would transfer urban street life to the high-rise building, Yamasaki claimed that the gallery would create a "vertical neighborhood" for the twenty families who had access to each elevator.[40]

In addition, Yamasaki designed a large open vestibule on the first floor with bathrooms, laundries, and recreation space similar to the galleries. Outside the high-rise buildings, a park of trees and grass would wind its way through the complex like a "river" of green as Yamasaki described it. In contrast to the active program of the 1947 plan for DeSoto-Carr and despite the fact that children would live in the project, these green areas were proposed for "passive recreation."[41]

By early 1951, when the plans for the two projects were sent to Washington for PHA approval, the scale and density of the public housing projects had grown. The skip-stop elevator buildings were now eleven stories tall, three stories higher than originally planned (although two stories shorter than the first

20. Open-air gallery in a Pruitt-Igoe high-rise. Architect Yamasaki designed these galleries to create common areas conducive to normal family life. Soon, however, they became known as "gauntlets" because of the danger posed by gangs of teenagers who took them over. (Photo courtesy of the Frances Loeb Library, Graduate School of Design, Harvard University)

plan for Cochran Gardens). The M-4 project, later known as Wendell Oliver Pruitt Homes, was planned as 1,522 dwellings distributed among twenty of the eleven-story structures and forty-one sets of two-story row houses; M-5, later William L. Igoe Apartments, would contain 1,222 units in sixteen apartment buildings and seventy row houses. The number of families on the two sites had swollen from 1,680 to almost 3,000, considerably more than the 723 families that occupied the land at the time. The new scheme also changed the earlier plan in another way: M-5 would be let to whites, not blacks.

In the following years, the Saint Louis Housing Authority scaled back the number of high-rises in the Pruitt and Igoe projects and omitted the row houses. When they were finally completed in 1955 and 1956, Pruitt and Igoe contained 1,736 and 1,134 dwelling units, respectively, (or a total of 2,870) in thirty-three high-rises at a density of 55 and 44.4 dwellings per acre. Following a Supreme Court order, the Saint Louis Housing Authority designated Igoe as a racially integrated project, but unable to attract white tenants, the entire Pru-itt-Igoe project soon had only black residents.

Pruitt-Igoe and High-Rise Redevelopment in Saint Louis

In contrast to the later history of Chicago public housing, the initial strategy of tall buildings and high densities in Saint Louis was not an attempt to restrict poor blacks to inner-city neighborhoods. To be sure, racial fears and bigotry abounded in mid-century Saint Louis—white residents protested that redevel-opment projects in their vicinity would bring blacks into their neighborhoods, and the housing authority officially segregated its housing projects by race (until 1954 when the Supreme Court barred de jure segregation) and made no attempt to disperse the African American population into white areas.

Yet in their plans for DeSoto-Carr, city officials attempted to recast the social character of the neighborhood by stabilizing or decreasing the number of poor African American residents. They first tried, but dropped, a scheme that would have produced a two-thirds majority of black middle-income resi-dents. In the final plan, they designated M-5 or William L. Igoe Apartments for whites who qualified for public housing but earned more income on average than did blacks. As for the low-income African Americans who would live in Pruitt-Igoe, the planners assumed that their new homes, a vast improvement on the decrepit slum dwellings, would somehow raise them out of poverty.

Nor did the federal government force the high-rises on the city. Indeed, far from being coerced to accept elevator buildings, Mayor Darst embraced

21. Saint Louis mayor Joseph M. Darst (left), visiting the construction site of W. O. Pruitt Homes in February 1953. Darst embraced the Pruitt-Igoe project and enthusiastically endorsed designs for high-rise buildings in the city's other redevelopment projects. (Photo courtesy of the Missouri Historical Society, Saint Louis)

them. In a May 1950 speech to the nation's mayors—fittingly delivered in Manhattan at the Waldorf-Astoria—Darst boasted about Cochran Gardens and the plans for skip-stop elevators and galleries of Pruitt-Igoe. While touring the site for the Mill Creek IBEC development, Darst suggested to William Zeckendorf and I. M. Pei that they reconsider their earlier plans for poured-concrete row houses and allow Hellmuth to prepare plans for eight-story apartment buildings like those at the Cochran and DeSoto-Carr public housing projects.[42]

The monumental high-rises were not seen as warehouses for the poor, the term later applied to them by critics of the public housing program, but as a great step forward, the kind of progress that would revitalize Saint Louis. Arthur Blumeyer, the head of the Saint Louis Housing Authority, approved an entire generation of elevator-building public housing projects that were built from 1953 to 1961. The George L. Vaughn Apartments on the De Soto-Carr redevelopment site and the Joseph M. Darst Apartments (an appropriate honor for the mayor who had promoted redevelopment and high-rise public housing), completed in 1956 and 1957, were both nine-story developments; the A. M. Webbe Apartments, opened in 1961, contained one eight-story, one twelve-story, and two nine-story buildings. Throughout the 1950s, the Saint Louis Housing Authority, the Chamber of Commerce, and the Saint Louis *Post-Dispatch* proudly reproduced plans, descriptions, and photographs of Pruitt-Igoe and the other high-rise public housing projects as examples of successful redevelopment that were contributing to the rebirth of the city.[43]

The planners of the new Saint Louis envisioned not just the poor, but people from the entire spectrum of income groups living in tall New York–style structures. Thus, when in 1951 the city's leaders planned a major slum clearance and urban redevelopment project near downtown for middle-income residences, the city's architects, Hellmuth, Yamasaki, and Leinweber, produced Corbusian sketches of giant apartment buildings that dwarfed those at Pruitt-Igoe. They envisioned three thirty-story slabs that held 1,200 apartments and towered over the two churches remaining on the clearance site. Over the next ten years, the Urban Redevelopment Corporation of Saint Louis, a group of business and civic leaders who raised $2 million for equity capital from local businesses, developed the site as Plaza Square Apartments, designed by Hellmuth, Obata, and Kassabaum (the new firm Hellmuth started in 1955 after he bowed out of the partnership with Yamasaki and Leinweber). Although not as monumental as originally conceived, these six thirteen-story apartment buildings in the tower and park configuration were still two stories higher than Pruitt-Igoe.[44]

For his part, Yamasaki, the architect of Pruitt-Igoe and other redevelopment and housing schemes for Saint Louis, strongly advocated the use of elevator buildings for urban living. Admitting that they were not ideal—his family lived in an old farmhouse with a large yard—Yamasaki insisted that high-rises were a practical necessity. He argued that the imperative of ridding the city of slums (which he called "the cancers of our cities"), the high cost of inner-city land, and the need for outdoor space required high-rise buildings. In Saint Louis, Yamasaki noted, the architects "chose to use high-rise buildings because we believed, and still believe, that they best suited the needs and limitations of the situation." Yamasaki even attacked low-rise buildings for their lack of privacy and open space and, in the case of three-story walk-ups, for their use of inconvenient and unhealthy stairs.[45]

The Failures of Pruitt-Igoe

As built, of course, Pruitt-Igoe fell short of the architect's vision for the project. Yamasaki blamed the higher densities and scale on the cost limits of the federal PHA, while the Saint Louis Housing Authority pointed to price inflation that raised building costs. In fact, as Eugene Meehan has shown, this inflation was peculiar to Saint Louis, where the unit cost of public housing projects was 60 percent above the national average and 40 percent above that of public housing construction in New York City. He concluded that by vastly overstating their bids, Saint Louis building contractors were committing what he termed "highway robbery." The inflated construction-contract bids completely negated the theoretical savings achieved by elevator buildings.[46]

The Pruitt-Igoe project became caught in a squeeze between the soaring building costs and the cost limits set by the federal PHA. When the PHA did not budge in its maximum limits, the authority raised the densities, the architects reduced room sizes and removed amenities, and the contractors cut corners.

Writing in 1965, James Bailey observed the effects: "The landscaping was reduced to virtually nothing, and such 'luxuries' as paint on the concrete block walls of the galleries and stairwells, insulation on exposed steam pipes, screening over the gallery windows, and public toilets on the ground floors, were eliminated." "But the basic scheme," Bailey concluded, "was built essentially as designed by the architects."[47] And was approved, he might have added, by the mayor, the head of the Saint Louis Housing Authority, and Saint Louis business leaders who hoped to rebuild their city into a Manhattan on the Mississippi.

Although for a few years life in the giant projects was uneventful, Pruitt-Igoe soon entered a downward spiral. As Roger Montgomery has shown, the departure of whites to Saint Louis's suburbs eased the postwar housing shortage and opened up living space for low-income blacks arriving in large numbers from the South. With alternative housing available, many migrants chose not to live in the newly built public housing project. In 1957, the year after both Pruitt and Igoe were occupied, 9 percent of the units remained empty. By 1960, the vacancy rate at Pruitt-Igoe had risen to 16 percent, while the rate for the city's low-rise public housing projects was only 3 percent and for all of Saint Louis only 5 percent. Ten years later, the high-rise project's vacancy rate

reached an astronomical 65 percent, compared with 8 percent for low-rise public housing and 10 percent for the city as a whole.[48]

As the working poor bypassed Pruitt-Igoe's apartments for other accommodations, the housing authority began renting to people supported by Missouri's
welfare program—a program with the ninth lowest payment scale in the nation.
By the mid-1960s, over 60 percent of the two thousand families living in Pruitt-
Igoe were female-headed households; the same proportion was on the welfare
rolls. Rental income fell far short of the amount needed to operate the projects,
forcing the Saint Louis housing authority to divert funds to subsidize the project and cut back on maintenance. A rent strike by public housing tenants in
1967 almost forced the agency into bankruptcy.[49]

Meanwhile, some of Pruitt-Igoe's tenants were wreaking havoc. Gangs of
teenagers and young men took over the public spaces and harassed and assaulted people who passed through them. Frightened residents renamed Yamasaki's galleries "gauntlets" and tried to avoid them. Thieves broke into the
storage rooms, vandals defaced the walls and smashed windows and lights, and
children urinated in the elevators. The projects gained a reputation for criminal
activity, and after several well-publicized robberies, some messengers and deliv-
ery workers refused to enter the giant complex.

As early as 1958, the Saint Louis Housing Authority had approached the
federal government to get funds to renovate and upgrade the physical plant of
Pruitt-Igoe. Finally in 1965, the federal government initiated a multimillion-
dollar rescue effort, which included restoring some of the amenities of the original plan. The remodeling program, however, failed to solve Pruitt-Igoe's severe
problems—many of which were social and economic in nature. Two years later,
the acting director of the housing authority requested that the federal government take control of the project or give the agency permission to demolish it.[50]

In 1972, the federal government acceded to the Saint Louis Housing Authority's request, and the dynamiting of Pruitt-Igoe began. The blanket coverage of the demolition by the news media bestowed a mythic quality to the ill-
fated housing project. In the years that followed, observers blamed the public
housing program, architecture, and racial attitudes, among other factors, for its
demise.

Yet lost in the debate and analysis of the demise of Pruitt-Igoe were the
reasons for constructing it in the first place. Most observers had forgotten
Mayor Darst and Saint Louis's leaders and their grand scheme to replace slums
with attractive, modernist-style high-rise buildings—including public housing—that would lure middle- and upper-class people back to Saint Louis.

True, the redevelopment campaign had succeeded in ridding the city of

22. Demolition of Pruitt-Igoe, which began in 1972. (Photo by Richard Moore courtesy of Missouri Historical Society, Saint Louis)

many slums—between 1950 and 1959, the number of substandard dwelling units in the metropolitan area was reduced by 79,000—but it had failed in its larger purpose. It had not reversed the drastic population loss that the postwar leaders of Saint Louis had found so disturbing. Between 1950 and 1970, the population of Saint Louis fell by over 234,000 people, and the proportion of the city's residents to those in the Saint Louis metropolitan area plummeted from 51 to 26 percent. Despite all the efforts at rejuvenating the city, the middle class did not return to Saint Louis, and the city's population continued to hemorrhage.

This was perhaps the greatest failure of the visionary postwar planners of the Gateway City. To transform Saint Louis into a gleaming, growing, modern metropolis was, after all, why they built Pruitt-Igoe.

Notes

1. Some examples of the press coverage of the failure of Pruitt-Igoe are "The Tragedy of Pruitt-Igoe," *Time*, December 27, 1971, 38; Jerome Curry, "Collapse of a Failure," *The National Observer*, May 20, 1972, 24; "Demolition Marks Ultimate Failure of Pruitt-Igoe Project," *Washington Post*, August 27, 1973; "Instant Demolition in a St. Louis Slum," *Life*, May 5, 1972, 6–7; Wilbur Thompson, "Problems That Sprout in the Shadow of No Growth," *AIA Journal* 60 (December 1973): 32; "St. Louis Blues," *Architectural Forum*, May 1972, 18; "The Experiment That Failed," *Architecture Plus* (October 1973).

2. Lee Rainwater, *Behind Ghetto Walls* (Chicago: Aldine, 1970), and "Fear and the House-as-Haven in the Lower Class," *Journal of the American Institute of Planners* 32 (January 1966); Oscar Newman, *Defensible Space* (New York: Macmillan, 1972); Charles Jencks, *The Language of Post-Modern Architecture* (New York: Rizzoli, 1977).

3. The literature on the fiasco of Pruitt-Igoe includes James Bailey, "History of a Failure," *Architectural Forum*, December 1965, 22–25; George McCue, "$57,000,000 Later," *Architectural Forum*, May 1973, 42–45; Roger Montgomery, "Pruitt-Igoe: Policy Failure or Societal Symptom," in Barry Checkoway and Carl V. Patton, eds., *The Metropolitan Midwest, Policy Problems and Prospects for Change* (Urbana and Chicago: University of Illinois Press, 1985), 229–43; Eugene J. Meehan, *Public Housing Policy—Convention Versus Reality* (New Brunswick: Center for Urban Policy Research, 1975); and idem, *The Quality of Federal Policymaking: Programmed Failure in Public Housing* (Columbia: University of Missouri Press, 1979); Katharine G. Bristol, "The Pruitt-Igoe Myth," *Journal of Architecture Education* 94 (May 1991): 163–71; and idem, "Beyond The Pruitt-Igoe Myth: The Development of American High-Rise Public Housing, 1850–1970" (Ph.D. dissertation, University of California at Berkeley, 1991); Mary C. Comerio, "Pruitt-Igoe and Other Stories," *Journal of Architectural Education* 34 (Summer 1981): 25–31.

4. Although Saint Louis built the original giant high-rise public housing structure, Chicago heedlessly followed. In 1963, the Chicago Housing Authority created the monstrous Robert Taylor Homes whose 4,230 dwelling units surpassed Pruitt-Igoe's 2,870 units.

5. Jon Teaford, *The Rough Road to Renaissance—Urban Revitalization in America, 1940–1985* (Baltimore: Johns Hopkins University Press, 1990), 10–43; Robert A. Beauregard, *Voices of Decline: The Postwar Fate of US Cities* (Cambridge, Mass.: Blackwell, 1993), 79–157.

6. Mark I. Gelfand, *A Nation of Cities: The Federal Government and Urban America, 1933–1965* (New York: Oxford University Press, 1975), 116–17, 137.

7. Gelfand, *A Nation of Cities*, 105–56; Richard Davies, *Housing Reform During the Truman Administration* (Columbia: University of Missouri Press, 1966).

8. For a summary of the act's provisions, see "Housing Act of 1949," *Architectural Forum*, August 1949, 83–85.

9. The others were Philadelphia, Boston, and Cleveland.

10. (Saint Louis) City Plan Commission, *Comprehensive City Plan, Saint Louis, Missouri* (Saint Louis, 1947), 5.

11. Ibid., 27–28, plate 13.

12. "Slum Surgery in St. Louis," *Architectural Forum*, April 1951, 135–36.

13. "Progress or Decay—Supplement," Saint Louis *Post-Dispatch*, March–May 1950; Teaford, *The Rough Road to Renaissance*, 54, 70; "Slum Surgery in St. Louis," 135–36.

14. Secondary sources on the garden-city movement and twentieth-century planning include Stanley Buder, *Visionaries and Planners: The Garden City Movement and the Modern Community* (New York: Oxford University Press, 1990); Howard Gillette Jr., "The Evolution of Neighborhood Planning: From the Progressive Era to the 1949 Housing Act," *Journal of Urban History* 9 (August 1983): 421–44; Peter Hall, *Cities of Tomorrow: An Intellectual History of Urban Planning and Design in the Twentieth Century* (Oxford: Basil Blackwell, 1988); Daniel Schaffer, *Garden Cities for America: The Radburn Experience* (Philadelphia: Temple University Press, 1982).

15. Catherine Bauer, *Modern Housing* (Boston: Houghton-Mifflin, 1934), 178–82.

16. (Saint Louis) City Plan Commission, *Comprehensive City Plan, Saint Louis, Missouri*, 30.

17. Teaford, *The Rough Road to Renaissance*, 54–66.

18. "Housing Action Democrats' First Platform Point," Saint Louis *Post-Dispatch*, March 19, 1949.

19. "Aldermanic Row Delays Inauguration; Darst Calls Slums City's Big Problem," Saint Louis *Post-Dispatch*, April 19, 1949.

20. "Joseph M. Darst Dies After Long Illness; Former St. Louis Mayor," Saint Louis *Post-Dispatch*, June 8, 1953; "Slum Surgery in St. Louis," 129.

21. Saint Louis *Post-Dispatch*, May 24, 1949, 3A; July 24, 1949, 3A.

22. Saint Louis *Post-Dispatch*, May 24, 1949.

23. Le Corbusier. *The City of Tomorrow and Its Planning* (from *Urbanisme*, 8th ed., trans. Frederick Etchells) (Cambridge, Mass.: MIT Press, 1971; first ed., London: John Roher, 1929; repr. ed., Architectural Press, 1947), and *The Radiant City* (London: Faber and Faber, 1933; repr. ed., 1967); Richard Plunz, *A History of Housing in New York City: Dwelling Type and Social Change in the American Metropolis* (New York: Columbia University Press, 1990), 184–89.

24. Plunz, *A History of Housing in New York City*, 210–27, 240–46; 264; "Public Housing, Anticipating New Law, Looks at New York's High Density Planning Innovations," *Architectural Forum*, June 1949, 87–90.

25. Saint Louis *Post-Dispatch*, May 24, 1949, July 1, 1949, 3A.

26. McCune Gill, *Library of American Lives, The St. Louis Story* (Saint Louis: Historical Record Association, 1952), 1034–36.

27. For his own account of Zeckendorf's experiences in Saint Louis, see *Zeckendorf: The Autobiography of William Zeckendorf* (New York: Holt, Rinehart and Winston, 1970), 231, 234–35.

28. Saint Louis *Post-Dispatch*, March 25, March 26, 1950.

29. Ibid., February 4, March 27, 1950.

30. Ibid., April 3, September 17, 1950.

31. Ibid., April 3, April 9, December 17, 1950.

32. Ibid., March 25, 1950, 1A.

33. Ibid., July 1, 1949; January 22, 1950; Harry Wilensky, "The Fight Against Decay," Special Progress Section, Saint Louis *Post-Dispatch*, September 9, 1956.

34. "Multi-Family Housing, Building Types Study Number 211," *Architectural Record* 115, June 1954, 185–87.

35. Saint Louis *Post-Dispatch*, December 25, 1949.

36. Ibid., January 22, May 12, 1950.

37. Ibid., January 18 (quotation), January 22, 1950.

38. Ibid., May 12, 1950. For examples of laudatory descriptions of Yamasaki's designs for public housing elevator buildings in architectural magazines, see "Slum Surgery in St. Louis," 128–35; "Four Vast Housing Projects for St. Louis," *Architectural Record* 120, August 1956, 180–89.

39. Yamasaki appears to have been the first architect to combine skip-stop elevators, deep corridors, and slab form in public housing. About 1950, architects of the Chicago Housing Authority were considering skip-stop elevators, but the authority rejected the idea. Julian Whittlesey, "The Skip-Floor Corridor Building Type Serves a Five-Fold Purpose," *Architectural Record* 112, February 1949, 124–28; idem, "New Dimensions in Housing Design," *Progressive Architecture* 32 (April 1951): 57–67.

40. "Slum Surgery in St. Louis," 128–35.

41. Ibid., 135.

42. Saint Louis *Post-Dispatch*, May 12, June 15, 1950.

43. See, for example, *Saint Louis Commerce* 28 (November 1954): 32–33.

44. "Slum Surgery in St. Louis"; Harry Wilensky, "Special Progress Section: The Fight Against Decay," Saint Louis *Post-Dispatch*, May 7, 1961, 1–3.

45. Yamasaki, Minoru, "High Buildings for Public Housing? A Necessity," *Journal of Housing* 9 (July 1952): 226, 229–32.

46. Meehan, *Public Housing Policy*, 36, 62–66.

47. Bailey, "History of a Failure," 22.

48. Montgomery, "Pruitt-Igoe: Policy Failure or Societal Symptom," 236–37.

49. D. J. R. Bruckner, "Public Housing Tenants in St. Louis to Strike," *Los Angeles Times*, February 2, 1967, 22; "Pruitt-Igoe Putting St. Louis in Deficit," *Journal of Housing* 68 (July 1968): 306–7.

50. Fred W. Lindecke, "PHA Approves $7 Million Plan to Mend Flaws at Pruitt-Igoe," Saint Louis *Post-Dispatch*, October 3, 1965; Montgomery, "Pruitt-Igoe Policy Failure or Societal Symptom," 231–32, 239.

10

Choosing Segregation
Federal Housing Policy Between *Shelley* and *Brown*

ARNOLD R. HIRSCH

The smoke and haze that enveloped the United States' riot-torn cities in the mid-1960s shrouded more than the smoldering remains that gave testimony to the racial, economic, and political failures of the postwar city. They also clouded judgment. So traumatizing was the ugliness of those years that social analysts and policymakers have since displayed an unwarranted tendency to interpret the contemporary urban plight primarily in the harsh light of the flames of that violent season. If not attributed solely to the riots themselves, the subsequent lurch to the right in our national politics, for example, has been blamed on a host of associated considerations: the rise of black nationalism, the baleful results of the War on Poverty, and the alleged excesses of 1960s-style liberalism in general. An almost inevitable corollary pointed a finger at the unintended consequences of social engineering and, with specific regard to programs such as public housing, the betrayal of good intentions. Softhearted, softheaded reformers meant well, conservatives in the post-riot era concluded, but the "real world" had a way of exposing their flawed assumptions and rendering

The author wishes to acknowledge the generous support of Chester Hartman and the Poverty and Race Research Action Council as well as the research assistance of Samuel Collins and Lynette Rawlings.

their efforts futile; they invariably made things worse by trying to make them better.[1]

Recent research, however, has undermined such conventional thinking. It is now clear that bitter white resistance to African American mobility appeared decades before the urban uprisings and Great Society programs supposedly provoked a well-justified "backlash." Whites not only protested black advances in the 1940s and 1950s, but—especially with regard to housing issues—resorted to violence as well.[2]

Less controversial, and hence less contested, has been the notion that in the 1960s something did, indeed, go wrong with the prevailing liberal paradigm. Even Kenneth T. Jackson's now-classic treatment of urban decentralization in the United States, *Crabgrass Frontier* (1985), concluded that the ghettoization of public housing reflected the "cost of good intentions" rather than design.[3] The discovery of early, and massive, white resistance to the deconcentration of urban African Americans, however, compels reassessment; and we would do well to distinguish the well known advocates who conceived of publicly assisted housing as social reform from the faceless bureaucrats who actually implemented the programs. Such a focused second look reveals that racial exclusion was neither an unforeseen by-product of grim economic realities nor the perversion of an otherwise "good" program. Moreover, the conscious construction of racially homogeneous communities following World War II resulted not only from the public housing program, but—even more important—from the influence of the Federal Housing Administration (FHA) in the private sector. Finally, civil rights forces, although thrown on the defensive early on, contested such segregated developments from both inside and outside the government's own offices. Dissenters in the bureaucracy especially raised explicit questions about the impact of new federal programs on the changing racial composition of urban neighborhoods. Their challenge—and its suppression—meant that a conscious, deliberate choice for segregation lay at the heart of national policy.

Between 1948 and 1954, a brief window of opportunity seemingly opened for those seeking to end government complicity in ghetto building. Framed by the Supreme Court's decisions in *Shelley v Kraemer* and *Brown v Board of Education, Topeka, Kansas*, the era promised great change. The former opinion, which rendered racially restrictive covenants unenforceable, represented a crest in the campaign waged against residential segregation by the National Association for the Advancement of Colored People (NAACP) and a host of allies. Hailed as a great victory, the voiding of restrictive covenants had particular relevance for the operations of the FHA, an agency that had earlier prescribed their use as a virtual precondition for federally insured mortgages. Similarly, although the *Brown* decision targeted schools, it challenged the sustainability of segregation in all public institutions and programs such as public housing. Alongside these judicial landmarks, new legislation—particularly the federal Housing Acts of 1949 and 1954—provided potential vehicles for resolving questions about the government's proper role in handling racial matters while rebuilding the nation's cities and fueling metropolitan growth. In the end, the hope to enlist government support for a policy of nondiscrimination proved illusory. The implementation of slum clearance and urban renewal, as authorized by the new laws, racially segmented the metropolitan United States in unparalleled fashion. More reflexive than anything else, the decision to reinforce traditional private practices with government sanction for racial segregation had nonetheless been made with a clear understanding of its consequences.

Democratizing Homeownership, Discriminating Policy

Confusion, or, at the very least, ambiguity, characterized the housing policy that emerged from the New Deal. In the private sector, President Franklin Delano Roosevelt modernized the concept of Jeffersonian democracy by broadening it to include homeowners in an industrial society as well as the idealized yeoman farmer. Building on the Lockean notion of propertied citizenship, Roosevelt's New Deal sought stability and security in a time of turmoil by making it easier to purchase—and keep—a house. The operations of the Home Owners Loan Corporation (HOLC), the FHA, and, later, the Veterans Administration (VA) proved wildly successful in democratizing homeownership in the United States, bringing it within the reach of millions who could only dream of it before. By 1950, the FHA and VA alone insured half of all new mortgages even as they, and other government agencies, standardized and rationalized real estate and financial practices for the market as a whole. Lengthened amortization periods, mortgage insurance, reduced monthly payments, lowered interest rates, and substantial tax benefits all brought homeownership within the grasp of the middle class for the first time. Ultimately, homeownership became more than an expectation for vast new segments of American society; it became an entitlement as well.[4]

The extension of homeownership, however, took place in a highly racialized context. As Kenneth Jackson's meticulous research has revealed, HOLC's appraisal system spawned the discriminatory practice of redlining, and the FHA's adherence to good "business" practice virtually excluded nonwhites from the enjoyment of the agency's benefits. Explicit racial references in the FHA's *Underwriting Manual* made it clear that the communities built and protected by the government were to be racially homogeneous (and almost always white), and through 1948 the agency promoted and insisted on the application of racially restrictive covenants to properties that sought government assistance. Given the government's concern with stimulating homeownership among those who could not earlier afford it, FHA's racial policies meant that whites who previously lacked the means to remove themselves to racially homogeneous communities could now do so with public support. As Gunnar Myrdal concluded in *An American Dilemma* (1944), New Deal programs extended racial " 'protection' to areas and groups of white people who were earlier without it." The result was that the emergent sense of entitlement that appeared after World War II embraced not merely the fact of property ownership, but a broader conception of homeowners' rights that included the assumption of a racially exclusive neighborhood.[5]

Similarly, the federal government's actions with regard to public housing exhibited both democratizing and restrictive tendencies. On the one hand, Secretary of the Interior Harold Ickes's Public Works Administration (PWA) initially showed a deep concern for "equity" in racial affairs. This concern manifested itself in two ways. First, Ickes placed a nondiscrimination clause in every PWA contract and guaranteed significant black employment on PWA projects through a labor quota system that placed the burden of proof on employers rather than on the government. After the creation of the United States Housing Authority (USHA) in 1937, Ickes's assistant, the African American economist Robert C. Weaver, instituted a similar program from his perch as race relations adviser in that agency. Second, Ickes also made certain that blacks enjoyed the benefits of the nation's low-income housing program. By 1940, more than one-third of such units were occupied by blacks, and the funding levels for the construction of all-black projects matched those of the others.[6] The administration simply concluded that low-cost housing "should be provided for Negroes according to their local population and needs."[7]

On the other hand, segregation remained the rule. Acutely aware of the possibilities for political reaction, Ickes adopted the "neighborhood composition" rule in the PWA's earliest developments, reassuring whites that no new project would alter the existing demographic balance in its area. After the creation of the USHA in 1937, localities assumed the power to select project sites and to determine racial occupancy. As one official later noted, "[T]he public housing program accepted the 'separate but equal' doctrine, and, through its equity policy, undertook to insist upon uniform enforcement of the 'equal' while

allowing local communities to decide upon the 'separate.' " Even more significant, he conceded that such action "rested upon no sound legal theory . . . but
rather reflected 'political expediency.' "[8]

Indeed, the politically irresistible move to restrain the New Deal's reformist
impulses ran through the Wagner-Steagall Act that gave birth to the USHA. If
housing reformers were pleased over the creation of a permanent, national
housing agency, there was little else in the bill to give them cheer. The refusal
to assist nonprofits and cooperatives, the elimination of demonstration projects,
the stringent containment of construction costs, the linkage to slum clearance,
the restriction of the program to poor people unable to afford market-based
shelter, strict local control of siting, and, indeed, the decision to participate in
the program all gave evidence of conservative influence in the legislative process. In sum, the law fleshed out the two-tier housing policy that framed government activity for the next generation. The top tier represented efforts to
channel cheap capital to producers and consumers of private housing through
the organization and subsidization of financial markets. Administered primarily
through the FHA and a host of supportive agencies (such as the Home Owners'
Loan Corporation, Home Loan Bank Board, and Federal National Mortgage
Association), this tier revolutionized homeownership in the United States. In
contrast, a truncated public housing program constituted the lower tier and
produced, in the words of Gail Radford, shelter that was "stingy, alienating, and
means-tested."[9] It became increasingly clear with each passing year that the
differing tracks held racial significance; the upper tier nourished a growing,
virtually all-white constituency while public housing struggled to support primarily a fragment of the minority community with which it became identified.

The USHA's openness to black participation reflected an institutional ves-
tige of the New Deal's early affinity for social experimentation and Harold
Ickes's recruitment of racial advisers who articulated minority interests in the
ranks of the administration. Although Ickes stirred controversy by first appoint-
ing Clark Foreman, a white, to head this effort, Robert C. Weaver soon became
Ickes's chief adviser on "Negro Affairs." In 1938, Weaver moved to the USHA
and, along with Frank S. Horne, established the Racial Relations Service (RRS)
to combat discrimination in the housing program.[10] There was no doubt in
Gunnar Myrdal's mind that subsequent USHA policy reflected the fact that the
agency had "a special division for nonwhite races, headed by a Negro who can
serve as spokesman for his people." Even more important, in 1947, the RRS and
its cadre of officers found a home in the Housing and Home Finance Agency
(HHFA), the umbrella organization created to coordinate and oversee all housing programs in the postwar era.[11]

Shelley and the Push for Nondiscrimination

In the summer of 1947, Frank S. Horne, now a special assistant to new HHFA Administrator Raymond M. Foley, prepared a report for President Truman's Committee on Civil Rights. Reflecting on the previous decade's experience, Horne noted that in the absence of legislation mandating nondiscrimination, restrictive practices had emerged that limited black access to the existing housing supply and "reduce[d] the number of areas and sites available for the location of new construction, resulting in uneconomical as well as inequitable expenditure of public funds." "These practices," he concluded, "contribute[d] to racial segregation and the development of the ghetto," and, in Horne's pointed words, "constitute[d] a drain upon the economic, social, and spiritual resources of the entire community." He hoped that now, under the aegis of the HHFA and with the Truman administration's expressed concern with civil rights, federal housing policy would make a "progressive contribution toward nondiscrimination and equitable participation in the extension of public benefits."[12]

In less than one year, events heightened Horne's optimism. First, in May 1948, the U.S. Supreme Court handed down its decision in *Shelley v Kraemer*, which rendered racially restrictive covenants unenforceable. The culmination of a long and bitter campaign, the legal victory appeared to particularly threaten the FHA's traditional operation and sparked an intense two-year debate in the HHFA about the revision of agency practices. Similarly, the passage of the federal Housing Act of 1949, by authorizing 810,000 new units of public housing in conjunction with a massive slum clearance campaign, offered the Public Housing Administration (PHA) the opportunity—depending on the design and implementation of the program—to enforce a policy of nondiscrimination in the rebuilding of American cities. In both cases, the RRS pushed vigorously for the liberalization of federal policy. Despite the strategic placement of such enterprising partisans, however, political resistance, bureaucratic foot-dragging, and institutional inertia made certain that the color line remained intact.

Bureaucratic opponents staked out their positions within days of the Supreme Court's announcement of its *Shelley* verdict. Two weeks after the judgment, Raymond M. Foley sent missives to his subordinates inquiring whether the rulings "in any way affect the programs of the HHFA." Within seventy-two hours, FHA Commissioner Franklin D. Richards fired back a response that the Court's action would "in no way affect the programs of this agency." In his estimation, the Court's decree would spark "no change either in our basic concepts or procedures."[13] In subsequent, more detailed statements, Richards emphasized the difficulty of enforcing nondiscrimination procedures, the threat such procedures posed to the agency's client base, and the need to maintain professional standards. In the end, he also asserted that it was not "the policy of the Government to require private individuals to give up their right to dispose of their property as they [saw] fit, as a condition of receiving the benefits of the National Housing Act."[14]

Horne respectfully dissented. The new legal environment, he said, raised "not only strictly legal questions but also considerations of public policy and of what Mr. Justice Frankfurter in his concurring opinion termed 'good conscience' which are not adequately covered by the FHA response."[15] Horne sensed the possibility of real change and went outside the agency to make it happen. The "FHA will need to be *blasted* high, wide, and handsome out of its barnacled position of hidebound medievalism," he wrote the NAACP's Walter White. He conceded that it was one "hell of a large order," but he believed that the "iron is hot now." "We've cracked the draft open and applied a spark or two on the inside," he said. "If the NAACP pours on the *proper oil*, applied at the *proper points*, we set this whole business afire."[16]

Horne hoped to move quickly enough to use the summer and fall political campaigns for additional leverage. The NAACP, however, did not dispatch Thurgood Marshall's lengthy memorandum renewing long-standing allegations of FHA discrimination until February 1, 1949. In it, Marshall and the NAACP recommended that the FHA "exclude all considerations predicated upon racial, religious, or national distinctions for the purpose of making commitments for insurance" and refuse mortgage insurance for properties covered by objectionable racial covenants and indeed for any development where "occupancy . . . will be limited by race, religion, or national origin." The White House forwarded the NAACP's indictment to the Attorney General, and subsequently, Philip B. Perlman, the solicitor general, held a series of conferences with both the FHA's legal staff and Thurgood Marshall. By the summer, Perlman believed he had worked out a formula that had "the approval of all parties" and would "eliminate entirely . . . all causes of complaint."[17]

Perlman announced the changes in FHA rules at a luncheon of the New York State Committee on Discrimination in Housing on December 2, 1949. In substance, the FHA agreed to render ineligible for mortgage insurance all property bound by racially restrictive covenants recorded after February 15, 1950 (an effective date announced in a press release two weeks after the luncheon). The intent, Perlman asserted, was "to bring the mortgage insurance operations of the Federal Housing Administration fully into line with the policy underlying the recent decisions of the Supreme Court of the United States in the covenant cases." The new rules, he stated, would "not effect [sic] mortgage insurance already in force and will apply only to properties where the covenant in question and the insured mortgage are recorded after the date to be specified."[18]

Almost immediately, the FHA began backpedaling. In a statement released one day after Perlman's, FHA Commissioner Richards contended that the amendments "do not attempt to control any owner in determining what tenants he shall have or to whom he shall sell his property." The agency also soothingly informed panicked lenders that their fears about changed procedures were "not warranted." Indeed, just three days after the solicitor general's speech, the FHA's executive board met and agreed that "it should be made entirely clear that violation [of the new rules] would not invalidate insurance." By 1951, responding to the charge that the FHA engaged in a "clear evasion" of the president's intent, a high agency official blandly responded that "it was not the purpose of these Rules to forbid segregation or to deny the benefits of the National Housing Act to persons who might be unwilling to disregard race, color, or creed in the selection of their purchasers or tenants."[19]

Thurgood Marshall and the NAACP expressed shock at press accounts quoting FHA officials to the effect that "there would really be no serious change in policy." Writing to Commissioner Richards, Marshall complained that "these newspaper reports give the impression that FHA is more interested in pointing out to prejudiced real estate interests ways and means of evading the clear intent of the Supreme Court decision and the Perlman announcement than in implementing an effective anti-discrimination policy." He added that the trumpeted February 15 implementation date gave "more than ample time and more than ample notice to persons who desire to flaunt the intent of the amendments to record covenants on land before the effective date of the amended rules."[20] Both Horne's sense of the moment's possibilities and Solicitor General Perlman's optimism about the outcome proved wildly unrealistic.

The FHA's continued recalcitrance on race manifested itself most clearly in its kid-glove handling of various Levittown developments. This resistance was particularly important because of the enormous impact that large residential builders, exemplified by Levitt and Sons, had on the postwar era and particularly on the growth of suburbia. FHA production advances enabled the Levitts to revolutionize the home-building industry by making use of the latest technology and mass-production techniques. First, in Long Island, New York, in the late 1940s, and then in Bucks County, Pennsylvania, outside Philadelphia, in the early 1950s, Levitt and Sons, with FHA assistance, made thousands of affordable homes on previously undeveloped land available only to whites.

Nearly six months after the *Shelley* decision—but before the announced

changes in FHA policy—Franklin Richards rejected Thurgood Marshall's request that FHA not insure mortgages for the Long Island development. The
agency, in Richards's view, lacked the statutory authority under the National
Housing Act or the legal basis under the recent Supreme Court decisions "to
withdraw its normal protection and benefits from persons who have executed
but do not seek judicial enforcement of such covenants."[21] The Perlman decree
hardly changed matters. In a 1952 visit to the Bucks County development,
Horne, an exceptionally fair-skinned African American, reported that a Levittown sales agent leaned over a counter to confide to him in a whisper: "You
know, we've got to keep the colored out." Horne repeatedly brought the situation to Foley's attention and claimed that the slur placed both himself and the
agency in an "untenable position." "[I]t is more than an anomaly," Horne wrote,
"that a representative of a Federal agency is subject to affront and insult by a
developer who is receiving assistance from that same Federal agency." Like
Marshall, he urged that federal aid "be withheld from Levitt until he shall cease
and desist from his brazen racial discrimination." Horne's complaints, like Marshall's, were brushed aside.[22]

Implementing the Housing Act of 1949

The potential for change embodied in the Housing Act of 1949 seemed even
greater than that promised by the Supreme Court, but it was dispatched just as
quickly. Carrying provisions for an unprecedentedly large public housing program, the bill provoked intense opposition from the real estate lobby. That
opposition manifested itself most dramatically in the legislative debates over
the Bricker-Cain amendment. Republican senators John Bricker of Ohio and
Harry P. Cain of Washington, ardent foes of public housing, determined that
the best chance of scuttling the legislation would be to write a flat prohibition
of racial segregation into it. Bringing their amendment to the Senate floor,
Bricker and Cain calculated that the measure would split northern liberals and
southern segregationists who joined in support of the housing bill, and, if
passed, their amendment would guarantee its defeat.

Democrat and legislative sponsor Allen Ellender of Louisiana, in fact, let it
be known that he would vote against his own bill if the amendment were
attached, and key Senate supporter John Sparkman of Alabama held African
Americans hostage to defeat it. If the antisegregation provision passed, Sparkman vowed that the South would shun the national housing program and deny
"the Negro" housing "in the very area where he needs it the most." The Senate

majority leader, Democrat Scott Lucas of Illinois, denounced the Bricker-Cain amendment as a thinly disguised attempt to kill the housing bill, and his liberal Democratic colleague from Chicago, Paul Douglas, agreed that its adoption would sound a "death knell" for slum clearance and redevelopment—measures he believed were in the interests of African Americans. In the end, Douglas agonized over his decision, but ultimately urged fellow civil rights advocates to defeat the ban on segregation. They did so and in the process handed President Truman and his Fair Deal a rare legislative achievement.[23]

Despite the rejection of the Bricker-Cain amendment, the Housing Act of 1949 still held forth the possibility of a direct and massive impact on racial living patterns. Implicit in the legislation was the choice, as Robert C. Weaver put it, of building "new and better segregated housing" or establishing neighborhoods that would be open to all. Indeed, one of the bill's framers, Senator Robert F. Wagner of New York, had earlier asserted that "we face the issue of whether we shall solidify or break down the ghettos of segregation in our cities." Lacking a ban on discrimination, however, the new law presented what Weaver called a "triple threat." Redevelopment initiatives in both public and private housing could be used, he noted, "as a guise for displacing minorities from desirable areas" or for "breaking up established racially democratic neighborhoods." They could also be used "to reduce even further the already inadequate supply of living space available" to African Americans.[24]

From within the HHFA, Horne issued the same warnings. As debate over the legislation droned on, Horne articulated the "necessity for adequate protection for racial minority groups in any bill or Title which extends Federal aid to communities for slum clearance and land assembly." He reminded Administrator Foley that the "theory under which Federal tax funds are made available under this program . . . is the national concern for the debilitating effects upon the total body politic of the consequences of slum living." The RRS subsequently believed that the HHFA's operations needed to reflect "modern housing and civil rights principles." "This would entail," Horne boldly concluded, "moving the human and civil rights considerations from the fringes into the very core" of the planning process.[25]

But Horne remained filled with trepidation. Despite the bill's requirements and assurances, the law did not, he noted "preclude the possibility of Federal funds and powers being utilized by localities to clear entire neighborhoods, change the location of entire population groups, and crystallize patterns of racial or nationalistic separation by allowing private developers—for whose benefit the legislation is primarily drawn—to prohibit occupancy in new developments merely on the basis of race." Fearing that "Federal funds and powers" would be used to "harden into brick and mortar the racially restrictive practices of private real estate and lending operations," he admonished Foley that minorities "could be exiled from entire city areas," and developers handed "a weapon more devastating than racial covenants in that the process would be afforded Federal sanction." "The central issue," he concluded, "is whether racial discrimination of any type is to be sanctioned in a program of city rebuilding which depends on *public* funds and powers as well as on private investment."[26]

Results were not long in coming. In a 1951 speech before the Richmond Civic Council, the NAACP's Clarence Mitchell produced a list of emergent horror stories under both Title I (slum clearance) and Title III (public housing) of the new Housing Act. Aiken, South Carolina, had a "varied housing pattern" but federal housing agencies there now supported "separate housing developments for colored people." Similarly, in Savannah, Georgia, planned public housing, Mitchell claimed, would "eliminate the slums, remove the colored people, and build a project for whites only." Nashville, Tennessee, also contemplated uprooting blacks in favor of whites, and Baltimore, Maryland, in its Waverly and Johns Hopkins Hospital redevelopment plans, did the same. George B. Nesbitt, a racial relations adviser in HHFA's new Division of Slum Clearance and Urban Redevelopment (DSCUR), noted that Baltimore's proposals manifested every facet of Weaver's "triple threat." They would, he wrote, effect "Negro clearance," convert a "racially flexible area to one of racial exclusion," and reduce the area "available to Negro residence."[27]

Responding to Mitchell's litany, Horne told Foley that early acceptance of the administrator's statements about sound Agency policy now gave way before "doubts as to the manner in which these policies are being implemented by operating officials in the constituent administrations." "The growing attitude toward the Baltimore program," Horne wrote, "simply reflects the growing fear that, if Title I is to follow the current practice of FHA regarding covenants and restrictive agreements, involuntary residential segregation by race will be reinforced and even spread under Federal sanction."[28] DSCUR's Nesbitt concurred. The division, he confessed in 1951, had "no adequate policy to implement the admitted major Federal responsibility" to expand, rather than reduce, the land area occupied by minorities, nor did it have "an adequate policy designed to prevent 'Negro clearance' or 'Negro containment.' "[29]

If Mitchell's concerns centered on the South, the doleful results of the Housing Act of 1949 were not confined to that region. The key slum clearance, redevelopment, and public housing program, particularly in terms of its early influence on national policy, could be found well north of Jim Crow's domain, in Chicago. Operating under state laws that antedated and yet mirrored the provisions of the Housing Act of 1949, the Windy City sought federal support for local initiatives already well underway. It sought Title I aid for the New York Life Insurance Company's Lake Meadows development, a slum clearance project on the near South Side; Title III public housing assistance was requested for construction of 11,500 to 15,050 units on a dozen mostly inner-city sites. Robert C. Weaver, now temporary chairman of the National Committee Against Discrimination in Housing, complained to HHFA that the program relied on a "preponderance of slum sites chosen on the basis of Negro containment" and was "insupportable." HHFA's own field officer agreed, commenting that it presented "insurmountable" relocation problems and "disproportionate Negro involvement" while incurring excessive costs and following "lines of least political and neighborhood resistance." "It not only . . . smack[s] of 'Negro clearance,' " the officer reported, "but at the same time buttresses up existing patterns of segregation."[30]

Weaver detected a pattern in Chicago whereby "local prejudice rather than rational land use has dictated the selection of sites in public housing programs." This massive initiative, moreover, came at a time when the HHFA was just establishing procedures under the new law. He knew the city would serve as a proving ground where "new standards safeguarding the equal treatment of minorities" could be developed or from which the disturbing "underlying pattern evolving there . . . [could] spread."[31]

When, in July 1951, a rampaging mob destroyed an apartment building that housed a single black family in the western suburb of Cicero, racial relations advisers Horne and Nesbitt seized the opportunity to campaign against the Chicago proposals. After linking the eruption of violence to the Windy City's own bloody racial history, its tradition of residential segregation, and its current redevelopment program, they sought rejection of the Chicago plans with an eye toward setting a national precedent. Citing pending applications from Detroit, Saint Louis, Baltimore, Norfolk, Tampa, New Orleans, Dallas, and a host of other cities, Horne contended that the "surrender to the various practices which have created and nurtured racial residential restriction is reflected in [their] current proposals" and that the "programs administered under HHFA have been increasingly drawn into the sordid scene." "Surely," he argued in a memorandum to Foley, "the vast powers, funds, and prestige of the Federal Government are not to be utilized to underwrite official irresponsibility and community immorality." Nesbitt agreed and reminded his superiors that the government could "condition its Federal aids . . . so as to induce Chicago to meet its responsibilities and hence lessen the likelihood of still more racial disorder in Chicago, Cicero, and other of its suburbs." "Indeed," he concluded, "if the Federal government extends its aid to Chicago without such conditions, it at once underwrites and reinforces the racism and the slum clearance sleight-of-hand now there."[32]

It was all to no avail. In what ultimately proved to be a showdown between local control and at least potentially coercive federal authority, the locals won hands down. Although HHFA delayed approval of four questionable sites, they were finally accepted after a series of intense discussions. In the end, Foley accepted the Chicago proposals with the warning that similar future initiatives would be disapproved. In a nod to the Racial Relations Service, the HHFA promised better coordination among its constituents and urged closer cooperation to open new housing opportunities for minorities. Still, DSCUR officials had no illusions about the practical consequences of the administrator's protestations. "It is difficult to feel," one of them wrote with the certainty of defeat, "that Chicago will at all readily respond" to Foley's urgings.[33]

Brown, Urban Renewal, and the Eisenhower Administration

The U.S. Supreme Court's historic decision in the school desegregation cases in May 1954 provided the occasion to revisit the federal government's housing policies. HHFA attorneys initially reacted nervously and circled their legal wagons in the attempt to circumscribe *Brown*'s reach. HHFA General Counsel B. T. Fitzpatrick doubted that the invalidation of the "separate but equal" doctrine in education applied to housing at all, while DSCUR's Associate General Counsel Joseph Guandolo voiced deep reservations about a potential "major extension of Federal Authority." RRS officials, however, rejected such temporizing and boldly displayed an expansive interpretation of *Brown*'s implications for housing policy.[34]

In a statement that reflected the "joint thinking and conscience" of race relations personnel in HHFA and its constituents (FHA, PHA, and DSCUR), new Racial Relations Adviser Joseph R. Ray sought to bring agency practice "into line with the public policy underlying the . . . Supreme Court decisions." The statement called for all multifamily residential projects and related facilities developed through federal subsidies, insurance, or other such powers to be rented or sold to families without regard to race, religion, national origin, or political affiliation. The policy would apply to federally aided public or private developments, as well as to community facilities erected on land assembled through federal grants or loans.[35] Horne, whose advocacy had earlier led to his demotion, unflinchingly goaded his superiors. The Supreme Court had "completely abandoned" the principle of "separate but equal" as being "inconsistent with the American way of life," he told them, and presented the "opportunity" for "this Administration to remove all restrictions from the housing market."[36] Horne's assertiveness led, this time, not to another demotion, but to his ultimate separation from government service—and the virtual gutting of the RRS itself.

Albert M. Cole, appointed by Dwight D. Eisenhower as Foley's successor in 1953, exemplified a more conservative regime that proved less tolerant of such insubordination. Cole stilled the voices of dissent in his agency and snuffed out what life remained in the New Deal's social legacy. A recently defeated congressman from Kansas, Cole had close ties to the real estate and home-building industries and had been an implacable foe of public housing in the legislative debates over the Housing Act of 1949. His nomination "deeply disturbed" the NAACP, which protested to no avail.[37] Once in office, he used the government's new presence in the housing arena to accelerate the racial segmentation of metropolitan America.

In July 1954, Cole met with the president's advisers and staff, along with the heads of PHA, FHA, and DSCUR, to devise a strategy for coping with the implications of *Brown*. Shortly thereafter, he announced the creation of an Advisory Committee on Minority Housing even as he explicitly rejected the use of government leverage to enforce nondiscrimination. Pointedly turning his back on his race relations advisers, he scorned the notion that he should "crack down" and "use our government aids as financial clubs."[38] Instead, HHFA embarked on a course of increasing the quantity and improving the quality of black-occupied housing while issuing no challenge to segregation. It seemed as though the administration believed that by finally addressing the physical housing needs of minorities, the pressure to dismantle "separate but equal" might be diminished—or, at least, safely ignored.

Cole revealed his determination to work in the existing racial framework in a carefully orchestrated Minority Housing Conference in December 1954 and in his brusque treatment of the RRS. In the first instance, his attempt to recruit private-sector assistance in alleviating the housing shortage for minorities generated proposals that Walter White deemed "appalling" because they were "so similar to the South African government's program of building separate communities for colored people."[39] In the second instance, Cole purged Horne and his chief assistant and isolated the RRS in his agency. By 1956, even Cole's handpicked replacement for Horne complained of the "gradual erosion of the duties and responsibilities" of the RRS and the fact that his staff had been "pre-cluded from or circumvented in discharging its designated functions."[40] A bold initiative in the New Deal, the RRS became irrelevant during the Cold War.

The centerpiece of the Eisenhower administration's housing policy, how-ever, was the Housing Act of 1954. Passed within weeks of the *Brown* decision, the law emphasized rehabilitation rather than mass demolition. Dubbed "urban renewal," the program sought slum prevention as well as clearance and prom-ised to spread resources to healthy, but threatened, neighborhoods, not just those already gripped by decay. In part, it attempted to tie the program's pros-pects to the expansion of the private minority housing market and liberalized FHA guidelines to accomplish that goal. The key to the program, however, was the role assigned to public housing by its earlier opponent, Albert M. Cole.

The administrator never conceived of public housing as a social reform that redistributed public benefits to poor people; he perceived, instead, only its use as relocation housing that would facilitate slum clearance, upgrade the inner-city housing stock, and relieve minority pressure on transitional communities. "[P]ublic housing for low-income families must be better integrated into a larger program," he asserted, "to improve the living standards and housing opportuni-ties of all segments of the community." "It cannot survive as a mission apart," he warned. The man who had earlier claimed that public housing could destroy the U.S. government now viewed it as "an integral part of the Administra-tion's overall housing program" that was "directly linked to the clearance of slums."[41]

Cole clearly understood the racial implications of the law's explicit linkage of displacement because of urban renewal and accessibility to public housing. "Since racial minorities constitute a high proportion of slum dwellers," he wrote one correspondent, "these circumstances orient the low-rent program signifi-cantly to serve their needs." Furthermore, bestowing such benefits on the mi-nority community confirmed, for Cole, the program's nondiscriminatory intent; nothing further needed to be done. Certainly, he would not permit civil rights advocates bent on desegregation "to strangle broad national progress until every last extreme aim has been satisfied." He knew, moreover, that the number of public housing units requested by the president could not meet the "probable total need" and that the "core planning and relocation problem in most commu-nities" involved "nonwhite families." Therefore, "major progress" could only be made in "rehousing the lowest income groups," thus making public housing inevitably an inner-city, minority program.[42]

These obvious racial realities prompted Frank Horne, shortly before his termination, to warn Cole against "yielding to 'expediencies' in order to get programs underway" and against compromising with city administrations "at the lowest level of racial relations." He also insisted that racial relations personnel review the localities' mandatory "workable programs" *before* they received certification. Urban renewal activities, instead, found themselves without such oversight. By 1955, Horne's successor, Joseph R. Ray, complained that commitments to furnish racial relations personnel to the new Urban Renewal Administration (URA) went unfulfilled. "To continue any longer the extended absence of racial relations services from the expanded and growing program of broad-gauged urban renewal activities that so predominantly involve Negroes," Ray informed Cole, "can only serve to place the Agency in an increasingly tenuous and not easily defensible position—indeed, render the Agency increasingly liable to charges of neglecting the needs of minorities."[43]

The harshest critics of Cole's actions charged that his "minority housing programs" were "conceived to counteract the effect of the United States Supreme Court's decisions calling for public school integration." Frances Levenson of the National Committee Against Discrimination in Housing alleged that some southern cities were "actually using the program to insure future school segregation by moving minority families out of presently integrated neighborhoods." By 1959, even the URA's own personnel admitted that "projects are accumulating which appear or can be made to appear motivated by the desire to effect 'Negro clearance' and frustration of desegregation in education in the one stroke with Federal aid." George Nesbitt had to concede that current practices left the government open to "charges of facilitating and sanctioning the racial conversion of residential areas in order to frustrate desegregation in educational and other public facilities."[44]

The intertwining of renewal and race proved no less striking outside the South. Concurrent with the Second Great Migration (1940–70), the age of urban renewal saw most of its projects conceived, planned, or built within a decade of the Housing Act of 1954. As early as 1957, the crucial role played by public housing became evident; indeed, virtually *all* (97 percent) such units built in urban renewal areas housed nonwhites. The new construction of densely packed high-rise projects, characterized by the concentration of "problem" families, the loss of local managerial control over tenant screening, and the removal of "over-income" households—all necessary outgrowths of a simultaneous policy of clearance and containment—perfectly articulated public housing's new mission and HHFA's social vision. They also gave rise to the stereotypical images that became so prevalent in the 1960s and 1970s. As Douglas Massey and Nancy Denton wrote in *American Apartheid*, after twenty years of urban renewal, "public housing projects in most large cities had become black reservations, highly segregated from the rest of society and characterized by extreme social isolation."[45]

If more than a trace of tragedy became evident here, there was also a considerable dose of irony. So often placed at the dawning of the civil rights era, the Supreme Court's renunciation of "separate but equal" in *Brown* brought to a close, instead, ongoing efforts to liberalize federal housing policy. In the government bureaucracy, the RRS represented the institutionalization of such sentiment and had been working, since the 1930s, to provide "equity" in the implementation of government programs. With the Supreme Court's invalidation of racially restrictive covenants in *Shelley*, the passage of the Housing Act of 1949, the promising ruling in the school desegregation cases, and the coming of urban renewal, the RRS moved beyond its earlier demands and pushed for a blanket policy of nondiscrimination. Thwarted at every turn, the RRS instead found itself isolated and ineffective. A brief season of postwar optimism had been eclipsed by the rapid onset of a sustained and overwhelming political reaction. At the very least, however, those protesting the reinforcement and expansion of federally sanctioned ghettos held a mirror up to policymakers and confronted them with the likely outcomes of their actions. Of all the adjectives that might be used to characterize the subsequent results, "unforeseen" and "unintended" should not be listed among them.

Notes

1. Thomas Byrne Edsall and Mary D. Edsall, *Chain Reaction: The Impact of Race, Rights, and Taxes on American Politics* (New York: Norton, 1991); Jim Sleeper, *The Closest of Strangers: Liberalism and the Politics of Race in New York City* (New York: Norton, 1990); Jonathan Rieder, *Canarsie: The Jews and Italians of Brooklyn Against Liberalism* (Cambridge, Mass.: Harvard University Press, 1985); E. J. Dionne, *Why Americans Hate Politics* (New York: Simon and Schuster, 1992); Charles Murray, *Losing Ground: American Social Policy, 1950–1980* (New York: Basic Books, 1984).

2. Dominic J. Capeci Jr., *Race Relations in Wartime Detroit: The Sojourner Truth Housing Controversy of 1942* (Philadelphia: Temple University Press, 1984); Raymond A. Mohl, "Making the Second Ghetto in Metropolitan Miami, 1940–1960," *Journal of Urban History* 21 (March 1995): 395–427; Thomas J. Sugrue, *The Origins of the Urban Crisis: Race and Inequality in Postwar Detroit* (Princeton: Princeton University Press, 1996); and idem, "Crabgrass-Roots Politics: Race, Rights, and the Reaction Against Liberalism in the Urban North, 1940–1964," *Journal of American History* 82 (September 1995): 551–78; Arnold R. Hirsch, *Making the Second Ghetto: Race and Housing in Chicago, 1940–1960* (New York, 1983); and idem, "Massive Resistance in the Urban North: Trumbull Park, Chicago, 1953–1966," *Journal of American History* 82 (September 1995): 522–50; John F. Bauman, *Public Housing, Race, and Renewal: Urban Planning in Philadelphia, 1920–1974* (Philadelphia: Temple University Press, 1987).

3. Kenneth T. Jackson, *Crabgrass Frontier: The Suburbanization of the United States* (New York: Oxford University Press, 1985).

4. Ronald Tobey, Charles Wetherell, and Jay Brigham, "Moving Out and Settling In: Residential Mobility, Home Owning, and the Public Enframing of Citizenship, 1921–1950," *American Historical Review* 95 (1990): 1395–422.

5. Jackson, *Crabgrass Frontier*, 190–218; Gunnar Myrdal, *An American Dilemma: The Negro Problem and Modern Democracy*, 2 vols. (New York: Harper and Row, 1944), 1:348–53, 2:622–27; Sugrue, *The Origins of the Urban Crisis*, 208–30.

6. Gail Radford, *Modern Housing for America: Policy Struggles in the New Deal Era* (Chicago: University of Chicago Press, 1996), 104; John B. Kirby, *Black Americans in the Roosevelt Era: Liberalism and Race* (Knoxville: University of Tennessee Press, 1980), 22–23.

7. Public Housing Administration, "The Negro in Public Housing, 1933–1953: Problems and Accomplishments" (Typescript, May 1954), Folder 4, Box 1, Record Group (hereafter RG) 196, National Archives II (hereafter NA II); "Minority Group Considerations in Administration of Governmental Housing Programs," attached to Frank S. Horne to Operating Staff of HHFA and Constituents [July 1947], Folder 3, Box 9, RG 196.

8. Radford, *Modern Housing for America*, 104–5; Martin Meyerson and Edward C. Banfield, *Politics, Planning, and the Public Interest: The Case of Public Housing in Chicago* (New York: Free Press, 1955), 121–22; Desmond King, *Separate and Unequal: Black Americans and the U.S. Federal Government* (Oxford: Oxford University Press, 1995), 190.

9. Radford, *Modern Housing for America*, 189–91, 197–98; Bauman, *Public Housing, Race, and Renewal*, 43–44.

10. Weaver, named HHFA administrator by President John F. Kennedy, went on to become the first secretary of the Department of Housing and Urban Development (HUD) under President Lyndon Johnson. His outspoken views generated opposition, slowing both his confirmation and the creation of the HUD itself. See Arnold R. Hirsch, " 'Containment' on the Home Front: Race and Federal Housing Policy from the New Deal to the Cold War," *Journal of Urban History* 26 (January 2000): 180; and Mark Gelfand, *A Nation of Cities: The Federal Government and Urban America* (New York: Oxford University Press, 1975), 312, 323–24.

11. Charles Abrams to the editor, August 16, 1955, *The New York Times*, August 23, 1955, 22; Kirby, *Black Americans in the Roosevelt Era*, 17–21, 121–22; Myrdal, *An American Dilemma*, 1:350.

12. "Minority Group Considerations in Administration of Governmental Housing Programs."

13. Raymond M. Foley to William K. Divers, May 18, 1948, and Franklin D. Richards to Raymond M. Foley, May 21, 1948, both in Reel 5, NAACP Papers, Part 5: Campaign Against Residential Segregation (University Publications of America).

14. Franklin D. Richards to Raymond M. Foley, February 14, 1949, Folder: Restrictive Covenants, 1949, Box 6, Commissioner's Correspondence and Subject File, 1938–1958, RG 31, NA II.

15. Frank S. Horne to Raymond M. Foley, n.d., in Reel 5, NAACP Papers, Part 5: Campaign Against Residential Segregation.

16. Frank [Horne] to Walter [White], July 20, 1948, in Reel 5, NAACP Papers, Part 5: Campaign Against Residential Segregation.

17. Walter White to Mr. President, February 1, 1949, and the attached "Memorandum to the President of the United States Concerning Racial Discrimination by the Federal Housing Administration"; Philip B. Perlman to David K. Niles, July 7, 1949, all in Folder: Restrictive Covenants, 1949, Box 6, Commissioner's Correspondence and Subject File, 1938–1958, RG 31.

18. "Statement by Solicitor General Philip B. Perlman at Luncheon Session of State-Wide Conference of New York State Committee on Discrimination in Housing, Hotel Martinique, 32nd Street, Broadway, Friday, December 2, 1949," Folder: Restrictive Covenants, 1949, Box 6, Commissioner's Correspondence and Subject File, 1938–1958, RG 31; FHA, Press Release, December 16, 1949, Folder 5, Box 4, RG 196.

19. FHA, Press Release, December 3, 1949, Folder 5, Box 4, RG 31; Walter L. Greene to Charles F. Crisp, December 22, 1949, and FHA, "Minutes—231st Meeting Executive Board—December 5, 1949," both in Folder: Restrictive Covenants, 1949, Box 6, Commissioner's Correspondence and Subject File, 1938–1958, RG 31; Abraham J. Multer Jr. to Walter L. Greene, September 4, 1951, and Walter L. Greene to Honorable Abraham J. Multer, September 11, 1951, both in Folder.

Racial Restrictive Covenants, 1950–1953, Box 6, Commissioner's Correspondence and Subject File, 1938–1958, RG 31.

20. Thurgood Marshall to Franklin D. Richards, December 7 and December 22, 1949, both in Folder: Restrictive Covenants, 1949, Box 6, Commissioner's Correspondence and Subject File, 1938–1958, RG 31.

21. Barry Checkoway, "Large Builders, Federal Housing Programs, and Postwar Suburbanization," in William K. Tabb and Larry Sawers, eds., *Marxism and the Metropolis: New Perspectives in Urban Political Economy* (New York: Oxford University Press, 1984), 152–71; David Halberstam, *The Fifties* (New York: Fawcett Columbine, 1993), 132–43; Franklin D. Richards to Thurgood Marshall, November 1, 1948, Folder: Restrictive Covenants, 1938–1948, Box 6, Commissioner's Correspondence and Subject File, 1938–1958, RG 31.

22. Frank S. Horne to the Administrator, March 19, 1952, and May 27, 1952, both in Folder: Racial Relations, Box 59, General Subject Files, 1947–1960, RG 207, NA II; Walter White to Mr. President, January 12, 1954, Folder: Racial Relations, Box 96, General Subject Files, 1947–1960, RG 207, NA II.

23. *The New York Times*, April 15, 1949, 15, and April 22, 1949, 1; Richard O. Davies, *Defender of the Old Guard: John Bricker and American Politics* (Columbus: Ohio State University Press, 1993), 137–38; and idem, *Housing Reform During the Truman Administration* (Columbia: University of Missouri Press, 1966), 107–8.

24. Robert C. Weaver, *The Negro Ghetto* (New York: Harcourt, Brace, 1948), 6, 324, note 361.

25. Frank S. Horne to B. T. Fitzpatrick, November 15, 1948, Folder: Racial Relations, Box 18, General Subject Files, 1947–1960, RG 207; Frank S. Horne to Raymond M. Foley, June 3, 1949, Folder 7, Box 748, Program Files–Racial Relations Files, RG 207.

26. Horne to Foley, June 3, 1949.

27. "Speech of Clarence Mitchell, director of the Washington Bureau, NAACP, Before the Richmond Civic Council, Moore Street Church Center, December 6, 1951," 3–4, Folder 11, Box 269, General Subject Files, 1949–1960, RG 207; Horne to Foley, December 18, 1951; George B. Nesbitt to N. S. Keith, August 30, 1951, Folder 11, Box 269, General Subject Files, 1949–1960, RG 207.

28. Horne to Foley, December 18, 1951.

29. Nesbitt to Keith, August 30, 1951.

30. Robert C. Weaver to Raymond Foley, February 6, 1951, Folder: Racial Relations, Box 53, HHFA General Subject Files, 1947–1960, RG 207; George B. Nesbitt to C. L. Farris, August 3, 1950, Folder 3, Box 749, Program Files–Racial Relations Files, 1946–1958, RG 207.

31. Weaver to Foley, February 6, 1951, and Robert C. Weaver to Raymond Foley, September 7, 1951, Folder 7, Box 4, Commissioner's Correspondence and Subject Files, 1938–1958, RG 31.

32. Frank S. Horne to the Administrator, July 27, 1951, Folder 11, Box 269, General Subject Files, 1947–1960, RG 207; George B. Nesbitt to N. S. Keith, July 30, 1951, Folder 3, Box 750, Program Files–Racial Relations Files, RG 207.

33. Raymond M. Foley to Honorable Martin H. Kennelly, October 18, 1951; Frank S. Horne to Raymond M. Foley, October 20, 1951, both in Folder: Racial Relations, Box 53, HHFA General Subject Files, 1947–1960, RG 207; George B. Nesbitt to N. S. Keith, November 8, 1951, Folder 11, Box 269, General Subject Files, 1949–1960, RG 207.

34. B. T. Fitzpatrick to Mr. Cole, June 10, 1954, Folder 5, Box 20, Subject Correspondence Files, Albert Cole, Administrator, 1953–1958, RG 207; Joseph Guandolo to J. W. Follin, August 24, 1954, and J. W. Follin to Albert M. Cole, May 28, 1954, both in Folder: Racial Relations, Box 284, General Subject Files, 1949–1960, RG 207.

35. Joseph R. Ray to Albert M. Cole, July 14, 1954, Folder: Racial Relations, Box 96, General Subject Files, 1947–1960, RG 207.

36. Frank S. Horne to Albert M. Cole, June 29, 1954, Folder 1, Box 748, Program Files–Racial Relations Files, 1946–1958, RG 207.

37. "Statement of Clarence Mitchell," March 2, 1953, in Reel 6, NAACP Papers, Part 5: The Campaign Against Residential Segregation.

38. "Address by Albert M. Cole at the Luncheon Meeting of the National Urban League, Pittsburgh, Pa., September 8, 1954," 4–5, in Reel 6, NAACP Papers, Part 5: The Campaign Against Residential Segregation.

39. Walter White to Herbert R. Brownell, December 22, 1954, Reel 6, NAACP Papers, Part 5: The Campaign Against Residential Segregation.

40. Joseph R. Ray to Albert M. Cole, April 16, 1956, Folder 1, Box 11, Subject Correspondence Files, Albert M. Cole, Administrator, 1953–1958, RG 207; Joseph R. Ray to Frank J. Meistrell, January 5, 1956, Folder 7, Box 134, HHFA Subject Files, 1947–1960, RG 207.

41. "Address by Albert M. Cole to the Annual Convention of the National Association of Housing Officials, Milwaukee, Wisconsin, October 15, 1953"; Albert M. Cole, "The Slum, the City, and the Citizen" (typescript speech delivered to the Saint Louis Chamber of Commerce, February 24, 1954); "Address by Albert M. Cole to the Annual Meeting of the Ohio Association of Real Estate Boards, September 15, 1954," all in Reel 6, NAACP Papers, Part 5. The Campaign Against Residential Segregation.

42. Albert M. Cole to Honorable Prescott Bush, May 3, 1956, Folder 7, Box 134, General Subject Files, 1947–1960, RG 207; "Address by Albert M. Cole to the Meeting of the Ohio Association of Real Estate Boards," 8; Albert M. Cole, "Address to the Mid-Atlantic Conference, National Association of Housing and Redevelopment Officials, New York, April 1, 1954," 11, in Reel 6, NAACP Papers, Part 5: The Campaign Against Residential Segregation. See also DSCUR, "Racial Relations Workshop: Report" (typescript, June 4, 1954), Folder 12, Box 745, Program Files–Racial Relations Files, 1946–1958, RG 207.

43. Frank S. Horne to Albert M. Cole, September 27, 1954, Folder: Racial Relations, Box 96, General Subject Files, 1947–1960, RG 207; Joseph R. Ray to Albert M. Cole, October 26, 1955, Folder 5, Box 116, HHFA Subject Files, 1947–1960, RG 207.

44. National Committee Against Discrimination, Press release, July 9, 1956, in Reel 8, NAACP Papers, Supplement to Part 5, General Office Files, 1956–1965; George B. Nesbitt to David M. Walker, September 30, 1959; Frances Levenson to David M. Walker, September 30, 1959; George B. Nesbitt to Sid Jagger, February 16, 1959, all in Folder: Racial Relations, Box 330, HHFA General Subject Files, 1949–1960, RG 207.

45. Robert Frederick Burk, *The Eisenhower Administration and Black Civil Rights* (Knoxville: University of Tennessee Press, 1984), 119–21; U.S. Commission on Civil Rights, *Report of the United States Commission on Civil Rights, 1959* (Washington, D.C.: GPO, 1959), 480–88; Elizabeth Wood, *The Beautiful Beginnings, the Failure to Learn: Fifty Years of Public Housing in America* (Washington, D.C.: National Center for Housing Management, 1982); Douglas S. Massey and Nancy A. Denton, *American Apartheid: Segregation and the Making of the Underclass* (Cambridge, Mass.: Harvard University Press, 1993), 57, 227. Nationally, there are roughly 1.3 million units of public housing, of which nearly 1 million were built before 1970 (at a time when civil rights obligations did not weigh heavily on the agency). Some 76 percent of the units occupied by blacks and 82 percent of those rented by Hispanics are located in central cities. See John Goering and Modibo Coulibably, "Public Housing Segregation in the United States," in Elizabeth D. Huttman, ed., Wim Blauw and Juliet Saltman, co-eds., *Urban Housing Segregation of Minorities in Western Europe and the United States* (Durham: Duke University Press, 1991), 305–34.

11

Planned Destruction
The Interstates and Central City Housing

RAYMOND A. MOHL

Few public policy initiatives have had as dramatic and lasting an impact on the late twentieth-century urban United States as the decision to build the Interstate Highway system. Virtually completed over a fifteen-year period between 1956 and the early 1970s, the building of the new Interstates had inevitable and powerful consequences for U.S. urban housing policy—consequences that ranged from the rapid growth of suburban communities to the massive destruction of inner-city housing in the path of the new urban expressways. Housing and highways were intimately linked in the post–World War II United States. In fact, this chapter contends that postwar policymakers and highway builders used Interstate construction to destroy low-income and especially black neighborhoods in an effort to reshape the racial landscapes of the U.S. city.

In metropolitan areas, the coming of urban expressways led very quickly to a reorganization of urban and suburban space. The Interstates linked central cities with sprawling postwar suburbs, facilitating automobile commuting while undermining what was left of inner-city mass transit. They stimulated new downtown physical development and spurred the growth of suburban shopping malls, office parks, and residential subdivisions. Oriented toward center cities, urban expressways also tore through long-established inner-city residential communities, destroying low-income housing on a vast and unprecedented scale. Huge expressway interchanges, clover leafs, and on-off ramps created enormous areas of dead and useless space in the central cities. The new expressways, in short, permanently altered the urban and suburban landscape throughout the nation. The Interstate system was a gigantic public works program, but it is now apparent that freeway construction had enormous and often negative consequences for the cities. As Mark I. Gelfand noted, "No federal venture spent more funds in urban areas and returned fewer dividends to central cities than the national highway program."[1]

Almost everywhere, the new urban expressways destroyed wide swaths of existing housing and dislocated people by the tens of thousands. Highway promoters and highway builders envisioned the new Interstate Highways as a means of clearing "blighted" urban areas. These plans actually date to the late 1930s, but they were not fully implemented until the late 1950s and 1960s. Massive amounts of urban housing were destroyed in the process of building the urban sections of the Interstate Highway system. According to the 1969 report of the National Commission on Urban Problems, at least 330,000 urban housing units were destroyed as a direct result of federal highway building between 1957 and 1968. In the early 1960s, federal highway construction dislocated an average of 32,400 families each year. "The amount of disruption," the U.S. House Committee on Public Works conceded in 1965, was "astoundingly large."[2] A large proportion of those dislocated were African Americans, and in most cities the Interstates were routinely routed through black neighborhoods.

Dislocated urbanites had few advocates in the state and federal road-building agencies. The federal Bureau of Public Roads and the state highway departments believed that their business was to finance and build highways and that any social consequences of highway construction were the responsibility of other agencies.[3] One federal housing official noted in 1957: "It is my impression that regional personnel of the Bureau of Public Roads are not overly concerned with the problems of family relocation."[4] Indeed, during most of the expressway-building era, little was done to link the Interstate Highway program with public or private housing construction or even with relocation assistance for displaced families, businesses, or community institutions such as churches and schools.

The victims of highway building tended to be overwhelmingly poor and black. A general pattern emerged, promoted by state and federal highway officials and by private agencies such as the Urban Land Institute, of using highway construction to eliminate "blighted" neighborhoods and to redevelop valuable inner-city land. This was the position of Thomas H. MacDonald, director of the U.S. Bureau of Public Roads (BPR) during the formative years of the Inter-

23. Expressways like this one in California permanently altered the urban and suburban landscape of America.

state system. It was also the policy of New York's influential builder of public works projects, Robert Moses. Highway builders were clearly conscious of the social consequences of Interstate route location. It was quite obvious that neighborhoods and communities would be destroyed and people uprooted, but this was thought to be an acceptable cost of creating new transportation routes and facilitating urban economic development. In fact, highway builders and downtown redevelopers had a common interest in eliminating low-income housing and, as one redeveloper put it in 1959, freeing "blighted" areas "for higher and better uses."[5]

The federal government provided most of the funding for Interstate Highway construction, but state highway departments working with local officials selected the actual Interstate routes. The consequence of state and local route selection was that urban expressways could be used specifically to carry out local race, housing, and residential segregation agendas. In most cities, moreover, the uprooting of people from central-city housing triggered a spatial reorganization of residential neighborhoods. Black population pressure on limited inner-city housing meant that dislocated blacks pressed into neighborhoods of "transition," generally working-class white neighborhoods on the fringes of the black ghetto where low-cost housing predominated. These newer "second ghettos" were already forming after World War II, as whites began moving to the suburbs and as blacks migrated out of the South into the urban North. Interstate Highway construction speeded up this process of second-ghetto formation, helping mold the sprawling, densely populated ghettos of the modern American city. Official housing and highway policies, taken together, helped to produce the much more intensely concentrated and racially segregated landscapes of contemporary urban America.[6]

Early Expressway Planning

The linkage between inner-city expressways and the destruction of urban housing actually originated in the BPR, the federal agency established in 1919. Thomas H. MacDonald, a highway engineer from Iowa, headed the BPR from its founding until early 1953. Over many decades, MacDonald relentlessly promoted his agency's road-building agenda.[7]

The automobile era demanded hard-surfaced roads. By the 1930s, mass transit was on the decline almost everywhere, as Americans seemingly preferred the convenience, flexibility, and privacy of automobile travel. Eyeing the enormous untapped urban market, the automobile industry had a major interest in express highways and in federal highway legislation. In particular, the extremely popular General Motors Futurama exhibit at the 1939 New York World's Fair, as Mark I. Foster noted, "stimulated public thinking in favor of massive urban freeway building." Norman Bel Geddes, the designer of the Futurama exhibit, also promoted the idea of a "national motorways system connecting all cities with populations of more than one hundred thousand."[8]

By the end of the 1930s, Thomas MacDonald and the BPR pushed for an interregional highway system linking the nation's largest metropolitan areas, an idea given initial form by President Franklin D. Roosevelt himself. According to Secretary of Agriculture Henry A. Wallace, at a 1938 meeting with MacDonald, the president sketched out on a map "a system of east-west, north-south transcontinental highways" and then requested that MacDonald make a report on the possibilities of building such a highway system. The BPR's subsequent report, *Toll Roads and Free Roads* (largely written by MacDonald and his assistant H. S. Fairbanks), completed in 1939, represented the first comprehensive effort to conceptualize what later became the Interstate Highway system. Significantly, the report acknowledged the obvious link between express highways and urban reconstruction. It made a strong case that highway planning should take place in the context of an ongoing program of slum clearance and urban redevelopment.[9]

Wallace reported to Roosevelt that the BPR's plan established nothing less than the basis for the complete physical rebuilding of American cities. The big problem, Wallace noted, was not transcontinental automobile traffic, but automobile congestion in the cities themselves. If new express highways penetrated and traversed the cities, traffic flow to the business centers would be facilitated. More than that, careful routing of these arterial highways could cut through and clear out blighted housing areas: "There exists at present around the cores of the cities, particularly of the older ones, a wide border of decadent and dying property which has become, or is in fact becoming, a slum area." Land acquisition in these slum areas for highway construction and urban redevelopment would result in "the elimination of unsightly and unsanitary districts where land values are constantly depreciating." As Wallace portrayed the situation, the BPR's highway construction plan could become a central element in the reconstruction and revitalization of the central cities.[10]

A second major highway report, *Interregional Highways*, was completed in 1944. It was prepared by the National Interregional Highway Committee, appointed by President Roosevelt, and headed by Thomas MacDonald. This report, which recommended an "interregional" highway system of 40,000 miles, actually mapped out a highway network that looks remarkably like the present Interstate Highway system. The 1944 report also made it clear that the new interregional or Interstate Highway system would penetrate the heart of metropolitan areas. Larger cities would be encircled by inner and outer beltways and traversed by radial expressways tying the urban system together. MacDonald believed these urban expressways essential to the future growth and development of the American city, especially modern slum clearance and urban reconstruction.[11]

Throughout the 1940s and into the early 1950s, MacDonald campaigned tirelessly for inner-city expressways that would clear out low-income housing and tenement districts, eliminating the "blighted districts contiguous to the very heart of the city." Dislocated urban residents, MacDonald suggested, could move to the new suburbs and commute to city jobs on new high-speed, multifunctional expressways.[12] In a 1947 speech to the U.S. Chamber of Commerce Conference on Urban Problems, MacDonald whimsically dismissed the inevitable housing destruction that accompanied urban expressway building: "It is a happy circumstance that living conditions for the family can be re-established and permit the social as well as economic decay at the heart of the cities to be converted to a public asset."[13]

To his credit, MacDonald also pushed for local planning policies and Congressional legislation requiring new housing construction for those displaced from their homes by expressway building. In an important statement in 1947, he made the case for relocation housing: "No matter how urgently a highway improvement may be needed, the homes of people who have nowhere to go should not be destroyed. Before dwellings are razed, new housing facilities should be provided for the dispossessed occupants." Ultimately, however, MacDonald's effort to forge a linkage between urban expressway construction and relocation housing was unsuccessful. In 1949, President Harry S. Truman rejected the coordination of highway and housing programs, citing anticipated high costs and difficulty of Congressional passage. By the early 1950s, the BPR had seemingly lost interest in the broader implications of highway building and focused instead on facilitating automobile and truck transportation. Highway engineers with their narrowly technical concerns were left in control of the BPR. MacDonald halted his speaking and writing crusade, and, after President Dwight D. Eisenhower failed to reappoint him director, he left the agency in 1953. Not until 1965, when much of the Interstate system had already been built, did the federal government require advance relocation housing for families and businesses displaced by Interstate Highway construction.[14]

Expressways and the Central Cities

The federal government rejected an urban policy that integrated highways and housing. However, other powerful interest groups were quick to recognize the implications of Interstate Highway construction at the cities' cores. Those interested at the time in the future of the central city—urban policymakers and planners, big city mayors, urban real estate interests, central city business groups—all sought a general rebuilding of the central cities during the contemplated postwar reconstruction. Urban expressway building was considered a necessary component of such urban policy and planning. The absence of any official interest in rebuilding inner-city housing for those displaced meant that huge sections of central-city land could be cleared for other uses. Expressway building was seen as a way of saving the central city from the creeping blight of an older and deteriorating housing stock. Because such housing accommodated mostly poor and minority residents, highway building often meant black removal from the central-city area. As early as 1949, one black housing official predicted—quite correctly, as it turned out—that "the real masters of urban redevelopment will be the forces intent on recapturing Negro living space for the 'right' people."[15]

Among the interest groups seeking to save the central business district, few were more important than the Urban Land Institute (ULI). Founded in 1936 to serve the interests of downtown real estate owners and developers, the ULI consistently pushed for central-city redevelopment. From the 1930s, downtown real estate professionals feared that suburbanization, and especially the decentralization of retailing, would ultimately sap the vitality of central-city economic activities. The automobile was largely to blame, because it both facilitated suburban growth and clogged downtown traffic arteries. As the respected urban planner and architect Victor Gruen put it in the mid-1950s, "the rotting of the core has set in in most American cities, in some cases progressing to an alarming degree." In the decade following World War II, the ULI's Central Business District Council focused on freeways as "the salvation of the central district, the core of every city."[16]

In a stream of pamphlets, newsletters, and technical bulletins, the Urban Land Institute sought to pave the way for central-city expressways. For James W. Rouse, a Baltimore real estate developer involved with the Urban Land Institute in the 1950s and later well known as a builder of "new towns" and festival marketplaces, the pattern of inner-city decay threatened the future of the central business district. According to Rouse, the solution for downtown America was clear: "Major expressways must be ripped through to the central core" as an integral aspect of extensive redevelopment efforts. Urban developer James H. Scheuer, in a 1957 ULI publication, envisioned inner belt expressways inevitably slicing through "great areas of our nation's worst slums." The ULI's monthly newsletter, *Urban Land*, urged urban governments to survey the "extent to which blighted areas may provide suitable highway routes." ULI consultant James W. Follin saw the 1956 Interstate Highway Act providing "wide open opportunity" to eliminate blighted housing and recapture central-city land for redevelopment. For the ULI, expressway building promised the salvation of the central business district.[17]

Using highways for slum clearance and urban redevelopment excited representatives of other interest groups. The American Road Builders' Association (ARBA) served as the major trade association for the nation's highway construction firms. As early as 1949, in a letter to President Truman, the ARBA defended the use of highway construction in slum clearance. Urban express highways, the ARBA contended, were necessary to alleviate traffic congestion, but through proper right-of-way planning they also could "contribute in a substantial manner to the elimination of slum and deteriorated areas." The elimination of urban slums would stimulate downtown businesses, contribute to an appreciation of property values, and counter the threat posed by slum housing to "the public health, safety, morals, and welfare of the nation." Similarly, as early as 1943 the American Concrete Institute (ACI), which had an obvious interest in highway construction, championed the use of urban expressways in "the elimination of slums and blighted areas." Build highways through the city slums, urged the ARBA and the ACI, and solve the problems of urban America.[18]

The automobile lobby joined the chorus touting the role of expressways in rebuilding urban America. Typically, in a 1956 pamphlet entitled *What Freeways Mean to Your City*, the Automotive Safety Foundation assured readers that freeways were desirable, beneficial, and beautiful; they stimulated rising land values and prevented "the spread of blight and . . . slums." Forward-looking communities used "the transportation potential of freeways to speed redevelopment of run-down sections along sound lines and to prevent deterioration of desirable sections." Similarly, in a 1962 article, the Highway Research Board contended that Interstate Highways were "eating out slums" and "reclaiming blighted areas." The inner-city freeway, in short, represented a "positive social good," especially if it was routed through blighted slum neighborhoods that might be reclaimed for more productive civic uses.[19]

The downtown developers, the automobile lobby, highway officials and experts, and planners and politicians at every level shared the urban expressway dream. Echoing his boss Thomas MacDonald, the BPR's urban road division

chief, Joseph Barnett, suggested in 1946 that properly located urban expressways would help immeasurably in "the stabilization of trade and values in the
principal or central business district." New York's Robert Moses pushed such
ideas vigorously. In a 1954 statement to the President's Advisory Committee
on a National Highway Program (generally known as the Clay Committee),
Moses argued that new urban expressways "must go right through cities and
not around them" if they were to accomplish their purpose. Expressways not
only addressed urban traffic problems, but through proper coordination they
could advance slum clearance plans and other aspects of urban redevelopment.
Moses concluded somewhat prophetically that city expressway mileage would
be "the hardest to locate, the most difficult to clear, the most expensive to
acquire and build, and the most controversial from the point of view of selfish
and shortsighted opposition." In other words, people whose homes would be
taken for expressways represented a highway problem, not a housing problem.[20]

Like New York, Detroit in the 1940s found expressways an "essential step
in slum clearance" that would "open up blighted areas and fit them for more
productive uses." Detroit's depressed inner-city expressways, Mayor Albert E.
Cobo told the Clay Committee in 1954, not only enhanced property values
along their right-of-way, but also were positively "a picture of beauty." A writer
in the *Western Construction News* in 1943 contended that urban expressways, "usually and best built through blighted areas," would solve traffic congestion, provide postwar employment, and revitalize city centers through slum clearance. A
1950 plan for expressways in Cleveland predicated revitalization of the central
business district on redevelopment of blighted "central residential areas." In the
early 1950s, Kansas City's city manager, L. P. Cookingham, stated that "no
large city can hope for a real future" without expressways that cleared slums
and preserved the central business district.[21]

Working within federal traffic engineering guidelines, highway builders at
state and local levels routed new urban expressways in directions of their own
choosing. Local agendas often dictated such decisions; the result was to drive
the Interstates through black and poor neighborhoods. Urban blacks were
heavily concentrated in areas with the oldest and most dilapidated housing,
where land acquisition costs were relatively low, and where organized political
opposition was weakest. Displaying a "two birds with one stone" mentality,
cities and states sought to route Interstate Highways through slum neighborhoods, using federal highway money to reclaim downtown urban real estate.
Inner-city slums could be cleared, blacks removed to more distant second-
ghetto areas, central business districts redeveloped, and transportation woes
solved all at the same time—and mostly at federal expense.[22]

It seems clear, then, that the Interstates were conceived of as more than just traffic arteries. To be sure, the highway engineers in the BPR and at the state level were interested in building highways that would move traffic efficiently, although many of them also shared the "two birds" theory. But business interests and government officials in the cities conceived of expressways as part of a larger redevelopment of the city centers. This rebuilding of the central city in many cases came at the expense of African Americans in the inner cities, whose neighborhoods—not just housing but churches, business districts, even entire urban renewal areas—were destroyed in the process of Interstate construction. In other instances, highway builders routed urban Interstates through white working-class and ethnic neighborhoods, historic districts, and parks, but building an expressway through a black community was the most common choice in the Interstate-building era.

Highway builders rarely mentioned African Americans specifically in their

24. Expressways were frequently used to eliminate "blighted" (i.e., black) neighborhoods and to segregate whites from blacks. This photograph of Chicago's Dan Ryan Expressway shows the demarcation line that became a common feature of many American cities. To the right are high-rise public housing units for blacks; to the left are white, working class bungalows.

discussions about blight and slums. The massive migration of southern blacks to northern and midwestern cities was well underway during the war years. Black newcomers moved into urban neighborhoods abandoned by whites as they departed for the suburbs. Southern cities already had large black populations. When the highwaymen talked about clearing out central-city blight in the postwar era, everyone knew what they meant. The intent, the goal, was clear to most, even if it was rarely stated directly. Their intentions were clear from their statements, actions, and policies—and the visible consequences of the highways they built are the best evidence of their intended goals.

Expressways and Inner-City Housing Destruction

From the late 1950s and well into the 1960s, urban expressway construction meant massive family dislocation and housing and community destruction. State highway engineers and consultants, usually working with local civic elites, determined the Interstate routes into the central cities. The routes they chose were consistent with perceptions and policies of the past. Highway builders had traditionally made clearing out housing blight at the center of the cities one of their goals. By the mid-1950s, after a decade and a half of heavy black migration into urban areas, most of those inner-city neighborhoods targeted by the highway planners' maps were predominantly African American. Consequently, most American cities faced serious community disruption and racial strife as the Interstate expressways ripped through urban neighborhoods and leveled wide swaths of inner-city housing. A few examples should serve to demonstrate the destructive impact of urban expressways.

In Miami, Florida, state highway planners and local officials deliberately routed Interstate-95 directly through the inner-city black community of Overtown. An alternative route using an abandoned railroad corridor was rejected, as the highway planners noted, to provide "ample room for the future expansion of the central business district in a westerly direction," a goal of the local business elite since the 1930s. Even before the expressway was built, and in the absence of any relocation planning, some in Miami's white and black press asked: "What About the Negroes Uprooted by Expressway?" The question remained unanswered, and when the downtown leg of the expressway was completed in the mid-1960s, it tore through the center of Overtown, wiping out massive amounts of housing as well as Overtown's main business district, the commercial and cultural heart of black Miami. One massive expressway interchange took up twenty square blocks of densely settled land and destroyed the housing of about 10,000 people. By the end of the 1960s, Overtown had become an urban wasteland dominated by the physical presence of the expressway. Little remained of the neighborhood to recall its days as a thriving center of black community life, when it was known as the Harlem of the South.[23]

In Nashville, Tennessee, highway planners went out of their way to put a "kink" in the urban link of Interstate-40 as it passed through the city. The expressway route gouged a concrete swath through the North Nashville black community, destroying hundreds of homes and businesses and dividing what was left of the neighborhood. The decision for the I-40 route had been made quietly in 1957 at a nonpublic meeting of white business leaders and state highway officials. By 1967, after years of denying that the expressway would adversely affect the community, the state highway department began acquiring right of way, displacing residents, and bulldozing the route. Outraged blacks in Nashville organized the Nashville I-40 Steering Committee to mount an opposition campaign, charging that routing an Interstate expressway through a black community could be legally classified as racial discrimination.[24]

The I-40 Steering Committee won a temporary restraining order in 1967, the first time a highway project had been halted by claims of racial discrimination. The Steering Committee's attorney alleged that "the highway was arbitrarily routed through the North Nashville ghetto solely because of the racial and low socio-economic character of the ghetto and its occupants without regard to the widespread adverse effects on the land uses adjoining the route." Ultimately, the I-40 Steering Committee lost its case in federal court, and the I-40 expressway was completed through Nashville's black community. However, the legal controversy in Nashville starkly revealed, if not a racial purpose, at least a racial outcome experienced by many cities.[25]

In New Orleans, enraged freeway opponents successfully waged a long battle against an eight-lane elevated expressway along the Mississippi River and through the edges of the city's historic French Quarter. The Riverfront Expressway originated in a 1946 plan proposed for New Orleans by the New York highway builder Robert Moses. The planned expressway was part of an inner-city beltway of the type that Moses favored and that the BPR had incorporated into its Interstate planning. After several years of hot debate and controversy, historic preservationists succeeded in fighting off the Riverfront Expressway plan. In 1969, the Department of Transportation secretary, John A. Volpe, terminated the I-10 loop through the Vieux Carré.[26]

However, while white New Orleans residents were fending off the highway builders, the nearby mid-city black community along North Claiborne Avenue was less successful. Highway builders there leveled a wide swath for

Interstate-10. At the center of an old and stable black Creole community, boasting a long stretch of magnificent old oak trees, North Claiborne served a variety of community functions such as picnics, festivals, and parades. The highway builders rammed an elevated expressway through the neighborhood before anyone could organize or protest. Some of the preservationists who fought the Riverfront Expressway gladly suggested North Claiborne as an alternative. By the 1970s, Interstate-10 in New Orleans rolled through a devastated black community, a concrete jungle left in the shadows by a massive elevated highway.[27]

Interstate construction in Montgomery, Alabama, also devastated a black community. In 1961, state highway officials recommended a route for Interstate-85 that traversed the city's major African American community. George W. Curry, a black minister and head of a Property Owners Committee, sent a petition with 1,150 signatures to local, state, and federal highway officials protesting that the expressway route would destroy an estimated 300 homes in black Montgomery and proposing an alternative route through mostly vacant land. At a public hearing, 650 people stood up to signify their opposition to the expressway. Curry argued that the route "was racially motivated to uproot a neighborhood of Negro leaders." An internal BPR "memorandum for record" spelled out the details:

> Rev. Curry alleges that the routing of this highway will uproot a Negro community, which has no place to relocate, and two Negro churches. It is claimed that there is a nearby alternate route which would cost $30,000 less. Rev. Curry charges that the proposed routing of the highway is designed by State and local officials to purposely dislodge this Negro community where many of the leaders of the fight for desegregation in Montgomery reside. Rev. Curry said that in a recent conversation with a Mr. Sam Englehardt, Alabama's Highway Director, Mr. Englehardt stated that it was his intention to get Rev. Abernathy's church.

Ralph Abernathy, a close adviser of Martin Luther King in the Montgomery bus boycott of 1956 and in other desegregation struggles, also complained about the Interstate-85 route in a telegram to President John F. Kennedy in October 1961. Abernathy's home stood in the path of the highway project, obviously targeted by Alabama highway officials.[28]

In Birmingham, Alabama, where three Interstates intersected, a black citizens' committee complained to the Alabama state highway department and the BPR in 1960 that proposed Interstate freeways "would almost completely wipe out two old Negro communities [in] eastern Birmingham with their 13 churches and three schools." Moreover, the public hearing held on the highway proposal had been segregated, and blacks were unable to present their grievances.[29] In 1963, as the start of Interstate construction neared in Birmingham, opposition flared again in the city's black community. A resident, James Hutchinson, protested to Alabama Senator John Sparkman that the Interstate (I-59) "bisects an exclusive colored residential area. In addition, it has a large interchange in the heart of this area." In the early days of the Interstates, the racial routing of the Birmingham expressway noted by Hutchison was rather typical. So was the response of Federal Highway Administrator Rex M. Whitton to Senator Sparkman. The route had been chosen by the Alabama state highway department and approved by the Bureau of Public Roads, Whitton wrote, "based on a thorough evaluation of all engineering, economic, and sociological factors involved." If that was the case, then it would seem that the destruction of the Birmingham black community was indeed a planned event.[30]

A similar pattern of planned destruction took place in Camden, New Jersey, bisected in the 1960s by Interstate-95, with the usual consequences for low-income housing. In 1968, the Department of Housing and Urban Development sent a task force to Camden to study the impact of highway building and urban renewal. It found that minorities made up 85 percent of the families displaced by the North-South Freeway—some 1,093 of a total of 1,289 displaced families. For the five-year period 1963 to 1967, about 3,000 low-income housing units were destroyed in Camden, but only about 100 new low-income housing units were built during that period.[31]

The Civil Rights Division of the New Jersey State Attorney General's Office prepared a second report on Camden. Entitled "Camden, New Jersey: A City in Crisis," the report made a similar case for the racial implications of expressway construction in Camden. As the report stated: "It is obvious from a glance at the renewal and transit plans that an attempt is being made to eliminate the Negro and Puerto Rican ghetto areas by two different methods. The first is building highways that benefit white suburbanites, facilitating their movement from the suburbs to work and back; the second is by means of urban renewal projects which produce middle and upper income housing and civic centers without providing adequate, decent, safe, and sanitary housing, as the law provides, at prices which the relocatee can afford." The central argument of the New Jersey civil rights report was that this outcome was purposely planned and carried out.[32]

The experience of Camden during the expressway-building era of the late 1950s and 1960s was duplicated in cities throughout the nation. A Kansas City, Missouri, midtown freeway originally slated to pass through an affluent neighborhood ultimately sliced through a racially integrated Model City area. It destroyed 1,800 buildings there and displaced several thousand people.[33] In Charlotte, North Carolina, Interstate-77 leveled an African American community, including four black schools.[34] Highway officials pushed ahead with a three-and-one-half-mile inner-city expressway in Pittsburgh, even though it was expected to dislocate 5,800 people.[35] In St. Paul, Minnesota, Interstate-94 cut directly through the city's black community, displacing one-seventh of St. Paul's black population. As one critic put it, "very few blacks lived in Minnesota, but the road builders found them."[36] Despite the fact that the Century Freeway in Los Angeles would dislocate 3,550 families, 117 businesses, and numerous schools and churches, mainly in black Watts and Willowbrook, the Department of Transportation approved the new expressway in 1968.[37]

The story was much the same in other cities. In Florida, Interstates in Tampa, Saint Petersburg, Jacksonville, Orlando, and Pensacola routinely ripped through, divided, and dislocated black neighborhoods.[38] In Columbus, Ohio, an inner-city expressway leveled an entire black community.[39] In Milwaukee, the North-South Expressway cleared a path through sixteen blocks in the city's black community, uprooting 600 families and ultimately intensifying patterns of racial segregation.[40] A network of expressways in Cleveland displaced some 19,000 people by the early 1970s.[41] In Atlanta, according to the historian Ronald H. Bayor, highways were purposely planned and built "to sustain racial ghettos and control black migration" in the metropolitan area.[42]

African Americans were not alone in suffering the destructive consequences of urban expressway construction. In Chicago, a whole range of ethnic neighborhoods gave way to expressways as they headed south, southwest, west, and northwest out of the downtown Loop area.[43] In Boston, an inner-city expressway tore through and destroyed the Chinatown district and part of the city's Italian North End.[44] In New York City, the Cross-Bronx Expressway ripped through a massive "wall of apartment houses" that stretched for miles, gouging "a huge trench" across a primarily working-class Jewish community.[45] As one transportation specialist suggested, "almost every major U.S. city bears the scars of communities split apart by the nearly impenetrable barrier of concrete."[46]

The devastating human and social consequences of urban expressway construction ultimately produced widespread opposition and citizen activism. Beginning in San Francisco in 1959, freeway revolts gradually spread throughout the country by the late 1960s.[47] Although state and federal highway planners coldly accepted citizen opposition as one of the costs of building roads, by the mid-1960s Congress became more sensitive to the political backlash created by massive housing destruction and the difficulties of relocating displaced families.

Political pressure on top staffers in the Federal Highway Administration and the new U.S. Department of Transportation (created in 1966) gradually led to a softening of the narrowly technocratic engineering mentality that had dominated the Bureau of Public Roads. As a result, some routes were altered to avoid neighborhood destruction, while other expressway projects were canceled altogether. In addition, new Congressional legislation required that for highway projects after 1965, relocation housing had to be provided in advance of construction. By that time, however, most of the urban Interstates had already been put into place; most of the damage had already been done.[48]

Conclusion

The historical record has demonstrated that highways and housing were closely linked in postwar urban policymaking. Early Interstate advocates conceived of new urban expressways as a means of rebuilding the central city by clearing away blighted housing. The Bureau of Public Roads advocated such ideas as early as the 1930s, and many of the pre-1956 urban expressways put these ideas into practice. After the landmark 1956 Interstate Highway legislation, highway officials at every level implemented expressway plans that destroyed enormous amounts of low-income, inner-city housing, especially in black neighborhoods where land acquisition costs were generally cheaper and where political opposition was minimal, particularly in southern cities. Thus, massive housing destruction—planned destruction—was the natural concomitant of expressway building in the central cities.

One thing the highway planners did not think through carefully, however, was where the hundreds of thousands of dislocated African Americans would find new housing. Some large-scale, high-rise public housing projects of the 1950s, such as the Robert Taylor Homes in Chicago or the Pruitt-Igoe Project in Saint Louis, absorbed many dislocated families, but highways and urban renewal were destroying more inner-city housing than was being built. In some places, public housing construction slowed in the politically reactionary 1950s. The new lily-white suburbs that sprouted in the postwar automobile era were unwelcoming to blacks. Essentially, most uprooted African American families found new housing in nearby low- and middle income white residential areas, which themselves were experiencing the transition from white to black. The expressway building of the 1950s and 1960s ultimately produced the much larger, more spatially isolated, and more intensely segregated second ghettos characteristic of the late twentieth century.

Notes

1. Mark I. Gelfand, *A Nation of Cities: The Federal Government and Urban America, 1933–1965* (New York: Oxford University Press, 1975), 222.

2. National Commission on Urban Problems, *Building the American City* (Washington, D.C.: U.S. Government Printing Office, 1969), 81; U.S. House of Representatives, Committee on Public Works, *Study of Compensation and Assistance for Persons Affected by Real Property Acquisition in Federal and Federally Assisted Programs* (Washington, D.C.: U.S. Government Printing Office, 1965), 24, 26, 105; Michael Sumich-ast and Norman Farquar, *Demolition and Other Factors in Housing Replacement Demand* (Washington, D.C.: National Association of Home Builders, 1967), 47–48, 76.

3. National Commission on Urban Problems, *Building the American City*, 91.

4. John P. McCollum to Albert M. Cole, May 23, 1957, Housing and Home Finance Agency Records (hereafter cited as HHFA Records), RG 207, Subject Correspondence Files, Albert Cole, Administrator, 1953–58, Box 18, National Archives II, College Park, Maryland.

5. William H. Claire, "Urban Renewal and Transportation," *Traffic Quarterly* 13 (July 1959): 417; Thomas H. MacDonald, "The Case for Urban Expressways," *The American City* 62, June 1947, 92–93; Robert Moses, "Slums and City Planning," *Atlantic Monthly* 175, January 1945, 63–68.

6. On the second ghetto, see Arnold R. Hirsch, *Making the Second Ghetto: Race and Housing in Chicago, 1940–1960* (Cambridge: Cambridge University Press, 1983), esp. 1–39; Raymond A. Mohl, "Making the Second Ghetto in Metropolitan Miami, 1940–1960," *Journal of Urban History* 21 (March 1995): 395–427.

7. W. Stull Holt, *The Bureau of Public Roads: Its History, Activities, and Organization* (Baltimore: Johns Hopkins University Press, 1923); Bruce E. Seely, *Building the American Highway System: Engineers as Policy Makers* (Philadelphia: Temple University Press, 1987).

8. Mark I. Foster, *From Streetcar to Superhighway: American City Planners and Urban Transportation, 1900–1940* (Philadelphia: Temple University Press, 1981), 153; Norman Bel Geddes, *Magic Motorways* (New York: Random House, 1940).

9. Henry A. Wallace to Franklin D. Roosevelt, February 13, 1939, copy in Bureau of Public Roads Records (hereafter cited as BPR Records), RG 30, Classified Central Files, Box 4107, National Archives II, College Park, Maryland; "Report of the Chief of BPR on the Feasibility of a System of Superhighways," undated typescript [1939], BPR Records, RG 30, Classified Central Files, Box 1949; U.S. Bureau of Public Roads (BPR), *Toll Roads and Free Roads*, U.S. House of Representatives, 76th Congress, 1st Session, 1939, House Document No. 272. The Department of Agriculture initially administered the Bureau of Public Roads, but in 1939 the BPR was transferred to the newly established Federal Works Agency. During the Truman administration, the BPR was shifted again, this time to the Department of Commerce.

10. Wallace to Roosevelt, February 13, 1939, BPR Records, RG 30, Classified Central Files, Box 4107.

11. U.S. National Interregional Highway Committee, *Interregional Highways* (Washington, D.C.: U.S. Government Printing Office, 1944); Thomas H. MacDonald to Albert B. Chandler, with accompanying notes, November 18, 1943, BPR Records, RG 30, Classified Central Files, Box 1892.

12. Thomas H. MacDonald, "Proposed Interregional Highway System as It Affects Cities," January 21, 1943, Thomas H. MacDonald Speeches, U.S. Department of Transportation Library, Washington, D.C.; Thomas H. MacDonald, "The Case for Urban Expressways," *The American City* 62, June 1947, 92–93; idem, "Future of the Highways," *U.S. News and World Report*, December 29, 1950, 30–33.

13. Thomas H. MacDonald, "The Federal-Aid Highway Program and Its Relation to Cities," September 11, 1947, speech typescript, BPR Records, RG 30, Classified Central Files, 1912–59, Box 1942.

14. MacDonald, "The Case for Urban Expressways," 92–93; Gelfand, *A Nation of Cities*, 225–30,

quotation on 226; Mark H. Rose, *Interstate: Express Highway Politics, 1941–1956* (Lawrence: Regents Press of Kansas, 1979), 61–62.

15. George B. Nesbitt, "Relocating Negroes from Urban Slum Clearance Sites," *Land Economics* 25 (August 1949): 285; George B. Nesbitt, "Break Up the Black Ghetto?" *The Crisis* 56 (February 1949): 48–52.

16. Victor Gruen, "The City in the Automobile Age," *Perspectives* 16 (Summer 1956): 48; Hal Burton, *The City Fights Back* (New York: Citadel, 1954), 78.

17. James W. Rouse, "Will Downtown Face Up to Its Future?" *Urban Land* 16 (February 1957): 4; James H. Scheuer, "Highways and People: The Housing Impact of the Highway Program," in *The New Highways: Challenge to the Metropolitan Region*, Technical Bulletin no. 31 (Washington, D.C.: Urban Land Institute, 1957); James W. Follin, "Coordination of Urban Renewal with the Urban Highway Program Offers Major Economies in Cost and Time," *Urban Land* 15 (December 1956): 3, 5.

18. Charles M. Upham to President Truman, February 16, 1949, and accompanying "Resolution of the American Road Builders' Association," BPR Records, RG 30, Classified Central Files, 1912–50, Box 183; "Planning for the Postwar Period: A Report of the Committee on Postwar Planning of the American Concrete Institute," n.d. (c. 1943), BPR Records, RG 30, Classified Central Files, Box 1892.

19. Automotive Safety Foundation, *What Freeways Mean to Your City* (Washington, D.C.: Automotive Safety Foundation, 1956), 32; Floyd I. Theil, "Social Effects of Modern Highway Transportation," *Highway Research Board Bulletin*, no. 327 (1962): 6–7; Gary T. Schwartz, "Urban Freeways and the Interstate System," *Southern California Law Review* 49 (March 1976): 484–85.

20. Joseph Barnett, "Express Highway Planning in Metropolitan Areas," *Transactions of the American Society of Civil Engineers* 112 (1947): 650; Robert Moses to Thomas H. MacDonald, June 11, 1946, BPR Records, RG 30, Classified Central Files, Box 2662, Statement of Robert Moses, Hearings, President's Advisory Committee on a National Highway Program, October 7, 1954, 47–51, in BPR Records, RG 30, Records Relating to National Highway and Defense Highway Programs, 1940–55, Box 1.

21. G. Donald Kennedy, *A Comprehensive Plan of Motorways for Detroit* (Lansing: Michigan State Highway Department, 1941), 14–15, copy in BPR Records, RG 30, Classified Central Files, Box 2448; Statement of Albert E. Cobo, Hearings, President's Advisory Committee on a National Highway Program, October 8, 1954, 249–75, in BPR Records, RG 30, Records Relating to National Highway and Defense Highway Programs, 1940–55, Box 1; Lynn Atkinson, "Freeways Solve Two Problems," *Western Construction News* (January 1943): 20–25, quotation on 22, reprint in BPR Records, RG 30, Classified Central Files, Box 1944; William B. Blaser, "Right-of-Way and Its Effect on Design," Proceedings of the Urban Highway Design Conference, February 13–17, 1950, mimeo, in BPR Records, RG 30, Reports of Highway Studies, Box 19; L. P. Cookingham, "Expressways and the Central Business District," *American Planning and Civic Annual* (1954): 140–46.

22. An extensive literature substantiates these generalizations. See, for example, Jon C. Teaford, *The Rough Road to Renaissance: Urban Revitalization in America, 1940–1985* (Baltimore: Johns Hopkins University Press, 1990); Bernard J. Frieden and Lynne B. Sagalyn, *Downtown, Inc.: How America Rebuilds Cities* (Cambridge, Mass.: MIT Press, 1989), 15–37.

23. Raymond A. Mohl, "Race and Space in the Modern City: Interstate-95 and the Black Community in Miami," in Arnold R. Hirsch and Raymond A. Mohl, eds., *Urban Policy in Twentieth-Century America* (New Brunswick: Rutgers University Press, 1993), 100–158.

24. Richard J. Whalen, "The American Highway: Do We Know Where We're Going?" *Saturday Evening Post*, December 14, 1968, 22–27, 54–64; John F. Seley, "The Kink in Nashville's Interstate-40," in John E. Seley, *The Politics of Public-Facility Planning* (Lexington, Mass.: Lexington Books, 1983), 57–66; Ben Kelley, *The Pavers and the Paved* (New York: Donald W. Brown, 1971), 97–107.

25. "Bias Is Charged in Highway Suit," *The New York Times*, November 27, 1967; Alan S. Boyd to Flournoy A. Coles Jr., April 8, 1968, Federal Highway Administration Records (hereafter cited as FHWA Records), RG 406, Central Correspondence, 1968–69, Box 131.

26. Priscilla Dunhill, "An Expressway Named Destruction," *Architectural Forum* 126 (March 1967): 54–59; Richard O. Baumbach Jr. and William E. Borah, *The Second Battle of New Orleans: A History of the Vieux Carré Riverfront-Expressway Controversy* (Tuscaloosa: University of Alabama Press, 1981).

27. *Vieux Carré Courier*, January 22, 1965; Claiborne Avenue Design Team, *I-10 Multi-Use Study* (New Orleans: Claiborne Avenue Design Team, 1976).

28. George W. Curry and the Property Owners Committee, A Petition Appeal, April 28, 1960, BPR Records, RG 30, General Correspondence, 1912–65, Box 1665; Berl I. Bernhard to Hyman Bookbinder, June 29, 1961, BPR Records, RG 30, General Correspondence, 1912–65, Box 1664; John W. Roxborough, Memorandum for Record, June 23, 1961, BPR Records, RG 30, General Correspondence, 1912–65, Box 1664; Ralph D. Abernathy to John F. Kennedy, October 3, 1961, telegram, BPR Records, RG 30, General Correspondence, Box 1664.

29. Lala Palmer to Alabama State Highway Department, April 11, 1960, telegram, BPR Records, RG 30, General Correspondence, 1912–65, Box 1665; Joe Davis to Luther Hodges, February 17, 1961, BPR Records, RG 30, General Correspondence, 1912–65, Box 1664.

30. James Hutchinson to John Sparkman, November 3, 1963, FHWA Records, RG 406, Federal-Aid System Correspondence, Box 3; Rex M. Whitton to John Sparkman, November 20, 1963, FHWA Records, RG 406, Federal-Aid System Correspondence, Box 3.

31. Steven H. Leleiko to Lowell K. Bridewell, December 4, 1968, FHWA Records, RG 406, F. C. Turner Files, Box 7.

32. Ibid.

33. Richard Leverone to Lowell K. Bridewell, May 16, 1968, FHWA Records, RG 406, L. K. Bridewell Files, Box 11.

34. *Charlotte Observer*, May 14, May 15, 1968, clippings, in FHWA Records, RG 406, L. K. Bridewell Files, Box 7.

35. Richard Leverone to Lowell K. Bridewell, May 21, 1968, FHWA Records, RG 406, L. K. Bridewell Files, Box 11.

36. Alan A. Aultshuler, *The City Planning Process: A Political Analysis* (Ithaca: Cornell University Press, 1965), 17–83; F. James Davis, "The Effects of a Freeway Displacement on Racial Housing Segregation in a Northern City," *Phylon* 26 (Fall 1965): 209–15; Frieden and Sagalyn, *Downtown, Inc.*, 28–29.

37. F. C. Turner to Lowell K. Bridewell, July 19, 1967, FHWA Records, RG 406, Central Correspondence, 1968–69, Box 140; Lowell K. Bridewell to Gordon C. Luce, March 20, 1968, FHWA Records, RG 406, Central Correspondence, 1968–69, Box 140; Kathleen Armstrong, "Litigating the Freeway Revolt: *Keith v Volpe*," *Ecology Law Journal* 2 (Winter 1972): 761–99.

38. Mohl, "Race and Space in the Modern City," 135.

39. Mark H. Rose and Bruce E. Seely, "Getting the Interstate Built: Road Engineers and the Implementation of Public Policy, 1955–1985," *Journal of Policy History* 2 (1990): 37.

40. Patricia A. House, "Relocation of Families Displaced by Expressway Development: Milwaukee Case Study," *Land Economics* 46 (February 1970): 75–78.

41. "Toward the Postindustrial City: 1930–1980," in David D. Van Tassel and John J. Grabowski, eds., *The Encyclopedia of Cleveland History* (Bloomington: Indiana University Press, 1987), xlix–li.

42. Ronald H. Bayor, "Roads to Racial Segregation: Atlanta in the Twentieth Century," *Journal of Urban History* 15 (November 1988): 3–21.

43. Elliott Arthur Pavlos, "Chicago's Crosstown: A Case Study in Urban Expressways," in Stephen Gale and Eric G. Moore, eds., *The Manipulated City* (Chicago: Maaroufa Press, 1975), 255–61.

44. Kenneth R. Geiser, *Urban Transportation Decision Making: Political Processes of Urban Freeway Controversies* (Cambridge, Mass.: Department of Urban Studies and Planning, Massachusetts Institute of Technology, 1970), 258–64; Alan Lupo, Frank Colcord, and Edmund P. Fowler, *Rites of Way: The Politics of Transportation in Boston and the U.S. City* (Boston: Little, Brown, 1971).

45. Robert A. Caro, *The Power Broker: Robert Moses and the Fall of New York* (New York: Knopf, 1974), 839–94; Marshall Berman, *All That Is Solid Melts into Air: The Experience of Modernity* (New York: Simon and Schuster, 1982), 290–312; Jill Jonnes, *We're Still Here: The Rise, Fall, and Resurrection of the South Bronx* (Boston: Atlantic Monthly Press, 1986), 117–26.

46. David Hodge, "Social Impacts of Urban Transportation Decisions: Equity Issues," in Susan Hanson, ed., *The Geography of Urban Transportation* (New York: Guilford, 1986), 303.

47. William H. Lathrop Jr., "The San Francisco Freeway Revolt," *Transportation Engineering Journal of the American Society of Civil Engineers* 97 (February 1971): 133–43; "The Revolt Against Big City Expressways," *U.S. News and World Report* 52, January 1, 1962, 48–51; James Nathan Miller, "We Must Stop Choking Our Cities," *Reader's Digest* 89, August 1966, 37–41; Priscilla Dunhill, "When Highways and Cities Collide," *City* 1 (July 1967): 48–54; "The War over Urban Expressways," *Business Week*, March 11, 1967, 4–5; Jack Linville, "Troubled Urban Interstates," *Nation's Cities* 8 (December 1970): 8–11; Juan Cameron, "How the Interstate Changed the Face of the Nation," *Fortune* 84, July 1971, 78–81, 124–25; and, for a general critique of the automobile culture, Jane Holtz Kay, *Asphalt Nation: How the Automobile Took Over America and How We Can Take It Back* (New York: Crown, 1997).

48. Raymond A. Mohl, "Federal Highway Policy and Housing Impacts, 1930s to the 1960s" (Unpublished research report for Poverty and Race Research Action Council, December 31, 1996), 60–69.

Jimmy Carter, Patricia Roberts Harris, and Housing Policy in the Age of Limits

JOHN F. BAUMAN

In 1976, newly elected President Jimmy Carter inherited the wages of federal urban housing, highway, and renewal programs, which, as Arnold Hirsch and Raymond Mohl have shown in earlier chapters, took a costly toll on the urban housing supply, further benighted public housing, helped fracture the New Deal political coalition, and hardened public animosity toward all liberal urban programs. Pessimism about the urban future enveloped cities in 1976. Especially among the urban working class, this despair was deepened by the macroeconomic changes overwhelming the nation in the mid-1970s. Globalization, for one, plunged the nation's share of world economic output from 35 percent in 1960 to 22 percent in 1980, eroding urban economies and rendering the United States more dependent than ever on imports and exports. Deindustrialization greatly accelerated in the 1970s as industrial firms left older manufacturing cities such as Philadelphia for the suburbs, the sunbelt, or low-wage foreign countries. Stagflation (an implacable combination of rising inflation and high unemployment, which bewildered economists schooled to believe that inflation remedied unemployment), along with the energy crisis, pummeled already reeling cities. These forces rent the already frayed urban social and political fabric, dividing it between a largely white and youthful technical, financial, managerial, and professional class seeking shelter in fashionable historic districts federally supported by tax credits and rehabilitation loans, and a growing, low-paid, often non-white, service sector nestled in old streetcar suburbs eviscerated in the 1970s and 1980s by epidemic housing abandonment. It was amid these later war-torn regions of American cities, North Philadelphia, the South Bronx, Watts, that the sociologist William Julius Wilson discovered a growing underclass that he preferred to call the "Truly Disadvantaged."[1]

The urban crisis seemingly called for a massive New Deal/Great Society–scale rescue mission. But since 1968, argues the historian Thomas Sugrue, the United States had entered a post–New Deal era, and the Carter administration represented an early milestone in this retreat from Neo-Keynsian economic solutions. Neo-Keynsians preached that large-scale government-spending programs such as urban renewal, Model Cities, and public housing fueled economic growth that produced jobs and general prosperity. Carter challenged what he saw as the Great Society "excesses" of the 1960s without surrendering his compassion for the dispossessed. He openly advocated the more limited government of the small Georgia town. Addressing Congress in 1978, Carter denied that government could "solve our problems, . . . It cannot eliminate poverty, or provide a bountiful economy, or reduce inflation, or save our cities, or cure illiteracy, or provide energy."[2]

This chapter explores the Carter housing policy, focusing especially on the actions of Carter's dynamic Secretary of Housing and Urban Development, Patricia Roberts Harris. In doing so, it examines such issues as the changing role of the state, which under Carter moved more forcefully to enlist the private sector in the city-rebuilding process. It looks at the Carter administration's emphasis on housing as part of "targeted" neighborhood revitalization, and the problem of dwindling low-income housing supply and affordability in an era when the federal government boldly retreated from its thirty-year-old commitment of "a decent home and a decent environment for all America."

Jimmy Carter and Urban Malaise

Jimmy Carter's 1976 presidential campaign had reluctantly engaged the issue of the urban crisis mainly in seeking votes in the northeastern cities where with the mayor by his side he pledged to be a "friendly ally and a partner in the White House." He also promised that he would shift or "orient" government monies "toward the more deprived areas, instead of to the suburbs where most of the political influence lies."[3] He downplayed his visceral preference for frugality, and he did not mention the sacrifice he expected from Americans in the

25. Patricia Roberts Harris, Secretary of Housing and Urban Development (HUD) during the Carter administration. Although Carter and Harris did not always see eye to eye, together they signaled an important shift away from the New Deal and Great Society visions for housing policy.

coming war against inflation. Asked about his views on housing and urban policy, Carter told the *Journal of Housing* that unlike Nixon and Ford, he believed that "public . . . and subsidized housing are not dirty words. . . . Traditional public housing can work when directed by professional local housing authorities, . . . and direct subsidies are essential for constructing and rehabilitating new low and moderate income housing and stimulating the construction industry."[4] These and other liberal views on urban rebuilding won large electoral victories in New York, Boston, Philadelphia, and other large cities, gaining him the allegiance of mayors such as Pittsburgh's Pete Flaherty.

While exciting unfounded liberal hopes for a new Great Society, Carter presaged the centrist ideology of the Democratic Party of the 1990s represented by President Bill Clinton, rather than the Lyndon Johnson tradition. Carter campaigned as a Washington outsider, unfettered by political apron strings, free to purge bureaucratic detritus. His homespun morality and his often brutal, impolitic honesty won Carter voter support. However, Carter's real passion lay not with reinvigorating America's distressed cities, places where he had won vital political support, but with balancing the federal budget. That uninspiring goal, not the scintillating vision of a New Deal, a New Frontier, or a Great Society, became the rude trademark of the Carter administration.[5]

Carter's urban policy reflected not only the president's antistatism and commitment to government frugality, but also the dynamism of his gifted Housing and Urban Development (HUD) secretary, Patricia Harris. Her appointment reflected at least in part Carter's deference to the critical support he had won from African Americans in places such as the East Bronx and North Philadelphia. A strong-willed African American, Harris determined to use her post to make the urban agency a servant of the inner-city poor rather than a creature of the building industry that dominated HUD and its predecessor, the Housing and Home Finance Administration (HHFA).

To the progovernment housing community untutored about Carter's post–New Deal mentality, his appointment of Harris seemed at first incomprehensible in light of her words to the *Journal of Housing*. Asked for her thoughts on public housing, Harris blurted out that she favored giving housing subsides directly to individuals: "I would rather have people in the marketplace purchasing their own shelter . . . than have the government put up the kind of public-housing monstrosities and the overly costly subsidized building programs that we've had in the past. We should make it clear that we're abandoning the whole notion of public housing."[6] The statement infuriated both housing reformers and the urban home-building industry that had thrived on the construction of government-subsidized housing. Her opponents protested that she lacked any housing background, a point reiterated by Senator William Proxmire during her Senate confirmation hearings. Noting her exquisitely fashionable attire and her partnership in a prestigious Washington, D.C., law firm, Proxmire questioned whether Harris knew anything about the poor. "Hurricane Pat," at her combative best, seized the rhetorical advantage. "Sir," she shot back, "I am one of them."[7]

Born, May 31, 1924, in Mattoon, Illinois, the daughter of a Pullman porter, Harris worked her way through Howard University. She directed programs for the Young Women's Christian Association and from 1949 to 1953 served as Associate Director of the American Council on Human Rights, whose work included bettering housing opportunities for minorities. She married a lawyer,

William Beasely Harris, in 1955 and in 1960 earned a law degree with honors from George Washington University where she later taught law. In 1963, President John F. Kennedy named her co-chairperson of the National Women's Committee for Civil Rights; President Johnson later appointed her ambassador to Luxembourg. In 1969, Harris served briefly as dean of the Howard University Law School before joining the law firm of Fried, Frank, Harris, Shriver, and Kampelman. Politically very active, Harris compiled an impressive list of memberships, including the National Association for the Advancement of Colored People (NAACP) Legal Defense Fund, but also directorships in IBM, Scott Paper, and the Chase Manhattan Bank. Asked in 1976 to sum up her career, Harris responded that she had been "involved for more than 30 years in the civil rights movement."[8]

Yet, outside her work for the American Council on Human Rights in the 1950s, her credentials reflected little housing expertise. That aside, Harris soon emerged as a strident and effective spokesperson for the professed mission of HUD: to rebuild cities and better the housing of the poor. She proclaimed the urban poor "HUD's number one client" and strenuously opposed threats to HUD's domain, especially from the budget ax–wielding chief of the Office of Management and Budget (OMB), Bert Lance. When Lance, Carter, and Health, Education and Welfare Secretary Joseph Califano proposed replacing welfare and housing subsidies with a version of Nixon's "guaranteed annual wage," Harris denounced the idea as "cashing out" public housing to the detriment of the poor. At HUD, where she installed a "new order" tilting toward cities and poor people, she was equally brazen, earning the sobriquets "the queen" and "iron-toed boot."[9]

Harris quickly won the esteem of many congressmen for her effectiveness. At first her opponent, in 1978 Wisconsin Senator William Proxmire praised Harris for her "substance and eloquence." Representative Henry Reuss hailed her as the "Best HUD Secretary ever." At the 1979 budget hearings, with inflation and the economy firmly ensconced as Carter priorities, Harris secured for HUD an 11 percent budget increase, up $1 billion from 1978. Others, however, scorned her as a "racist who only wants to help blacks." Undoubtedly, Harris did press the cause of the black urban poor in the face of Carter's tightfisted budget policies. The NAACP's Clarence Mitchell adored her.[10] Yet Harris was neither a racist nor a black militant. She was a corporate lawyer who chose Jay Janis, a Florida developer with ties to David Rockefeller, as undersecretary of HUD. Her natural sympathies with the urban poor aside, she, like her predecessors, cultivated warm ties with private developers.[11]

Budget differences notwithstanding, like Carter, Harris shared an ideologi-

cal commitment to urban neighborhoods, viewing them as nuclei for the revitalization of urban America. They particularly shared a belief in the empowerment
of people, neighbors helping neighbors, the vital community. This idea incorporated elements of the community-control movement of the 1960s and traditional Christian communitarianism implicit in the millennial fervor of the
nineteenth-century reformist social gospel. The idea also drew heavily on the
progressive environmentalism inherent in the Settlement House Movement
brought from England to the United States in the 1880s by Jane Addams and
Graham Taylor and the school-centered urban neighborhood–rebuilding
schemes of the journalist and housing reformer Jacob Riis and the educator
John Dewey. Revitalized neighborhoods served as laboratories for citizenship
where once-disaffected poor people mobilized into voluntary organizations
that empowered them to take control of their lives and become productive
members of society. In the Carter administration, the Domestic Policy Staff-
member and former Chicago community organizer Marcia Kaptur and HUD
Assistant Secretary Geno Baroni pressed for policies to make neighborhood
associations central to the urban rebuilding effort. Kaptur and Baroni likewise
sensitized Carter and Harris to the concerns of poor working-class white communities deeply alienated by their perception that Johnson's Great Society had
failed to include them.[12]

Therefore, like many Americans in the 1970s, neither Carter nor Harris
believed any longer in the power of government-redesigned physical environments to cure urban problems. Instead, Carter's housing secretary shared the
president's vision of revitalized neighborhoods, bustling with entrepreneurial
vigor, where—aided by government grants and generous tax breaks—poor
black families in concert with white, childless, middle-class professionals
opened neighborhood businesses, refurbished historic houses, scrubbed clean
graffiti-defaced walls, and excited drab streetscapes with spring plantings. She
recognized the persistence of American apartheid and knew that government-
subsidized neighborhood revitalization might potentially spawn gentrification
and uproot the very families it intended to help.[13]

Both Carter and Harris also believed that the federal government could not
decree city rebuilding as President Lyndon Johnson had attempted in the
1960s. It required a partnership involving government, newly empowered residents, private bankers, corporate officers, and developers. Government ignited
and helped coordinate the process. However, Harris's vision of HUD's role in
urban revitalization dwarfed Carter's. He wanted merely economy and efficiency at HUD, not costly new programs.

Nevertheless, Carter owed his presidency to cities for which he had prom ised new urban legislation. In January 1976, he asked Harris for her latest thoughts on "Housing and Urban Development" for a fireside chat. "Cities where citizens are suitably shelter[ed] . . . in dignified surroundings are the mark of a civilized and humanistic society," she wrote. Using words that may have shocked the inflation-minded Carter, she advised him to "[t]ell Americans that [the administration] will use all the tools available [to rebuild cities, including the] . . . construction of publicly-owned housing. . . . This administration also has pledged itself to . . . take all steps necessary to make certain that federal aid is provided so that all citizens can look proudly on our urban centers as symbols of a vibrant America."[14]

She would revamp HUD for that task. Unabashedly partisan, Harris believed that previous Republican administrations had used the agency's past tribulations "to shut down projects designed by Democratic congresses to aid the housing and community development needs of American cities." Under Presidents Richard Nixon and Gerald Ford, an enfeebled HUD had refused to deal with the problem of "dual housing markets," substantial, well-financed suburbs and gentrified neighborhoods for well-heeled mainly white families, and, for less affluent white and black families, aging urban hulks often excluded from improvement by the persistence of redlining, the practice whereby banks and real estate agents place poor sections of the city off limits to mortgage money. Moreover, local public housing policies reinforced patterns of racial segregation, aggravating the housing problem of African Americans. Blacks made up 39 percent of Philadelphia's population in 1980, but the average African American family in that city lived in a census tract that was 82 percent black. Rows of moldering brick row houses made up much of segregated black Philadelphia, where over 20,000 units sat abandoned, gutted, and boarded up. The Ford administration had subverted the 1974 Community Development Block Grant program meant to give states and localities greater latitude to ameliorate such conditions, ignoring the act's low-income housing requirements and its mandate to eliminate urban slums and blight.[15]

In contrast to prevailing public opinion, Harris for one rebuffed the idea that urban renewal had been a failure. Renewal, asserted Harris, had stemmed the worst tide of urban blight, bettered low-income housing, and strengthened the urban economy. She regarded HUD as an arsenal for city rebuilding and a supermarket for urban revitalization.[16] Neighborhoods took center stage in her strategy. However, she was a brilliant corporate lawyer, not an architect or planner. Names such as Jacob Riis and ideas about neighborhood units eluded her. She shared instead the sensibilities of the journalist and architecture critic Jane Jacobs for whom the neighborhood fabric of streets, storefronts, and sandlots made up a cultural construct. Human interaction, neighbor to neighbor, the give and take of the marketplace, not architects and planners, built neighborhoods. From these forces, especially the vital commercial sector, arose economic and social order and opportunity.[17]

Revitalizing stricken urban communities involved not only private investment, but also a bevy of dedicated people and dynamic social organizations. Neighborhood Housing Services (NHS), pioneered by the Urban Reinvestment Task Force in Pittsburgh's North Side in the late 1960s, offered a model. In this aging section of the Steel City, founded during the Mexican-American War of the 1840s, a partnership of neighbors, banks, and businesses spurred on by the city's Pittsburgh History and Landmarks Foundation and aided by NHS helped preserve the threatened neighborhood.[18]

Harris considered the mid-1970s propitious for neighborhood revitalization. The imminence of the nation's Bicentennial, the rise of the Organization of Petroleum Exporting Countries (OPEC) with its implication for rising gasoline prices, and the public disillusionment with congested expressways actually rekindled interest in old urban neighborhoods studded with ornate, turreted Italianate and Queen Anne Victorian housing stock. The housing appealed to young, childless couples, who found charm in the blemished but comfortable and convenient old dowager residences whether in Pittsburgh's North Side or Boston's South End.

Unlike Carter, however, Harris harbored unyielding faith in the durability and necessity of HUD to facilitate the betterment of urban communities. To be economically stable, struggling inner-city neighborhoods, white and black, required programs such as Section 8, Community Development Block Grants, below-market interest rates on mortgage loans, and tax incentives to encourage business investment, rebuild unsafe housing, and create jobs. Section 8 loomed as HUD's biggest housing tool for urban revitalization. It had emerged in August 1974, two days after Nixon's resignation speech, and resembled HUD's older Section 23 leased housing program.[19] The same 1974 Housing and Community Development Act created the Community Development Block Grant (CDBG), a child of Nixon's "New Federalism," which lumped Great Society categorical programs such as sewer grants into a single grant giving communities greater "flexibility" in spending federal money. After January 1, 1975, Section 8 became the nation's primary vehicle for housing low- and moderate-income families. Under Section 8, HUD invited Local Housing Authorities (LHAs) to ask for a number of new or existing units to be supplied by the private sector. In fact, Section 8 played a major ideological role in shifting responsibility for low-income housing to the private sector. It limited HUD's role to inspecting units, warranting them acceptable, and paying landlords the difference between 25 percent of the tenants' income and the fair market rent of the unit. Pittsburgh's housing authority stated the Section 8 procedure succinctly: The Authority "assure[s] that it [the house] meets code standards, and . . . contracts with the landlord. . . . The whole concept of this program is that the individual goes out and finds his house."[20]

Critics complained that many Section 8 existing housing units barely met HUD's minimum standards for occupancy. Expanding the housing supply was another matter. The housing expert and liberal gadfly Cushing Dolbeare decried the meager new construction under Section 8. In Pittsburgh as elsewhere, private developers could secure only risky twenty-year bank financing for Section 8 projects, the duration of HUD's fiscal commitment. Pittsburgh used the safe housing market for older people to cajole developers into Section 8 "new construction."[21] In 1976, elderly housing accounted for 70 percent of all Section 8 new construction.[22]

The image of conventional public housing, projects such as Chicago's grim, high-rise Robert Taylor Homes, built and owned by Local Housing Authorities, remained benighted; but image and reality sometimes differed. In Pittsburgh, more elderly "blue chip" tenants than families with children lived in high-rise units in 1975. Nationally, barely 9 percent of high-rise complexes presented problems. Low-rise units such as Pittsburgh's Arlington Heights homes— tucked away in the city's South Side—accounted for 62 percent of HUD's "troubled" projects. For many poor families, only conventional public housing contained subsidies deep enough to shelter them.[23]

Yet in city after city, operating such conventional housing projects inexorably bankrupted local authorities. Rent receipts failed to cover project operating costs, especially for maintenance. Confronted by an aging public housing stock beset by fractured gas lines, warped window frames, and ancient appliances, big city housing authorities from Boston to Los Angeles faced ruin.[24] In response to skyrocketing maintenance costs and escalating tenant rents, the 1969 (Senator) Edward Brooke Amendment had fixed rents at 25 percent of tenant income and ordered HUD to subsidize LHA operating expenses.[25] Not only did Congress inadequately fund the Brooke subsidies, but it also neglected to underwrite the various modernization programs designed to mend HUD's leaking dikes.[26] To prod LHAs toward greater management accountability, HUD next pegged operation subsidies to evidence of increased efficiency. Stagflation, however, choked all federal efforts to modernize troubled housing projects. The mid-1970s energy crisis further exacerbated urban housing problems.[27]

Harris fought the tight-fisted Carter administration for the resources to refurbish these tools, to enlarge the number of certified Section 8 units, to expand the Section 312 housing rehabilitation program, and to modernize public housing. She imagined HUD leading neighborhood revitalization, ending the invidious concentrations of poor people, and promoting rehabilitation by preserving existing housing and making the city a reasonable alternative to suburban living. Cities, argued Harris, could no longer rely on manufacturing for economic growth; they must seize the advantage by developing strong service sectors and appealing neighborhoods.[28] She assailed redlining, a policy of deliberate bank-sponsored disinvestment in black neighborhoods rooted in FHA's blatantly racist appraisal practices of the 1930s. Harris accused the Federal National Mortgage Association (Fannie Mae) of being "lily white" and prejudicial in its mortgage-purchasing policies to the interests of blacks and urban neighborhoods. A main purpose of Carter's and Harris's urban policy aimed to target public and private money back into battered cities.[29]

The administration previewed its new urban policy immediately when the impending expiration of the CDBG program forced HUD to take action to have it renewed. Carter's Housing and Community Development Act of 1977, aggressively shepherded through Congress by Harris, reauthorized the 1974 Community Development Block Grant program for another three years, but used a dual formula to target the aid from otherwise healthy cities with pockets of poverty, such as Denver and Atlanta, to distressed urban areas suffering both poverty and population decline.

Harris proclaimed housing "the single most important physical component of national urban policy."[30] The 1974 CDBG program had embodied a strong housing component, ordering participating cities to file Housing Assistance Plans. Harris, however, deplored the insufficiency of past CDBG housing activity, the unnecessary demolitions of sound public housing stock, and the failure of HUD to coordinate housing efficiently with community development. In 1977, Harris pushed Congress not only to increase the level of new and substantially rehabilitated Section 8 housing by 164,200 units, but to authorize Annual Contribution Contracts for 56,000 units of public housing and to increase public housing operating subsidies to $665,000,000.[31] The Urban Development Action Grant (UDAG), the centerpiece of the 1977 housing legislation, allocated 20,000 Section 8 "substantially rehabilitated" housing units for neighborhood revitalization effort in distressed urban areas.[32]

Targeting federal dollars toward these wasting urban regions lay at the heart of the strategy being shaped in 1977 by Carter's Urban and Regional Policy Group (URPG). Carter at first had attempted to ignore the costly, albeit pressing issues of urban decay. When black leaders and organized labor denounced the administration's laxity, Carter responded by creating URPG. The president personally selected the membership made up of the secretaries of HUD, Treasury, Commerce, Labor, Health, Education, and Welfare, and Transportation and chaired by Harris. URPG's agenda emphasized redistributing or targeting resources to disadvantaged urban populations, modernizing old central cities, and strengthening the social and economic foundations of "urban communities and opening suburbs so that every race and class can live close to where they work."[33]

Harris and her group met regularly over the course of one year and elicited input from interested citizens, state and local officials, and such prominent urban scholars and housing experts as Bernard Frieden and William Wheaton. The group produced a giant study containing over seventy proposals for attacking the urban crisis.[34] Submitted by Harris on March 23, 1978, the final, pared-down but still turgid 128-page URPG Report contained forty-three urban policy initiatives. Carter unveiled the report with considerable fanfare four days later, declared cities "vital to the health of the nation," and committed the administration "to provide leadership to conserve the rich urban heritage . . . and expand the job, housing, and neighborhood choice of millions of disadvantaged urban residents."[35] The report exuded optimism as well as engineer Carter's conviction that the solution to difficult problems lay in a comprehensive approach.

Although basic elements of URPG's exuberant urban agenda would infuse Carter's "Urban Policy Initiatives of 1978," the policy group's vision nevertheless reflected the president's more limited, fiscally conservative view of government. Washington should act more as catalyst and orchestrator; it provided incentive grants to help states develop their own policy initiatives and offered tax incentives and low-interest loans to attract investment to economically fallow urban areas. URPG mainly refocused federal policy on preserving the health and vitality of central cities, a goal explicit in the 1937, 1949, and 1954 federal housing laws, but derailed by the suburban agenda of the Nixon-Ford presidencies. Significantly, URPG rejected the traditional liberal faith in environmentalism, dismissing it as "salvation through bricks—that we can bulldoze away urban problems." Nor, asserted URPG, can government rebuild cities unilaterally as Lyndon Johnson attempted or retreat in disarray as Nixon did. Rehabilitating battered urban neighborhoods required a "New Urban Partnership" wherein government leveraged private investment to increase economic opportunity, restore a sense of community, and lure the middle class back into the cities.

Here lay the real importance of Carter's urban housing program. It unveiled a grand design for replacing government leadership and dollars with corporate funds in leading the city-rebuilding process, a major retreat from the New Deal and Great Society strategy. Carter's 1978 "New Urban Initiatives," the legislative version of the URPG report, focused more on partnerships and economic development than on housing. Bearing a $4.4-billion-dollar price tag, it brandished such new programs as a National Development Bank and $1.7 billion in tax incentives and loan guarantees designed to encourage private business to relocate office and production facilities in distressed urban areas. Strengthened Community Development Corporations, new Neighborhood Reinvestment Centers, and efforts to increase minority participation in federal contracts by luring government defense contractors into aging city neighborhoods buttressed the initiatives.[36]

Immediate reaction to Carter's urban initiatives was favorable. Speaking before Congress, Wisconsin Representative Henry Reuss commended Carter for "sett[ing] in motion a policy process that if sustained holds the promise of halting the deterioration of our urban centers." Reuss praised Carter's plan to review existing urban aid programs and to "target" tax credits, but, he added, "[W]e lack details. . . . Active White House leadership will be required . . . to put them into effect." However, because Carter's real goal was fighting inflation, he never exercised that leadership.[37]

The targeting component of the Carter-Harris urban program, albeit modest and clearly within the post–World War, pro-growth, urban renewal tradition, lacked political viability. Targeting CDBGs at the distressed neighborhoods of big cities (made possible under the 1977 dual formula) ignored small cities, growing cities, and, of course, suburbs, which had benefited from the Nixon-Ford policies. It also foundered on the rocks of continuing stagflation and a stubborn energy crisis worsened by Carter's standoff with Iranian Islamic revolutionaries. A rising antigovernment tide, deepened by concerns about fiscal austerity, emboldened the growing ranks of western and southern congressmen to oppose Harris's inner-city agenda. In 1978, Congress lopped off 115 HUD staff positions needed to monitor the targeting of CDBG funds.

Congressional discomfiture aside, that same 1978 legislation betrayed Congress's and HUD's deepening interest in conserving the nation's existing urban housing stock, a concern visible in the 1977 law. In 1978, Congress tripled the Section 312 housing rehabilitation loan program and awarded independent corporation status to the Reinvestment Task Force. It also broadened and expanded Section 8 as a revitalization tool by approving 39,000 units as part of a new "moderate rehabilitation" program, which required landlords to invest minimally (under $3,000) to upgrade moldering inner-city housing.[38] Eligible cities with CDBG programs such as Pittsburgh, where Section 8 proved vital to neighborhood revitalization, embraced the Moderate Rehabilitation program, using it to acquire seventy desperately needed additional Section 8 housing units.[39]

Nor did Congress in 1978 ignore HUD's appeal to conserve the nation's 1.2 million units of public housing branded "troubled." Harris had once denounced "the projects"; now converted, she halted demolitions, swore to salvage "troubled" projects as part of the comprehensive reclamation of city neighborhoods, and determined to increase tenant participation in maintenance and management. "We care about our troubled projects," wrote Harris in January 1979, "because we care about the people who live there. Ours is not a bricks or mortar response, it is a compassionate human response."[40] "Urban Initiatives" for public housing built on HUD's earlier Target Projects Program. In addition to funding necessary roof repairs and window replacements and recovering fire- and vandal-damaged units, it endeavored to design away "indefensible space," retrain authority staff, and even provide low-cost driver training to enhance tenant mobility and job opportunity. Consistent with the Carter-Harris emphasis on targeting, "Urban Initiatives" provided $256 million to upgrade thirty-three of the most severely distressed public housing authorities, including those in Boston, Chicago, New York, and Pittsburgh. Like earlier modernization programs, "Urban Initiatives" aimed to expunge the negative image of public housing. Harris stressed tenant participation in management, insisting that tenants' views be given "full and serious consideration."[41] Urban Initiatives also balanced intensive physical rehabilitation with social initiatives, such as the anticrime program that operated in Pittsburgh's three older, inner-city projects plagued by vandalism, fire, and rodent infestation. HUD awarded the Boston Housing Authority $10 million in modernization monies to rehabilitate the notorious oceanside Columbia Point project and added $450,000 to improve basic management systems there.[42]

The Carter-Harris Urban Policy Critique

Over time, Harris and HUD won numerous kudos from Congressman William Proxmire, the National Association of Housing and Redevelopment Officials, and others, especially for the secretary's stellar performance in shifting HUD's focus back toward problem-ridden big cities and the housing-starved poor.[43]

Being brash, an unequivocal champion of black opportunity, and an advocate of increased federal spending for housing in a tight-fisted administration, however, Harris courted trouble. She barely muffled her sharpest differences with the administration over Carter's and Budget Director Bert Lance's efforts to collapse housing into welfare through a voucher system, over Carter's refusal to back her in her crusade to oust the head of Fannie Mae, and over the stiff budgetary limitations imposed on HUD spending. Harris's refusal to air her frustrations with Carter openly as Califano did won her points for loyalty in the administration, but rebuke from liberals such as Cushing Dolbeare.[44]

In the late 1970s, housing reformers like Dolbeare and experts such as George and Eunice Grier attacked HUD on several fronts. Such critics viewed "targeted" neighborhood revitalization, UDAGs and all, as "gentrification," which by raising property values and rents, displaced more low-income families than it housed. Urban reinvestment and revitalization, argued the Neighborhood Reinvestment Corporation's Philip Clay, "should not lead inevitably to a decline in improved housing opportunities for low- and moderate-income households."[45]

Critics also assailed the administration's parsimony. Early in her tenure at HUD, Harris battled Bert Lance's stern orders to "eliminate . . . ineffectual programs, cut back, . . . eliminate unnecessary costs, and hold programs to the lowest feasible level."[46] Her failure to subdue OMB and to win significant increases in the amount of new or low- and moderate-income housing irked and dismayed her natural allies in the black and white liberal community. Harris's retort that economy, greater efficiency, and bureaucratic legerdemain enabled the agency to serve more needy families proved unconvincing.[47]

Carter's rhetoric about urban reconstruction had heightened liberal expectations, only to dash them when he acted more the budget slasher than champion of the urban poor. Liberals deplored the halfheartedness and insufficiency of his urban policy agenda. Speaking for a wide range of pro-housing groups, including church groups, the Americans for Democratic Action, the National Committee Against Discrimination in Housing, and the National Urban League, Dolbeare protested HUD's 1980 budget that programmed fewer than 300,000 units of Section 8. He understood Carter's concern for curbing inflation and lowering the federal deficit, but urged that Carter not do it on the backs of ill-housed poor people. In March 1980, Dolbeare gently chided Harris. "Dear Pat," wrote Dolbeare, "there is really nothing wrong with the HUD budget . . . that doubling it would not cure."[48] A month later, he voiced a complaint, common among public housers, that the administration appeared "to be focussed [sic] not on the desperate housing conditions of low-income people and their need for jobs and for better neighborhoods, but on more abstract notions of 'fiscal viability,' 'leveraging,' or improving 'coordination' and 'effectiveness.'"[49]

Even the vaunted "Urban Initiatives" for modernizing public housing fizzled on paper. Reviewing modernization policies, one critic disclosed "a discouraging picture of poor structures, and multiple disincentives." He cited a study of 41,000 public housing units needing at least $2,600 per unit to restore habitability. Yet, from 1976 to 1980, Congress had appropriated just $2 billion or a mere $1,600 per dwelling.[50]

Few—certainly not the growing ranks of conservatives in Congress—heeded the outcries. Dolbeare's pleas in the late 1970s came amid an America fleeing the welfare state. Little remained of progressive environmentalism and the radiant faith of garden-city and modern housing apostles that publicly built, well-designed housing would provide safe and sanitary communities radiating civic values. Although she was a firm believer in positive government, Harris's neighborhood vision of scrubbed storefronts, clean streets, good police protection, and plentiful jobs little resembled the 1920s–1930s modern housing schemes of Catherine Bauer or Clarence Stein. In the "age of limits," government no longer built; instead it coaxed, coordinated, leveraged, and assisted private-sector initiatives. Neither Carter nor Harris pioneered a public-private partnership at HUD; instead, they built on the Eisenhower, Kennedy, Johnson, and Nixon legacy. Carter strengthened an existing public-private partnership and refocused it on neighborhood and downtown revitalization.[51]

Carter's urban policy bore results, if not those that Harris envisioned. By 1980, banks and insurance companies, prodded and encouraged by HUD and its pallet of CDBG, Section 312 housing rehabilitation loans, tax credits for historic preservation, and other FHA and tax incentive programs, were pumping millions of dollars into downtowns and into increasingly fashionable old neighborhoods such as Baltimore's Federal Hill, Philadelphia's Rittenhouse Square and Queens Village, and Pittsburgh's Mexican War Streets, where young "urban pioneers" as Harris both sought and feared, discovered the charm and cost-effectiveness of living in revitalized neighborhoods.[52] Big city downtowns, Philadelphia, Boston, Baltimore, and Detroit, rebounded to such a degree in the 1980s that one magazine article wondered: "Where is the urban crisis?"

Carter, indeed, launched a new urban renaissance; only low-income housing lagged.[53] While the downtown flourished, the old streetcar suburbs, the isolated languishing haunts of William Julius Wilson's underclass, attracted few dollars. In 1980, Philadelphia's black mayor, W. Wilson Goode, pledged to spend half the city's $60 million Community Development Block Grant to spur private investment in decaying North Philadelphia. He lured hardly a cent to the region.

Goode's gesture to the critics of his neglectful inner-city policy aside, nationwide the bulk of CDBG monies went to downtown revitalization, not to distressed neighborhoods. Carter's targeted programs and his embrace of corporate partnerships produced the needed fillip to restart the engines of the 1950s pro-growth coalition, which had unveiled the original urban renaissance. Philadelphia announced planning for Gallery II and a new waterfront extravaganza. Pittsburgh undertook Renaissance II, and Boston Government Center.

The Carter administration, strapped by inflation and the energy crisis and politically weakened, quickened the retreat from the problems of the ill housed. Carter's Commission for a National Agenda for the 1980s actually proposed a "triage" approach to withhold funding for neighborhoods deemed unredeemable. Carter's successor, President Ronald Reagan, merely pursued these policies of limited urban aid and the encouragement of corporate-led downtown rebuilding more aggressively. In the neighborhoods, Reagan's policies, according to one historian, replaced Nixon's policy of "benign neglect" with one of "malign neglect." Reagan cut Carter's 1981 budget request for $30 billion in Section 8 housing certificates nearly in half. By 1985, Reagan had gutted the Department of Housing and Urban Development budget by two-thirds.[54] In the 1983 Urban and Rural Renewal Act, Reagan terminated both Section 8 new construction and substantial rehabilitation programs, leaving local housing authorities with a downscaled Section 8 and aging housing projects where refrigerators failed, gas lines still leaked, and vermin reigned. In the late 1980s and early 1990s, "vouchers," "tenant ownership," and "privatization," all terms current during the Harris years, held sway at the Department of Housing and Urban Development.[55]

Therefore, if Carter and his compassionate, albeit irascible HUD secretary bequeathed an urban legacy of scintillating, boutique-lined streets, they also—albeit inadvertently—helped deepen the isolation and misery of urban neighborhoods. In the dusk of the Carter presidency, the sociologist William Julius Wilson first exposed the existence of an isolated "truly disadvantaged," the black poor left behind by urban revitalization. Dolbeare warned of the trend, but so did Harris, who feared that neighborhood rebuilding without rigorous enforcement of fair housing laws would further concentrate the minority poor.[56] Unfortunately, neither she nor any housing policymaker—past or present—has dealt with the consequences of what scholars have called American Apartheid; nor have they constructed a plan sought by Harris for truly diverse neighborhoods in a nation still divided by race and still in search of a workable low-income housing policy.

Notes

1. See Thomas Sugrue, "Carter's Urban Policy Crisis," in Gary M. Fink and Hugh Davis Graham, eds., *The Carter Presidency: Policy Choices in the Post–New Deal Era* (Lawrence: University Press of Kansas, 1998), 137–45; David W. Bartelt, "Housing the Underclass," in Michael B. Katz, ed., *The Underclass: Views from History* (Princeton: Princeton University Press, 1993), 118–23; and Gregory D. Squires, "Public-Private Partnership: Who Gets What and Why," in Gregory D. Squires, ed., *Unequal Partnership: The Political Economy of Urban Redevelopment in Postwar America* (New Brunswick: Rutgers University Press, 1989).

2. Quoted in William E. Leuchtenburg, "Jimmy Carter and the Post–New Deal Presidency," in Gary M. Fink and Hugh Davis Graham, eds., *The Carter Presidency: Policy Choices in the Post–New Deal Era* (Lawrence: University of Kansas Press, 1998), 16; Fink and Graham, eds., The Carter Presidency, 16.

3. For quote, see Sugrue, "Carter's Urban Policy Crisis," 138.

4. "Presidential Candidates State Their Positions on Housing Issues," *Journal of Housing* (March 1976): 125; Berry Glad, *Jimmy Carter: In Search of the Great White House* (New York: Norton, 1980).

5. On fiscal conservatism, see Peter G. Bourne, *Jimmy Carter: A Comprehensive Biography from Plains to Postpresidency* (New York: Scribners, 1997), 369–74, 430–40; on Carter as a "centrist," see Leuchtenburg, "Jimmy Carter and the Post–New Deal Presidency"; and Bruce J. Schulman, "Slouching Toward the Supply Side: Jimmy Carter and the New American Political Economy," both in Fink and Graham, eds., *The Carter Presidency*, 16–40.

6. "Patricia Robert Harris Is President-Elect Carter's Choice for Secretary of the Department of Housing and Urban Development," *Journal of Housing* (November 1976): 536.

7. Susan McBee, "Forceful HUD Secretary Is Turning Her Critics Around," clipping from *The Washington Post*, n.d., in Box 77, Harris Personal File, May 1978, The Papers of Patricia Harris, Manuscript Division, Library of Congress, Washington, D.C. [hereafter HP].

8. See a Department of Housing and Urban Development biographical portrait, edited by Harris, n.d., Box 8, Chronological File, February 1977, HP; and McBee, "Forceful HUD Secretary Is Turning Her Critics Around," HP.

9. On HUD tilting toward the poor, see p. 17 of Harris's "Briefing Book: Policy Development for Distressed Cities," n.d., 1977, in Box 28, Briefing Books, Policy Development and Research, 1977, HP; "Hurricane Pat, Iron-Toed Boot at HUD," *Washington Star*, n.d., c. December 1977, news clipping in Box 76, Chronological File, January 1978, HP.

10. William Proxmire to Harris, January 18, 1977, Box 8, Chronological File, February 1977, HP; Clarence Mitchell to Harris, August 26, 1977, Box 76, Patricia Harris Subject File, Personal, July–August 1977, HP; and McBee, "Forceful HUD Secretary Is Turning Her Critics Around," HP.

11. McBee, "Forceful HUD Secretary Is Turning Her Critics Around," HP; Harris Memorandum on Janis, February 3, 1977, Box 8, Chronological File, March 1977, HP.

12. Sugrue, "Carter's Urban Policy Crisis," 142–43; on Riis and the neighborhood idea, see Allen F. Davis, *Spearheads for Reform: The Social Settlements and the Progressive Movement, 1890–1914* (New York: Oxford, 1967); and Elisabeth Lasch-Quinn, *Black Neighbors: Race and the Limits of Reform in the American Settlement House Movement, 1890–1945* (Chapel Hill: University of North Carolina Press, 1993).

13. "Profile of Patricia Robert Harris," in Box 8, Chronological File, February 1977, HP; John H. Mollenkopf, *The Contested City* (Princeton: Princeton University Press, 1983), 273; Bourne, *Jimmy Carter*, 367.

14. Harris, "Memorandum to the President, Re: Proposed Section on Housing and Urban Development for Fireside Chat," January 26, 1977, in Box 8, Chronological File, January 1977, HP.

15. Patricia Harris, "Summary Paper for HUD Briefing with President," July 27, 1977, Box 21, Briefing Books, Housing Residential-President Meeting, 1977, HP; and Bourne, *Jimmy Carter*, 373; on Philadelphia, see Caroline Adams, David Bartelt, David Elesh, Ira Goldstein, Nancy Klenawsky, and

William Yancey, eds., *Philadelphia: Neighborhoods, Division, and Conflict in a Postindustrial City* (Philadelphia: Temple University Press, 1991), 90–91.

16. Memo to Bill Wise and Peggy Grant, March 11, 1978, Box 9, Chronological File, March 1978, HP; Memo to Bert Lance, February 14, 1977, Box 8, Chronological Files, February 1977, HP.

17. Howard Gillette, "The Evolution of Neighborhood Planning: From the Progressive Era to the 1949 Housing Act," *Journal of Urban History* 4 (August 1983): 395–421.

18. Jon Teaford, *Rough Road to Renaissance: Urban Revitalization in America, 1940–1985* (Baltimore: Johns Hopkins University Press, 1990), 242; Roy Lubove, *Twentieth-Century Pittsburgh, Volume Two: The Post-Steel Era* (Pittsburgh: University of Pittsburgh Press, 1996).

19. On moratorium, see Fred Rosenbaum to Senator Bob Packwood, October 31, 1973, Box 141, PRO 9-1, Leased Housing, 1973, Record of the Department of Housing and Urban Development, National Archive, Washington, D.C. [hereafter HUD Records].

20. Rachel G. Bratt, Chester Hartman, and Ann Meyerson, eds., *Critical Perspectives on Housing* (Philadelphia: Temple University Press, 1986), 312; Bartelt, "Housing the Underclass," 152; Housing Authority of the City of Pittsburgh, May 15, 1975, in Housing Authority Office, Pittsburgh, Pa. [hereafter HACP Mins.].

21. HACP Mins., October 21, 1976; Cushing Dolbeare to Carla Hills, October 5, 1976, Box 25, PRO 9, Low-Rent Housing October–December 1976, HUD Records.

22. Memorandum, Carla Hills to Federal Housing Commissioner, November 15, 1976, Box 25, PRO 9, Low-Rent Housing, October–December 1976, HUD Records.

23. Bratt, "Public Housing," in Bratt et al., eds., *Critical Perspectives on Housing*, 357.

24. HACP Mins., January 16, 1975; February 20, 1975; September 18, 1975; January 15, 1976.

25. Carla Hills to Honorable Lindy Boggs (Mrs. Hale Boggs), May 3, 1976, Box 25, PRO 9, Low-Rent Housing, June–September 1976, HUD Records; HACP Mins., July 22, 1976.

26. Veronica Chicadel, "NAHRO TPP Service Program," *Journal of Housing* (November 1976): 551; Arthur D'Amato, "TPP," *Journal of Housing* (January 1976): 40–41. Congress approved a $91.5 million program called Target Projects Program (TPP), effective April 1, 1975. TPP provided intensive, short-term assistance to improve "the physical conditions and general liveability of individual public housing projects . . . facing serious operational and environmental problems." Under TPP, Pittsburgh, for example, got $660,000 to modernize its aging Arlington Heights complex; it then asked for $8 million to completely rehabilitate the project. HUD gave it $1,800,000. Arlington remained "troubled." See HACP Mins., August 22, 1976; "Low Income Public Housing Modernization Program—PHA-Aided Projects, Notice of Proposed Rulemaking," n.d., c. 1976, Box 25, Low-Rent Public Housing, HUD Records.

27. Bratt, "Public Housing," in Bratt et al., eds., *Critical Perspectives on Housing*, 337–40.

28. See Harris to Chicago Daily News, November 30, 1977, Box 138, Chronological File, November 1977, HP.

29. See Carl Holman to "Pat" Harris, June 15, 1978, and Harris to Parren Mitchell, July 17, 1978, all in Box 46, PRO 7, Neighborhood Associations, January–December 1978, HUD Records.

30. Lawrence Simons to Harris, November 21, 1977, Box 8, National Urban Policy, Chronological File, November 1977, HP.

31. Mary Nenno, "Fiscal Year 1978 Budgets for the Department of Housing and Urban Development," *Journal of Housing* (February 1977): 65–72.

32. On the 1977 legislation, see Harris, "Summary Paper for HUD Briefing with President," July 27, 1977, Box 21, Briefing Book, Housing Residential, HP; Harris, "Statement of Patricia Harris Before Subcommittee on Banking and Housing and Urban Affairs (Proxmire Committee)," March 4, 1977, Box 23, Briefing Book, Block Grant Program, HP.

33. "Draft Progress Report to the President by URPG," August 1977, Box 34, Subject File, Briefing Books, June 20, 1977, HP.

34. Dr. Melvin Webber (School of Architecture, Berkeley), to Harris, April 21, 1978, and Harris to Webber, April 17, 1978, both in Box 77, Patricia Harris Personal, HP.

35. "Urban and Regional Policy Group Report," March 27, 1978, Box 34, Briefing Books, URPG, March 27, 1978, HP.

36. "Briefing Book, URPG," March 27, 1978, Box 34, Press Release Briefing Book, Policy Announcing New Partnerships to Conserve American Communities, President Jimmy Carter, HP; a good treatment of the URPG report can be found in Sugrue's "Carter's Urban Policy Crisis," 148–53.

37. Harris to Henry Reuss, May 27, 1998, Box 77, Subject File, Personal, April 1977, HP; Mary K. Nenno, "President Carter's 1978 Urban Policy Initiatives," Journal of Housing (May 1978): 217–21.

38. "1978 Housing Legislation: An Overview and Analysis," Journal of Housing 36 (January 1979): 15.

39. HACP Mins., March 7, 1978; February 22, 1979; February 28, 1980.

40. For quotation, see Harris, "Successful Housing Policies Depend on Meshing Private Investment and Public Expenditure," Journal of Housing 36 (January 1979): 40; and Memorandum, Harris to Lawrence Simon, Box 35, PRO 8, November 1977, HUD Records.

41. "Memorandum, "John B. Rinelander on Issuance of Modernization Regulations," January 13, 1977, Box 35, PRO 8, January–May 1977, HUD Records.

42. On Columbia Point, Harris to Edward W. Brooke, December 4, 1978, Box 34, Subject File, Columbia Point, HP; on Pittsburgh, HACP Mins., January 4, 1979, and May 24, 1979.

43. See Proxmire to Harris, October 24, 1978, Box 78, Harris Personal, October 1, 1978, HP.

44. "Carter's Cutters vs. the Bulge," Time, December 4, 1978, 33.

45. Philip Clay, "Managing the Urban Reinvestment Program," Journal of Housing (October 1979): 453.

46. Bert Lance to Harris, June 2, 1977, Box 21, Briefing Books, Housing Residential 1977, HP. See also Henry B. Schechter, "Economic Squeeze Pinches the Future of Housing," Journal of Housing (April 1980): 192.

47. Harris to Lawrence Simons, January 4, 1940, Box 10, Chronological File, January 1940, HP.

48. Dolbeare to Harris, March 8, 1978, Box 11, Ad Hoc Low-Income Housing Coalition, 1977–1978, HP.

49. Dolbeare, "Housing Policy in the 1979 Budget," March 1978, manuscript found in Box 11, Ad Hoc Low-Income Housing Coalition, 1977–1978, HP.

50. Raymond Struyk, "Public Housing Modernization: An Analysis of the Problem," Journal of Housing (October 1980): 492.

51. Peter Marcuse, "Housing Policy and the Myth of the Benevolent State," in Bratt et al., eds., Critical Perspectives on Housing, 248–58.

52. See Adams et al., eds., Philadelphia, 87.

53. Teaford, Rough Road to Renaissance, 255–307.

54. Bartelt, "Housing the Underclass," 154; June Manning Thomas, "Detroit: The Centrifugal City," in Squires, ed., Unequal Partnership, 151–53.

55. Hartman, "Housing Policies Under the Reagan Administration," in Bratt et al., eds., Critical Perspectives on Housing, 362.

56. See William Julius Wilson, The Declining Significance of Race: Blacks and Changing American Institutions (Chicago: University of Chicago Press, 1980); Douglas S. Massey and Nancy A. Denton, American Apartheid: Segregation and the Making of the Underclass (Cambridge, Mass.: Harvard University Press, 1993).

Epilogue

ROGER BILES

In July 1998, the Chicago Housing Authority (CHA) demolished the three southernmost high-rises in the Robert Taylor Homes, the nation's largest public housing project. The CHA planned eventually to raze all the Taylor Homes, thereby eliminating 4,321 apartments in twenty-eight structures. In a city whose housing projects contained eleven of the nation's fifteen poorest census tracts, the Taylor Homes project stood out as especially hopeless—"the worst slum area in the United States" by the CHA's own estimate. The 11,000 residents of the Taylor Homes—a population 99 percent black, 96 percent unemployed, 84 percent earning less than $10,000 annually, and 70 percent under the age of 21—would have to be relocated somewhere else in Chicago. Moreover, within fifteen years, the housing authority planned to eliminate 11,000 low-income units citywide.

Chicago is perhaps the foremost among U.S. cities that are losing their most infamous high-rise public housing projects under the auspices of a program called Hope VI. According to the Hope VI blueprint, the federal government would provide financial assistance for the elimination of 100,000 apartments by the year 2000, construction on the same sites of smaller housing developments for mixed-income occupancy, and relocation of the uprooted tenants to privately owned buildings. As the twentieth century drew to a close, policymakers in Washington had clearly repudiated the high-rise public housing experiment. The *New York Times* concluded: "The Federal Government is helping cities clear slums again, but this time they are slums it helped create."[1]

The demolition of high-rise public housing projects immediately spawned new challenges, however. The enormous high-rises housed many more people than the townhouses designed to replace them, and because of the substantial cost of constructing new units, housing experts predicted that the overall low-income housing stock would inevitably shrink. Housing officials also worried about the difficulty of dispersing the former residents without creating problems in their new neighborhoods. Not surprisingly, public housing authorities found that stable, middle-class neighborhoods failed to welcome refugees from notorious places like the Robert Taylor Homes. Although public housing projects had tolerated the aberrant habits of unemployed tenants with criminal records, drug habits, and trails of angry creditors, such behavior disqualified them from obtaining new housing elsewhere. Local housing authorities used part of their Hope VI grant awards to employ social service agents to find landlords in respectable surroundings willing to accept these tenants, but successes came grudgingly. A pattern soon emerged whereby the tenants settled for housing in poor black enclaves only marginally safer and better kept than the highrises they had vacated.[2]

The advent of Hope VI came at a time that the declining availability of low-income housing portended a crisis for U.S. cities. During the 1970s, a decade that turned out to be a golden age for the provision of housing for needy families, the Department of Housing and Urban Development (HUD) provided financing for 400,000 apartments annually. In the 1980s, however, dramatic changes in politics and the economy resulted in a drastically reduced federal presence and a concomitant loss in low-income housing. In keeping with his crusade to decentralize government and reduce federal spending on social welfare initiatives, President Ronald Reagan cut back funding for urban programs. The urbanologist Anthony Downs remarked, "Reagan's constituency is mostly suburban and rural, so why bother?" As Secretary of HUD, Reagan appointed Samuel R. Pierce Jr., an innocuous bureaucrat so invisible to the public that he became widely known as "Silent Sam." Pierce kept such a low profile that, at a White House reception for urban luminaries, Reagan erroneously greeted him as "Mr. Mayor." The absence of spirited advocacy on the part of HUD left public housing interests without a significant voice in the Reagan cabinet. Low-income housing starts dropped from 183,000 in 1980, to 119,000 in 1983, to 28,000 in 1985. The Housing and Urban-Rural Recovery Act of 1983 stipulated that, unless HUD could prove that building new units would be cheaper, it must acquire existing housing; by 1986, new construction accounted for less than 20 percent of subsidized housing units authorized by the federal government. From 1980 to 1988, federal funding for day-to-day maintenance, rehabilitation, and new construction declined from $35 billion to $7 billion.[3]

To substitute for public housing, the Reagan administration offered housing vouchers. Under this form of privatization, low-income families secured apartments in the private market and paid rent equal to 30 percent of their annual incomes. Acting on the recommendation of the 1982 *Report of the President's Commission on Housing*, Reagan initiated the voucher program as an experiment in 1984 and made it available to all local housing authorities two years later. In the first three years of operation, Congress appropriated funds for 148,000 vouchers, but low-income families used fewer than 30,000. Bureaucratic logjams and the difficulty in finding an adequate number of units at acceptable rent levels seemed to have curtailed the program. In an age of fiscal belt-tightening, charged critics of the voucher system, Congress failed to allocate a fraction of the amount necessary to compensate for the abandonment of public housing construction.[4]

In the 1990s, the situation worsened. Responding to the highly publicized instances of corruption and mismanagement in Philadelphia and Chicago, HUD seized control of those local housing authorities. Less visible but more important, the shrinking stock of low-income housing continued to contract. In the early years of the decade, the federal government financed the construction of a paltry 36,000 new units a year, and in 1996 President Bill Clinton signed housing legislation authorizing no new construction at all. At least in part, Clinton's draconian cut resulted from the rising cost of preserving the existing public housing stock. In 1996, HUD spent almost $2.5 billion (out of a total budget of $20 billion) to maintain existing public housing projects—repairing broken elevators, patching leaky roofs, replacing defective boilers, and the like. In addition to the rising cost of coaxing continued use out of aging structures, housing officials spent increasing sums on security and social services for a tenant population rife with problems and prone to antisocial behaviors.[5]

Financial crisis loomed as well because of the delayed costs inherent in the Section 8 program. Created in 1974 in the first wave of privatization efforts, the program allowed tenants to choose their own lodging in the private market and to pay rent and utilities (up to 30 percent of their income) with Section 8 certificates provided by the government. The system became so popular that, by the mid-1990s, about twice as many aid recipients lived in private dwellings under Section 8 as lived in conventional public housing. The government financed the certificates through long-term contracts—usually twenty years in length—that cost vast amounts to renew. In the year 2000, for example, HUD would need to renew 2.5 million low-income apartments at an estimated cost of $17 billion. Absent a dramatic infusion of funds, the cost of renewing Section 8 alone would essentially consume all of HUD's operating budget.[6]

In such a foreboding climate, HUD Secretary Henry G. Cisneros labored valiantly to maintain the federal government's commitment to low-income housing. Fully endorsing the replacement of the nation's most blighted high-rise projects with smaller, mixed-income developments, he touted the virtues of an alternative kind of public housing. Donning hard hats at the construction sites around the country where explosive charges and bulldozers leveled high-rise complexes, Cisneros proselytized on behalf of the "New Urbanist" doctrine that propounded the mainstreaming of low-income populations in units that looked nothing like "the projects." In theory, at least, low-income housing would be decentralized, integrated into mixed-income buildings, and situated in a variety of neighborhoods with diverse ages, races, and incomes. Critics of the New Urbanism questioned whether policymakers and the American populace intended to underwrite such an expensive enterprise on behalf of low-income families. In 1996, skeptics noted, the federal government spent $66 billion on mortgage-interest and property tax deductions, more than two-thirds of which benefited families with yearly incomes above $75,000 and about one-fourth the total spent on low-income housing.[7] Some contemporary critics espoused "Third Sector," "non-market," "Progressive" solutions to the problem of "affordable" housing. They assumed Washington's abdication from low-cost housing supply and urged that community-based, nonprofit housing corporations fill the void. Indeed, in places like Hartford, Connecticut, Cleveland, Ohio, and Burlington, Vermont, nonprofit housing corporations in the 1990s, often aided by state and local grants and HUD's tax and below-market interest rate programs, played a critical role in supplying affordable housing to low-income families.[8]

By the late 1990s, the federal government continued to exercise a considerable impact on the private housing market. Thanks to the continued activity of the Federal Housing Administration (FHA), approximately 65 percent of U.S. households owned or were purchasing their homes. Although potential home buyers relied less on FHA and Veterans Administration loans than they had in the decades immediately following World War II, certain categories of borrowers still depended on government aid. For example, first-time home buyers with little capital for down payments necessarily remained FHA customers. On the other hand, because of the maximum cost of a house available with government insurance, more expensive homes could not be obtained through FHA involvement. The federal agency experimented with variable-rate loans, reverse-equity mortgages, and other innovative methods of making mortgage money available to meet the demand of a population that eagerly sought new housing. As the twentieth century came to an end, advancing suburban sprawl remained clear evidence of government's studied attention to the housing interests of the affluent middle class.[9]

What of the sense of community that housers in the early twentieth century sought when they argued for an expanded government role in the provision of low-income housing? The importance of the neighborhood echoed through the writings of Clarence Perry and Jacob Riis; Clarence Stein's and Henry Wright's designs of Sunnyside, New York, and Radburn, New Jersey;

Roger Biles   269

the tireless political activism of Catherine Bauer; and the abortive attempts at
fashioning new towns in the 1970s. Despite the persistent setbacks encountered
at every turn in a society infused with an individualistic ethos, communitarians
persevered in arguing for an alternative vision that made good housing accessible to all citizens. Receiving modest allocations when more generous funding
was needed and accepting compromises in the form of federal legislation that
routinely deferred to real estate and building interests, housers fruitlessly argued
for a more holistic approach to housing, one that never materialized.

In the 1990s, proponents of the New Urbanism similarly emphasized the
centrality of community building, underscoring the importance of regional
planning, strong neighborhoods, and scattered-site low-income housing. Although still alive, however, the communitarian vision seemed no closer to realization in an age of dwindling federal budgets for low-income housing. The
plans for the destruction of projects like Techwood Village in Atlanta and Ca-
brini Green in Chicago prominently featured lucrative redevelopment schemes
but alarmingly little housing on the same sites. Could vouchers and other private remedies provide for the uprooted public housing tenants? The government's subsidization of public housing construction seemed thoroughly
discredited, but it remained unclear that any private solutions would be more
successful in meeting the housing needs of all the people.[10]

In her classic 1934 study *Modern Housing*, Catherine Bauer advocated the
creation of a noncommercial housing sector in the United States for the benefit
of those whose housing needs were not adequately served by the private real
estate market. Fifteen years later, she lamented the continued lack of opportunities for cooperative homeownership and other nonprofit housing ventures for
families who either could not afford to or did not want to purchase a home.
Housing had become a "straight consumer issue," no longer a tool of economic
and social class reform. For Bauer, the failure of reformers to establish a nonprofit housing sector was a key factor in explaining where urban housing had
gone wrong. The noncommercial housing sector offers no panacea, to be sure,
but it does provide a means of reconnecting housing back to the larger issues
of economic and social reform.[11]

Notes

1. *The New York Times*, September 6, 1998.
2. Ibid.; Jerry Adler and Maggie Malone, "Toppling Towers," *Newsweek*, November 4, 1996, 72.
3. "The Unsheltered Life," *U.S. News and World Report*, November 11, 1996, 29; William Fulton,
"HUD at 20 Faces a Midlife Crisis," in American Planning Association, *The Best of Planning: Two Decades
of Articles From the Magazine of the American Planning Association* (Chicago: Planners Press, 1989), 586

(quotation); Jun Hyun Hong, "Dispersal of Public Housing in the U.S.: An Analysis of Intra- and Inter-Metropolitan Variations in the Location of Public Housing" (Ph.D. dissertation, University of Pittsburgh, 1995), 20; Stanley Ziemba, "Is Public Housing on Its Last Legs," in American Planning Association, *The Best of Planning*, 286.

    4. Chester Hartman, "Housing Allowances: A Bad Idea Whose Time Has Come," in J. Paul Mitchell, ed., *Federal Housing Policy and Programs, Past and Present* (New Brunswick, N.J.: Center for Urban Policy Research, 1985), 383–89; Robert K. Landers, "Low Income Housing," *Congressional Quarterly's Editorial Research Reports* 1 (May 8, 1987): 219–22.

    5. *The New York Times*, February 24, 1997; Jason DeParle, "Slamming the Door," *The New York Times Magazine*, October 20, 1996, 68.

    6. Ibid. Vouchers were created under the aegis of the Section 8 program.

    7. Jerry Adler and Maggie Malone, "Toppling Towers," 71; Jason DeParle, "Slamming the Door," 53; U.S. Department of Housing and Urban Development, *Urban Policy Brief*, September 1994, 6.

    8. John Emmeus Davis, ed., *The Affordable City: Toward a Third Sector Housing Policy* (Philadelphia: Temple University Press, 1994).

    9. Willem van Vliet, ed., *The Encyclopedia of Housing* (Thousand Oaks, Calif.: Sage Publications, 1998), 182.

    10. Adler and Malone, "Toppling Towers," 72.

    11. Catherine Bauer, "The Middle Class Needs Housing Too," *The New Republic*, August 29, 1949, 18.

Bibliographic Essay

Pre-1900:

Gwendolyn Wright's *Building the Dream: A Social History of Housing in America* (Cambridge, Mass.: MIT Press, 1981) remains the only comprehensive historical survey of housing in the United States. As Wright's title implies, she focuses mainly on the social and cultural roots of American housing from the seventeenth into the twentieth century. She does, however, discuss the emerging role of the federal government as a supplier of housing, including a chapter on public housing.

No scholarly study looks exclusively at the provision of housing in colonial America. However, several key works dealing with the rise of popular political consciousness and the social and economic conditions of the laboring classes in colonial America explore housing conditions, among them Gary Nash's detailed study of Boston, New York, Charleston, and Philadelphia, *The Urban Crucible: Social Change, Political Consciousness and the Origins of the American Revolution* (Cambridge, Mass.: Harvard University Press, 1979), and Billy G. Smith, *The "Lower Sort": Philadelphia's Laboring People, 1750–1800* (Ithaca: Cornell University Press, 1990). Both books emphasize that a long period of colonial warfare, a growing ethnically diverse population, and nascent capitalism spawned increasingly wretched housing for America's eighteenth-century urban poor.

In her *Manhattan for Rent, 1785–1850* (Ithaca: Cornell University Press, 1989), Elizabeth Blackmar links New York's burgeoning early nineteenth-century speculative housing market to both unbridled young capitalism and rising class segregation. Stuart Blumin argues similarly in his brilliant *Emergence of the Middle Class: Social Experience in the American City, 1760–1900* (Cambridge: Cambridge University Press, 1989), a book that contains excellent chapters detailing the evolution of bourgeois housing standards in early Victorian America. A good discussion of the rise of the urban tenement and the early philanthropic effort to mitigate the worst housing conditions experienced by the poor, especially in New York, can be found in Robert Bremner's *From the Depths: The Discovery of Poverty in the United States* (New York: New York University Press, 1956). Stanley Buder's *Pullman* (New York: Oxford University Press, 1967) examines one ill-fated corporate effort to better working-class housing. In *Atlantic Crossings: Social Politics in a Progressive Era* (Cambridge, Mass.: Harvard University Press, 1998), Daniel T. Rodgers deftly explores what he regards as the preponderant influence of European housing ideas on the gestation of an early housing reform movement.

1900–1932:

The emergence of housing as a public policy issue around the turn of the century was in part a result of the publication of Jacob Riis's *How the Other Half Lives: Studies Among the Tenements of New York* (New York: Charles Scribner's, 1890). In the decade preceding World

War I, working-class housing and living conditions were major focuses of Paul U. Kellogg, ed., *Pittsburgh Survey*, 6 vols. (New York: Russell Sage Foundation, 1909–1914), and of professional social work and public administration publications such as *Charities and Commons* (later *Survey*) and *The American City: Housing Betterment*. The periodical published by Lawrence Veiller's National Housing Association, should be read in conjunction with the proceedings of its annual meetings; see also Lawrence Veiller, *The National Housing Association: A New Organization to Improve Housing Conditions, Both Urban and Suburban* (New York: National Housing Association, 1910).

For an introduction to housing between 1900 and 1932, see Robert G. Barrows, "Beyond the Tenement: Patterns of American Urban Housing, 1870–1930, *Journal of Urban History* 9 (August 1983): 395–420; and Michael Doucet and John C. Weaver, "Material Culture and the North American Home: The Era of the Common Man, 1870–1920," *Journal of American History* 72, no. 3 (1985): 1395–1422. Works that illuminate the progressive roots of federal housing policy include Howard Gillette, "The Evolution of Neighborhood Planning from the Progressive Era to the Housing Act of 1949," *Journal of Urban History* 9, 4 (1983): 421–44; John F. Bauman, *Public Housing, Race, and Renewal: Urban Planning in Philadelphia, 1920–1974* (Philadelphia: Temple University Press, 1987); and Robert Fairbanks, *Making Better Citizens: Housing Reform and the Community Development Strategy in Cincinnati, 1890–1960* (Urbana: University of Illinois Press, 1988); see also Edith Elmer Woods's classic *Recent Trends in American Housing* (New York: Macmillan, 1931). A number of books focus on Chicago. See Edith Abbott's *The Tenements Of Chicago, 1908–1935* (Chicago: University of Chicago Press, 1936); Deveraux Bowley's richly illustrated *The Poorhouse: Subsidized Housing in Chicago, 1895–1976* (Carbondale: Southern Illinois University Press, 1978); and Thomas Philpot, *The Slum and the Ghetto: Neighborhood Deterioration and Middle Class Reform, Chicago, 1880–1930* (New York: Oxford University Press, 1978). On New York, see Anthony Jackson, *A Place Called Home: A History of Low-Cost Housing in Manhattan* (Cambridge, Mass.: MIT Press, 1976), and Richard Plunz, *A History of Housing in New York City: Dwelling Type and Social Change in the American Metropolis* (New York: Columbia University Press, 1990).

Important works for placing housing reform during this era in a broader economic and social context are Roy Lubove, *The Progressives and the Slums: Tenement House Reform in New York City, 1890–1917* (Pittsburgh: University of Pittsburgh Press, 1962), Alan F. Davis, *Spearheads for Reform: The Social Settlement and the Progressive Movement, 1890–1914* (New York: Oxford University Press, 1967); Dolores Hayden, *Designing the American Dream: The Future of Housing, Work, and Family Life* (New York: Norton, 1984); and Gwendolyn Wright, *Moralism and the Model Home: Domestic Architecture and Cultural Conflict in Chicago, 1873–1913* (Chicago: University of Chicago Press, 1980).

The most recent comprehensive analysis of company-sponsored housing is Margaret Crawford's *Building the Workingman's Paradise: The Design of American Company Towns* (New York: Verso Press, 1995). On housing during World War I, see Richard Candee, *Atlantic Heights: A World War I Shipbuilders' Community* (Portsmouth, N.H.: Portsmouth Marine Society, 1985); and two key articles, Roy Lubove, "Homes and a 'Few Well-Placed Fruit Trees': An Object Lesson in Federal Housing," *Social Research* (Winter 1960): 469–86; and Christian Topalov, "Scientific Planning and the Ordering of Daily Life: The First 'War Housing' Experiment in the United States, 1917–1919," *Journal of Urban History* 17, 1 (1990): 14–45. See also Bruce Bustard, "Homes for War Workers: Federal Housing Policy During World

War I," *Prologue* 24, 1 (Spring 1992): 33–43; and Kristin M. Szylvian, "The Industrial Housing Reform and the Emergency Fleet Corporation," *Journal of Urban History* 125, 5 (1999): 647–90.

On the influence of British garden cities on American planned communities, see Daniel Schaffer, *Garden Cities for America: The Radburn Experience* (Philadelphia: Temple University Press, 1982); Wayne Attoe and Mark Latus, "First Public Housing: Sewer Socialism's Garden City for Milwaukee," *Journal of Popular Culture* 10, 1 (1976): 142–49; and Margaret Ripley Wolf, *Kingsport, Tennessee: A Planned American City* (Lexington: University Press of Kentucky, 1987).

Works on race and racial discrimination in housing during the 1900–1932 era include James Borchert, *Alley Life in Washington: Family, Community, Religion, and Folklife in the City, 1850–1970* (Urbana: University of Illinois Press, 1980); and James Andrew Wiese, "The Other Suburbanites: African American Suburbanization in the North Before 1950," *Journal of American History* 85 (March 1999): 1495–524.

On housing in the 1920s, see James Ford's classic *Slums and Housing* (Cambridge, Mass.: Harvard University Press, 1936); and Roy Lubove, *Community Planning in the 1920s: The Contributions of the Regional Planning Association* (Pittsburgh: University of Pittsburgh Press, 1963). Suburbanization during the 1920s is examined in Kenneth T. Jackson's *Crabgrass Frontier: The Suburbanization of the United States* (New York: Oxford University Press, 1985); Robert Fishman's *Bourgeoise Utopias: The Rise and Fall of Suburbia* (New York: Basic Books, 1987); and Margaret Marsh, *Suburban Lives* (New Brunswick: Rutgers University Press, 1990). See also Marc A. Weiss, *The Rise of the Community Builders: The American Real Estate Industry and Urban Land Planning* (New York: Columbia University Press, 1987); and Janet Hutchison, "Building for Babbitt: The State and the Suburban Home Ideal," *Journal of Policy History* 9, 2 (1997): 184–210.

1933–1976:

The best general treatments of federal housing policy beginning in the New Deal era are Mark I. Gelfand, *A Nation of Cities: The Federal Government and Urban America, 1933–1965* (New York: Oxford University Press, 1975); R. Allen Hays, *The Federal Government and Urban Housing: Ideology and Change in Public Policy* (Albany: State University of New York Press, 1985); Lawrence M. Friedman, *Government and Slum Housing* (New York: Rand McNally, 1968); Nathaniel Keith, *Politics and Housing Crisis Since 1930* (New York: Universe Books, 1973); and Henry J. Aaron, *Shelter and Subsidies: Who Benefits from Public Housing* (Washington, D.C.: The Brookings Institution, 1972). The crucial role played by the Home Owners Loan Corporation and the Federal Housing Administration is explicated in Kenneth T. Jackson, "Race, Ethnicity, and Real Estate Appraisal: The Home Owners Loan Corporation and the Federal Housing Administration," *Journal of Urban History* (August 1980): 419–52. On the passage of the landmark Wagner-Steagall Act, see Timothy McDonnell, *The Wagner Housing Act: A Case of the Legislative Process* (Chicago: Loyola University Press, 1957); and J. Joseph Huthmacher, *Senator Robert F. Wagner and the Rise of Urban Liberalism* (New York: Athenaeum, 1971). An alternative vision for housing in the 1930s was offered in Catherine Bauer, *Modern Housing* (Boston: Houghton Mifflin, 1934); a more recent analysis is provided in Gail Radford's superb *Modern Housing for America: Policy Struggles in the New Deal Era* (Chicago: University of Chicago Press, 1996). The architecture of the New Deal public housing projects is discussed in Richard Pommer, "The Architecture of Urban Housing in the

United States During the Early 1930s," *Journal of Society of Architectural Historians* 37 (December 1978): 235–64. The best sources on the New Deal's decentralization programs are Joseph Arnold, *The New Deal in the Suburbs: A History of the Greenbelt Town Program, 1935–1965* (Columbus: Ohio State University Press, 1971); and Paul K. Conkin, *Tomorrow a New World: The New Deal Community Program* (Ithaca: Cornell University Press, 1959).

The best overall view of federal housing programs during World War *II* is Phillip J. Funigiello, *The Challenge to Urban Liberalism: Federal-City Relations During World War II* (Knoxville: University of Tennessee Press, 1978). On the fate of the U.S. Housing Authority and public housing during World War II, see Roger Biles, "Nathan Straus and the Failure of U.S. Public Housing, 1937–1942," *The Historian* 53 (Autumn 1900): 33–46. For an instructive case study of federally constructed housing after the Lanham Act but before entry into the war, see Kristin M. Szylvian, "Bauhaus on Trial: Aluminum City Terrace and Federal Defense Housing Policy During World War II," *Planning Perspectives* 9 (July 1994): 229–54.

On urban redevelopment and urban renewal, begin with Richard O. Davies, *Housing Reform During the Truman Administration* (Columbia: University of Missouri Press, 1966). A general overview of these programs is provided in Jon C. Teaford, *The Rough Road to Renaissance: Urban Revitalization in America, 1940–1985* (Baltimore: Johns Hopkins University Press, 1990). Especially influential contemporary criticisms of renewal were Jane Jacobs, *The Death and Life of Great American Cities* (New York: Vintage Press, 1961); and Catherine Bauer, "The Dreary Deadlock of Public Housing," *Architectural Forum*, May 1957, 140–42, 219–21. Later critical assessments are Martin Anderson, *The Federal Bulldozer: A Critical Analysis of Urban Renewal, 1949–1962* (Cambridge, Mass.: MIT Press, 1964); Marc A. Weiss, "The Origins and Legacy of Urban Renewal," in J. Paul Mitchell, ed., *Federal Housing Policy and Programs, Past and Present* (New Brunswick: Rutgers University Press, 1985), 253–76; and Oscar Newman, *Defensible Space* (New York: Macmillan, 1973). The important case study of New York City is examined in Joel Schwartz, *The New York Approach: Robert Moses, Urban Liberals, and Redevelopment of the Inner City* (Columbus: Ohio State University Press, 1993).

The construction in the 1950s and 1960s of high-rise public housing projects in one of the nation's largest cities is detailed in Devereaux Bowly Jr., *The Poorhouse: Subsidized Housing in Chicago, 1895–1976* (Carbondale: Southern Illinois University Press, 1978). The quality of life in these projects is described in Gerald D. Suttles, *The Social Order of the Slum: Ethnicity and Territory in the Inner City* (Chicago: University of Chicago Press, 1968); Oscar Lewis, *La Vida: A Puerto Rican Family in the Culture of Poverty* (New York: Random House, 1966); and Lee Rainwater, *Behind Ghetto Walls: Black Family Life in a Federal Slum* (Chicago: Aldine Press, 1970). The contentious literature on black families and public housing is discussed in John F. Bauman, Norman P. Hummon, and Edward K. Muller, "Public Housing, Isolation, and the Urban Underclass: Philadelphia's Richard Allen Homes, 1941–1965," *Journal of Urban History* 17 (May 1991): 273–86. The story of the federal government's primary decentralization scheme in the 1960s is told in Roger Biles, "New Towns for the Great Society: A Case Study in Politics and Planning," *Planning Perspectives* 13 (April 1998): 113–32.

The principal overview of postwar suburbanization and federal housing policy is Kenneth T. Jackson's *Crabgrass Frontier: The Suburbanization of the United States* (New York: Oxford University Press, 1985). Contemporary critiques of suburban life are found in William Whyte, *The Organization Man* (New York: Simon and Schuster, 1956); and John

Keats, *The Crack in the Picture Window* (Boston: Houghton Mifflin, 1956). The Los Angeles experience is presented in Greg Hise, *Magnetic Los Angeles: Planning the Twentieth Century Metropolis* (Baltimore: Johns Hopkins University Press, 1991).

A number of historical studies have examined the intersection of race and housing. See Arnold Hirsch, *Making the Second Ghetto: Race and Housing in Chicago, 1940–1960* (Cambridge: Cambridge University Press, 1983); John F. Bauman, *Public Housing, Race, and Renewal: Urban Planning in Philadelphia, 1920–1974* (Philadelphia: Temple University Press, 1987); Dominic J. Capeci Jr., *Race and Inequality in Postwar Detroit: The Sojourner Truth Housing Controversy of 1942* (Philadelphia: Temple University Press, 1984); Thomas J. Sugrue, *The Origins of the Urban Crisis: Race and Inequality in Postwar Detroit* (Princeton: Princeton University Press, 1996); Raymond A. Mohl, "The Second Ghetto and the 'Infiltration Theory' in Urban Real Estate, 1940–1960," in June Manning Thomas and Marsha Ritzdorf, eds., *Urban Planning and the African American Community* (Thousand Oaks, Calif.: Sage, 1996): 58–74.

The broad contours of transportation and housing policy are sketched in the following: Mark Rose, *Interstate: Express Highway Politics, 1941–1956* (Lawrence: University of Kansas Press, 1979); and Bruce L. Seely, *Building the American Highway System: Engineers as Policy Makers* (Philadelphia: Temple University Press, 1987). Case studies of the impact of freeway construction in specific cities are Raymond A. Mohl, "Race and Space in the Modern City: Interstate-95 and the Black Community in Miami," in Arnold R. Hirsch and Raymond A. Mohl, eds., *Urban Policy in Twentieth Century America* (New Brunswick: Rutgers University Press, 1993); and Ronald H. Bayor, "Roads to Racial Segregation: Atlanta in the Twentieth Century," *Journal of Urban History* 15 (November 1988): 3–21.

1976–1990:

Few historians have examined the shaping of U.S. housing policy in the post-Nixon era. Most studies of federal housing policy that focus on the retreat from public housing have emanated from social and political scientists such as R. Allen Hays, whose *Federal Government and Urban Housing: Ideology and Change in Public Policy* (Albany: State University of New York Press, 1985) includes both the Carter and the Reagan years. A good historical assessment of Carter's housing policy appears in Thomas Sugrue's "Carter's Urban Policy Crisis," in Gary M. Fink and Hugh Davis Graham, eds., *The Carter Presidency: Policy Choices in the Post–New Deal Era* (Lawrence: University of Kansas Press, 1998). Also useful for understanding the history of housing policy during the Carter-Reagan years are Rachel G. Bratt's "Public Housing: The Controversy and Contribution," and Chester Hartman's "Housing Policies Under the Reagan Administration," both in Rachel G. Bratt, Chester Hartman, and Ann Meyerson, eds., *Critical Perspectives on Housing* (Philadelphia: Temple University Press, 1986). A number of recent books have examined recent housing policy in the context of persistent housing segregation patterns and the emergence of an urban underclass. Most of these studies have implicated federal policy in isolating poor black families in urban regions barren of economic opportunity. Noteworthy among these studies are William Julius Wilson, *The Truly Disadvantaged: The Inner City, the Underclass, and Public Policy* (Chicago: University of Chicago Press, 1987); David Bartelt, "Housing the Underclass," in Michael Katz, ed., *The Underclass Debate: Views from History* (Princeton: Princeton University Press, 1993); and Douglas S. Massey and Nancy A. Denton, *American Apartheid: Segregation and the Making of the Underclass* (Cambridge, Mass.: Harvard University Press, 1993).

Contributors

John F. Bauman is a Visiting Research Professor in Community Planning and Development at the Muskie School of Public Affairs at the University of Southern Maine, and Professor Emeritus of History at California University of Pennsylvania. He has authored or co-authored numerous articles and books, including *Public Housing, Race, and Renewal: Urban Planning in Philadelphia, 1920–1974* (1987). He is currently at work with Edward K. Muller on a book on the history of urban planning in Pittsburgh, 1880–1943.

Roger Biles is Professor of History at East Carolina University. His most recent book is *Richard J. Daley: Politics, Race, and the Governing of Chicago* (1995). He has published articles related to housing policy in such journals as *Planning Perspectives, The Historian, and Mid-America.*

Robert B. Fairbanks is Professor of History at the University of Texas at Arlington and also editor for the Americas for *Planning Perspectives.* He has written several books, including *Making Better Citizens: Housing Reform and the Community Development Strategy in Cincinnati* (1988), and, most recently, *For the City as a Whole: Planning, Politics, and the Public Interest in Dallas, Texas, 1900–1965* (1998). He is currently writing a book on public housing in Texas.

John S. Garner is Professor of Architecture at the University of Illinois at Urbana–Champaign, where he teaches urban history and historic preservation. He is the author of *Model Company Town: Urban Design Through Private Enterprise in Nineteenth-Century New England* (1984), and he has edited *The Midwest in American Architecture* (1991), and *The Company Town: Architecture and Society in the Early Industrial Age* (1992).

Thomas W. Hanchett is staff historian for the Museum of the New South in Charlotte, North Carolina. He previously taught American history at Youngstown State University and at Cornell University. His doctoral dissertation won the Urban History Association's annual prize in 1993 and was published as *Sorting Out the New South City: Race, Class, and Urban Development in Charlotte, 1875–1975* (1998). Other publications include a 1996 *American Historical Review* article on the rise of the shopping center, which won the Catherine Bauer Wurster Prize from the Society for City and Regional Planning History.

Arnold R. Hirsch at present is Research Professor of History at the University of New Orleans, where he has served since 1979. He is best known for his book, *Making the Second Ghetto: Race and Housing in Chicago, 1940–1960* (1983). It was republished in a paperback edition in 1998. In addition to a host of articles and chapters, he has co-edited *Creole New Orleans: Race and Americanization* (1992) and *Urban Policy in Twentieth-Century America* (1993).

Janet Hutchison is a Research Associate at the National Museum of American History, Smithsonian Institution. Her articles on housing policy and the American home have been published in *Journal of Policy History, Agricultural History,* and *Perspectives in Vernacular Architecture.* In her forthcoming monograph on the Better Homes in America Movement she considers local case studies and national directives to understand how civic activism and state housing policy promoted the American dream.

Eric J. Karolak is currently a policy analyst with the nonpartisan Ohio Legislative Budget Office. He received his Ph.D from Ohio State University in 1997. From 1995 to 1997 he taught history at the University of Alaska, Southeast. His research interests include labor history and twentieth-century public policy. This chapter is his first major publication.

Raymond A. Mohl is Professor of History and Chairman of the Department at the University of Alabama at Birmingham. He is the author, editor, or co-editor of ten books, including *The New City: Urban America in the Industrial Age, 1860–1920* (1985), *Searching for the Sunbelt* (1990), and *The New African American Urban History* (1996). He was the founding editor of the *Journal of Urban History* and the President of the Urban History Association in 1998. He is currently completing a history of race relations in Miami and a book on the Interstates and the cities.

Gail Radford teaches U.S. history at the State University of New York at Buffalo. She did her graduate work at Columbia University, where she studied under Kenneth Jackson. Her book, *Modern Housing for America: Policy Struggles in the New Deal Era,* was published in 1996. Currently she is researching the origins of semi-autonomous agencies, such as public authorities, which came to be used extensively at all levels of government in the United States during the twentieth century.

Kristin M. Szylvian is Associate Professor of History at Western Michigan University. Her most recent articles on housing policy have appeared in the *Journal of Urban History* and *Planning Perspectives*. Szylvian, who is currently working on a monograph on wartime housing, has visited and collected oral history testimony at numerous World War I, New Deal, and World War II federal housing developments nationwide.

Alexander von Hoffman is a Senior Research Fellow at the Joint Center for Housing Studies at Harvard University. Previously he was an associate professor of urban planning and design at the Graduate School of Design of Harvard University. He is currently writing two books, one on the community development movement and the revival of the inner city, the other on the history of low-income housing reform in the United States. Von Hoffman is the author of *Local Attachments: The Making of an American Urban Neighborhood, 1850–1920.*

Index

Aaron, Henry J., 171
Abernathy, Rev. Ralph, 238
Abrams, Charles, 14, 112
accelerated depreciation, 172
Ackerman, Fred, 69
Addams, Jane, 11
African Americans, 37, 60; and World War II housing, 131; postwar suburbs, 174, postwar federal housing policies, 206–22; highway policy, 234–41; Philadelphia, 252
Akron, Ohio, 44, 52–55
Ambrose, Stephen, 146
American Apartheid, 221
American Concrete Institute (ACI), 233
American Individualism, 83
American Institute of City Planning (AICP), 7–8
American Institute of Planning (AIP), 48, 146
American Road Builders' Association (ARBA), 233
American Town Planning Association, 48
Americans for Democratic Action, 259
An American Dilemma (1944), 209
Anderson, Martin, 153
Architect's Small House Service Bureau, 90–91, 93
Architectural Forum, 190
Aronovici, Carol, 10, 62
Augur, Tracy, 58
Automotive Safety Foundation, 233
Atterbury, Grosvenor, 47
Avion Village, 128

Bailey, James, 200
Baltimore, 232; and Bethlehem Steel plant, 67
Barnett, Joseph, 234
Baroni, Geno, 251
Bartholomew, Harland, 185, 187
Bath, Maine, 63
Bauer, Catherine (Wurster), 12–13, 102–4, 109, 111, 116, 140, 193, 144, 187
Bauman, John F., 15, 151

Beard, Charles and Mary, 94–95
Bel Geddes, Norman, 230
Bellamy, Edward, 9
Bethlehem Steel, and World War I housing, 63
Better Homes in America, 12, 88–90, 93
Bier, Thomas, 171
Biles, Roger, 13
Birmingham, Alabama, 238–39
Blandford, Robert, 130–31
Blivens, Bruce, 86
Boston, 6, 11, 21, 30, 49
Brace, Charles Loring, 7
Breuer, Marcel, 133, 190
Bricker, Senator John, 145
British Royal Town Planning Institute, 48
Brooke (Edward) Amendment (1969), 151, 254
Brown, Edwin, 82, 89
Brown v. Board of Education, 15, 174, 207–8, 222
Brooklyn, 49
Buffalo, New York, 30, 31, 33–34, 153
Bureau of Public Roads (BPR), 227–29, 233, 241
Burgess, Ernest, 22
Butterick Company (and the *Delineator*), 88
Byrd, Senator Harry, 111–12

Califano, Joseph, 250
Camden, New Jersey, 9; and Yorkship Village, 70–72; Highways, 239
Carl Mackley Homes, Philadelphia, 104–5
Carter, President Jimmy, 12, 246–62; housing policy, 248, 256–57; urban policy, 249; Urban Policy Initiatives (1978), 256–57
Celebration, Florida, 175
Chamber of Commerce, 87, 89, 109, 231
Charity Organizing Society (COS), 23, 26, 31
Chicago, 11, 36, 57, 149–50, 154–55, 169, 235; tenements in, 29–30; City Homes Association, 27; postwar housing and civil rights in, 217–18; highways in, 240; public housing in, 258
Chicago Housing Authority (CHA), 149, 215

Childrens' Aid Society, 7
Churchill, Henry S., 58, 94
Clay Commission (President's Advisory Com-
    mission on a National Highway Program,
    1954), 234
Cleveland, 30, 240
Clinton, President William Jefferson, 267
Cobbett, William, 6
Cobo, Mayor Albert, 151, 234
Cold War, 170–72
Cole, Albert M., 219–21
Columbus, Ohio, 240
Commission for a National Agenda for the
    1980s, 261
Commission on Living Conditions of the
    Emergency Fleet Corporation, 73
Committee on Civil Rights, 211
Committee on Community Planning of AIA,
    38
Community Development Block Grant
    (CDBG), 253, 255, 258, 260–61
Community Reinvestment Act (1977), 175
Congress of Industrial Organizations (CIO),
    127
cooperative housing, 145
Council of National Defense (CND), 63–64
Crabgrass Frontier, 207
Curry, George W., 238

Daley, Mayor Richard J., 149–54
Dallas, Texas, 31–32
Darst, Mayor Joseph M., 181, 188–89, 191,
    197–98
Davis, James J., Secretary of Labor, 89
Death and Life of Great American Cities, 153
decentralization, 144, 183, 246–47
Defense Homes Corporation (DHC), 124
Defense Housing Coordinator (World War II),
    123–24
Defense Housing Division (DHD), 125–26
Defensible Space, 148
DeForest, Robert W., 32, 47
Denton, Nancy, 221
Department of Commerce, 81, 87–88, 91
Department of Housing and Urban Develop-
    ment (HUD), 140–41, 157, 223, 249–59,
    261, 266–67
Department of Labor, 61, 76
DeSoto-Carr Redevelopment Area, St. Louis,
    186–88, 194–96

Detroit, 35, 234
Dilworth, Mayor Richardson, 151
Division of Slum Clearance and Urban Rede-
    velopment (DSCUR) of the Housing and
    Home Finance Administration (HHFA),
    216, 219
Dolbeare, Cushing, 254, 259–61
Douglas, Senator Paul, 157, 159, 215
Downing, Andrew Jackson, 13
Downs, Anthony, 266
Draper, Earl, 44

East River Houses, New York, 189
Eccles, Marriner, 107–8
Eclipse Park, Wisconsin, 10, 44, 53–54
École des Beaux Arts, 46
Eidlitz, Otto M., 64, 75
Eisenhower, Dwight D., 145–47, 169, 220,
    231
Ellenbogen, Henry, 109, 111
Ellender, Allen, 214
Elliot, Charles, 8, 48, 51
Emergency Fleet Corporation, 19, 61–76, 82,
    85
Emmerick, Herbert, 130–31
England. See Great Britain
environmentalism, 7
Executive Order 11063, 140–51
expressways. See highways

Fahey, John, 107
Fairbanks, H. S., 230
Fairbanks, Robert B., 11
Fair Deal, 144, 215
Fair Housing Act (1968), 175
Federal Aid Highway Act (1944), 169
Federal Bulldozer, 153
Federal Highway Administration, 241
Federal Home Loan Bank Act (1932), 107, 110
Federal Housing Administration (FHA), 14,
    145; and Better Housing Movement, 91, 94,
    creation of, 107–8; impact on mortgage
    market and housing standards, 115–16; and
    World War II housing, 124; and postwar
    suburbanization, 164–68, 174–75; and civil
    rights, 207–14, 216, 220, 268
Federal National Mortgage Association (Fan-
    nie Mae), 118, 210, 255
Federal Public Housing Authority, 129–30, 13
federal tax policy and housing, 171, 122

Federal Works Agency (FWA), and World War
    II housing, 124–25, 130
Fishman, Robert, 13
Flower, B. O., 7
Foley, Raymond M., 211, 216
Follin, James W., 233
Ford, George B., 47
Ford, President Gerald, 252
Ford, Henry, 129
Ford Motor Company and Willow Run, 128,
    131
Foreman, Clark, 126–27, 210
Forest Hills Gardens, 47–48
Fort Green Houses, 152
Foster, Mark I., 230
Frankfurter, Felix, 71, 74
French industrial housing, 46–47
Fried, Marc, 154
Frieden, Bernard, 256
Funigiello, Philip J., 134
Futurama (GM exhibit, 1939), 230

Gans, Herbert, 154
Garden City Movement, 43–58; garden sub-
    urbs, 43; Greenbelt, Maryland, 44; Saint
    Louis plan, 186–88
Garden Homes Development (Cincinnati), 86
Garner, James S., 10, 12
Gelfand, Mark I., 227
gentrification, 259
George, Henry, 9
George-Healy Act, 106
George Washington Carver Court, 130
German housing experiment, 86, 187
G.I. Bill, 134, 164
Goode, Mayor W. Wilson, 260–61
Goodyear Heights, 44, 52–54, 57
Goodyear Tire and Rubber, 51–52
Gilder, Richard Watson, 11
Gould, Elgin R. L., 8, 25, 47
Great Britain, 9, 10, 37, 44–45, 48, 186
Great Depression, 13, 39, 92–93, 102–16
Great Society, 157
Greenbelt, Maryland, 44, 132
Gropius, Walter, 126, 133, 187, 190
Grier, George and Euncie, 259
Gruen, Victor, 232

Hanchett, Thomas W., 14
Harris, Patricia, 247; Secretary of HUD, 249,

biography, 248–50; vision for HUD,
    251–53; and Fannie Mae, 255–59; and
    Urban and Regional Planning Group
    (URPG), 255–57
Hartman, Chester, 154
Hellmuth, George F., 191, 193
Henry Hudson Parkway, 169
Hester Street, 27
high-rise housing projects, 147
Highway (Interstate) Act of 1956, 140,
    169–233
highways, and suburbanization, 168–71; and
    housing, 226–41
Hiss, Philip, 63–64
Hirsch, Arnold H., 14, 150
Home Builder's Clinic, 90
Home Modernization Bureau, 82, 92–93
homeownership, 66–67, 81–96
Home Owners Loan Corporation (HOLC)
    (1933), 107, 118, 208, 210
Homes Registration Information Service, 89
Hoover, President Herbert, and "Own Your
    Own Home Movement," 12, 19, 81–83; and
    Better Homes Movement, 81–96, and Fed-
    eral Home Loan Board Act, 107
Hoover's Conference on Home Building and
    Home Ownership (1931), 93
Hoovervilles, 81
Hope VI, 265–66
Hopkins, Harry, 107
Hopkins, Mary, 50
Horne, Frank S., 210–11, 215–20
housers, 70
housing, in eighteenth century, 4; in nine-
    teenth century, 4–7; and republican tradi-
    tion, 5; and emerging middle class, 5;
    reformers, 9–10; housing evils, 29; garden
    city housing, 43–58; and World War I,
    62–65; industrial housing, 60–77; post–
    World War I housing crisis, 62; public hous-
    ing, 102–18, 139–59, 180–202; suburban
    housing, 163–76
Housing Act of 1934 (National Housing Act),
    93
Housing Act of 1937 (Wagner Steagall Act),
    xii, 109–12, 117, 118, 124, 139, 210, 184,
    214–15, 217
Housing Act of 1949 (Taft-Ellender-Wagner
    Act), xii, 139, 143–45, 147, 159, 184, 188,
    214–18, 222

Housing Act of 1954, 140, 146, 220–21
Housing Act of 1961, 155
Housing and Community Development Act of 1977, 255
Housing and Home Finance Administration (HHFA), 140, 147, 151, 210–11, 215–19, 221
Housing and Urban Development Act of 1965 (HUD), 140, 156. *See also* Department of Housing and Urban Development
Housing and Urban Development Act of 1968, 141, 156–57
Housing Division of the Public Works Administration, 20
Housing Reform: A Handbook for Practical Use in American Cities, 31–32
How the Other Half Lives, 11, 23
Howard, Ebenezer, 12, 44–45
Howe, Frederic C., 9
Howe, George, 125
Hutchinson, Janet, 12

Ickes, Harold L., 104, 109, 209, 210
Ihlder, John, 10
Indian Head, Maryland, 126
Internal Revenue Service, 171–73
International Basic Economy Corporation, 191–92
international housing congresses, 45–50
Interregional Highways, 230–31
interstate highways, 15, 140, 169–70, 226–41

Jackson, Kenneth T., 2, 115, 165, 207–8
Jacob Riis Houses, 190
Jacobs, Jane, 14, 140, 153, 175, 252–53
Janis, Jay, 250
Jencks, Christopher, 181
John J. Cochran Gardens, 189, 191, 193, 196–98
Johnson, Lyndon B., 15, 140, 156, 249, 251, 256, 260
Jordan, Marguerite Walker, 73
Journal of the American Institute of Architects, 37–38, 63
Journal of Housing, 248–49

Kaiser shipyard, 132
Kahn, Louis I., 125
Kansas City, Missouri, 239
Kaptur, Marcia, 251

Kennedy, President John F., 16, 140–41, 151, 238, 250, 260
Kincaid, Illinois, 10, 12, 44, 54, 57
King, Martin Luther, Jr., 238
Kingsport, Tennessee, 49
Kistler, Pennsylvania, 49
Kohler, Wisconsin, 89
Korean War, 133, 145
Krammer Homes, 125

Labor Housing Conference (LHC), 103, 108–9, 111, 115, 116
Ladies Home Journal, 87
Lake Meadows, 217
Lakeview Terrace, 104
Lake Shore Drive, 169
Lance, Bert, 250, 259
Lanham, Fritz, 124
Lanham Act, 13, 124–25, 128, 131–32, 139
Lantz, Simon, 92, 94
LeClaire, Illinois, 47
LeClaire, Jean-Edmund, 47
Le Corbusier, 148, 168, 174, 181, 190, 195
Leinweber, Joseph W., 191, 199
Letchworth, England, 44–45, 52, 186
Levenson, Frances, 221
Levitt, William, 165–66
Levittowns, 96, 135, 165–67, 213–14
Lewis, Oscar, 152
Lewis, Sinclair, 95
Lincoln Center for the Performing Arts, 152
Linda Vista, 122

McGuire, Marie, 140
McMurtry, George, 8
Meehan, Eugene, 200
Meloney, Marie, 88–89, 93
Miami, Florida, 236
Miller, Wallace E., 30
Miller, Zane, 38–39
Milwaukee, 86, 240
Minority Housing Conference, 219
Mitchell, Clarence, 216, 250
Mitchell, J. Paul, 134
Minneapolis, Minnesota, 90, 153
Model Tenement House Law, 35
Modern Housing, 103, 144, 187, 269
Montgomery, Alabama, 238
Montgomery, Roger, 200
Morgenthau, Henry, Jr., 107

Moses, Robert, 148–49, 190, 229, 234, 237
Moynihan, Daniel Patrick, 152
Muller, Emil, 45–47
Mumford, Lewis, 58, 113–14, 143
Mutual Home Ownership Plan, 127–28, 130, 133
Mutual Ownership Defense Housing Division, 125, 127
Myrdal, Gunnar, 209–10

Napoleon III, 46
Nashville, Tennessee, 237
National Association for the Advancement of Colored People NAACP), 174, 207, 212, 250
National Association of Home Builders, 145
National Association of Housing and Redevelopment Officials (NAREB), 258
National Association of Housing Officials (NAHO), 139
National Association of Real Estate Boards (NAREB), 85–87, 109–10, 140, 145, 183–84
National Commission on Urban Problems, 157–58, 227
National Committee Against Discrimination in Housing, 217, 221, 259
National Committee on the Housing Emergency, 127
National Conference of Charities, 29, 33
National Conference on City Planning, 51
National Development Bank, 257
National Federation of Business and Professional Women's Clubs, 89
National Housing Act (1934), 93, 107, 212–14
National Housing Agency, 20, 122, 126, 129, 131, 140
National Housing Association (NHA), 22–23, 32–39, 48
National Housing Conference (NHC), 146
National Industrial Recovery Act (NIRA) (1933), 20, 104
National Mortgage Corporation for Housing Cooperatives, 115
National Municipal League (NML), 48
National Public Housing Conference (NPHC), 108–9
National Recovery Administration (NRA), 104
National Register of Historic Places, 175
National Retail Lumber Dealers Association, 109

National Urban League, 259
Neighborhood Housing Services, 253
Neighborhood Retirement Centers, 257
Neimeyer, Oscar, 195
Nelson, Herbert U., 110
Nelson, Nelson O., 47
Neponsit Garden Village, 49
Nesbitt, George B., 216–17, 221
Neutra, Richard, 127–28, 130
New Deal, 12, 93–94, 96, 104–18, 134, 163–65, 187, 208–9, 257
New Earswick, England, 44
New Harmony, Indiana, 5
New London, Connecticut, 36, 68
New Orleans, 237–38
New Republic, 86
new towns, 44–45, 157, 268
New York Association for Improving the Condition of the Poor, 7, 8
New York City, 5, 6, 10, 15, 23, 26, 105, 113, 148–49, 153, 189–90, 240, 258
New York City Housing Authority, 112
New York City Tenement Law of 1868, 10
New York City Tenement Law of 1895, 26
New York City Tenement Law of 1901, 11, 23, 26, 30, 163
New York Times, 152, 265
New Yorker, 113
Newark, New Jersey, 15
Newman, M. W., 149
Newman, Oscar, 148
Nixon, President Richard, 15, 141, 143, 157, 159, 248, 250, 252–53, 256, 260–61
Nolen, John, 8, 48–49, 58, 63, 69, 74
Norfolk, Virginia, 166
Norris, Tennessee, 44
North American Phalanx, 5
Northgate Shopping Center, 170
Noyes, John Humphrey, 5

O'Dwyer, William, 189–90
Office of Management and Budget (OMB), 250, 259
Olmstead, Frederick Law, 8, 33
Olmstead, Frederick Law, Jr., 34, 47, 51–52, 54
Olmstead, John C., 8
Oneida, New York, 5
Operation Breakthrough, 159
Organization Man, 174

Organization of Petroleum Exporting Countries, 15, 253
Orth, George, 8
Overtown, 236–37
Owen, Robert, 5
"Own Your Own Home" Campaign, 12, 81–82, 85, 87–88, 91, 95

Paine, Robert Treat, 8
Palmer, Charles F., 123–24, 127, 129
Paris Expositions, 26, 45–46
Parker, Barry, 44
Parkridge Homes, 125–26
Parrish, Helen, 8
Patterson, James T., 110–11
Peabody, Francis S., 54, 56
Pei, I. M., 198
Perkins, Frances, 107
Perlman, Philip B., 212–14
Perry, Clarence, 186–87, 268
Philadelphia, 5, 6, 8, 15, 35, 67, 104, 141, 151, 156, 181, 247, 252, 260–61, 267
Pierce, Samuel R., Jr., 266
Pico Gardens, 126
Pine Ford Acres, 125
Pittsburgh, 253–54, 258, 260–61
Pittsburgh Survey, 9
Plaza Square Project, 189
Plunz, Richard, 104
Pope, Robert Anderson, 66
Post, George B., 54–55
President's Advisory Committee on a National Highway Program, 234
Progress and Poverty, 9
Proxmire, William, 249–50, 258
Pruitt-Igoe, 14, 180–205, 241
Public Buildings Administration, 126
Public Housing Administration (PHA), 181, 193, 196, 200, 211, 218
Public Works Administration (PWA), 39, 104–6, 108, 110, 112–13, 116, 125, 132, 147, 150, 156, 159, 181, 209
Pullman, Illinois, 8, 10
Pullman, George, 8
Purdue University, 90

Queensbridge, 113, 114

racial segregation, 13–16, 115–16, 131, 133, 139–40, 150–59, 160–67, 181, 193–202, 206–22, 226–41, 246–61

Radburn, New Jersey, 38, 44, 127, 186, 187, 268
Rapp, Frederick, 5
Ray, Joseph R, 218, 221
Raymond, Antonin, 125
Reagan, Ronald, 261, 266
Reconstruction Finance Corporation, 81
Red Hook, 113–14
Regional Planning Association of America (RPAA), 186, 187
Republican opposition to housing, 145–47, 157, 188, 214–15, 252
Resettlement Administration (RA), xi, xii, 20, 111
Reuss, Henry, 250, 257
Reuther, Walter, 128, 129
Richards, Franklin D., 211–14
Riis, Jacob, 10, 11, 23, 251, 252, 268
Riverside, Illinois, 54
Robert Taylor Homes, 1, 149, 150, 241, 254, 265
Rockefeller, David, 250
Rockefeller, Nelson, 191, 192
Romney, George, 159
Roosevelt, President Franklin D., 20, 39, 93, 104, 107–10, 112, 122–24, 129, 187, 230
Roosevelt, Theodore, 26
Rosenman, Samuel I., 129
Rosenwald, Julius, 86
Rouse, James W., 232
Rowntree, Joseph, 44
Rural Electrification Administration, 125
Russell Sage Foundation, 31, 32, 47

Saarinen, Eero, 125
Saarinen, Eliel, 125
Sackett, H. S., 92
St. Louis, Missouri, 14, 165, 180–202, 217, 241
St. Louis Housing Authority, 180–81, 193–201
Salomon, Sidney, 191
San Francisco, 240
San Diego, 121–22
Savannah, Georgia, 175
Schever, James H., 233
Schmidlapp, Jacob, 35, 37
Schmidt, Walter, 110
Scheuers, Edwin, 125
Sears Roebuck Company, 90

Section 8 of Housing Act of 1974, xiii, 253–55, 257, 259, 267
Seiberling, Frank, 51–52
Servicemen's Readjustment Act of 1944, 134
settlement house movement, 11, 22, 251
sewerage, 170–71
Shelly vs. Krammer (1948) 14–15, 207, 211–14, 222
shopping centers and malls, 170, 173, 226
Shurcliff, Arthur, 48
Simkhovitch, Mary, 108
Simonds, Ossian Cole, 56–58
South Bend, Indiana, 127
South Carolina, 216
Sparkman, John, 214, 239
Stein, Clarence, 44, 58, 143, 174, 186, 187, 260, 268
Stelzle, Charles, 31
Sternberg, George, 1, 8
Stockbridge, Massachusetts, 50
Straus, Nathan, 112–13
Stuyvesant Town (New York City), 190
Subsistence Homesteads, 132
suburbanization, 14–16, 51–58, 67–70, 83–85, 94–96, 134–35, 163–76, 183–85, 226–41
Sunnyside Gardens (Queens, New York City), 38, 186, 268
Swanson, J. Robert, 125

Taft-Ellender-Wagner Act. *See* United States Housing Act of 1949
tax incentives, 172–73
Taylor, Graham, 74, 251
Taylor Homes. *See* Robert Taylor Homes
Taylorville, Illinois, 56
Techwood Homes (Atlanta, Georgia), 187, 269
Temiscaming, Ontario, 53
Tenement House Laws (New York), xi, 10, 23–32, 35, 163
Tennessee, Nashville, 216, 237
Tennessee Valley Authority, 44
Texas, 31–32, 127–28, 157–58, 175, 176
Tigert, John James, 89
Truman, Harry S., 128, 133, 144–45, 184, 189, 211, 231, 233
Tugwell, Rexford G., 107, 111
Tyson's Corner, Virginia, 176

United Automobile, Aircraft, and Agricultural Implements Workers of America, 128

United Nations, 190
United States Association of Building and Loan Societies, 45
United States Building and Loan League, 109
United States Bureau of Public Roads (BPR), 227, 229–38, 241
United States Chamber of Commerce, 89, 109, 231
United States Conference of Mayors, 146
United States Department of Agriculture, 90, 94
United States Department of Commerce, 81–83, 87–88, 91, 93
United States Department of Housing and Urban Development, 3, 140, 151, 156–59, 181, 247–61, 266–67
United States Department of Interior, 111
United States Department of Justice, 175
United States Department of Labor, xi, 19, 61–77
United States Department of Transportation, 241
United States Housing Act of 1937. *See* Housing Act of 1937
United States Housing Act of 1949. *See* Housing Act of 1949
United States Housing Act of 1950, 145
United States Housing Act of 1954. *See* Housing Act of 1954
United States Housing Act of 1961. *See* Housing Act of 1961
United States Housing Authority (USHA), xii, 20, 111–15, 123, 125–27, 209–10
United States Housing Corporation (USHC), xi, 19, 37, 61–77, 82, 85
United States Savings and Loan League, 145
United States Shipping Board, xi, 37, 61–77, 82, 85
United States Supreme Court, 15, 154, 164, 167, 174, 197, 207, 211–18, 221–22
Union Park Gardens, Wilmington, Delaware, 69
Unwin, Raymond, 44, 57
Urban and Regional Policy Group (URPG) (1977), 255–57
Urban and Rural Renewal Act, 261
Urban Land Institute, 227, 232–33
Urban Renewal, 8, 13–15, 139, 140, 143–59, 172, 181–202, 221–22, 226–41, 252, 261

Van Pelt, John, 75

Vanport City, Oregon, 132
Vandergrift, Pennsylvania, 8, 10
Vaux, Calvert, 54
Veiller, Lawrence, xi, 1, 9, 10, 11, 20, 23–39, 70–71
Veterans Administration, 14, 139, 164–68, 208, 268
Veterans of Foreign Wars, 145
village improvement societies, 50–51
Volpe, John A., 237

Wagner, Robert, 108–11, 118, 144, 215
Wagner-Steagall Act. See United States Housing Act of 1937
Walker, Hale, 44
Wallace, Henry, 89, 107, 230
Walling, Wilbur, 86
Walsh, David, 105
War Industries Board, 63, 71
War on Poverty, 206
Warburton, C. W., 94
Waring, George, 51
Washington, D.C., 8, 33, 156, 165
Washington Terrace, Cincinnati, Ohio, 37
Water Pollution Control Act, 171
Weaver, Robert, 140, 209–10, 215–17
Welwyn Garden City, 45
Westbrook, Lawrence, 127, 130, 133
Weyerhauser Forest Products Company, 91
Wheaton, William, 256
Whitaker, Charles H. 63

White, Alfred T., 8, 37, 49
White, Walter, 212
Whitton, Rex M., 239
Whyte, William H., 14
Wilhelm, Donald, 88
Williams, David R., 128
Willow Run, Michigan, 128–29
Wilmington, Delaware, 69
Wilson, William B., 64
Wilson, President Woodrow, 12, 60, 65, 82
Wisconsin Act (1919), 86
Wisconsin, Milwaukee, 240
Wood, Edith Elmer, 58, 62, 86
Wood, Elizabeth, 150
Woods, Robert, 11
Works Progress Administration, xi, 126–27
World Trade Center Towers, 191
World War I, 12, 19, 22, 37, 43, 51, 60–77, 96
World War II, 13, 20, 121–35, 165–66, 174, 207
Wright, Frank Lloyd, 57, 126, 174
Wright, Henry, 44, 58, 143, 186, 187, 268
Wuster, Catherine Bauer, 139–40. See also Bauer, Catherine
Wyatt, Wilson, 20, 134

Yamasaki, Minoru, 182–83, 191–200
Yorkship Village, Camden, New Jersey, 70, 72

Zeckendorf, William, 191, 192, 193, 198
Zeilenbau, 187